THE UNEASY ALLIANCE

THE UNEASY ALLIANCE

AMERICA, BRITAIN,
AND RUSSIA, 1941–1943

by ROBERT BEITZELL

Alfred A. Knopf / New York / 1972

THIS IS A BORZOI BOOK
PUBLISHED BY ALFRED A. KNOPF, INC.

Copyright © 1968, 1972 by Robert Egner Beitzell
All rights reserved under International and Pan-American
Copyright Conventions. Published in the United States
by Alfred A. Knopf, Inc., New York, and simultane-
ously in Canada by Random House of Canada, Limited,
Toronto. Distributed by Random House, Inc., New York.
Manufactured in the United States of America

Library of Congress Cataloging in Publication Data:
Beitzell, Robert. The uneasy alliance.
Bibliography: p. 1. World War, 1939–1945—Diplomatic history. I. Title.
D748.B35   940.53′2   78–136332
ISBN 0–394–44193–1   1- 19-73
FIRST EDITION

To Margharetta and Peter

Contents

Contents   *ix*

Introduction

The Second World War was the most destructive conflict in history. In terms of lives lost, cities laid waste, geographical extent or any other quantitative measurement, the war defies rational comprehension. Fire storms at Dresden and Hamburg, human shadows etched into cement at Hiroshima and Nagasaki by the heat of atomic explosions, missiles aimed in the general direction of London and Antwerp, unrestricted submarine warfare in the Atlantic and Pacific, kamikaze pilots who left behind letters of apology to their parents, mass murder in the forest at Katyn and the far larger, unspeakable horrors of Belsen and Buchenwald—all these things happened. Soldiers died fighting for their countries, but people were also killed because of their nationality, or their religion, or the social class to which they belonged. In some nations what started as resistance to the foreign enemy became instead even more terrible civil war. Millions upon millions died in Europe and Asia. More millions fled from their homes, never to return, as armies advanced and retreated. Villages partly burned in one campaign were leveled in the next. In Germany and in Japan cities, the centers of civilization, were systematically reduced to ashes and rubble. Though this book describes the actions of statesmen and generals, the reader should not forget that the final reality was the suffering of individuals.

The Uneasy Alliance is a history of the often acrimonious relationship which existed between the United States, Great Britain, and the Soviet Union during part of the Second

World War. The period covered extends from Pearl Harbor
to the conclusion of the conferences at Cairo and Tehran in
December, 1943. Events occurring within these twenty-four
months largely determined the course of the remaining two
years of war and deeply influenced, even conditioned, the
following three decades of uncertain peace.

When Japan and Germany declared war on the United
States in December, 1941, the Axis powers possessed the
strategic initiative. America, Great Britain, and the Soviet
Union were simply cobelligerents. Even this cobelligerency
was incomplete, for the Soviet Union and Japan remained at
peace with each other until 1945. America was building an
army, an air force, and a new navy, but Washington was not
prepared for war. This meant that London and to a much
greater extent Moscow had at first to carry the main burden
of the struggle. America and Great Britain had publicly sub-
scribed to the vaguely worded Wilsonian principles of the
Atlantic Charter, which called for national self-determination,
free trade, and democracy. The Soviet Union with certain
reservations also endorsed the Charter. But there were no
concrete territorial or political agreements between the three
powers, no common plan for victory. America and Great
Britain did not even recognize the frontiers of the Soviet
Union. Roosevelt, Churchill, and Stalin knew what they
wanted in the postwar settlement, however. They were well
aware that their desires conflicted. Most of all they knew
that to survive they had to cooperate. At times during the
dark months of 1942, as Japan occupied Southeast Asia, as
U-boats pillaged the Atlantic, as German armor drove ever
deeper into the Soviet Union, the issue of survival appeared
to be in jeopardy.

When Roosevelt, Churchill, and Stalin left Tehran in
December, 1943, the war had been transformed. The Soviet
Union had mastered the German army and was driving the
invader from its territory. The United States and Great
Britain had created a unique instrument of wartime col-

laboration, the Combined Chiefs of Staff, and America possessed what amounted to a surplus of military power. The U-boat menace was defeated. Japan stood on the defensive. Italy had surrendered. Peace feelers were being received from other enemy states. America and Great Britain were almost masters of the air over Europe. Germany would fight on in desperation, but Roosevelt, Churchill, and Stalin shared a common certainty of her destruction. At Tehran Stalin also gave pledges concerning the war against Japan.

Similar progress apparently characterized the political relations between the three powers. Great Britain and the Soviet Union were linked by a treaty promising twenty-five years of future friendship. Great Britain and the United States jointly demanded the unconditional surrender of Germany and Japan, though Stalin believed the policy simply prolonged the war. The three powers were sponsors of a new world organization to replace the League of Nations. At Tehran, Roosevelt, Churchill, and Stalin redrew the map of Eastern Europe. There also, Stalin accepted certain territorial changes in Asia previously agreed to by Roosevelt, Churchill, and Chiang Kai-shek. Indeed, in the politics of the war, Tehran, not Yalta or Potsdam, was the seat and center of decision. But the cooperation between Washington, London, and Moscow had been marred by bitter disputes and conscious falsehoods. The unity had become superficial; the differences real. This also was mirrored in the conversations between the three leaders at Tehran.

The fact of the cobelligerency of the United States, Great Britain, and the Soviet Union after surviving the crises of 1942 and launching their own attacks in 1943 promised the eventual defeat of Germany and Japan. The way in which that cobelligerency was conducted during that same period, by acts of commission and omission, raised serious questions about the nature of the postwar period. The mistake of Germany and Japan was that they fought entirely separate wars in Europe and Asia—and so shared a common fate.

America, Great Britain, and the Soviet Union fought a joint war first in Europe and then in Asia, but the conflict of their ambitions prevented the achievement of peace.

I would like to acknowledge, with thanks, the suggestions and assistance of Josef Anderle and Carl Hamilton Pegg in preparing an earlier version of this book. I want also to acknowledge the encouragement and patience of Ashbel Green, who waited while necessary revisions were made. Mrs. Eleanor Starzyk acted as prodder, typist, grammarian, and friend. I am further indebted to the many archivists, librarians, and colleagues who helped find answers to what must have seemed an endless number of questions. Finally I would like to say that without the continuous aid of my wife, Margharetta, this book could not have been written.

                                                    Robert Beitzell

PART ONE

THE DIPLOMACY AND
STRATEGIC PLANNING OF
THE GRAND ALLIANCE
December 1941–August 1943

I

SOVIET TERRITORIAL AMBITIONS AND BRITISH STRATEGY FOR FIGHTING WORLD WAR TWO
December 1941–January 1942

The morning of December 8, 1941, found the British Foreign Secretary, Anthony Eden, at the port of Invergordon in the north of Scotland. He had just arrived after an all-night train ride from London. For the first and only time during the war, Eden was feeling sick. At eight o'clock he called upon a local doctor; the diagnosis was gastric influenza. The news was most unwelcome since Invergordon marked the beginning, not the end, of his journey. Waiting at the dock stood the destroyer H.M.S. *Somali*, whose destination was Scapa Flow, and the British cruiser *Kent*. The *Kent*, in turn, was to carry Eden to Russia for high-level political and military discussions between the Soviet Union and Great Britain.[1]

1. Anthony Eden: *The Memoirs of Anthony Eden, Earl of Avon* (3 vols.; Boston: Houghton Mifflin; 1960–65), II, 330–1. Cited hereafter as *Memoirs*, followed by volume numbers.

Shortly after leaving the doctor, Eden was told that the Prime Minister wanted to speak with him on the telephone. The messenger, a naval officer, explained that this meant going to his headquarters, where a secure line was available. Eden felt reluctant since he wanted to board the *Somali* and head for the relative comfort of the *Kent*. The Prime Minister's request, however, could not be ignored, and Eden was also informed that the American Ambassador to Great Britain, John G. Winant, was on the phone with Churchill. Eden went to the headquarters, took the call, and so learned of the Japanese attack on Pearl Harbor.

The Prime Minister was greatly excited and had earlier talked with Roosevelt over the trans-Atlantic cable to confirm the news. The President answered with the words: "It's quite true. They have attacked us at Pearl Harbor. We are all in the same boat now." Churchill later recalled replying: "This certainly simplifies things. God be with you."[2]

Although it was not yet clear whether the Japanese had struck at any British possessions in the Far East, Churchill told Eden that he intended to declare war on Japan immediately. If confirmed, reported landings on Malaya would justify his action; if the reports proved false, the Prime Minister said he would refer to a speech made a few weeks earlier in which he promised to treat an attack on the United States as an attack on England.

Eden's reaction was one of intense relief. For both, the news ended a week of mounting anxiety about events in the Pacific. In 1940 Roosevelt had ordered that London be supplied with four code machines developed by the American Signal Intelligence Service, which deciphered top-secret radio dispatches to and from the Japanese Foreign Ministry and its embassies overseas. Between December 1 and 6, British intercepts revealed that Japan might soon declare war

2. Winston S. Churchill: *The Second World War* (6 vols.; Boston: Houghton Mifflin Company; 1948–53), III, 605. Cited hereafter as *Second World War*, followed by volume numbers.

on the United States and Great Britain.[3] This decision had been communicated to Japan's Axis partners, Germany and Italy. Even though it precluded Japan's intervention in Germany's war against Russia, Hitler seemed to welcome the news. The Japanese Ambassador in Berlin, General Hiroshi Oshima, informed Tokyo that the German Foreign Minister, Joachim von Ribbentrop, had quoted Hitler as saying he too was ready to break with the United States. Nor could the day of action be long away as the British, on December 3 and 4, deciphered messages from the Japanese Foreign Minister, Shigenori Togo, ordering the destruction of code machines, message files, and all confidential documents in the embassies in London and Washington. The following day the order was extended to include all consular offices in the United States and Great Britain and their overseas possessions, and also consular offices in the Dutch Empire.

Churchill wanted a German declaration of war on the United States. He did not desire a war with Japan, but if one brought the other he was willing to accept it. What upset the Prime Minister and Eden was that ordinary military intelligence raised the possibility of an Anglo-Japanese conflict without American participation. For several months Japan had been increasing the strength of her garrison in the southern part of French Indochina. On the afternoon of December 5, British air reconnaissance from Malaya reported two or possibly three large Japanese convoys about eighty miles southeast of Cambodia Point in the Gulf of Siam. They were escorted by a mixed force of cruisers and destroyers.[4] It could be maneuvers; it could presage an

3. For the texts of some of the British intercepts for the period November 21, 1941, to December 22, 1941, see U.S. Senate and House of Representatives, Joint Committee on the Investigation of the Pearl Harbor Attack: *The Pearl Harbor Attack*, Hearings and Exhibits of the Joint Committee, 79th Congress, 1st and 2nd sessions (39 parts; Washington: Government Printing Office; 1946), pt. 35, 668–93.

4. James R. M. Butler and J. M. A. Gwyer: *Grand Strategy, June 1941–August 1942* (London: H.M. Stationery Office; 1965), p. 303. This is Volume III in the official British history of the higher direction of the war and will be cited hereafter as *Grand Strategy*, III.

attack on the Kra Isthmus in Thailand; it could also mean an attack on British Malaya or the Dutch East Indies. The British Far Eastern Military Command in Singapore ordered a general alert. No direct military evidence pointed toward a Japanese strike at any American possessions. A worried Churchill asked Ambassador Winant and Roosevelt's Lend-Lease Coordinator, Averell Harriman, to come to the Prime Minister's country estate, Chequers, for the weekend to discuss the situation. Churchill said the British were willing to delay their response to Japanese aggression, even accept some military sacrifice, if only they could coordinate their actions with Washington.[5] The phrasing was awkward but the intention was clear; if attacked, the British wanted a joint Anglo-American declaration of war. Winant and Harriman were sympathetic but could give no assurances.[6] The news of Pearl Harbor ended British anxieties.

Since neither Churchill nor Eden yet knew the extent of the disaster which had overwhelmed the American Pacific Fleet on Sunday morning, their sense of relief was accompanied by feelings of exhilaration. Had they known, it would probably have made little difference, for four battleships sunk and two hundred aircraft destroyed—even the loss of naval mastery in the Pacific—were as nothing compared with having America in the war. As Churchill put it: "Hitler's fate was sealed. Mussolini's fate was sealed. . . . As for the Japanese, they would be ground to powder."[7] Eden, too, felt that "whatever happened now, it was merely a matter of time." Before, he had believed in British victory but had "never seen the means, now both were clear."

5. Harriman informed Washington of Churchill's position by cable on December 6, 1941. See Robert Sherwood: *Roosevelt and Hopkins: An Intimate History* (New York: Harper and Brothers; 1950), p. 424. Cited hereafter as *Roosevelt and Hopkins*.

6. "Winant could only reply that the responsibility for declaring war rested solely with Congress." Gerald Pawle: *The War and Colonel Warden; Based on the Recollections of Commander C. R. Thompson, Personal Assistant to the Prime Minister, 1940–1945* (New York: Alfred A. Knopf; 1963), p. 134. Cited hereafter as *Colonel Warden*.

7. Churchill, *Second World War*, III, 607.

Churchill said he was going to the United States at once. Eden agreed the trip was necessary, but wondered if the Americans would want a visit from Churchill so soon. He also worried about the effects of the Prime Minister's journey upon his own plans. Only a month earlier, Churchill, in the presence of Brendon Bracken, British Minister of Information, and James Stuart, Chief Whip of the Conservative Party, had named Eden as his political heir. Eden asked, in light of the dangers involved, whether he should not cancel his trip to Moscow. He did not see how both he and the Prime Minister could undertake hazardous journeys at the same time. Churchill demurred. The whole perspective of the war had changed. What mattered to Great Britain was "the intentions of our two great allies." Eden was to go on. At the end of the conversation, Churchill put Ambassador Winant on the line to wish Eden Godspeed. Eden felt that he heard relief in Winant's voice, too.

Eden arrived in Moscow late on the evening of December 15, 1941. He had been accompanied from England by Sir Alexander Cadogan, the Permanent Under Secretary for Foreign Affairs; Major General Archibald Nye, Vice Chief of the Imperial General Staff; and Ivan Maisky, the Soviet Ambassador to Great Britain. He was met by Vyacheslav Molotov, the Soviet Foreign Minister, and Sir Stafford Cripps, the British Ambassador to Moscow. There were also a guard of honor, scores of klieg lights, and a battery of still and motion picture cameras. The Russians were giving his visit maximum publicity.

The following day, December 16, Eden saw Stalin and noted in his diary that he found the Soviet Premier to be a "quiet dictator."[8] Maisky served as interpreter. Stalin began the meeting by handing Eden drafts of two short treaties. One was for an Anglo-Soviet military alliance against Germany and her European allies and pledged the powers to no separate peace. The other called for cooperation in postwar

8. Eden, *Memoirs*, II, 334.

affairs.[9] Both were innocuous and were to be published immediately. There was also, however, a Most Secret Protocol detailing what the Soviet Union regarded as a just European peace settlement. As he translated the third paper, Maisky believed Stalin was making a mistake.[1]

In the Secret Protocol, Stalin asked for British recognition of his 1940 annexation of Latvia, Lithuania, and Estonia and his 1939 occupation of half of prewar Poland. Poland would be compensated with East Prussia less Tilsit and German territory north of the Nieman, which must go to Russia. He further desired Petsamo from Finland, and Bessarabia and Northern Bukovina from Rumania. Finland and Rumania were to permit Soviet military bases within their territory. Turning to Germany, Stalin called for her dismemberment. Not only would she lose East Prussia, but the Rhineland and possibly Bavaria would become separate states. The truncated parts would pay reparations. Austria was to regain her independence and her 1938 frontiers. Indeed, except for the changes mentioned, Europe would return to the boundaries of 1937. Stalin described the new arrangement as "practical arithmetic." His position altered very little during the next four years.

Eden was not surprised by the terms of the protocol. Indeed, as far as the Soviet Union's western frontier was concerned, the British Government on October 15, 1940, had offered to recognize the *de facto* sovereignty of the Soviet Union over Estonia, Latvia, Lithuania, Bessarabia, Bukovina, and "those parts of the former Polish State now under Soviet control."[2] The price then was only that "the

9. For the full text of the Soviet proposals and a summary of the protocol, see U.S. Department of State, *Foreign Relations of the United States. Diplomatic Papers*, 1942, III (Washington, D.C.: U.S. Government Printing Office; 1961), 497–501. Cited hereafter as *U.S. Foreign Relations*, followed by various years and volume numbers.

1. Ivan Maisky: *Memoirs of a Soviet Ambassador: The War*, 1939–43 (New York: Charles Scribner's Sons; 1968), pp. 231–2. Cited hereafter as *Memoirs*.

2. Llewellyn Woodward: *British Foreign Policy in the Second World War* (London: H.M. Stationery Office; 1962), p. 145. Cited hereafter as *British Foreign Policy*.

Soviet Union would apply to Great Britain a neutrality as benevolent as that applied to Germany." The sponsor of this policy was Sir Stafford Cripps, who attended the present meeting and, as Eden noted in his diary, was the only person to enjoy the tea and cakes which followed the conversation. In October, 1940, however, Britain stood alone in expecting a German invasion in the spring. Now she was allied with the United States; and it was Russia, not England, whom Hitler had attacked. There was no immediate necessity for concessions. The Foreign Office had never regarded Cripps' call for collaboration with Russia as realistic. The ideological gulf between the two countries was too great. Churchill was expressing more than his own opinion when he began his speech of June 22, 1941, about the German attack on the Soviet Union with this sentence: "The Nazi regime is indistinguishable from the worst features of Communism."[3]

Nevertheless, Eden could put the responsibility for saying no upon Washington. On December 4, 1941, Cordell Hull, the American Secretary of State, after learning of Eden's impending trip to Moscow, instructed Winant to call upon the Foreign Secretary. Like Eden, Hull had few doubts about what the Russians wanted; and, in case the British might be tempted, Winant was to remind Eden of Britain's obligations under the Atlantic Charter of August 12, 1941. The charter set forth Anglo-American views on the peace, and its first two articles called for "no aggrandisement" and "no territorial changes that do not correspond to the freely expressed wishes of the people concerned."[4] Winant was also to tell Eden that there must be no secret accords.[5]

In Moscow Eden answered Stalin by citing Roosevelt's opposition to any secret agreements. The Foreign Secretary could make no territorial commitments before consulting

---

3. Churchill, *Second World War*, III, 371.
4. For the text of the Atlantic Charter, see ibid., III, 443–4.
5. Cordell Hull: *The Memoirs of Cordell Hull* (2 vols.; New York: Macmillan Company; 1948), II, 1162. Cited hereafter as *Memoirs*, followed by volume numbers. See also Hull's cable to Winant printed in *U.S. Foreign Relations*, 1941, I, 192–205.

the Prime Minister, the Americans, and the British Dominions. Instead of a treaty or treaties, Eden proposed a joint
declaration proclaiming Anglo-Soviet collaboration in making and maintaining the peace settlement. It was this proposal that produced Stalin's remark about treaties being
practical arithmetic; he regarded declarations as algebra.
Stalin also thought it only proper that a great power like
Britain should establish military bases in Denmark, Norway,
and France. Eden resisted the bribe and maintained he was
not empowered to deal with the questions raised by the
Soviet protocol. Maisky asked, "Not even the Soviet frontiers?"[6] Eden insisted on consultation with London and
doubted that the United States would like the Russian
proposals. After some further badgering, Stalin reluctantly
accepted Eden's position.

Conversation shifted to other topics. Stalin held that
Poland's western border should be moved to the Oder River.
He believed Germany was supplying Japan with planes and
pilots. He also said that the Red Army had gained the initiative over the Germans. Eden feared the effect of America's
entry into the war upon lend-lease deliveries to Russia and
Great Britain. About the other questions Stalin had raised
Eden gave open support to only one, the restoration of
Austria. German dismemberment and reparations, like the
Soviet frontiers, required consultation and careful study.
Eden did not directly challenge Stalin's ideas about Poland
either, but by talking about the danger of irredentist movements, the Foreign Secretary issued a muted warning. In his
diary Eden recorded that when the meeting ended, "All was
friendly."

The atmosphere changed the next day when Stalin, reversing himself, informed Eden that he must accept the protocol, or at least that section dealing with Russia's frontier.
Unless he did, there would be no declaration and no treaty.
Eden's counter offer to recognize the Russian boundary of

6. Eden, *Memoirs*, II, 337.

1938 did not improve matters. The deadlock continued through the next three days. Churchill cabled Eden to stand firm and thought it would "be inexpedient" even to tell Roosevelt informally of the Russian demands.[7]

Finally, Eden resorted to a new device in the history of diplomacy: negotiation by hidden microphones. Eden was staying at a hotel and assumed that his room came equipped with electronic ears. He believed that the one place free of these devices was the embassy car. On December 18, while driving back to the hotel after a fruitless interview with Stalin, Eden proposed to Cripps and Cadogan that the three of them put on a little act using undiplomatic language. This was agreed; and when he got to his room, the Foreign Secretary loudly lamented ever coming to Moscow. The Russians were declared to be impossible as partners even against a common foe. Cripps and Cadogan joined in the chorus.[8]

What did it—the secret listeners or his persistent loyalty to the principles of the Atlantic Charter in his talks with Stalin—Eden never knew, but a few hours later Maisky called and the atmosphere changed once again. Eden had asked earlier to see the scene of some recent fighting. Maisky told Eden that Stalin had given the necessary orders and that the trip was arranged for the following day. Moreover, when Eden returned to Moscow, Stalin told him that he understood the "necessity for . . . consulting with the United States." Discussions, while still unproductive, were again friendly. Stalin insisted on a treaty containing explicit recognition of his forcible annexations of the Baltic States and portions of Finland, but he was willing to have the negotiations continue in London. The Polish frontier might be treated as a separate question, but he wanted the 1941 line. Interestingly, at no point in the conference did the Soviet Premier use either of the two arguments ordinarily advanced to justify the annexations: namely, that the lands

7. Churchill, *Second World War*, III, 631.
8. Eden, *Memoirs*, II, 345.

in question had been part of the Russian Empire prior to 1914 and that by giving the Soviet Union additional defense in depth, they had helped her survive the German assault in 1941. Stalin would tolerate no debate on the merits of the Soviet position. With the sound of German guns audible in Moscow, he offered no hint of compromise. The British were asked to recognize the Soviet frontier of June, 1941; the frontier itself was not negotiable.

Eden left Moscow on December 22. The Foreign Secretary cabled Churchill that his visit had allayed some of the Soviet suspicions and that Stalin "sincerely wants military agreements but he will not sign until we recognize his frontiers." Eden predicted future "badgering." Despite his initial misgivings, Churchill believed Roosevelt should be informed, and as soon as he reached England, Eden gave Winant a full report on what had happened at Moscow. One thing must have pleased Eden; there were no extended lectures on a British cross-channel attack, a subject Stalin raised in his first message to Churchill after the German invasion in June, 1941, and for which the Soviet Union maintained a drumfire of varying intensity over the next three years.[9] Instead, in the military talks the Russians were sympathetic about Britain's plight in the Far East, although they made it clear that the Soviet Union could not declare war on Japan.

While Eden was building his shaky bridge to Moscow, Churchill traveled to Washington. The Prime Minister left England aboard the battleship *Duke of York* on December 12, 1941. His party included Lord Beaverbrook, Minister of Aircraft Production, member of the War Cabinet, and a

9. For the text of the first message dated July 18, 1941, see Ministry of Foreign Affairs of the U.S.S.R., *Correspondence Between the Chairman of the Council of Ministers of the U.S.S.R. and the Presidents of the U.S.A. and the Prime Ministers of Great Britain During the Great Patriotic War of 1941–45* (2 vols.; Moscow: Foreign Language Publishing House; 1957), I, no. 3, 12–13. Cited hereafter as *Stalin's Correspondence*, followed by volume number.

specialist in supply problems. Present also were Admiral of the Fleet Sir Dudley Pound, the First Sea Lord; Air Chief Marshal Sir Charles Portal; and the former Chief of the Imperial General Staff, Field Marshal Sir John Dill.

By December 12 London had received full information on Pearl Harbor. The Americans, as Churchill cabled Eden, had "only two battleships effective in [the] Pacific against ten Japanese." On December 8 Japanese troops landed in northern Malaya, and that same day Britain declared war on Japan. On December 10, while steaming to attack the landings in Malaya, the only British capital ships in the Far East, the *Prince of Wales* and the *Repulse*, were sunk by Japanese aircraft flying from Saigon. Churchill was deeply distressed by these sinkings, as he had sent the ships to Singapore against the advice of Pound.[1] When added to the American losses, this loss meant that the Japanese were masters of the Pacific; and Malaya, the Philippines, Burma, and the Dutch East Indies—even India and Australia—all lay open to assault.

Except for the Russian front where the Red Army had launched its first winter offensive, the only good news during the second week of December—and it was good only in simplifying the struggle—came from Berlin. As Churchill and Roosevelt hoped, Hitler kept his pledge to General Oshima; on December 11, 1941, Germany declared war on the United States. Probably a German-American war was unavoidable after Pearl Harbor, but Hitler's action brought it on within four days. Mussolini followed Hitler's lead, also on December 11. With one exception, all the great powers were now locked in combat. The exception was in the Far East, where Japan's fight to get and keep her new Pacific Empire and Russia's attempt first to contain and then to drive out the Germans preserved an uneasy peace in Man-

1. S. W. Roskill: *The War at Sea, 1939–1945* (3 vols.; London: H.M. Stationery Office; 1954–58), I, 556–7. Cited hereafter as *The War at Sea,* followed by volume numbers.

churia for the next four years. Nevertheless, the war which started at 4:45 in the morning of September 1, 1939, on the plains of Poland had become truly global in scope.

Common foes, however, do not automatically produce a common strategy. Churchill crossed the Atlantic in a state of "some anxiety."[2] Pearl Harbor had been more than a military defeat; it had been a severe blow to American pride. He feared that the "U.S. might pursue the war against Japan and leave (Britain) to fight Germany and Italy." Churchill arrived in Washington on December 22, 1941, and stayed until January 14, 1942. When this conference, which was given the code name Arcadia, had ended, Churchill had largely succeeded in persuading Roosevelt to accept British strategy and even British staff procedures for the opening phase of the war.[3]

During February and March, 1941, there had been highly secret Anglo-American military talks in Washington. Their subject was joint strategy in the event that the two countries became engaged in a common war against Germany and Japan.[4] Among the many tentative decisions reached, it was agreed that there should be unity of supreme military control and unity of field command in cases of joint operations. It was also agreed that "the Atlantic and European area is considered to be the decisive theater." The military posture in the Far East would be defensive. In Europe the Allies would conduct a sustained air offensive, effect the early elimination of Italy, and build up forces for an eventual assault on Germany. Zones of strategic responsibility were assigned: the Pacific and western Atlantic went to the United States; the Far East, eastern Atlantic, and Middle

2. Churchill, *Second World War*, III, 641.
3. Documents relating to Arcadia have been published by the Department of State. See U.S. Department of State: *Foreign Relations of the United States. The Conferences at Washington, 1941–1942, and Casablanca, 1943* (Washington, D.C.: U.S. Government Printing Office; 1968), pp. 3ff. Cited hereafter as *U.S. Foreign Relations, Washington and Casablanca Papers.*
4. Mark S. Watson: *Chief of Staff: Prewar Plans and Preparations* (Washington, D.C.: U.S. Government Printing Office; 1950), pp. 367–82. Cited hereafter as *Prewar Plans.*

East went to England. Great emphasis was placed on the role of air power.

However, these commitments were not in any sense binding. Both governments kept discussions at a low level; no official of cabinet rank was present at any of the meetings. General George Marshall, the United States Army Chief of Staff; General Henry Arnold, American Army Air Force Chief of Staff; Admiral Harold Stark, American Chief of Naval Operations—all stayed away. American isolationist sentiment was still too strong, and the political risks were too great. On August 12, 1941, the day Roosevelt and Churchill issued the Atlantic Charter, legislation extending the American draft passed in the House of Representatives by a single vote.

Pearl Harbor undercut isolationism, but it did not alter the provisional status of the military agreements. Churchill received a sharp reminder of this as soon as America became a belligerent. In the staff conversations of early 1941, Britain had been promised 50 percent of American aircraft production even if the United States entered the war. On December 7, however, the American War Department issued a preemptory order stopping all lend-lease shipments. Churchill was able to get this order rescinded before leaving London, but it was a vivid demonstration of the necessity for Arcadia.

While crossing the Atlantic, Churchill and his military advisers prepared three papers detailing British views on how the war should be fought. Churchill gave them to Roosevelt on December 23. Like Stalin's position on Soviet frontiers, Churchill's opinions changed very little in the next two years. His first paper dealt with Anglo-American strategy against Germany in 1942.[5] The Prime Minister began by stressing the importance of supplies for Russia. The Anglo-Americans had no other role to play in that gigantic struggle between Germany and Russia which Churchill named "the

5. For the full text as given to Roosevelt, see Churchill, *Second World War*, III, 646–51.

prime fact in the war at this time." All promises made must
be kept as "in this way alone shall we [America and Britain]
hold our influence over Stalin and be able to weave the
mighty Russian effort into the general texture of the war."

While the Soviet Union tied down the bulk of German
forces, Great Britain and the United States would launch
two attacks in 1942. One was a combined bomber offensive,
subsequently named Pointblank. Churchill asked that
twenty American bomber squadrons be sent to England to
reinforce the Royal Air Force. No target limitations were
placed on Pointblank. Churchill referred to "accurate"
bombing; but the targets were "cities," and the hope was for
"internal reactions upon the German government."

The second operation, the main Anglo-American effort of
the year, was to be the occupation and control of the whole
North African coast from Cairo to the Strait of Gibraltar.
General Claude Auchinleck, the British Commander in the
Middle East, was about to launch an offensive in Cyrenaica
which Churchill hoped would result in "the total destruction of the enemy force in that area." This would be followed by Operation Acrobat, the clearing of Libya. As
Auchinleck advanced westward from Egypt, Great Britain
and the United States would invade French North Africa.
The operation's code name was Super-Gymnast. The British
contribution would be 45,000 men; the American, 150,000.
Hopefully, before 1942 ended, Super-Gymnast and Acrobat
would link up, and the African coast of the Mediterranean
would be cleared.

Unprovoked attack upon the African possessions of Vichy
France, a neutral state recognized by Washington though
not by London, disturbed Churchill not at all. He described
it as forestalling the Germans, but admitted that Super-
Gymnast would probably result in a Nazi occupation of
European France. This was inconsequential since, according
to the Prime Minister, conditions in Paris and Vichy were
much the same anyway. The Vichy Government itself was
to be offered a choice. The Prime Minister would extend "a

blessing or a cursing." If Vichy and French North Africa declared for the Allies, the United States and Great Britain would promise "to reestablish France as a Great Power with her territories undiminished." In the paper Churchill left his course undefined, but during Arcadia he said if France failed to cooperate she would "be ignored entirely in the peace settlement."[6] He titled his 1942 program "Closing the Ring" around Germany.

The Prime Minister's second European paper dealt with the campaign for 1943. It should produce, Churchill hoped, a "German collapse . . . at the end of 1943 or 1944." It presupposed Soviet survival and Anglo-American success in the African campaign. Turkey, too, "though not necessarily at war, would be definitely incorporated in the American-British-Russian front." With the Mediterranean secured and the ring closed, Churchill planned to hurl forty armored divisions upon the Continent. Behind would be "another million men of all arms." However, in flat violation of the foremost canon of war—concentration of forces—Churchill would attack everywhere. Norway, Denmark, Holland, Belgium, France, Italy, and the Balkans were all named as suitable landing points.

The reason for the dispersion was that Churchill did not intend to fight the German Army; instead, as he put it, the landings would "enable the conquered populations to revolt against the Germans." In short, Europe would free itself, with America and Britain supplying arms and a small mobile force in each country sufficient to throw the German occupying garrison off balance. Leaving aside the logistical problem of nourishing a number of simultaneous or near-simultaneous invasions and the even larger question of the effectiveness of civil risings, the whole operation rested on the assumption that Russia alone would either contain or defeat the bulk of the German Army. It was not so much a plan as a wish. The proposal did, however, have one great advantage

6. *U.S. Foreign Relations, Washington and Casablanca Papers*, p. 72.

in British eyes: by relying on Russia and the conquered populations, England would escape another bloodbath like that of the First World War. This was London's constant nightmare. As Churchill put it at Arcadia, "It need not be assumed that great numbers of men are required [for victory]." Germany would succumb to tank brigades to which Britain would contribute 300,000 men. Churchill hoped that even this move might not prove necessary. Twice in his paper he referred to the possibility of a German collapse before any invasion at all.

When it came to Japan, the subject of his third paper, Churchill was bluntly realistic. The enemy had command of the sea and the Allies "must expect, therefore, to be deprived one by one of [their] possessions and strong-points in the Pacific." The only thing to be done was to make the Japanese pay as high a price as possible for their conquests, while concentrating on naval construction, particularly aircraft carriers, to make good the losses of Pearl Harbor and the South China Sea. He believed that Great Britain and the United States might challenge the Japanese fleet as early as May, 1942. Even so, the Asian war would remain defensive. He warned against "a needless dissipation on a gigantic defensive effort of forces which have offensive parts to play." His Pacific paper also contained a more general appraisal of the American war effort.

After Russia was attacked in June, 1941, Roosevelt had instructed his Secretary of War, Henry L. Stimson, and his Secretary of the Navy, Frank Knox, to explore "at once the overall production requirements required to defeat our potential enemies."[7] The result was a plan named the Victory Program, which was nothing if not grandiose. According to the Victory Program, America should have the largest air force and navy in the world, together with an army of 215 divisions, including 61 armored divisions. If implemented, this would mean the end of aid to Russia and

7. For the full text of Roosevelt's letter dated July 9, 1941, see Watson, *Prewar Plans*, pp. 338–9.

England. Churchill became aware of the American plans during a lend-lease conference held in London in September, 1941. In terms of armament manufacture, he wanted the Victory Program expanded, but he did not want a large American army. In his third paper, Churchill asked that Washington think in terms of a coalition war. "What," he said, "will harm us is for a vast U.S. Army of ten millions to be created which for at least two years while it is training would absorb all the available supplies and stand idle defending the American Continent." Except in the air and at sea, America was to remain the arsenal for others. Churchill used the language of twentieth-century warfare, but his strategy of closing the ring and helping Europe free itself was that of Castlereagh against Napoleon.

Churchill, during Arcadia, soon discovered that his main anxiety—that America, in reaction to Pearl Harbor, would go for Japan first—was groundless. Both Roosevelt and his principal military adviser, General Marshall, supported a Europe-first strategy. Until Hitler's defeat the Pacific was to be a secondary and defensive theater. One of the military papers approved at Arcadia was entitled "American-British Grand Strategy." It said: "Notwithstanding the entry of Japan into the War, our view remains that Germany is still the prime enemy and her defeat is the key to victory. Once Germany is defeated, the collapse of Italy and the defeat of Japan must follow."[8]

The British also succeeded in greatly increasing the pace of American armament manufacture. Beaverbrook represented England in the supply discussions. He bombarded Roosevelt, Roosevelt's friend and adviser, Harry Hopkins,

8. *U.S. Foreign Relations, Washington and Casablanca Papers*, p. 214. For additional material on the military discussions at Arcadia, see also Maurice Matloff and Edwin M. Snell: *Strategic Planning for Coalition Warfare, 1941–1942* (Washington, D.C.: U.S. Government Printing Office; 1953), pp. 96–102. Cited hereafter as *Strategic Planning, 1941–1942*. Ray S. Cline, *Washington Command Post: The Operations Division*. "United States Army in World War II." Office of the Chief of Military History, Department of the Army (Washington, D.C.: U.S. Government Printing Office; 1951), p. 144. Cited hereafter as *Washington Command Post*.

and Vice President Henry Wallace with memorandums
calling for ever-larger production quotas. Wallace, who was
given the job of trying to coordinate the work of the various
American agencies involved, later wrote: "Out of all these
[meetings at Arcadia] I have no recollection whatsoever
except the dynamism of Lord Beaverbrook. He was a power
house with regard to what could be done and what had to be
done."[9] By the end of the conference, an enlarged Victory
Program, which called for the manufacture of 100,000 aircraft in 1943 and 45,000 in 1942, and 75,000 tanks in 1943
and 45,000 in 1942, had been approved. According to his
doctor, Sir Charles Wilson, Churchill visualized "in detail
what this programme means to the actual conduct of the
war [and he was] . . . drunk with the figures."[1]

Churchill had nearly equal success with Super-Gymnast,
to which Roosevelt became an immediate and enthusiastic
convert.[2] Marshall, however, had doubts, and though Super-
Gymnast was discussed many times at Arcadia, when the
conference ended the Americans had not agreed to any
specific operational plan. Marshall believed that the British
estimate of forces required was much too low. He felt
French cooperation was a necessity and feared a German
counterattack through Spain. Nevertheless, the paper on
American-British grand strategy said that in 1942 the Allies
would close and tighten the ring around Germany by "sustaining the Russian front, by arming and supporting Turkey,
by increasing our strength in the Middle East, and by
gaining possession of the whole North African coast." A
separate memorandum gave the date of May 25, 1942, as
that fixed with "certain reservations" for American combat
loading to commence in New York for some sort of North

9. *U.S. Foreign Relations, Washington and Casablanca Papers*, p. 136,
note 2.
1. Sir Charles Wilson: *Churchill: The Struggle for Survival, 1940–1965*
(Boston: Houghton Mifflin; 1966), p. 24. Cited hereafter as *Churchill*.
2. Henry L. Stimson and McGeorge Bundy: *On Active Service in Peace
and War* (New York: Harper and Bros.; 1948), pp. 419, 425. Cited hereafter
as *On Active Service*.

African campaign.[3] The United States, at least in theory, was committed to a Mediterranean attack and a policy of closing the ring.

The British—and this was probably their greatest achievement at Arcadia—also won Roosevelt over to their staff procedures. By December, 1941, Churchill had developed a fairly efficient machine for the direction of the war.[4] Its heart was the Chiefs of Staff Committee, consisting of the Chief of the Imperial General Staff, General Alan Brooke; the First Sea Lord, Admiral Dudley Pound; Air Chief Marshal, Charles Portal; and the Chief of Staff to the Prime Minister, General Hastings Ismay. With one exception, its personnel remained the same from Arcadia to the end of the war. The exception was Admiral Sir Dudley Pound, who suffered a stroke in September, 1943. His successor as First Sea Lord was Admiral Sir Andrew Cunningham. Under the supervision of the Prime Minister and the War Cabinet, the Chiefs of Staff were responsible for planning Britain's military effort. They had direct access to the Prime Minister without going through the Service Secretaries. They also possessed a command function. They issued orders to subordinates in the field with the assistance of a Secretariat, a Vice Chiefs of Staff Committee, a Joint Planning Staff, and a Joint Intelligence Subcommittee.

There was no comparable American organization. As George Marshall, the Army Chief of Staff, put it two days after Pearl Harbor, Washington was "a poor command post."[5] The closest thing to the British Chiefs of Staff Committee in 1941 was the Army-Navy Joint Board, consisting of Admiral Harold Stark, Chief of Naval Operations, and General Marshall. General Henry Arnold, Army Air Force Chief of Staff, attended their meetings; but in terms

3. Matloff and Snell, *Strategic Planning, 1941–1942*, pp. 105–7.
4. For a description by Churchill's personal Chief of Staff of the machinery for war direction, see Hastings Ismay: *The Memoirs of General the Lord Ismay* (New York: Viking Press; 1960), pp. 159–78. Cited hereafter as *Memoirs*.
5. Cline, *Washington Command Post*, p. 90.

of the chain of command, Arnold was a subordinate of General Marshall. Until July, 1939, the Joint Board had no right of access to the President, being subordinate to the Secretary of the Navy and the Secretary of War. Nor did it have any command function. The Joint Board issued no orders. If Marshall and Stark agreed, all was well; if they disagreed, the Army and the Navy went their separate ways until the dispute was resolved at the Cabinet level. By a military order in July, 1939. Roosevelt put the Joint Board under the newly organized Executive Office of the President. This move resulted in some improvement, but meetings were infrequent and the Joint Board lacked that most elementary of institutions, its own Secretariat. If the American military machine responded well to the crisis of December, 1941, it was a tribute to the personalities and characters of the men in the higher levels of command and not to the organization itself, which, by British standards, was headless.

During Arcadia all this was changed, although the Americans probably would have done it themselves; Marshall certainly was aware of the inadequacies, and after Arcadia he went on to reorganize the War Department. He was also indirectly responsible for the Arcadia reform. Marshall wanted one man to be the commander of all American, British, Dutch, Australian, and New Zealand forces in Southeast Asia. He hoped this unity of command would help stem the tide of Japanese advance. He also sought to establish a precedent for subsequent Allied operations. To make the proposal more attractive to the British, Marshall suggested General Sir Archibald Wavell, then Commander in Chief, India. As Wavell could expect little but defeat, Churchill was not very happy with the idea. Roosevelt, however, supported Marshall; Churchill gave way and cabled the War Cabinet for their approval. In his message the Prime Minister said that Wavell "would receive his orders from an appropriate joint body, who will be responsible to me as Minister of Defense and to the President of the

United States, who is also Commander-in-Chief of all United States Forces."[6]

The War Cabinet accepted Wavell's appointment, and he became the first Anglo-American Supreme Commander of the Second World War. The area of his authority was given the acronym ABDA, standing for American-British-Dutch-Australian theater. London also wanted additional information about the "joint body." Churchill was visiting Canada when this reply came in, and on their own the British Chiefs of Staff drafted a memorandum entitled "Higher Direction of War in the ABDA Area," which was given to Marshall, Stark, Arnold, and King on December 29.[7] This was followed by a second and more carefully written British memorandum entitled "Post-Arcadia Collaboration," circulated on January 10. Both papers were egocentric. The joint body would be the British Chiefs of Staff Committee, or their representatives, meeting with their American opposites. It would be called the Combined Chiefs of Staff. What the British achieved by this was not merely a joint body but, as one presupposed the other, greater coherence in the American command structure. Until he made sure that the normal home of the Combined Chiefs would be in Washington and that it would control the allocation of war material, Marshall threatened to resign if the British plan was implemented. Once he secured what he wanted, Marshall threatened to resign if it wasn't. When Arcadia ended, Churchill agreed to try out the new arrangement for one month. Frail at birth, the Combined Chiefs of Staff emerged by 1943 as the supreme body for the planning and execution of the Anglo-American war program.

The Combined Chiefs of Staff, in turn, fathered the American Joint Chiefs of Staff. Since the British regarded

6. *U.S. Foreign Relations, Washington and Casablanca Papers,* pp. 277–9. For the text as sent to London, see Churchill, *Second World War,* III, 675.

7. For the text of this memorandum, see *U.S. Foreign Relations, Washington and Casablanca Papers,* p. 277.

the air arm as a separate and equal service with the Army and the Navy, General Arnold became Portal's counterpart. Even the device of a personal representative of the head of government to the Chiefs of Staff was imitated. By mid-summer of 1942, Roosevelt found his equivalent for Ismay in Admiral William Leahy, who at the time of Arcadia was American Ambassador to Vichy France. After his appointment Leahy had an office at the White House and also served as Chairman of the Joint Chiefs of Staff.[8] Curiously, no official charter or directive establishing the Joint Chiefs of Staff ever appeared. Its first formal meeting occurred on February 9, 1942. It issued orders; represented America on the Combined Chiefs of Staff; and developed its own Secretariat, Planning Staff, and Intelligence Committee—yet on paper it never existed.

Like the British Chiefs of Staff, the membership of the Joint Chiefs was remarkably consistent. In March, 1942, when Admiral Stark was moved to London, his replacement as Chief of Naval Operations and the Navy representative on the Joint Chiefs was Admiral Ernest J. King. In July, 1942, Admiral Leahy was added to the Joint Chiefs as Chairman of Staff to the President. From then until the end of the war, Leahy, Marshall, Arnold, and King directed the American military machine.

Since the British Chiefs of Staff and the American Joint Chiefs were responsible for the day-by-day operations of their forces, it was impossible for them to be away from London or Washington except for short periods of time. This in turn meant relatively few meetings of the actual Combined Chiefs of Staff. To provide continuity between these meetings, a permanent subcommittee of the Combined Chiefs was established in Washington. It consisted of the American Joint Chiefs of Staff, who attended its sessions in person, and a high-level British Military Mission, which was in constant contact with London. Subordinate to this

8. William D. Leahy: *I Was There* (New York: McGraw-Hill; 1950); pp. 95–7. Cited hereafter as *I Was There*.

body were a Combined Chiefs of Staff Intelligence Committee, a War Plans Committee, a Secretariat, and, eventually, numerous other joint boards handling such matters as shipping and the allocation of munitions production.

The head of the British Military Mission was also a full member of the Combined Chiefs of Staff. Churchill selected Field Marshal Sir John Dill, a former Chief of the Imperial General Staff, for the job. Dill's presence at Arcadia was almost accidental, since he was out of favor with Churchill. Indeed, the Prime Minister had secured Dill's resignation as Chief of the Imperial General Staff in October, 1941, and intended to appoint him Governor of Bombay. It was Dill's successor, General Alan Brooke, who persuaded Churchill to bring Dill to Arcadia, where Churchill observed that he fitted in well with the Americans. When the Prime Minister left Washington, Dill stayed behind to help ease the then-experimental Combined Chiefs through its "teething" troubles.[9]

Dill, quiet, courteous, and good-humored, became a close friend of Marshall. In the early days of his mission, Dill once described himself as providing neutral ground for the meeting of the American Army and Navy, but he provided much more than that. With great tact, he explained Washington's views to London and London's views to Washington. By 1943 Dill personified Allied unity. At the height of the controversy over the cross-channel attack, George Marshall told Roosevelt that he was willing to let a Britisher command the operation provided Dill was chosen.[1] When Dill died in 1944, Roosevelt asked that he be buried in Arlington National Cemetery, and the American Joint Chiefs served as his honorary pallbearers.

9. Arthur Bryant: *A History of the War Years Based on the Diaries of Field Marshal Lord Alanbrooke, Chief of the Imperial General Staff*, Vol. I: *The Turn of the Tide* (New York: Doubleday; 1957), p. 227. Cited hereafter as *The Turn of the Tide*.

1. U.S. Department of State: *Foreign Relations of the United States. Diplomatic Papers. The Conferences at Cairo and Tehran, 1943* (Washington, D.C.: U.S. Government Printing Office; 1961), p. 209. Cited hereafter as *U.S. Foreign Relations, Tehran Papers*.

Although the American Joint Chiefs of Staff was patterned after the British Chiefs of Staff, it differed from its model in two significant respects: one involved power; the other, institutional structure. Roosevelt did not pretend to the art of generalship. Only once during the war did he overrule the advice of the Joint Chiefs on a major operation—when he insisted on Super-Gymnast in 1942. Otherwise, the Joint Chiefs were left alone to win the war quickly and with the minimum cost in casualties. The Joint Chiefs, as a body, and, in particular, General Marshall, who rapidly emerged as the dominant personality in the Joint Chiefs, thus determined Washington's military strategy. They had an authority and an independence denied the British Chiefs of Staff. Rarely did Roosevelt attend their meetings; almost always he accepted their guidance.

With Churchill, the picture was reversed. He met daily with his Chiefs of Staff and was perfectly willing to give advice on everything from grand strategy to the question of which contingents in the Home Guard should be issued steel helmets. On occasion he even went behind the backs of his Chiefs of Staff and sent urgings, if not orders, to commanders in the field. Brilliant, eccentric, erratic—he believed himself capable of directing Britain's war effort. General Brooke, who became Chairman of the British Chiefs of Staff in March 1942, sometimes wondered which caused him more difficulty, the enemy or his impetuous Prime Minister.

The institutional difference between the British and American organizations was equally striking. On graduating from Staff College in 1922, Ismay had written: "The soldier must realize that war is the instrument of policy, and that, in so far as any subservience is necessary, he must be subservient to the statesmen."[2] Certainly, taken as a maxim, neither George Marshall nor any of the American Joint Chiefs would have disagreed. Unfortunately, throughout most of the Second World War, Ismay's principle remained

2. Ismay, *Memoirs*, pp. 40–1.

in Washington just that—a maxim believed in but never implemented. In part, this again reflected personalities. Cordell Hull, the American Secretary of State, was not a member of Roosevelt's inner circle. Moreover, Hull was inclined to turn Ismay's words upside down. Shortly after Pearl Harbor Hull circulated a memorandum within the State Department stating: "They [the Army and Navy] are the fellows who are taking responsibility for the strategy and conduct of the war."[3] The State Department was to subordinate itself to the requirements of the War Department. In short, foreign policy was the servant, not the master, of military policy. There was also a difference in machinery between Washington and London. Under the British system, the Chairman of the Intelligence Committee of the Chiefs of Staff came from the Foreign Office. For Cordell Hull to ask for, or for George Marshall to accept, a similar arrangement in the American Joint Chiefs would never have occurred to either man, whereas the one agency which did exist to coordinate foreign and military policy, the Standing Liaison Committee of the War, Navy, and State Departments, decayed into a low-level messenger service as the war progressed. Hull had no influence on the decisions of Marshall. The War Department created while the State Department dreamed.

3. Hull, *Memoirs*, II, 1109.

II

CROSS-CHANNEL ATTACK OR TERRITORIAL CONCESSIONS, THE FIRST BROKEN PROMISE
January–July 1942

With at least the outlines of an agreed strategy and methods of command, it might be supposed that when Churchill left Washington on January 14, the Anglo-Americans had achieved a mutually acceptable pattern of operations for the coming year. Actually, the reverse was true; events overtook the planners. On December 23 Churchill had requested that four American divisions be sent to Northern Ireland. Roosevelt and Marshall agreed. The troop movement was to be called Operation Magnet. Its purpose was largely psychological, to demonstrate to both the British and the Germans that America intended to fight in Europe. Relief of the existing British garrison would also enable London to send more troops to the Middle East to replace Australian divisions being recalled to defend their homeland. The necessary convoy began to assemble at New York; but on January 12, with British approval, the convoy was rerouted to the South Pacific. The reason lay in the speed and magnitude of the Japanese advance.

Churchill had spoken of the loss of strongholds in the Pacific, but at Arcadia it was hoped that the Japanese could be held north and east of the line of the Malay Peninsula and the Netherlands Indies and that communications with the Philippines, which Japan had invaded on December 10, 1941, could be reestablished. To this end ABDA had been created. No one had much faith in ABDA, but neither did they expect it to dissolve in six weeks, which was what actually happened.

On December 22 Japan landed in the Philippines in force. Although numerically superior to the attackers, the Philippine Army proved unreliable; and within twenty-four hours General Douglas MacArthur, Commander of United States Forces in the Philippines, ordered a retreat into the Bataan peninsula. There followed an effective, if hopeless, defensive battle which lasted in Bataan until April 9 and then in the island fortress of Corregidor until May 6, 1942. By the Bataan campaign, General MacArthur and his successor, General Jonathan Wainwright, prevented Japan from using one of the best harbors in Asia—Manila Bay—for six months. But in ordering the withdrawal, MacArthur handed over the Philippines-proper on December 23, 1941, without any real fight.[1]

If anything, the story in Malaya was worse. Churchill called it the greatest disaster in British military history. The Japanese landed on the peninsula early on the morning of December 8, 1941. By a series of bold and skillful maneuvers, they succeeded in sealing up a large British army in the

---

1. Douglas MacArthur: *Reminscences* (New York: McGraw-Hill; 1964), pp. 123–7. For a critical discussion of MacArthur's decision by the official historian of the Philippine campaign, Louis Morton, see Kent Roberts Greenfield, ed.: *Command Decisions* (New York: Harcourt, Brace; 1959), pp. 110–29. Cited hereafter as *Command Decisions*.

supposed fortress of Singapore, where there were no significant landward defenses even though the British had been working on the base since 1921. On February 15, 1942, General Allan Percival surrendered with over 70,000 men.

The fall of Singapore sealed the fate of the Netherlands Indies. During January and February, the weak United States Asiatic Fleet and the even weaker Dutch and Australian naval forces were destroyed piecemeal. Only four destroyers escaped. Invaded from the north, west, and east and lacking air and naval protection, the Netherlands Indies was not so much conquered as occupied. On March 9 the last Allied ground forces there, at one point numbering 100,000 men, surrendered. With this collapse, Australia itself lay open to assault. On the day the Dutch gave up the Indies, 800 miles away in Burma the British evacuated Rangoon and retreated northward and westward toward the Indian frontier. The loss of Rangoon and Burma meant the cutting off of the Burma Road. Henceforth, China would depend upon the trickle of supplies air-ferried from India over "the Hump" of the Himalayan Mountains.[2]

In just ninety days, from January to April, 1942, Japan wrested the whole of Southeast Asia from the Allies. At the time, it was believed that immense Japanese forces were involved. Actually, only a handful of divisions, together with superior air and sea power, had seized and held the initiative over much larger defensive ground forces. The key to Japan's whirlwind success was mobility and concentration. In short, General Wavell and his disintegrating ABDA command received a "capsule course of instruction in the principles of war."[3] The effect of the Asian collapse was to negate the strategy of Arcadia. Europe might come first, but Australia and India had to be held.

Nor was the Pacific the sole scene of Allied misfortune.

2. Unless otherwise noted, the dating of military events is that given in Mary H. Williams: *Chronology, 1941–1945* (Washington, D.C.: U.S. Government Printing Office; 1960).

3. U.S. Department of the Army: *American Military History* (Washington, D.C.: U.S. Government Printing Office; 1959), p. 386.

On December 19, 1941, in one of those feats of individual bravery which characterize Italian military history, three Italian human torpedoes managed to penetrate the defenses of Alexandria Harbor and explode mines beneath the British battleships *Queen Elizabeth* and *Valiant*. The ships settled in shallow water and on an even keel, so the British were able to dissemble their misfortune, but naval initiative in the Mediterranean passed to the enemy for the next several months.[4]

Although lacking cover on his sea flank, General Auchinleck decided to go ahead with his Egyptian offensive. On December 29 he reached the long-isolated British garrison at Tobruk and, during January, advanced through Cyrenaica to Benghazi. By January 21 Cyrenaica was cleared and the Libyan frontier crossed. The Germans, however, had taken advantage of the changed naval situation. General Rommel and his Afrika Corps were reinforced to the point of parity with their attackers. Parity proved sufficient; the British retreated 300 miles in five days. Auchinleck was able to form a front around Tobruk and offered to try again later in the year, but only if the Prime Minister could guarantee him a two-to-one superiority over his opponent.

The setback in Africa, however, was nothing compared with the rout in the Atlantic. Churchill, quite properly, described the American sea frontier in the opening months of the war as "the U-boat paradise."

In November 1941, the British lost 104,212 gross tons of shipping to German attack. The figures for the Allies in the succeeding four months were as follows: December, 485,985 tons; January, 207,102 tons; February, 384,110 tons; and March, 480,185 tons.[5] Of this amount, almost all was sunk

4. Andrew B. C. Cunningham: *A Sailor's Odyssey: the Autobiography of Admiral of the Fleet, Viscount Cunningham of Hyndhope* (London: Hutchinson & Co.; 1951), pp. 433–5. Cited hereafter as *A Sailor's Odyssey*.
5. The figures are from a table printed in Churchill, *Second World War*, IV, 126. See also Samuel Eliot Morison: *History of United States Naval Operations in World War II* (15 vols.; Boston: Little, Brown; 1947–57), I, 114–54. Cited hereafter as *U.S. Naval Operations in World War II*, followed by volume number.

less than 300 miles from the American coast and the remainder in other parts of the Atlantic under United States
Navy patrol. It was not until April that Washington insti-
tuted coastal convoys.

Asian collapse, African setback, Atlantic difficulties—all
were met by improvisation. The Australian Government
recalled its divisions from North Africa. Roosevelt and
Churchill pleaded that they be diverted at least momentarily
to Burma in an attempt to salvage land communications
with China. The Australians refused and Burma fell.
Britain, too, rushed reinforcements eastward, first to Singapore, then to Burma, and finally to India. The British,
however, still fearing invasion of England and already over-
extended, possessed no strategic reserve. The fifty Hurricane
fighters sent to Singapore in January, 1942, represented a
maximum effort for London.

Under the circumstances, the task of stemming the tide,
particularly in the Far East, fell upon Washington. George
Marshall chose General Dwight Eisenhower, then a member
of the Army's War Plans Division, to find the men, the
shipping, and the supplies.[6] As a psychological gesture more
than anything else, Roosevelt in mid-March ordered General
MacArthur to Australia to lead the defense of the southwest
Pacific. Arcadia had decided that the main effort of the war
should be in Europe; but between January and March,
90,000 American troops were dispatched to the Pacific as
against 20,000 to Iceland and Northern Ireland. No one was
unhappier about the situation than the man responsible for
the Pacific deployment: General Eisenhower. On January
22, in a note to himself, he had written: "We've got to go to
Europe and fight—and we've got to quit wasting resources
all over the world—and still worse—wasting time. If we're
to keep Russia in, save the Middle East, India, and Burma,

6. Eisenhower was ordered to Washington in December 1941 as an Asian
specialist. He had served under MacArthur for four years in the Philippines,
attempting to build up a Philippine Army. Dwight D. Eisenhower: *Crusade
in Europe* (Garden City, New York: Doubleday; 1948), p. 14. Cited hereafter as *Crusade in Europe*.

we've got to begin slugging with air at West Europe; to be followed by a land attack as soon as possible."[7] A month later, on February 28, the personal note had expanded into a formal memorandum. Eisenhower and the Army War Plans Division drew a sharp distinction between what was "necessary" and what was "desirable" in winning the war. To protect the security of the United States, Hawaii, and the Caribbean area, the U.S. had to master the North Atlantic sea-lanes, keep Britain and Russia in the war, and prevent a German-Japanese linkup in the Middle East or India. Everything else, including holding Australia, Alaska, and South America below Natal, was just "highly desirable."[8]

Eisenhower accepted the basic premise of Arcadia: Germany first. He had no interest, however, in the British plan for "closing the ring." Instead, he felt that America and Britain should "engage from the middle of May onwards" an increasing proportion of the German Air Force over Northwest Europe and "by late summer" launch a cross-channel attack. The advantages of such a program were twofold. First, on the logistic level, it would stem drainage to the Pacific and, through the preinvasion buildup, both secure England and compel the clearing of the North Atlantic. Second, on the military level, it would mean launching the attack on Europe while the Russian Army was still an effective fighting force. Indeed, many in the War Department were convinced that unless sizable portions of the German Army were drawn off the Russian front the Soviet Union could not survive a second year of war. Eisenhower wanted detailed planning with the British to begin at once.

Much more than the plan for an attack in Africa, the Eisenhower memorandum reflected current thinking in the War Department. As early as the summer of 1941, War Department planners, in drawing up the Victory Program, had held that the United States "must prepare to fight

7. Alfred Chandler, ed.: *The Papers of Dwight David Eisenhower: The War Years* (5 vols.; Baltimore: Johns Hopkins University Press; 1970), I, 73.
8. Cline, *Washington Command Post*, pp. 147–51.

Germany by actually coming to grips with and defeating her ground forces."[9] During the Arcadia Conference, Major General Stanley Embick, then George Marshall's senior adviser on strategy, had warned that "acceptance of a commitment in North West Africa at this time would prove to be a mistake of the first magnitude." Marshall neither accepted nor rejected Embick's views. Seeing Roosevelt's interest in Super-Gymnast, he remained noncommittal and raised only technical objections. But the twin notions of closing the ring and Europe's liberating herself were alien to the American military mind. By March 16 the Eisenhower memorandum had been accepted by the Joint Chiefs of Staff. By March 16, too, it was evident that Super-Gymnast was dead for the immediate future. Super-Gymnast constituted only half of a larger operation: the clearing of the whole southern coast of the Mediterranean. At Arcadia Churchill talked of Auchinleck's seizing Libya and Tripoli from the west while Gymnast forces advanced east through Algeria.

In January the Libyan campaign (Acrobat) failed. In February the withdrawal of Australian and New Zealand divisions from Egypt meant that Auchinleck could not renew his offensive for many months. Without Acrobat and the prospects of a linkup with British forces advancing westward out of Egypt, Super-Gymnast made little sense. Moreover, there was the attitude of the Vichy Government to take into account. Churchill talked of going ahead with Super-Gymnast regardless of the position of the French authorities in North Africa. In Washington, however, Dill and the British planners on the Combined Chiefs of Staff readily admitted that Super-Gymnast presupposed "whole-hearted French cooperation." Ironically, this was on January 22, one day after Auchinleck's attack, which might have been decisive for French opinion in North Africa, had been turned into a defeat by Rommel. On March 3 the Com-

9. Matloff and Snell, *Strategic Planning, 1941–1942*, p. 61.

bined Chiefs of Staff agreed that, "far from cooperating, the Vichy French will continue to aid the Axis."[1] The obstacles to Super-Gymnast appeared insuperable.

In March Eisenhower and the Army War Plans Division converted his memorandum into a simple sketch of the cross-channel operation, giving the area of assault, the timing, and the forces necessary. At first, it was hoped that D-Day could be scheduled sometime between July 15 and August 1, 1942; but the continuing demands of the Pacific and the need to replace the Australians and New Zealanders in the Middle East with fresh troops from Britain made this date impossible. Fall and winter were poor times to navigate the Channel. Thus when Eisenhower's sketch appeared, D-Day had been shifted to April 1, 1943. The place of landing would be between Le Havre and Boulogne. America proposed to furnish 30 divisions and 3,000 aircraft; the British would be asked to supply 18 divisions and 2,500 aircraft. The code name for the invasion itself was Roundup; for the preinvasion buildup, Bolero.[2]

The sketch also included a plan for a second, contingency operation, called Sledgehammer, in case Russian collapse appeared imminent. This emergency invasion, which also could be used in the unlikely event of a German collapse, should be readied for any time after September, 1942. For Sledgehammer the majority of the forces would be British. Enough landing craft would be available to transport only five divisions, and, although the word "sustaining" was used, Sledgehammer clearly constituted a sacrifice. The Eisenhower outline was completed on March 27. Marshall approved; and after minor changes of wording, he and Henry L. Stimson, the American Secretary of War, presented it to Roosevelt on April 1. The President was now as enthusiastic over Roundup as he had been before about Gymnast. Although it had been discussed by the Combined Chiefs of Staff, he decided to bypass Dill and the infant organization

1. Ibid., p. 175.
2. Ibid., pp. 182–7; Cline, *Washington Command Post*, pp. 152–8.

in Washington. Instead, he asked his close friend and adviser, Hopkins, and Marshall to fly to London immediately
and show the plan to Churchill. No consideration at any
point was given to the political implications of a cross-
channel assault.

Hopkins and Marshall arrived in London on April 8.
Churchill found the American proposal "momentous" and
cabled Roosevelt that "our two nations are resolved to
march forward into Europe together in a noble brotherhood
of arms on a great crusade for the liberation of the tor-
mented peoples."[3] Both Roundup and Sledgehammer were
approved by the British Chiefs of Staff and, with Hopkins
and Marshall in attendance, by the War Cabinet Defense
Committee on April 14. Marshall noted that "many if not
most" of the participants had "reservations regarding this or
that."[4] Hopkins, however, seems to have been almost totally
taken in and believed that an agreement "in principle"
constituted a binding contract. Both men left London feeling that the British had switched from closing the ring to a
head-on assault upon Hitler's Fortress Europe.

Actually, nothing of the sort had occurred. Roundup,
much less Sledgehammer, was exactly what the British intended to avoid. This was the first meeting of the two top
Anglo-American military leaders. Brooke, Chairman of the
British Chiefs of Staff, had been studying Marshall during
their talks. His conclusion was that, although Marshall
might be a good administrator, as a strategist he was impossible. Marshall was equally unimpressed. He decided that
Brooke "may be a good fighting man, [but] he hasn't got
Dill's brains."[5] Such thoughts, however, were confided to
diaries and friends; on the surface all were in agreement.
Ismay admits that he and his colleagues were less than
candid with their visitors. Churchill insisted that all was
aboveboard but also noted that "there were other alternatives

3. Churchill, *Second World War*, IV, 321.
4. Matloff and Snell, *Strategic Planning, 1941–1942*, p. 189.
5. Sherwood, *Roosevelt and Hopkins*, p. 523.

which lay in my mind."[6] The first was "the descent on French Northwest Africa."

By April 14, however, cross-channel attack had already ceased to be strictly an Anglo-American problem. The Russians were involved, and it was Roosevelt's fault. On April 2 the President had cabled Churchill announcing the Hopkins and Marshall visit. Roosevelt also said that as soon as the Prime Minister approved Marshall's plans, the President would ask Stalin to "send two special representatives to [Washington] at once."[7] On April 12 Churchill replied that he regarded Roundup and Sledgehammer as "masterly . . . in principle." In a muted fashion, Churchill referred to "day-to-day emergencies in the East and Far East" and the necessity of facing them. The Prime Minister said nothing about the Russians.

If this reply was meant as a warning, it was already too late. As Churchill dictated his message, Stalin was reading that Roosevelt wanted him to send Molotov and a general to Washington "in the immediate future."[8] The President had in mind a "very important military proposal involving the utilization of [Anglo-American] armed forces in a manner to relieve [Stalin's] critical Western Front." Whether it was done intentionally or not, Roosevelt had already contacted the Russians before receiving the consent of the British Government. Perhaps Roosevelt believed that in not using the expression *cross-channel attack*, he had kept. all his options open. If so, Stalin soon disabused him of the notion and also proved his skill as a negotiator. On April 20 the Soviet Premier accepted Roosevelt's invitation. Molotov, said Stalin, would arrive in Washington not later than May 15 for "an exchange of views on the organization of a second front in Europe in the near future."[9] Roosevelt was also informed that "it goes without saying that Molotov will also

6. Churchill, *Second World War*, IV, 323.
7. Ibid., p. 314.
8. *Stalin's Correspondence*, II, No. 17, 22–3.
9. Ibid., II, No. 18, 23–4.

go to London." The message was an excellent example of preemptive diplomacy. What Roosevelt offered was a "military proposal"; what Stalin assumed was "a second front in Europe." What Roosevelt intended to propose was the invasion of Europe in 1943; what Stalin asked for was an attack "in the near future." Nor was this all. The seemingly casual reference to a Molotov visit to London brought to a head Anglo-American controversy over Soviet territorial claims.

In December Washington and London agreed in refusing Russia recognition of her 1941 frontier. London, however, rapidly changed its mind. On January 28 Eden circulated a memorandum to the War Cabinet in which he pointed out that after a German defeat "Russia's position on the European continent will be unassailable."[1] In this same memorandum, United States foreign policy was described as "exaggeratedly moral, at least where non-American interests are concerned." When the war ended, Soviet forces would be much deeper into Europe than they had been in 1941. It seemed to Eden only "prudent to tie the Soviet Government to agreements as early as possible." Lord Halifax, the British Ambassador to Washington, was instructed in February "to speak in this sense to the State Department." On March 7 Churchill cabled Roosevelt "that the principles of the Atlantic Charter ought not to be construed so as to deny Russia the frontiers she occupied when Germany attacked her."[2] By the end of the month, Halifax was saying that London would negotiate a treaty with Russia that would give implicit recognition to Soviet claims other than that to Poland. Roosevelt and Hull strongly objected, preferring that all territorial settlements await the holding of a peace conference. There were to be no secret arrangements in the Second World War.

Molotov visited London first, arriving on May 20. By then, the German summer offensive in Russia was gathering

1. Eden, *Memoirs*, II, 370.
2. Churchill, *Second World War*, IV, 327.

momentum. Molotov indicated that he was more interested in an immediate cross-channel attack than in the frontier question. He did not moderate Russian territorial claims but spoke pessimistically about the Soviet Union's ability to survive the German assault and asked the British to draw off at least forty German divisions from the Russian front. Churchill was sympathetic but noncommittal. In fact, the Prime Minister stressed the shortage of landing craft and pointed out to Molotov that "it was unlikely that any move we could make in 1942 . . . would draw off large numbers of enemy land forces from the Eastern Front."[3]

Molotov was equally unsuccessful with the frontiers. Washington exerted extreme pressure. When Halifax said that London intended to accept the Russian demands, Sumner Welles, the American Under Secretary of State and a close friend of Roosevelt, wrote: "The attitude of the British Government is . . . not only indefensible from every moral standpoint, but likewise extraordinarily stupid."[4] This was in April; in May at the time of the Molotov visit to London, Hull threatened public denunciation if the British carried out their plans. The Foreign Office gave way, and Molotov was presented with an innocuous treaty draft pledging Great Britain and the Soviet Union to no separate peace and to postwar cooperation.[5] Molotov argued for three days with a sympathetic but unyielding Eden. Then, on the evening of May 24, the American Ambassador, John Winant, paid a call on the Soviet Foreign Minister. Winant explained that America and Russia were "both interested in a second front."[6] He also told Molotov that Roosevelt was "set against introducing frontier questions at this time." Washington seemed to be linking the question of a second front to a Russian backdown on the frontiers. The Soviet

3. Ibid., IV, 333.
4. *U.S. Foreign Relations*, 1942, III, 541–2.
5. For the text presented to Molotov by Eden on May 23, 1942, see *U.S. Foreign Relations*, 1942, III, 561–3.
6. Ibid., III, 560.

Union was in no position to bargain so Molotov immediately became reasonable. Two days later, on May 26, he accepted the British draft with only a few minor changes.

Molotov arrived in Washington on Friday, May 29. He was preceded by a warning from Churchill. The Prime Minister was "proceeding ceaselessly" with "all preparations" for the cross-channel attack. However, he was also sending Lord Louis Mountbatten, British Chief of Combined Operations, to Washington "to explain to [the President] the difficulties of 1942." Churchill further believed that he and Roosevelt must never let the invasion of French Northwest Africa pass from their minds. He noted that Auchinleck was resuming his offensive.[7]

The warning was disregarded. As he had in London, Molotov talked of a Russian collapse unless the Anglo-Americans invaded Europe soon. Where London had been only sympathetic, Washington was far more forthcoming. On Saturday, May 30, Roosevelt and Molotov met with General Marshall and Admiral King. To his earlier arguments, Molotov now added this statement: "If the answer [on the immediate launching of a second front] should be . . . affirmative, the war would be decided in 1942."[8] Roosevelt asked Marshall whether developments were clear enough so that he could say to Molotov that America and Britain were preparing a second front. Marshall answered yes, whereupon Roosevelt "authorized Mr. Molotov to inform Mr. Stalin that [the President] expected the formation of a second front this year." Nor was there any ambiguity about the point of attack; the phrase used was "across the Channel."[9] Perhaps Roosevelt was thinking of an enlarged Sledgehammer or perhaps he was saying what he felt was necessary to keep Russia in the war. In any case, when Molotov left Washington he carried with him a press release which the Soviet Foreign Minister himself had drawn up. It

7. Churchill, *Second World War*, IV, 340.
8. *U.S. Foreign Relations*, 1942, III, 576.
9. Sherwood, *Roosevelt and Hopkins*, p. 564.

included this sentence: "In the course of the conversations, full understanding was reached with regard to the urgent tasks of creating a second front in Europe in 1942."[1] Not only Stalin but the whole world was to know of the American pledge. To his credit, Marshall objected, asking that there be no reference to 1942, for which no real plans existed; but Roosevelt overruled him.

Molotov arrived back in London on June 9 and left for Moscow on June 11. Churchill found the Soviet Foreign Minister "full of plans for creating a second front by a cross-channel operation in 1942."[2] Roosevelt, too, was sounding optimistic. On May 31 the President sent Churchill a vague outline for an invasion of Europe in 1942. The Americans and the British would land a few troops in France early in August in an effort to draw the German Air Force into combat. If the Germans came out, the Americans and the British would try to defeat them; if the Germans stayed away, the Allies might make the lodgment permanent.

Churchill would have none of it. On June 11 the War Cabinet voted "not to move to France . . . except to stop there, and . . . not go . . . unless German morale is deteriorating."[3] Molotov was not informed of this decision. Instead, to protect themselves from Soviet reproaches, Molotov was given an *aide-mémoire* which Churchill handed to him personally. On the subject of Roundup, Churchill was unequivocal. The British "are concentrating our maximum effort on the organization and preparation of a large-scale invasion of the Continent of Europe by British and American forces in 1943. We are setting no limit to the scope and objective of this campaign, which will be carried out in the first instance by over a million men . . . with air forces of appropriate strength."[4] About Sledgehammer, an

1. For the text of the press release issued on June 11, 1942, see *U.S. Foreign Relations, 1942*, III, 593–4.
2. Churchill, *Second World War*, IV, 341.
3. Bryant, *The Turn of the Tide*, p. 316.
4. For the full text of the *aide-mémoire*, see Butler and Gwyer, *Grand Strategy*, III, Appendix IV, 682–3.

operation now pledged by Washington, Churchill was more discreet. "We are making preparations for a landing on the Continent in August or September, 1942." He noted that "the main limiting factor to the size of the landing force is the availability of special landing-craft . . . [and warned] . . . it would not further the Russian cause . . . if . . . we embarked on some operation which ended in disaster." The conclusion of the Sledgehammer paragraph was, nevertheless, guardedly optimistic. "We can therefore give no promise in the matter, but, provided that it appears sound and sensible, we shall not hesitate to put our plans into effect." As soon as he read it, Maisky believed the British were saying no.[5] Molotov apparently placed more weight on the word of Washington. According to Churchill, he "sailed off into the air . . . apparently well satisfied with the results of his mission." Ironically, the Soviet-American press release and the British veto carried the same date.

On Saturday, June 13, General Brooke received a phone call from Churchill, who "considered Roosevelt was getting a little off the rails, and [that] some good talks as regards [the] Western Front were required."[6] He intended to fly across the Atlantic and wanted Brooke and the British Chiefs of Staff to go with him. The Prime Minister landed in Washington on June 18 and stayed until June 26. The meeting generated an Anglo-American strategic debate which was not finally resolved until July 23, 1942. When it was over, Churchill's strategy of closing the ring had triumphed over the American demand for immediate cross-channel assault. By July 23 Sledgehammer and very probably Roundup were dead. In their places stood Super-Gymnast and a policy of Mediterranean attack. But the debate also produced suspicions and animosities between Washington, London, and Moscow which continued throughout the war.

For one thing, however, the Anglo-Americans could be

5. Maisky, *Memoirs*, p. 282.
6. Bryant, *The Turn of the Tide*, p. 320.

thankful: between June 3 and 6 the Japanese lost the initiative in the Pacific. Early in May American naval intelligence concluded on the basis of intercepted radio traffic that the Japanese were planning a major amphibious operation. At the time, it was not known whether the attack was headed for Alaska, Hawaii, or Australia, since all were vulnerable. Only three American carriers—the *Hornet, Enterprise,* and *Yorktown*—were available and, of these, the *Yorktown* was still disabled from damage inflicted in the battle of the Coral Sea. Facing them would be Vice Admiral Chuichi Nagumo's four carriers and the largest battleship in the world. By May 20, again on the basis of radio intercepts, it seemed that the Japanese were headed for Midway Island. The fall of Midway would give Japan defense in depth for her Pacific conquests. The Americans had no choice but to fight, and the battle opened on June 4. By nightfall all the Japanese carriers had been sunk, as was the *Yorktown*. The Japanese battleships retreated without firing a shot. The Americans could rapidly make good their losses; the Japanese could not. The tide had turned in the Pacific.

Midway, however, was the only bright spot. In the Atlantic losses rose in June to over 800,000 tons. In Russia the German attack moved forward toward the Don and the all-important oil fields of the Caucasus. In Africa General Auchinleck's second offensive of the year fared no better than his first. On June 13 Rommel destroyed the British armor in the battle of Knightsbridge. On June 21 Tobruk fell, and it seemed that Auchinleck, far from winning Libya, might lose Egypt. The fall of Tobruk also ended the Washington Conference and sent Churchill hurrying home to meet a storm of criticism concerning his leadership. Lacking only the final ignominy of total defeat in the desert, these events served as the background for Churchill and Roosevelt's second meeting since Pearl Harbor. Actually, the Washington Conference of June 18 to 26 involved two geographically separate meetings. In the sweltering heat of Washington,

the Combined Chiefs of Staff gathered; in the relative
coolness of the Hudson River valley, Roosevelt and Churchill talked at Hyde Park.

On Friday, June 19, the Combined Chiefs of Staff held
their first meeting. Marshall opened the session by asking
that Brooke "give an outline of the present situation as seen
by the British Chiefs of Staff."[7] Although he was to change
his position within a few hours, Brooke acted as a loyal
spokesman for the Prime Minister. He said Gymnast should
be reconsidered; he wanted to study the possibility of sending American forces to the Middle East. The British were
also interested in offensives based on Australia against the
Japanese. As for Sledgehammer, it was being studied; but,
with equal interest, so were landings in northern Norway
and hit-and-run raids in the Pas-de-Calais. When Brooke
finished his presentation, Marshall did not argue. Instead
he asked Brooke, Dill, and Ismay to go with him to the War
Department. During this more informal session, an Anglo-
American memorandum was drafted. Brooke now reversed
himself. The memorandum condemned Gymnast as a diversion, reaffirmed Roundup, and stressed the importance of
Bolero—the American buildup in England. On Saturday,
June 20, Brooke explained his action to the Combined
Chiefs. He said that he feared a Soviet collapse and that
"the Bolero Plan fitted into the [strategic] pattern because
it contemplated putting American troops into England in
sufficient strength to insure the safety of the United Kingdom."[8]

There was a tendency on everyone's part to steer away from
Sledgehammer. Brooke, of course, was bound by the War
Cabinet decision of June 11. But Marshall, too, was having
second thoughts. Allied landing-craft capacity in September,
1942, would limit the assault force to two divisions. For the
entire operation the Americans could contribute between

7. For the minutes of the June 19 meeting, see *U.S. Foreign Relations,
Washington and Casablanca Papers*, pp. 422–6.
8. Ibid., pp. 429–30.

four and six divisions; the British, only a slightly larger number. Twelve divisions with two in assault hardly sounded like
a second front. The Germans already had twenty-five divisions in France and, considering Allied strength, it was unlikely that Hitler would have to draw on the Russian front for
reinforcements. The Combined Chiefs decided to postpone
any decision on Sledgehammer and to continue Bolero and
shipments to Russia. The experts ignored the promise to
Molotov and hoped nothing untoward would happen on the
Russian front which might force their hands. Brooke and
Marshall wanted to keep Super-Gymnast dead, and both
worried about what might be going on at Hyde Park.

At Hyde Park Super-Gymnast was very much alive. Churchill insisted that he was ready to keep his end of the bargain
with Molotov—six to eight divisions would be ready by fall.
However, he defied anyone, American or British, to come up
with a workable plan. Should he and Roosevelt turn the
Channel into a river of blood just for the sake of a contract
which, even if kept, would do the Russians no good? Failure
in 1942 would spoil all chance of success in 1943. At the
same time, Churchill asked: "Can we stand idle in the Atlantic theater during the whole of 1942?" The answer, of
course, was no. "It is in this setting and on this background,"
said Churchill, "that the French Northwest Africa operation
should be studied."[9] Roosevelt did not commit himself, but
he found Churchill's argument persuasive. At Arcadia he
had told Marshall that he wanted American troops fighting
the Germans in 1942. This would help overcome the American tendency, natural after Pearl Harbor, to think of Japan
as the primary enemy. He had also warned Marshall that
this first encounter must end in victory. Super-Gymnast
seemed to meet both requirements. Also, the British were
unwilling to put Sledgehammer into effect, and the President had promised Molotov a second front in 1942.

Roosevelt and Churchill returned to Washington on Sunday, June 21. Churchill had barely settled into his air-conditioned room at the White House when the news arrived of the fall of Tobruk. The Prime Minister was shocked. After the defeat at Knightsbridge on June 13, it was apparent that Auchinleck's second attempt to take Cyrenaica in 1942 had failed. What Churchill and Brooke expected was that Auchinleck would regroup his forces in western Egypt while holding the advanced supply base and port of Tobruk in Libya as a threat to Rommel's flank. Such was the role Tobruk had played under similar circumstances in 1941 when it successfully withstood a six-month siege. Before leaving London, Churchill and the War Cabinet sent their view about Tobruk to Auchinleck in Cairo. Unfortunately, Auchinleck, Commander in Chief in the Middle East, did not make this strategy clear to General Neil Ritchie, Eighth Army Commander and the man responsible for the tactical handling of British forces. Ritchie failed to prepare Tobruk's defenses, and the fortress was taken by Rommel. The Germans and Italians at one stroke acquired a port, immense supplies of oil and equipment, and a forward base for a campaign against Egypt. Even worse was the manner of the loss—33,000 Allied troops surrendered to less than half their number of Germans. As Churchill later put it: "Defeat is one thing; disgrace is another."[1]

Like the rapid advance of the Japanese six months earlier, the fall of Tobruk and the threat to Egypt transformed the Second Washington Conference from a strategic review into a logistic command post. The Combined Chiefs devoted themselves to finding ways to meet the emergency. Marshall offered to send the only operational American armored division, the Second Armored Division, to Egypt. This offer raised a number of administrative problems, however, and it was decided instead to send Auchinleck by special convoy 300 Sherman tanks and 100 self-propelled guns. To provide the material, the Second Armored Division was stripped of

1. Ibid., IV, 383.

its equipment. The British diverted from India to the Middle East 127 tanks and 24 fighter planes. Production enthusiasts talked in tens of thousands; but in mid-1942 the Combined Chiefs faced a much more grim reality.

The fall of Tobruk also meant political trouble for the Prime Minister. During 1941 Tobruk became a symbol of British tenacity; the ignominy of its collapse brought sharp and widespread criticism. It was the culminating blow—the *Prince of Wales* and the *Repulse*, Hong Kong, Malaya, Singapore, Burma, and now Tobruk. Moreover, defeat in the Far East was excusable because the Far East had been starved to protect England and Egypt. Defeat in the desert was inexcusable because the British enjoyed a clear superiority in numbers. It seemed British tanks were inferior to German tanks; British generals, rank amateurs when compared with Rommel. Before leaving Washington, Churchill knew he would have to face a sharp debate in the House of Commons. Sir John Wardlaw-Milne, an influential Conservative and Chairman of the Finance Committee, made the motion on June 25. It read: "That this House, while paying tribute to the heroism and endurance of the Armed Forces of the Crown in circumstances of exceptional difficulty, has no confidence in the central direction of the war."

Despite his troubles, Churchill at the White House still labored for Gymnast. After learning of the Brooke-Marshall memorandum with its criticism of the North African expedition and its support of Bolero, Churchill informed Brooke that he was dissatisfied with the "do-nothing attitude" of the staffs.[2] On June 20 Roosevelt sent Marshall a paper asking him to suggest where, on the assumption that the Russians were hard pressed, American and British ground forces could engage the Germans before September 15, 1942. Neither Brooke nor Marshall was happy. Marshall liked things even less when after a meeting at the White

2. Bryant, *The Turn of the Tide*, p. 328.

House with Roosevelt and Churchill on June 21, General Ismay circulated an *aide-mémoire* stating that Gymnast was the "best alternative in 1942" to Sledgehammer should it prove impossible to mount the latter operation.[3] The *mémoire* was approved by Brooke, which showed that the Chief of the Imperial General Staff was again falling in step behind the Prime Minister.

Marshall was particularly upset by the implications of Gymnast. Where did one go from French North Africa? He feared that Gymnast would signal the demise not merely of Sledgehammer but of the invasion of France in 1943 as well. To protect the principle of cross-channel attack and at the same time to meet the President's September deadline, Marshall felt compelled to advocate Sledgehammer not only as a sacrificial attack to ward off Soviet collapse, but also as a practical military operation. On June 23 Marshall sent a memorandum to Roosevelt calling for a landing in the Pas-de-Calais.[4] Since there were no troops for 1942, Marshall retreated into the mysteries of air power; the Royal Air Force would provide an umbrella under which the Allies could survive months of superior German counterattacks. As Marshall put it: "The potential power of the immense Air Force concentrated in the UK, alone introduces many possibilities for new departures. The use of bombers for transport, smoke, protective barriers, feints, etc., is yet to be exploited." Marshall urged Roosevelt to imitate the Germans, who "by clever utilization of every conceivable method, overcame what were commonly accepted as insurmountable obstacles in virtually all of their great thrusts . . ., Norway, Flanders in 1940, Crete, etc." The idea was to secure a permanent lodgment in September, 1942, which would subsequently be exploited by the larger resources available in 1943. To Churchill's complaint about the difficulties of finding a commander, Marshall's answer was that one could be

3. *U.S. Foreign Relations, Washington and Casablanca Papers*, pp. 434–5, 468–9.
4. For the full text of the memorandum, see ibid., pp. 473–5.

discovered in the United States. Marshall ended his memorandum with a warning about Gymnast. Besides the familiar cry of diversion, he added: "An outstanding disadvantage is the fact that the operation, even though successful, may not result in [the Germans] withdrawing planes, tanks, or men from the Russian Front."

Churchill and Marshall were deadlocked and the Prime Minister had to return to England. The conference ended with a compromise. Although the Combined Chiefs had approved the Brooke-Marshall memorandum on June 20, this was set aside and replaced with a slightly watered-down version of Ismay's *mémoire*. It was agreed that although the preinvasion buildup would continue, the Anglo-Americans would have "to act offensively in 1942." It was further agreed that "Operations in France or the Low Countries . . . would, if successful, yield greater gains than operations in any other theatre." Plans for Sledgehammer were to be "pressed forward with all possible speed, energy, and ingenuity." But if it appeared impossible, then "the possibilities of operation Gymnast will be explored carefully and conscientiously, and plans will be completed in all details as soon as possible."[5] The Combined Chiefs also said they would look into operations in Norway and Spain. Thus when Churchill left on June 26, the debate was unresolved, but Roosevelt seemed to favor Gymnast.

Marshall felt so strongly about what he regarded as a diversionist debauch that in early July he suggested to Roosevelt that the British be presented with an ultimatum: either they carry out Sledgehammer or the Americans would abandon the European war and fight Japan first. Dill reported the situation to London and added that such a decision would be "immensely popular with the United States Navy, Australia, New Zealand and China."[6] Roosevelt disagreed; he did not believe the choice was between the North African invasion and the cross-channel attack in 1943. Ulti-

5. Ibid., p. 479.
6. Butler and Gwyer, *Grand Strategy*, III, 631.

matums were out as was a change in the Europe-first strategy. He was, however, willing to give Marshall one last
chance to persuade the British to undertake an invasion of
Europe in 1942; but, if Churchill held his ground, Marshall
must accept some alternative operation, which could only
mean Gymnast. The American promise to Molotov was to
be kept, if not quite in the way the Russians expected.

Marshall, King, Eisenhower, and Hopkins left Washing-
ton on July 16. They arrived in London on Saturday, July 18.
The political prospects of the mission were poor. On June 25
Auchinleck removed Ritchie and assumed command of the
Eighth Army. The change came too late. Rommel pressed his
attack and Auchinleck retreated 400 miles. In July the
British stood at bay at El Alamein—the last defensive line
before Alexandria and Cairo. Wardlaw-Milne's motion of
"No Confidence" failed by 475 votes to 25 on July 2.[7] Yet
Churchill's margin of victory was deceptive. The government had not been shaken, but there was a great deal of
popular discontent; further defeat in the desert might cost
the Prime Minister his office. An aborted landing in France
would bring about his fall. Marshall argued that the operation would be a success. He had modified the plan as presented in the memorandum to Roosevelt. The Pas-de-Calais,
with its excellent communication net, had been abandoned
as the assault site. Instead, Marshall selected the more limited objectives of taking the Channel Islands. Guernsey and
Jersey, and the port of Cherbourg on the Cotentin Peninsula. Surprisingly, Marshall's plan resembled a scheme which
Churchill had proposed during the fall of France: that the
remnants of the French Army hole up in the Cotentin
Peninsula. Marshall now believed that the Allies could do
the same thing with the skimpy forces available in the fall of
1942. Air power could protect them during the winter

---

7. Nigel Nicolson, ed.: *Harold Nicolson, Diaries and Letters, Volume II:
The War Years, 1939–1945* (New York: Atheneum; 1967), 229–32. Cited
hereafter as *Diaries and Letters*, II.

months, and in the spring they would provide a bridgehead
for the larger assault in 1943.

According to Hopkins, "Marshall and King pushed very
hard," but they failed to convince the British.[8] Roosevelt
was informed of the impasse, and he cabled Marshall that
some agreement involving the use of American troops
against the Germans in 1942 must be reached. On July 24
Sledgehammer gave way to Super-Gymnast, now rechris-
tened Torch by the Prime Minister. Marshall was bitterly
disappointed and felt that the British had been leading him
on when they accepted his plans back in April. Marshall also
insisted that the British face the full consequences of their
action. Churchill and Roosevelt talked about invading
North Africa in 1942 and France in 1943. In Marshall's
opinion this was nonsense; Torch meant the end of
Roundup. Churchill at first demurred, but then gave way.
The Combined Chiefs of Staff memorandum setting forth
the new strategy included this sentence: "That it be understood that a commitment to this operation [Torch] renders
'Round-up' in all probability impracticable of successful
execution in 1943 and therefore that we have definitely
accepted a defensive encircling line of action for the Continental European theatre."[9] Brooke, having been asked to
attack the Germans with what amounted to bare hands
while Egypt was endangered, remained convinced that the
Americans were no strategists. Eisenhower later admitted
that Sledgehammer, even in its Cotentin version, would
have failed.

Although the final decision for Torch was not taken until
late in July, Stalin already knew the cross-channel attack
planned for 1942 had been called off. On July 18 Churchill
addressed a long message to the Soviet Premier about the
Arctic convoys. The July convoy had met with disaster, with

8. Sherwood, *Roosevelt and Hopkins,* p. 611.
9. For the full text of this memorandum, see Butler and Gwyer, *Grand
Strategy,* III, Appendix V, 684–5.

twenty-three ships sunk out of the thirty-three dispatched. The Admiralty decided to postpone further sailings until the long Arctic nights set in. In the course of explaining the bad news, Churchill noted that he was "building up [for] a really strong second front in 1943."[1] In short, with the Germans crossing the Don River, the commitments given to Molotov only a month earlier were no longer valid. Churchill said his message had been seen by Roosevelt.

Stalin's reply, sent on July 23, was harsh and bitter. After accusing the British of cowardice over the Arctic convoys, he stated "most emphatically that the Soviet Government cannot tolerate the second front in Europe being postponed till 1943."[2] Nor were the Russians alone in their anger. Hopkins, Eisenhower, Stimson, and Marshall—all had fought against Gymnast to the end. Even the normally Anglophile Winant was furious. Roosevelt, whose responsibility for the crisis and particularly for the Russian involvement in it was greater than Churchill's, kept discreetly in the background. His July communications to Stalin dealt with such innocuous subjects as survey flights in Alaska to prepare a new supply route to Russia. He did, however, advise Churchill to handle Stalin "with great care" and to put himself in the Soviet Premier's place. Clark Kerr, the new British Ambassador to Moscow, was more explicit: it would be best if the Prime Minister came to the Soviet Union. Churchill asked Stalin for an invitation on July 31, 1942. He said he would bring with him the Chief of the Imperial General Staff, General Allan Brooke. Acting with unusual speed, Stalin replied that same day inviting the Prime Minister to come to Moscow. Churchill left London feeling like a man "carrying a large lump of ice to the North Pole."

1. *Stalin's Correspondence*, I, No. 56, 52–5.
2. Ibid., I, No. 57, 56.

III

CROSS-CHANNEL ATTACK VERSUS THE MEDITERRANEAN, FROM MOSCOW TO CASABLANCA

August 1942–January 1943

C hurchill's first meeting with Stalin took place a little after 7 P.M. on Wednesday, August 12, 1942.[1] The Prime Minister was accompanied by Clark Kerr and Averell Harriman, the latter serving as Roosevelt's special representative. Present also were Molotov and Marshal Kliment Voroshilov, the Soviet Defense Minister. According to Churchill, the first two hours of the four-hour conference were "bleak and somber." Churchill began with a frank and lengthy explanation of the reason for canceling Sledgehammer. He talked about the scarcity of

1. For the Prime Minister's account of the meeting, see Churchill, *Second World War*, IV, 477–83. See also Herbert Feis: *Churchill, Roosevelt, Stalin: The War They Waged and the Peace They Sought* (Princeton, N.J.: Princeton University Press; 1957) pp. 73–80. Cited hereafter as *Churchill, Roosevelt, Stalin*. William H. McNeill: *America, Britain, and Russia: Their Cooperation and Conflict, 1941–1946* (London: Oxford University Press; 1953) pp. 197–200. Cited hereafter as *America, Britain and Russia*.

landing craft, the inability of the Anglo-American air forces
to provide adequate cover in the Channel, and, finally, the
small size of the assault force compared with the German
garrison in France. Churchill depicted Sledgehammer as an
invitation to disaster which even in the form of a sacrificial
attack would not help the Russians because Hitler could
defeat it without pulling a single man, plane, or gun from
the eastern front. The longer Churchill talked, the gloomier
Stalin looked. Finally Stalin interrupted Churchill to say
that "a man who was not prepared to take some risks could
not win a war." With insulting bluntness Stalin accused the
British of being afraid to fight the Germans. He admitted he
could not force his allies to undertake Sledgehammer, but
he did not accept the arguments for its postponement.
Harriman later cabled Roosevelt that so far in the meeting
there had been "no agreement on any point and the atmosphere was tense."[2]

Despite the provocation, Churchill kept his temper. Indeed, the Prime Minister had put his bad news first, the
cancellation of Sledgehammer, in order to make his good
news, the invasion of North Africa, seem all the better. To
improve Soviet spirits, Churchill described the increasing
effectiveness of the Allied bomber campaign against Germany. Stalin's frowns lessened, and the two men, although
only in words, rapidly destroyed all the cities of Germany.
The proper mood established, Churchill asked the rhetorical
question "What is a second front?" The Prime Minister
then unfolded a map of the Mediterranean and explained
Torch.[3] A now smiling Stalin watched as Churchill drew a
picture of a crocodile. The Prime Minister declared that
Nazi Europe was like the crocodile, with France as its hard
snout and the Mediterranean its soft underbelly. The Anglo-
Americans were unprepared as yet to attack the snout, but
they were ready and intended to cut into the vulnerable

2. For Harriman's report to Roosevelt, see *U.S. Foreign Relations*, 1942,
III, 618–20.
3. Churchill, *Second World War*, IV, 480–1.

Mediterranean underbelly. This, said Churchill, was Torch, and the assault was scheduled to begin no later than October 30.

With a quickness of mind that amazed both Churchill and Harriman, Stalin grasped the strategic advantages and disadvantages of Torch. Stalin recounted four main reasons for Torch. First, Torch would hit Rommel in the back; second, it would overawe Spain; third, if in reaction the Germans moved into French North Africa or unoccupied France, this move would produce fighting between the French and Germans; fourth, the conquest of the African shore of the Mediterranean would expose Italy to the full brunt of the war. Stalin saw two disadvantages: first, to be a success, Torch required Spanish neutrality; otherwise, the expedition's communications might be cut at Gibraltar. Second, there was the danger of an adverse reaction to the landings on the part of the Vichy officials in North Africa. Stalin urged Churchill to be very careful in handling these aspects of Torch. Stalin also asked that the timing of Torch be pushed forward to the first week of October. Considering that Stalin had never before heard of Torch, the Soviet Premier's performance was astonishing.

The last two hours of the meeting were now as warm as the first two hours had been cold. Churchill and Harriman assured Stalin they would be careful with the French. Harriman told Stalin that reports from American agents in North Africa indicated it was unlikely the French would fire on American troops. Churchill and Harriman also said they would try to advance the date for Torch. As for Stalin, he became Torch's enthusiastic supporter. At one point the Soviet Premier declared: "May God prosper this undertaking."[4] According to Churchill everyone parted "in an atmosphere of good will." Harriman cabled Roosevelt that night that "the relationship between [Stalin and Churchill] had reached a most friendly basis."[5]

4. Ibid., IV, 481.
5. *U.S. Foreign Relations, 1942,* III, 620.

As both Churchill and Harriman soon discovered, however, their optimism was premature. Churchill stayed in Moscow four more days, but it was only on his last night, Saturday, August 16, that the Prime Minister again had a really friendly meeting with Stalin. During the interim Churchill, and to a lesser extent Harriman, endured ceaseless badgering over Sledgehammer's cancellation. Torch receded into the background. It was Sledgehammer and Sledgehammer alone which interested the Russians. The new Soviet attitude was apparent at the start of Churchill's second meeting with Stalin on Thursday, August 14. Churchill came expecting to continue the previous day's discussions about Torch. Instead, Stalin handed Churchill and Harriman a harshly worded memorandum castigating Sledgehammer's postponement.[6] The memorandum started with Molotov's visit to London in June where, according to Stalin, "the decision to open a second front in Europe in 1942 was reached." It alleged that the failure to implement this decision dealt a "mortal blow to . . . Soviet public opinion, . . . complicates the situation of the Red Army . . . and prejudices the plan of the Soviet Command." With the German Army concentrated in Russia, Stalin and his colleagues were of the opinion that the second front should come in 1942. The memorandum ended with the statement that Stalin was "unfortunately unsuccessful in convincing the Prime Minister . . . [of this], while Mr. Harriman . . . fully supported the Prime Minister."

Churchill described the ensuing discussion as "most unpleasant." He said he would give Stalin a formal reply to the Soviet memorandum the following day. Stalin, however, was not to be put off. Without becoming angry or even animated, the Soviet Premier spent almost the entire meeting trying to persuade Churchill to undertake Sledgehammer. What Stalin wanted was six or eight divisions landed on the

6. For the text of the Soviet memorandum, see *Stalin's Correspondence*, I, No. 65, 60–1.

Cherbourg peninsula in the fall. He accused the British of cowardice. He accused them of defaulting on lend-lease deliveries. But most of all Stalin accused Churchill of breaking his word over Sledgehammer.

According to Brooke, who was present, Churchill took it for a time but finally crashed his fist down on the table and began an impassioned reply. Stalin stood up and with a broad grin stopped Churchill's interpreter and said: "I do not understand what you are saying, but by God, I like your sentiment."[7] Thereafter the meeting was quieter, with an end to insults but with an atmosphere that remained frigid. Churchill asked Stalin whether the Red Army could stop the Germans short of the all-important oil fields of the Caucasus. Stalin assured Churchill the Caucasus would be held. Stalin also discoursed at length on the merits of Soviet rocket artillery. About Sledgehammer, however, neither man changed his position. Stalin wanted it, whereas Churchill denied the practicality of a cross-channel attack in 1942 and offered Torch instead. They agreed to let the staffs examine the problem. Stalin also asked Churchill and Harriman to come to a banquet the next day. Churchill accepted but added he would have to leave Moscow the morning of the day after, Saturday, August 15. A disconcerted Stalin requested that Churchill stay through Sunday. Churchill acquiesced and when the meeting ended the two men shook hands, an event Churchill found notable enough to record in his memoirs. Upon returning to his dacha, State Villa No. 7, the Prime Minister complained that he was "downhearted and dispirited" and talked of leaving Stalin alone "to fight his own battles."[8]

Friday morning, Churchill, Cadogan, and Brooke prepared an *aide-mémoire* answering Stalin's memorandum.[9]

7. Bryant, *The Turn of the Tide*, p. 374.
8. Wilson, *Churchill*, pp. 63–4.
9. For the text of the British *aide-mémoire*, see *Stalin's Correspondence*, I, No. 66, 61–3.

It, together with a brief supporting letter from Harriman, was handed to Molotov later in the day.[1] The British *mémoire* denied that any promise of a second front in 1942 had been given to Molotov during his visit in London. Churchill called Stalin's attention to the note the Prime Minister had handed Molotov on June 10, 1942, shortly before the Soviet Foreign Minister left for Moscow. Churchill quoted the sentence in the earlier note that read: "We can therefore give no promise in the matter [of implementing Sledge-hammer]." He averred that in several conversations with Molotov, he had made it quite clear that Sledgehammer was only a plan and one with little prospect of being adopted.

Having at least to his own satisfaction answered Stalin's charge of broken promises, Churchill then discussed the operations themselves. Sledgehammer was declared a military impossibility, whereas Torch became "the best second front in 1942 and the only large-scale operation possible from the Atlantic." Churchill again offered to have Brooke "go into [the military] details with the Russian commanders to any extent that may be desired." He ended the *mémoire* with a pledge to aid his "Russian Allies by every practicable means." Harriman's supporting letter was very brief. Roosevelt's representative stated that he had studied Stalin's memorandum and Churchill's *mémoire*. Harriman wrote that he did not believe "any useful purpose would be served in comments by me additional to what the Prime Minister has said." Harriman, however, did reaffirm Churchill's statement that "no promise has been broken regarding the second front."

Under the circumstances the staff conversations were an exercise in futility. Marshal Kliment Voroshilov, the Soviet Defense Minister, and Marshal Boris Shaposhnikov, former Chief of the Soviet General Staff, represented Russia. Brooke spoke for the Anglo-Americans. Voroshilov asked for Sledgehammer; Brooke offered Torch. Brooke later wrote

1. For the text of Harriman's letter, see *U.S. Foreign Relations*, 1942, III, 622.

that after two and a half hours of discussion he "saw clearly that [he and Voroshilov] could go on arguing till the cows came home without making any headway." Brooke also discovered that the Russians were unwilling to give him any information as to the real situation on the eastern front. The meeting ended with an agreement to disagree.[2] Nor was the banquet Friday night any more productive. Stalin was personally friendly to Churchill, but, as the Prime Minister cabled Roosevelt, there was "no opportunity of talking about serious things." It was a night of toasts and suckling pig. Churchill proposed Stalin's health and Cadogan proposed death and damnation to the Nazis. Harriman felt that Stalin seemed to be entirely oblivious of the unpleasant discussions of the night before. Brooke found the whole scene, with its sham conviviality, disgusting. Churchill left about 1:30 A.M.

Saturday evening, August 15, Churchill again called on Stalin. As he himself admits, the Prime Minister was not in the best of moods. Churchill had come to Moscow fully expecting to have a difficult time with Stalin over the cancellation of Sledgehammer, but what had transpired was almost beyond belief. Stalin had accused the British Army of cowardice and Churchill himself of duplicity. There had been no political discussions and, except for the first night, no real military discussions either. Instead, Churchill had been faced with hours of invective made more telling by the cold, almost impersonal manner in which it had been delivered. Even during the friendly banquet, Stalin had referred to Churchill's role in the British intervention in Russia after the First World War and expressed a liking for "a downright enemy."[3]

Churchill, of course, made allowance for Russia's military position which in August, 1942, was truly desperate and which must have placed Stalin under great strain. On August 9, 1942, Field Marshal Ewald von Kleist's Army

2. Bryant, *The Turn of the Tide*, pp. 378–81.
3. Churchill, *Second World War*, IV, 493.

Group A took Maikop in the Caucasus, where the Germans could see the first Russian oil derricks, while that same day Field Marshal Friedrich Paulus lined up the whole of his Sixth Army on the right bank of the Don River facing Stalingrad, whose factory smoke smudged the horizon. The German Army, confident of victory and 300 miles east of Moscow, was preparing for what it believed would be the last battle. Churchill felt, however, that the abuse he had been subjected to was excessive. He was also puzzled by the sudden shift from Wednesday's cordiality to Thursday's bitterness. Moreover, he had completely failed to reach any understanding with the Soviet Premier, a fact which boded ill for the future of the Alliance.

Churchill arrived at the Kremlin at seven o'clock in the evening. He was accompanied only by his interpreter, Major Birse, and he regarded the visit as a short courtesy call to say goodbye to Stalin. He did not, however, leave the Kremlin until seven hours later, and during the intervening time, as Churchill put it, "a relationship was established."[4] During the first hour, Churchill and Stalin discussed the situation in the Caucasus, and Stalin again expressed the opinion that the Red Army would stop the Germans. Stalin also said he had heard rumors that Turkey intended to enter the war on the German side in the near future, but he was prepared to meet that contingency, too. Churchill expressed surprise about the Turkish news and doubted if it were true, as his understanding was that Ankara desired to keep out of the war, nor did he believe the Turks would provoke a fight with Great Britain, which was inevitable if they attacked Russia.

At this point Churchill started to say goodbye, and Stalin suddenly seemed embarrassed. Using the most cordial tone Churchill had yet heard in Moscow, Stalin invited the Prime Minister to join him in his personal quarters for drinks and dinner. Churchill accepted and Stalin became as affable as he had been unfriendly before. Stalin showed Churchill his

4. For Churchill's account of this meeting, see ibid., IV, 495-9.

apartment, which was small and simple. He introduced the Prime Minister to his daughter, and he himself uncorked the bottles.[5] Stalin asked Churchill if he should not invite Molotov, who was described as struggling over the conference communiqué and a companionable drinker. Churchill agreed and also had Major Birse put through a call for Cadogan and inform the Prime Minister's party that he might not be back until late. Molotov arrived immediately; Cadogan did not show up until one in the morning.

The dinner was obviously improvised with various dishes being brought in and out at intervals. The conversation, too, seems to have been rambling although Stalin was obviously trying to be friendly, and at one point, when the talk lagged, he began teasing Molotov about the Soviet Foreign Minister's alleged gangster friends in Chicago. Aside from the chaffing of Molotov, the main impressions Churchill brought away from the meeting were that he had established a friendly intimacy with Stalin and that the Soviet Premier was confident he could defeat the Germans. Churchill and Stalin also discussed the possibility of some sort of combined Anglo-Soviet military operation in northern Norway to relieve German pressure on the Arctic convoys. It was agreed the operation would be worthwhile if the forces could be found. Out of curiosity Churchill asked Stalin which struggle he found harder, the present fight against the Germans or carrying through the policy of the collective farms. Holding up his hands, Stalin answered the collective farms. "Ten millions [killed]," he said, "it was fearful and four years it lasted."[6] Stalin defended collectivization as necessary to mechanize Soviet agriculture and so avoid periodic famines. To himself, Churchill recalled Burke's maxim: "If I cannot have reform without injustice, I will not have reform."

When Cadogan arrived, everyone turned his attention to the conference communiqué. What resulted was a short

5. Svetlana Alliluyeva: *Twenty Letters to a Friend* (New York: Harper and Row; 1967), p. 171.
6. Churchill, *Second World War*, IV, 498.

document of two paragraphs. In the first were listed the main participants in the negotiations. In the second paragraph it was declared that the Moscow discussions had been carried on "in an atmosphere of cordiality and complete sincerity" and had provided an opportunity for "reaffirming the existence of the close friendships and understanding between the Soviet Union, Great Britain, and United States of America." The Allied governments were "determined to carry on [the war] . . . until the complete destruction of Hitlerism and any similar tyranny has been achieved."[7] Churchill, Cadogan, and Birse left the Kremlin at 2:30 on the morning of August 16, 1943.

The following day, while flying back to London, Churchill sent a message to Roosevelt summarizing the results of the Prime Minister's Moscow visit. Churchill believed the trip was necessary as only he personally could have imparted the bad news about Sledgehammer "without leading to really serious drifting apart [of the Alliance]." Stalin was described as "entirely convinced of the great advantages of Torch." By the end of the conference, Churchill said he "had got on to easy and friendly terms [with Stalin]."[8] What Churchill did not say was that for the second time in ninety days the Russians had been deceived about the cross-channel attack.

Churchill in his message to Stalin of July 18, 1942, had mentioned "the building up of a really strong second front in 1943." This was the first time Stalin had learned of the cancellation of Sledgehammer, and it produced the explosion which brought Churchill hurrying to Moscow. It also contained the explicit promise of a cross-channel attack in 1943. During the Moscow meetings nothing was said by either Churchill or Harriman that cast any doubt on this promise. In fact, the reverse was true. During their first meeting on August 12, Churchill informed Stalin that

7. For the full text of the communiqué, see *U.S. Foreign Relations, 1942*, III, 623–4.
8. Churchill, *Second World War*, IV, 501–2.

Roundup, the invasion of France planned for 1943, would be launched the following spring. He even enumerated the forces involved—twenty-seven American and twenty-one British divisions, half this force being armor. Churchill described Torch as a prelude to Roundup. Harriman, in his message to Roosevelt about the August 12 meeting, also records that Churchill told Stalin of "the plans and strength of Roundup."[9] Roundup was again discussed during the bitter meeting of August 13, and the British *aide-mémoire* of August 14 declared that Torch "prepares the way for 1943." Indeed, the *mémoire* stated that one of the main reasons for abandoning Sledgehammer was that it would "use up wastefully and wantonly the key men and the landing craft required for real action in 1943." In short, Stalin was given to understand that while Sledgehammer was off, Torch and Roundup were on; and that of the latter two operations, Torch was subordinate to Roundup. He was not told that the Combined Chiefs believed that Torch canceled Roundup or that the only plan for the invasion of France in 1943 required Germany's collapse.

Perhaps in early August Churchill sincerely believed in Roundup, although neither Brooke nor Marshall shared his opinion. Two events, however, reduced the possibilities of the operation. One, the Dieppe raid, demonstrated the effectiveness of German defense measures at a French channel port; the other was Hitler's decision to fight for North Africa. The Dieppe raid took place on August 19, 1942.[1] The British decided to test the propositions that a landing in France would provoke an air battle with the Luftwaffe and that the landing could be protected by fighters and bombers. The plan called for a six-hour occupation of the town. Dieppe was garrisoned by one regiment of the 302d Infantry Division. Attacking were two brigades of the 2d Canadian

9. *U.S. Foreign Relations*, 1942, III, 619.
1. For a contemporary account of the Dieppe raid, see Hilary A. S. G. Saunders: *Combined Operations* (New York: Macmillan; 1943), pp. 110–46.

Division, a Canadian tank regiment, 1,000 British Commandos, and 50 American Rangers—about 6,300 troops in all, of whom 5,000 were Canadian. The naval force contained 237 ships, albeit only six destroyers and no larger vessels. To make up for the paucity of ship-to-shore fire support and to engage the Luftwaffe, the Royal Air Force allocated 67 squadrons (60 were fighter squadrons) to the operation—more planes than had fought in the Battle of Britain. The Commandos and Rangers were to silence German coastal batteries located east and west of Dieppe while the town itself would be taken by the Canadians. One Commando action was a complete success, the other only partially so; but despite extreme gallantry, the main force never got over the Dieppe seawall. Three quarters of the Canadians were either killed, wounded, or missing. Many could not be reembarked, and the Germans took 2,000 prisoners. The RAF lost 106 aircraft; the Germans lost 48. Churchill claimed a victory; but British anxieties about a cross-channel attack increased.

Whatever its psychological effect, Dieppe was only an incident of war from which valuable lessons were learned. As Marshall predicted, it was Torch and North Africa which eliminated Roundup. Churchill saw the campaign as an Anglo-American exercise in the art of lightning warfare. The basic plan remained a double envelopment with the Eighth Army advancing westward from Egypt and destroying Rommel's Afrika Corps while the Americans and British landed in Algeria. Churchill and Brooke doubted Auchinleck's ability to defeat Rommel; the Eighth Army appeared mesmerized by its antagonist. On their way to Moscow, Churchill and Brooke stopped in Cairo, and Auchinleck was relieved. His replacement as British Commander in Chief in the Middle East was General Harold Alexander; the Eighth Army command was given to General Bernard Montgomery. Montgomery's orders were to fight the battle; Alexander would take care of administration and support.

Montgomery attacked at El Alamein on October 23,

1942.[2] By Wednesday, November 4, he had broken through Rommel's lines; the Germans, however, successfully withdrew their mobile forces. Torch began on November 8, 1942, with landings at Casablanca, Oran, and Algiers; but it was not until May 13, 1943, that the last Axis forces in Africa laid down their arms. The British blamed Marshall and to a lesser extent General Eisenhower, who had been chosen to command Torch, for vetoing a strong landing at Bône and thus failing to close the doors of Bizerte and Tunis to German reinforcements. Marshall still feared Spain would allow the Germans to block the Strait of Gibraltar and cut Torch's communications, so he insisted on the landing at Casablanca; the British rightly judged Franco would do nothing.[3] Stung by the criticism, the Americans wondered if it was only the sudden rains which prevented Montgomery from destroying Rommel at El Alamein. In any case, Hitler had enough time and sufficient manpower to transform Torch into exactly the sort of extended campaign Marshall feared. Instead of lightning warfare, the battle lasted eight months. However, the 150,000 men and the new Fifth Panzer Army which Hitler sent to Africa weakened the German offensive in Russia. Hitler kept Tunis but lost Stalingrad. In the end, of course, he lost them both. German resistance at Stalingrad ended on February 2, 1943; 90,000 prisoners of war were taken. When the encirclement had been completed in November, 1942, the Russians estimated there were 330,000 men trapped in von Paulus's Sixth Army. Tunis fell on May 7, 1943; 275,000 prisoners of war were taken; 125,000 were Germans. Psychologically and militarily, Stalingrad was the greater Allied victory. In terms of strategy

2. Sir Bernard Montgomery: *The Memoirs of Field-Marshal the Viscount Montgomery of Alamein, K.G.* (New York: World Publishing; 1958), pp. 106–26. Cited hereafter as *Memoirs.*

3. For the participants' account of this debate, see Churchill, *Second World War*, IV, 525–45; Eisenhower, *Crusade in Europe*, pp. 74–94. See also George F. Howe: *Northwest Africa: Seizing the Initiative in the West*, Office of the Chief of Military History, Department of the Army (Washington, D.C.: U.S. Government Printing Office; 1957), pp. 25–31. Cited hereafter as *Northwest Africa.*

and the wastage of Axis resources, Tunis was more immediately productive.

During the first week of December, Roosevelt and Churchill asked Stalin to meet them in Africa for the "planning of joint operations in 1943."[4] Stalin was unable to go because of the Stalingrad battle, but he issued a blunt warning about "the promises . . . of a second front in 1943."[5] The promise died at the African conference of Roosevelt and Churchill, which was held at Casablanca between January 14 and 24, 1943.[6] Indeed, it was the necessity for the Anglo-Americans to reach some sort of decision on what to do after Torch which caused the conference to be held, whereas it was the debate as to what this decision should be which took up most of the time and energy of the participants. By comparison the two other major events of Casablanca, Roosevelt's enunciation of the doctrine of unconditional surrender and the President's and Prime Minister's efforts to unite the French Generals Charles de Gaulle and Henri Giraud, had a quality of improvisation about them. This does not mean, however, that the French negotiations or unconditional surrender was unimportant.

In January, 1943, Frenchmen fighting the Germans were divided into two factions: General Charles de Gaulle's Free French Movement organized with Britain's help in London in June, 1940, and those civil servants and officers in Algeria, Morocco, and French West Africa who since November, 1942, had cooperated with Torch. The leader of the North Africans was General Henri Giraud. Uniting the two factions at Casablanca proved difficult.

The trouble was not so much between de Gaulle and Giraud as between de Gaulle and Giraud's followers. Giraud

4. *Stalin's Correspondence*, I, No. 92, 81; II, No. 55, 42.
5. Ibid., I, No. 93, 82; II, No. 58, 44.
6. For material on the Casablanca Conference, see *U.S. Foreign Relations, Washington and Casablanca Papers*, pp. 487ff. For other descriptions of the conference, see Churchill, *Second World War*, IV, 675–95; Bryant, *The Turn of the Tide*, pp. 439–76; Sherwood, *Roosevelt and Hopkins*, pp. 667–97.

was nonpolitical. From the French Armistice in 1940 to April, 1942, he was a prisoner of the Germans. For the Free French this was the decisive period when joining the movement meant armed struggle against the Vichy Government in metropolitan France. For Giraud's followers these were the years when they had remained loyal to Vichy and its elderly Chief of State, Marshal Henri Pétain. Indeed some, like Pierre Boisson, the Governor-General of French West Africa, had actively fought de Gaulle. It was Boisson who handed the Free French a humiliating defeat at Dakar in September, 1940. To de Gaulle the North Africans were men who had stained the honor of France by not carrying on the war against Germany. To the North Africans de Gaulle was a man who had set Frenchmen against Frenchmen when unity in the face of disaster was all important.

Nor was this history of animosity between the Free French and the North Africans the only complicating factor at Casablanca. Roosevelt disliked de Gaulle. Until Torch, Washington had recognized the Vichy regime as the government of France. It did this in part at London's request. The French Fleet in 1940 and 1941 was believed to hold the balance of power in the Atlantic and the Mediterranean. The Navy was loyal to Vichy. To influence Vichy, Washington ignored and sometimes opposed the Free French. The result was criticism of Roosevelt and his Secretary of State Cordell Hull by many American liberals. Roosevelt and Hull blamed de Gaulle for the criticism.[7] This situation produced mutual estrangement and a background of suspicion between de Gaulle and Roosevelt.

Torch, of course, broke the American connection with Vichy. It did not, however, still liberal criticism of Roosevelt. Instead, in the months preceding Casablanca, that criticism reached a new peak because of the fortunes of war. Upon deciding to undertake Torch, Roosevelt and Churchill arranged for General Giraud's escape from France, hoping

7. Hull, *Memoirs,* II, 1130.

that as a nonpolitical war hero Giraud might rally the North Africans to the Allies.[8] Neither the President nor the Prime Minister doubted for a moment that if Torch had had the slightest Gaullist flavor, the French in North Africa would have fought.

Unfortunately, at the time of the landings, the North Africans spurned Giraud. Quite by accident Admiral Jean François Darlan, Commander in Chief of the French Navy and Marshal Pétain's acknowledged political heir, happened to be in Algiers when Torch was launched. General Alphonse Juin, the French Military Commander in North Africa, felt himself bound by Darlan's authority. Darlan offered to cooperate with Torch. Anything more than token French resistance might have jeopardized the operation, so an unhappy Eisenhower decided to deal with Darlan, and a storm of criticism broke over Washington. Cold and formal relations with an aged Pétain were one thing; active collaboration with Admiral Darlan was an entirely different proposition. Roosevelt backed Eisenhower and found himself accused of supporting Fascism.[9] Churchill also supported Eisenhower and was similarly attacked. De Gaulle was, naturally, one of the most vociferous critics.

Darlan was assassinated on December 24, 1942, under circumstances that have never been fully explained. Eisenhower was able to persuade the North Africans to accept Giraud as their leader, and criticism of Anglo-American policy, though not stilled, was at least diminished. Then, just before the opening of the Casablanca Conference, Roosevelt and Churchill came under renewed fire. Shortly before his death Darlan had asked that a former member of the French administration then in exile in Argentina, Marcel Peyrouton, be brought to North Africa as Darlan's political assistant. Giraud, although an able soldier, proved inept in government. Eisenhower allowed Peyrouton to come to Al-

8. Robert Murphy: *Diplomat Among Warriors* (New York: Doubleday; 1964), p. 116.
9. Sherwood, *Roosevelt and Hopkins*, p. 653.

giers, and he was made Governor-General. Peyrouton's credentials, however, turned out to be almost as poor as Darlan's. He had been Minister of the Interior in Vichy France and had broken with Pétain only for personal reasons. Rather unfairly, as Peyrouton's appointment had never been brought to their attention until it was already a subject of controversy, Roosevelt and Churchill again came under attack. Unity of all Frenchmen fighting the Germans was, of course, a good thing in itself, but there can be no doubt that at the time of the Casablanca Conference some sort of Gaullist blessing upon the North Africans would have been politically useful to the President and the Prime Minister. Roosevelt arranged for Giraud's presence at Casablanca. Churchill was to induce de Gaulle to come.

Churchill did not find his task an easy one. De Gaulle, then in London, took the position that his relations with Giraud were strictly a French affair. De Gaulle said he would be happy to have "simple and direct talks with Giraud" but not in "the atmosphere of an exalted Allied forum."[1] Roosevelt, who at this stage in the war regarded de Gaulle's posturings as amusing, chaffed Churchill about the bad behavior of the Prime Minister's "bridegroom," de Gaulle, as compared with the good behavior of the President's "bride," General Giraud.[2] Churchill joined in the bantering with Roosevelt, but he also cabled de Gaulle a blunt warning that "the position of His Majesty's Government toward your movement . . . [might] . . . be reviewed." Since the British were financing the Free French, the threat was not an idle one.

Despite the pressure de Gaulle did not come to Casablanca until January 22, and once there he remained intransigent. Indeed the conference was prolonged for two days beyond its planned ending just so the de Gaulle and Giraud

---

1. *U.S. Foreign Relations, Washington and Casablanca Papers*, pp. 814–16.
2. Roosevelt cabled Hull that de Gaulle "is showing no intention of getting into bed with Giraud." Ibid., p. 816.

talks could take place.[3] The American Secret Service seemed to regard de Gaulle as a potential Presidential assassin; armed with submachine guns, they hid behind the curtains during Roosevelt's meeting with de Gaulle on January 22. The General himself was subjected to alternate lectures by the President and Prime Minister on the theme of Allied unity. What Roosevelt wanted was de Gaulle's agreement to put himself in a subordinate position under Giraud. The President did not advance his case when he described France as being "in the position of a little child unable to look out and fend for itself and that in such a case, a court would appoint a trustee to do the necessary."[4] De Gaulle knew who was the trustee of France, and it was neither Roosevelt nor Giraud.

It was not until the last hours of the conference, on January 24, that de Gaulle and Giraud finally achieved some semblance of unanimity, and even then an element of trickery was involved. De Gaulle was having what he supposed was a private conversation with Roosevelt; nearby Churchill was saying farewell to Giraud. Acting on his own, Hopkins decided that if the four men could be gotten together in the same room an agreement might result. He led Churchill and Giraud to where Roosevelt and de Gaulle were meeting. According to Hopkins, Churchill "grunted," de Gaulle "was a little bewildered," and a "surprised" Roosevelt "took it in his stride."[5] The President and Prime Minister tried to get de Gaulle to sign a declaration of unity with Giraud. The most de Gaulle would concede was to issue an innocuous statement saying that he and Giraud had

3. For de Gaulle's description of his conversations with Giraud, see Charles de Gaulle: *Mémoires de Guerre*, tome II: *L'Unité, 1942–1944* (Paris: Librairie Plon; 1956), pp. 77, 81–3, 85–6. Cited hereafter as *Mémoires*, II. For Giraud's description, see Henri Giraud: *Un Seul But, la victoire: Alger 1942–1944* (Paris: René Julliard; 1949), pp. 101–3, 105–7, 109–10.

4. *U.S. Foreign Relations, Washington and Casablanca Papers*, pp. 694–6. See also note 1, p. 694.

5. Sherwood, *Roosevelt and Hopkins*, p. 693.

met and exchanged views. With this the President and Prime Minister had to be satisfied.

De Gaulle was then conducted to the courtyard of the building where the talks had taken place. Here another surprise awaited him. The courtyard was filled with reporters, cameramen, and newsreel photographers. The correspondents were there for the press conference which was to end the Casablanca Conference. According to Hopkins, before de Gaulle could catch his breath Roosevelt suggested that de Gaulle and Giraud shake hands.[6] To the accompaniment of flashbulbs, de Gaulle acquiesced and shortly thereafter left for London. Eden later wrote that nothing was accomplished by the "shotgun wedding" at Casablanca except a reduction of public agitation over Allied policy. He was wrong. During the unexpected meeting, Giraud agreed to have exploratory talks with representatives of the Free French at Algiers. Under the guise of these negotiations, de Gaulle's movement penetrated French North Africa. As Eisenhower put it to the Combined Chiefs of Staff, Giraud "might be a good Division Commander but he had no political sense and no idea of administration. He was dictatorial by nature and seemed to suffer from megalomania. In addition he was very sensitive and always ready to take offense." Eisenhower believed: "It had been far easier to deal with Admiral Darlan."[7] He was soon to deal with de Gaulle.

It was at this same press conference on Sunday, January 24, that Roosevelt for the first time announced the policy of demanding the unconditional surrender of Germany, Japan, and Italy. Roosevelt always maintained that his use of this momentous phrase was entirely accidental. According to the President, he had had so much difficulty getting de Gaulle

6. Sherwood, *Roosevelt and Hopkins*, p. 693. Harold Macmillan: *The Blast of War, 1939–1945* (New York: Harper and Row; 1967), p. 203. Cited hereafter as *The Blast of War*.

7. *U.S. Foreign Relations, Washington and Casablanca Papers*, pp. 568–9.

and Giraud together that he was reminded of the meeting of
Grant and Lee at Appomattox. This in turn brought to his
mind General Grant's nickname of "Old Unconditional Surrender." When the press conference was held, this association of ideas resulted in the phrase's more or less popping
out of the President's mouth. In short, one of the more
decisive events of the Second World War was the product of
pure happenstance.

The tale was a good one but untrue. Giraud and de Gaulle
may have brought to mind Grant and Lee; but unconditional surrender had long been discussed in Washington. On
April 15, 1942, the Subcommittee on Security Problems of
the Advisory Committee on Post-War Foreign Policy held
its first meeting at the State Department. The original
members were Norman Davis, Chairman; Green H. Hackworth; Breckinridge Long; John MacMurray; and, *ex officio*,
Leo Pasvolsky; all were close associates of Cordell Hull.[8]
Among the topics dealt with by the subcommittee were
armistice terms for Germany, Italy, and Japan. A representative from the War Department, General George Strong, and
from the Navy Department, Admiral Arthur Hepburn,
joined the subcommittee at its second session. During the
third meeting, on May 6, 1942, it was agreed "to begin . . .
discussion of the armistice period with the assumption that
unconditional surrender will be exacted of the principal
defeated states."[9] The subcommittee doubted this would be
achieved but considered it preferable to an armistice and a
negotiated peace. Hull was flatly opposed to the whole idea
and believed unconditional surrender as an announced policy might prolong the war by solidifying Axis resistance into
desperation. Davis, however, spoke to Roosevelt privately
about the subcommittee's position.

8. For the organization of the subcommittee, see Harley A. Notter:
Postwar Foreign Policy Preparation, 1939–1945 (Washington, D.C.: U.S.
Government Printing Office; 1949), pp. 124–5. Cited hereafter as *Postwar
Foreign Policy Preparation*.
9. *U.S. Foreign Relations, Washington and Casablanca Papers*, note 2,
p. 506.

Before leaving Washington for Casablanca, Roosevelt, on January 7, 1943, told the American Joint Chiefs of Staff that "he was going to speak to Mr. Churchill about the advisability of informing Mr. Stalin that the United Nations were to continue on until they reach Berlin, and that the only terms would be unconditional surrender."[1] He thought this information would give a boost to Russian morale. He did not ask the Joint Chiefs' opinion, and none was offered. He did not tell Cordell Hull. At Casablanca the concept of a private message to Stalin was expanded into a public declaration which would apply the principle of unconditional surrender to Germany, Italy, and Japan. With two reservations, Churchill agreed and, on January 18, 1943, the Prime Minister informed the Combined Chiefs of Staff that at the end of the conference a paper would be released "to the effect that the United Nations are resolved to pursue the war to the bitter end, neither party relaxing its efforts until the unconditional surrender of Germany and Japan has been achieved."[2] Like Roosevelt, Churchill did not ask the Combined Chiefs for their comment. His two reservations were that he would have to clear the statement with the War Cabinet in London and that he preferred to exclude Italy. The War Cabinet approved and believed Italy should be mentioned along with Germany and Japan. Knowing Hull's stand, Roosevelt still said nothing to his Secretary of State.[3] Instead, to forestall Hull's criticism, he pretended his use of the phrase was accidental. During the news conference on January 23, 1943, the President said:

Another point I think we have all had it in our hearts and heads before, but I don't think that it has ever been put down on paper by the Prime Minister and myself, and that is the determining that peace can come to the world only by the total elimination of German and Japanese war power.

Some of you Britishers know the old story—we had a General

1. Ibid., p. 506.
2. Ibid., p. 635.
3. Hull, *Memoirs*, II, 1570.

called U. S. Grant. His name was Ulysses Simpson Grant, but in my, and the Prime Minister's, early days he was called "Unconditional Surrender Grant." The elimination of German, Japanese, and Italian war power means the unconditional surrender of Germany, Italy and Japan. That means a reasonable assurance of future world peace. It does not mean the destruction of the population of Germany, Italy, or Japan, but it does mean the destruction of the philosophies in those countries which are based on conquest and the subjugation of other people.[4]

Roosevelt used a prepared text and, except for the introductory sentence and the reference to Grant, he closely followed his notes. On the same subject Churchill said: "Even where there is some delay there is design and purposes, and as the President has said, the unconquerable will to pursue this quality [Allied unity], until we have procured the unconditional surrender of the criminal forces who plunged the world into storm and ruin."[5] Curiously, although Roosevelt called Casablanca the " 'unconditional surrender' meeting," the phrase was not used in the conference communiqué. The policy itself had certain advantages for Roosevelt and Churchill. It would reassure the Russians that America and Britain had no intention of making any deals with Hitler and Mussolini. It, together with the photograph of Giraud and de Gaulle shaking hands, would show domestic critics that the Darlan episode was closed and would never be repeated. Unconditional surrender was, however, a mistake. Very probably, as Churchill later maintained, it had no effect on Hitler; but it stiffened the will to fight of the average German soldier. The Italians may have ignored it, but the Japanese did not. Churchill himself was never inhibited by the slogan. Later in the war, however, Roosevelt substituted the call for unconditional surrender

---

4. *U.S. Foreign Relations, Washington and Casablanca Papers*, p. 727.
5. Ibid., p. 729. It is often overlooked, but neither Italy nor Japan surrendered unconditionally: the Italians became our allies in the war against Germany; the Japanese insisted on the right to retain their monarchy.

for the less congenial task of making up his mind as to what sort of peace settlement America desired. The Russians also believed the policy was a mistake and were embarrassed by the reference to Japan with whom they were not at war. Unconditional surrender made a good slogan, but it was an error in the politics of conflict.

IV

CROSS-CHANNEL ATTACK VERSUS THE MEDITERRANEAN, THE SECOND BROKEN PROMISE

January–August 1943

Unconditional surrender and French affairs were peripheral issues at the Casablanca Conference. This was essentially a military meeting to decide what Anglo-American forces should do in 1943. Before arriving at Casablanca, both sides had circulated position papers. Washington's came out first on December 26, 1942; London replied on January 2 and 3, 1943.[1] Despite his July reservation that Torch killed Roundup, Marshall was again calling for a cross-channel attack. According to the American Joint Chiefs of Staff, the correct strategy was to build up "as rapidly as possible adequate balanced forces in the United Kingdom in preparation for a land offensive against Germany

1. For the texts of these papers, see *U.S. Foreign Relations, Washington and Casablanca Papers*, pp. 735–52.

in 1943." This would insure that "the primary effort of the United Nations is directed against Germany rather than against her satellite states." The cross-channel attack gave "timely and substantial support of Russia . . . [whose] . . . continuance as a major factor in the war is of cardinal importance." Except as a base for bombing operations against Italy and Germany, the North African theater should be closed down when Axis troops had been driven out. Excess Allied forces from North Africa would be transferred to England to participate in the invasion.

The Joint Chiefs also considered the problem of the U-boat menace. During 1942 sinkings amounted to 7,790,697 tons, compared with 4,328,558 tons in 1941. Enemy submarines in November, 1942, sank 729,160 tons of Allied and neutral shipping—the highest monthly total of the war. Losses were sharply down in December, but this decline was rightly attributed to bad weather in the North Atlantic, which worked in favor of the convoys and against the U-boat packs. In their memorandum the Joint Chiefs pointed out that "a prerequisite to the successful accomplishment of the strategic concept for 1943 is an improvement in the present critical shipping situation by intensified and more effective anti-submarine warfare."

Since Churchill talked about bringing Turkey into the war once Torch had been completed and using that country as a base for a Balkan campaign, the Americans gave their own opinions on the subject. The Joint Chiefs believed that Turkey should be maintained "in a state of neutrality favorable to the United Nations until such time as she can, aided by supplies and minimum specialized forces, insure the integrity of her territory and make it available for our use." Once that condition was achieved, the Joint Chiefs favored "offensive air operations from bases on her [Turkey's] northern coast, in aid of Russia and against German controlled resources and transportation facilities in the Balkans." There was no mention of any land offensives, either

Turkish or Allied; the eastern Mediterranean, like the western Mediterranean, would be the scene only of air attacks on Europe.

From a British viewpoint, the most disturbing sections of the American memorandum were those dealing with the war against Japan. It had always been agreed that until Germany's defeat Allied campaigns in the Pacific and in the Far East would be limited to what was called the strategic defensive. At the insistence of the Navy Department, Washington now questioned this maxim. According to the Joint Chiefs of Staff, Anglo-American forces should "conduct a strategic offensive in the Atlantic–Western European theater directly against Germany, employing the maximum forces consistent with maintaining the accepted strategic concept in other theaters." The new accepted strategic concept in the war against Japan was to "continue offensive and defensive operations in the Pacific and in Burma to break the Japanese hold on positions which threaten the security of our communications and positions." The Joint Chiefs also noted: "It is well understood that the strategic concept contained herein is based on the strategic situation as it exists and can be foreseen at this time, and that it is subject to alternation in keeping with the changing situation." The sentences appeared innocuous, but Sir John Dill warned London that Marshall wanted a cross-channel attack and that King wanted increased resources for offensive operations in the Pacific, and should this not be accepted, both were talking about turning their backs on Europe and going all out against Japan.

In their reply the British Chiefs of Staff Committee supported only one of the American proposals—that dealing with the U-boats. London, like Washington, agreed that "the defeat of the U-boat menace [is] to remain a first charge on our resources." Elsewhere, the British argued for a program of Mediterranean attack in 1943 with "a view to—(1) knocking Italy out of the war, (2) bringing Turkey into the war, and (3) giving the Axis no respite for recuperation."

Concerning the revival of Roundup, Brooke maintained that a maximum Bolero effort would still make available only twenty-five divisions, thirteen British and twelve American, for any cross-channel attack even if the operation was delayed to August, 1943. A September or later landing was risky due to deteriorating weather conditions. Moreover, shortages in shipping and landing craft would limit the size of the assault force to six divisions. Facing them would be forty German divisions in prepared fortifications, capable of rapid reinforcement because of the highly developed transport facilities of northwestern Europe. "To make a fruitless assault [in France] before the time is right would," said the British, "be disastrous for ourselves, of no assistance to Russia and devastating to the morale of occupied Europe." It would prevent all attacks in other theaters, including the Pacific, and slow the Allied bomber offensive as shipping space would have to be devoted to troops and their supplies rather than to aircraft. Most important, and this the British put in italics: "*Russia would get no relief for another 7 or 8 months and the Axis would have a similar period to recuperate.*"[2]

Pessimism gave way to optimism when the British discussed the Mediterranean. They believed Anglo-American

> success in North Africa opens up wide possibilities of offensive operations against the Southern flank of the Axis. In particular we may be able to detach Italy from the Axis and induce Turkey to join the Allies. If we force Italy out of the war and the Germans try to maintain their line in Russia at its present length, we estimate that they will be some 54 divisions and 2,200 aircraft short of what they need on all fronts. If the defection of Italy were followed by that of other satellite powers, these deficiencies would be still larger.

The British wanted to retain the American troop buildup in England, Operation Bolero, to take advantage of any sudden

2. Ibid., p. 739.

German collapse; but in 1943, except for the bomber offensive, Anglo-American armies would campaign in the Mediterranean. When it came to specific operations, however, London was reticent. After clearing North Africa, "it will be necessary to seize one or other of the island bases—Sicily, Sardinia or Corsica—in order to increase the pressure on Italy." Since Corsica could only be taken after the fall of Sardinia, the strategic choice narrowed to an operation against Sicily or Sardinia. London did not "feel able at this stage to express a definite opinion as to which of the two alternatives should be chosen."

In the war against Japan, the British Chiefs of Staff insisted that there be no change from the Arcadia Conference decision, namely, "that we should bend all efforts to the early and decisive defeat of Germany, diverting only the minimum force necessary to hold Japan." They recognized the difficult position of China, which since the closing of the Burma Road in April, 1942, was dependent upon its own meager resources and the few supplies which could be airlifted across the Himalayas. The British favored opening the Burma Road by the reconquest of Burma but gave no date for the operation. The Chiefs of Staff Committee added: "Important though China is as an ally against Japan, Russia is far more important as an ally against Germany. Moreover, after the defeat of Germany, Russia might be a decisive factor in the war against Japan, whereas China could never help us in the war against Germany." London's program was one of defense in the Pacific, offense in the Mediterranean, and the assembling of "British and United States forces in the United Kingdom for the invasion of the Continent in the event of a sudden crack in German military power."

The Combined Chiefs of Staff met fifteen times at Casablanca. As usual the British were well prepared; documentation for their policies was provided by a 6,000-ton ship carrying "an elaborate staff, cipher and planning organization, with the technical mechanism for presenting every quantitative calculation that might be called for."[3] By comparison the American Joint Chiefs were not well prepared; they were not even all there. Admiral Leahy, Chairman of the Joint Chiefs, had developed a severe case of bronchitis at the last minute and was left behind at a naval hospital in Trinidad. Nor was the American delegation a large one. Brigadier Ian Jacob, Assistant Military Secretary to the War Cabinet, noted in his diary that "when the U.S. Chiefs saw how the land lay and the size of our party, they suddenly woke up to the fact that they had left most of their clubs behind." A British triumph appeared inevitable, but Churchill counseled Brooke to go slowly. The Chief of the Imperial General Staff was to adopt a policy toward the Americans of "the dripping of water on a stone."[4]

Not surprisingly the conferees deadlocked for four days, from January 14 through 18.[5] Ismay detected an atmosphere of veiled antipathy and mistrust. Brooke spoke at length on the advantages of a Mediterranean attack and the disadvantages of Roundup. He ended the ambiguity concerning Sicily and Sardinia. Brooke favored the Allied undertaking of Operation Husky, the code name for an attack on Sicily, rather than Operation Brimstone, the code name for an attack on Sardinia. He said he "did not favor [land] operations in Italy from Sicily in 1943 unless Italy collapsed completely." The British believed Italy would be brought down by the invasion of Sicily and by bombing. Brooke was very frank about the main thrust of London's strategy. He stated that "on the Continent, Russia is the only ally having large land forces in action. Any effort of the other allies must necessarily be so small as to be unimportant in the overall picture. He felt that ground operations by the United States and the United Kingdom would not exert any great influence until there were

3. Bryant, *The Turn of the Tide,* p. 441.
4. Ibid., p. 445.
5. For minutes of the meetings, see *U.S. Foreign Relations, Washington and Casablanca Papers,* pp. 536–626.

definite signs that Germany was weakening."[6] The British Chiefs of Staff buttressed their arguments with elaborate quantitative calculations.

Marshall, however, remained unpersuaded. He did not want to send American troops to England so that they could sit idly by waiting for Russia to win the war. What disturbed the Joint Chiefs was the seemingly improvisatory nature of British thinking. In their opinion the invasion of Sicily was being pushed by Brooke simply because once the Axis had been expelled there would be an excess of Allied forces in North Africa. Marshall and King regarded British talk about the start of "a crumbling process in Germany . . . [and] . . . the terrific latent power of the oppressed people" as wishful dreams. As King put it in a meeting of the American Joint Chiefs with Roosevelt: ". . . the British have definite ideas as to what the next operation should be but do not seem to have an overall plan for the conduct of the war." Marshall was equally blunt in the sessions of the Combined Chiefs of Staff. He said that "the United States Chiefs of Staff were anxious to learn the British concept as to how Germany is to be defeated." Marshall "thought it important that we now reorient ourselves and decide what the 'main plot' is to be. Every diversion or side issue from the main plot acts as a 'suction pump.' "[7]

For Marshall the main plot was the English Channel, and the suction pump was the Mediterranean.

Unfortunately for their position, the Americans were not prepared to argue with British manpower statistics. Marshall was further shaken when Eisenhower, the only American commander experienced in amphibious attack in the European theater, criticized the planned assault force for Roundup as wholly inadequate. Nor were the Joint Chiefs themselves united. King wanted more resources for the Pacific and was impressed by British figures on the savings in shipping which would be achieved by opening the Mediter-

6. Ibid., p. 583.
7. Ibid., p. 583.

ranean. General Arnold was equally interested in Portal's arguments about the use of North African and Sicilian air bases for attacking Germany's southern flank.[8] More important was Roosevelt's position. Even before Casablanca, the President's attitude on the issue of cross-channel versus Mediterranean operations in 1943 was one of wait and see. At Casablanca he continued being neutral, whereas the Prime Minister, who in November seems to have toyed with the idea of going ahead with Roundup, was now emphatic as to the advantages of the Mediterranean.

Lacking firm support, Marshall told Roosevelt he was willing to undertake the invasion of Sicily provided the British agreed to American plans for the Pacific. This agreement was reached in a meeting with the President and the Joint Chiefs on January 16, 1943—two days after the Casablanca Conference opened.[9] In the sessions of the Combined Chiefs of Staff, however, Marshall continued to call for Roundup. He defended the operation by retreating into the arcane world of air power. Although Washington's memorandum referred to balanced forces, Marshall said he "felt that if a bridgehead [in France] were established and Germany did not attempt to meet our air superiority, the bridgehead could be expanded. On the other hand, if they did meet our air superiority, it would necessitate withdrawing large air forces from the Russian front." Marshall also mentioned "a suggestion by Mr. Molotov that we send a ground force to the Continent sufficient to divert forty German divisions from the Russian front. He said this was out of the question and that our aim should be to weaken German air power in the Russian theater rather than ground forces."[1] Brooke was uninterested, and King and the Chief of the Imperial General Staff engaged in increasingly acrimonious discussions about the Far East, where the Ameri-

8. Henry H. Arnold: *Global Mission* (New York: Harper and Bros.; 1949), pp. 397–8. Cited hereafter as *Global Mission*.
9. For the minutes of the meeting, see *U.S. Foreign Relations, Washington and Casablanca Papers*, pp. 594–600.
1. Ibid., pp. 583–4.

cans wanted to start on the recapture of Burma and Rabaul and to conduct operations against the Marshall and Caroline Islands in 1943. Dripping water proved ineffective, and on January 17 Brooke wrote in his diary: "A desperate day. We are further from obtaining agreement than we ever were."[2]

Sir John Dill broke the impasse. Close to Marshall and King, he knew the real American position. On the afternoon of January 18, after a fruitless morning meeting of the Combined Chiefs of Staff, Dill told Brooke he could get everything he wanted in Europe if he would yield in the Pacific. Brooke was inclined to resist, but Portal joined the discussion and supported Dill. Portal also had with him a memorandum prepared by Air Marshal Sir John Slessor, Commander in Chief elect of Coastal Command, which, although it accepted the American Pacific program, stated that "these operations must be kept within such limits as will not, in the opinion of the Combined Chiefs of Staff, prejudice the capacity of the United Nations to take any opportunity that may present itself for the decisive defeat of Germany in 1943."[3] It included a more general Germany-first clause as well. Brooke, Portal, and Dill drafted a brief paper which combined the British European program, the American Pacific program, and Slessor's limiting conditions. Dill offered to take it to Marshall, who accepted it with minor changes. That same afternoon it was approved by the Combined Chiefs of Staff and presented to Roosevelt and Churchill.[4]

The meeting with the President and the Prime Minister started at 5 P.M.; present were the Combined Chiefs of Staff and Harry Hopkins. Marshall, who had been acting as Chairman of the Combined Chiefs, asked Brooke to present their report. After mentioning the U-boat threat and renewal of the Germany-first decision, Brooke said: "Our

2. Bryant, *The Turn of the Tide*, p. 449.
3. Ibid., note 11, p. 450.
4. For the text, see *U.S. Foreign Relations, Washington and Casablanca Papers*, pp. 760–1.

efforts in defeating Germany will be concerned first with efforts to force them to withdraw ground and air forces from the Russian front. This will be accomplished by operations from North Africa by which Southern Europe, the Dodecanese Islands, Greece, Crete, Sardinia, and Sicily will all be threatened, thus forcing Germany to deploy her forces to meet each threat. The actual operation decided upon is the capture of Sicily."[5] Brooke then mentioned the buildup in England and the American program of Pacific operations. Concerning an attack across the Channel, Brooke stated it would be undertaken "in the event that the German strength in France decreases, either through withdrawal of her troops or because of an internal collapse."

The discussion which followed was relatively brief, and only a few new points were raised. Churchill offered to sign a treaty with the United States pledging British all-out aid in the war against Japan once Germany had been defeated. This pledge Roosevelt refused as being unnecessary. The President said he was, however, interested in obtaining an engagement from Russia. Churchill also asked that a planning staff, including the appointment of a commander, be set up in London in case a return to the Continent became possible during the summer. The Prime Minister used the code word Sledgehammer—an operation which envisaged reduced German resistance. Roosevelt agreed to the creation of the planning staff. The President himself requested that the Combined Chiefs of Staff send some 200 to 250 aircraft to China. This he said "would have a tremendously favorable effect on Chinese morale." Concerning Turkey, the Prime Minister noted that she "will be in a weak position at the peace table following the war if she has not participated in it." Since the British were supplying the equipment necessary to bring Turkey into the war, Churchill asked that London "be allowed to play the Turkish hand, just as the United States is now handling the situation with reference

5. For the minutes of this meeting, see ibid., pp. 627–37.

to China." The President "concurred in this view." Marshall was disturbed by the optimism of Roosevelt and Churchill. About the planes for China, Marshall remarked that some increase was planned but that "it is a tremendously expensive operation." About the return to the Continent, Marshall stated that "unless there is a complete crack in German morale, operations across the Channel will have to be extremely limited." Marshall also said that there would have to be a second meeting of the Combined Chiefs before summer "to make the necessary readjustments in the decisions made now." Churchill approved and later cabled the War Cabinet that there would be "another Conference . . . withing the next six months."

From January 19 to 23, the Combined Chiefs of Staff continued their daily, sometimes twice daily, discussions at Casablanca. These sessions were devoted to fleshing out the January 18 agreement with operational orders, plans, and more exact definitions of what was contained in the memorandum. The Combined Chiefs made Eisenhower responsible for the invasion of Sicily and suggested the operation be mounted during the favorable July moon—a period of maximum darkness—in order to provide cover for the approach of the landing fleet.[6] Although the Americans did not know it, the British planning staff had reversed themselves and now pressed for an assault on Sardinia rather than on Sicily; Brooke put down the revolt. Having convinced Marshall and King to attack Sicily, Brooke believed any wavering "would irrevocably shake their confidence in our judgement."[7] The Combined Chiefs also placed Montgomery's Eighth Army under Eisenhower's command, to become effective when Montgomery's forces reached Tunisia. Since the move raised to ten the number of British or British-controlled divisions under Eisenhower's authority, as opposed to two American divisions, the Combined Chiefs

6. For the text of the directive to Eisenhower, see ibid., pp. 799–800.
7. Bryant, *Turn of the Tide*, pp. 455–6.

revised Eisenhower's staff. General Sir Harold Alexander, Commander in Chief of British Forces in the Middle East, became Deputy Allied Supreme Commander and was charged with coordinating land operations in Tunisia and with the detailed planning for Husky.[8] Air Marshal Sir Arthur Tedder, like Montgomery and Alexander another officer from Cairo, was made Allied Air Commander for the Sicilian invasion. Admiral Sir Andrew Cunningham retained his position as Allied Sea Commander. Eisenhower would lead a British team.

On other operations the Combined Chiefs of Staff reached compromise agreements. The British paper on Turkey, submitted on January 19, stressed that that country "will be of value to the Allies as an offensive base for air rather than land operations," which was Marshall's position.[9] The paper also illustrated the nature of British military thinking. Since the British Planning Staff had very little to offer the Turks in terms of military hardware, they argued for political inducements to obtain her entry into the war. "British and American diplomacy," they said, "should be directed to exploit Turkish fears of Russia." Not planes and guns but rather a voice in the peace settlement would bring Turkey to battle. The British planners even expressed opinions about the nature of the postwar settlement. According to them, "whether it would be wise for His Majesty's Government to oppose Russian desires regarding passage of the Straits [of the Bosporus and Dardanelles] seems a matter for urgent consideration, for if we thwarted Russia in that respect we should probably be confronted with a claim for rights of transit through Persia to a port on the Persian Gulf. This, from our point of view, would be most undesirable." In the discussion of the paper, Marshall kept completely

8. Eisenhower offered to serve under Alexander, but the Combined Chiefs were still concerned with French opinion in North Africa, which was strongly anti-British. Eisenhower, *Crusade in Europe*, pp. 138–9.

9. For the text of the memorandum, see *U.S. Foreign Relations, Washington and Casablanca Papers*, pp. 764–73.

quiet on the subject of political considerations, but he insisted that any hardware allocations be subject to review and approval by the Combined Chiefs of Staff. Brooke agreed and the British were free to play their Turkish hand.

Elsewhere in Europe, the Combined Chiefs of Staff agreed to the continuation and expansion of Pointblank—the Allied bomber offensive against Germany. By early 1943 the Americans had established a 500-plane daylight bomber force in England. It had seen little action because of the inevitable vicissitudes of buildup and because of British doubts as to the ability of the B-17 Flying Fortress aircraft to move across the skies of Europe in the face of German fighter resistance. The British themselves bombed at night, when darkness and the primitive state of German radar afforded maximum protection to their planes and crews. At Casablanca, after a personal meeting between Churchill and Major General Ira Eaker, who commanded the American bomber force in England, daylight attack was approved.[1] The Germans were to be hit around the clock. The object was "the progressive destruction of the German military, industrial and economic system, and the undermining of the morale of German people."

In keeping with the decision about the U-boat threat, submarine operating bases and construction yards were given first priority as aerial targets. The man in charge of the bomber offensive, Pointblank, Air Chief Marshal Arthur Harris, Deputy Chief of British Air Staff, disliked attacking the operating bases, many of which were located in France. He felt it would cause excessive civilian casualties and doubted bombs could penetrate the concrete bunkers protecting the submarines. Both Churchill's and Harris's fears proved correct. Flying Fortress raids in daylight resulted in high losses and were called off until long-range escort fighters became available. The bombing of Brest, Lorient, Saint-Nazaire, and Bordeau failed to damage, much less sink, a

1. Churchill, *The Second World War*, IV, 678–80.

single U-boat.[2] Other Casablanca decisions concerning the Atlantic battle, however, were more effective. Increased escort and merchant ship construction; continuous aircraft protection for convoys; and the formation of hunter-killer groups of destroyers, corvettes, and small carriers put the Germans on the defensive by the spring of 1943.

The British Joint Planning Staff also submitted a report entitled "Continental Operations in 1943."[3] The paper discussed Operation Hadrian—a plan drawn up in November, 1942, for an assault on the Cotentin Peninsula in Normandy. The objective was "seizing and holding a bridgehead and, if the state of German morale and strength of her resources permit, of exploiting success." According to the British, "with the resources available in 1943, neither the size of the seaborne and airborne assault forces nor the rate of buildup can approach the requirements of the Combined Commanders. It is clear, therefore, that no operation to seize and hold a footing in the Cotentin Peninsula has any prospect of success unless the German reserves have been very greatly reduced. Similar considerations would apply to a limited operation anywhere on the French coast." Having admitted Hadrian to be an impossibility, the British still wanted planning to continue, with a target date of August 1, 1943. The report also called for raids and operations "on a larger scale to take advantage of German disintegration." The Combined Chiefs agreed that the Sicilian operation would have priority over Hadrian and suggested that any raids, the one mentioned being an attack on the Channel Islands, be coordinated with Husky. With these changes the report was approved. Britain and America would invade Europe as soon as Germany collapsed.

Turning to the war against Japan, the British agreed to prepare for the reconquest of Burma in 1943. Since the

2. See Hans-Adolf Jacobsen and Jürgen Rohwer, eds.: *Decisive Battles of World War II: The German View* (London: André Deutsch Ltd.; 1965), p. 288.

3. For the text, see *U.S. Foreign Relations, Washington and Casablanca Papers*, pp. 785–9.

campaign would be mounted from India, it was their responsibility. The decision reflected strong American pressure. The planners envisaged a three-phase operation. Phase one involved securing the airport at Akyab in South Burma by land and sea assault to provide advanced air cover for future attacks. Phase two called for the recapture of Northern Burma and the building of a road to link the Burma Road with India. The final action, code name Anakim, would hopefully see all of Burma in Allied hands and would reopen the port of Rangoon, the best entry point for supplies moving over the Burma Road. The Combined Chiefs set "November 15, 1943, as the provisional date for the Anakim assault." The other operations, which were really local attacks, would be undertaken earlier. The Combined Chiefs also agreed that "it will be necessary to decide in July 1943 whether to undertake or postpone the [Anakim] operation."[4] British reservations concerning Burma were caused by the fact that the campaign involved the use of large landing craft. These ships were in short supply, and except for a minimal allocation to the Pacific, London wanted them concentrated in European waters. They dropped the reservation when Admiral King offered to provide landing craft, crews, and naval support forces from American sources. Reference to the provisional date for the capture of Burma showed, however, that the British, while agreeing, remained unconvinced.

On Friday, January 22, Admiral King gave the Combined Chiefs a full briefing on American plans for the Pacific.[5] After the victory at Midway, the American Joint Chiefs approved a two-pronged attack on the Japanese naval and air base at Rabaul on New Britain Island. Rabaul had been

4. Ibid., p. 673.
5. For the text of the American memorandum on Pacific operations, which King presented to the Combined Chiefs, see Louis Morton: *The War in the Pacific. Strategy and Command: The First Two Years* (Washington, D.C.: U.S. Government Printing Office; 1962), Appendix H, pp. 627–9. Cited hereafter as *Strategy and Command*.

occupied by Japan on January 23, 1942. The occupation threatened sea communications between the United States and Australia. One line of advance toward Rabaul ran through the Solomon Islands; the other, through New Guinea. The first step in the campaign was to drive the Japanese out of the island of Guadalcanal in the Solomons and the port of Buna in New Guinea. Unknown to Washington, the Japanese planned to mount attacks from both places themselves. The resulting struggle produced a crisis in the Pacific which lasted from August to November, 1942. By mid-November the Allies held Guadalcanal, and the Japanese were penned in at Buna. King informed the Combined Chiefs that the advance to Rabaul would continue. It was hoped that Rabaul would be taken in May, 1943, which would free American landing craft for participation in operations against Burma.

King also told the Combined Chiefs that the Americans intended in 1943 to open a second line of operations against Japan. Though the Army and Navy had long considered Japan to be America's most likely enemy, Washington had never planned to attack her from Australia. Pearl Harbor, the Japanese advance to the south, and the Arcadia Conference decision to hold Australia and New Zealand put strong American forces in places undreamed of by the prewar Joint Board. The Rabaul campaign was in part the exploitation of the fortunes of war. Now new ship construction and Japanese losses at Midway and in the South Pacific combined to open the way for a more traditional approach to the question of how to defeat Japan. Before the war the American Navy had expected to fight its way directly across the Pacific in a series of operations based on Hawaii and Midway. This strategy involved the conquest of some of the Japanese mandated islands in Micronesia which flanked the line of advance. King announced that the campaign would begin in the summer of 1943. King was not specific about targets, but he mentioned the Gilbert, Marshall, and Caroline Islands.

The British disliked the plan, but the Pacific theater came under the authority of the American Joint Chiefs, and British approval was the agreed price for a program of Mediterranean attack. According to the Secretariat the Combined Chiefs "took note of the proposals of the Joint U.S. Chiefs of Staff for the conduct of the war in the Pacific theater in 1943."[6]

The following day, January 23, the Combined Chiefs met with Churchill, Roosevelt, and Hopkins to present their final report.[7] Derived from the January 18 memorandum, the final report was a much more lengthy document. Although Roosevelt suggested that the paper be considered "paragraph by paragraph," only four topics were actually discussed. They constituted, however, the crucial issues: assistance to Russia, operations in the Mediterranean, operations from the United Kingdom, and operations in the Pacific. As in the meeting of January 18, Roosevelt and Churchill were inclined to be optimistic while their professional advisers tended toward pessimism.

Concerning aid to Russia, by which the Combined Chiefs meant lend-lease deliveries, the report stated: "It will be possible to meet full commitments by the end of the calendar year 1943; and we have approved a program of shipments on this basis subject to the proviso that supplies to Russia shall not be continued at prohibitive cost to the United Nations effort." Roosevelt agreed that the limiting clause should stand and asked Hopkins for his opinion. Hopkins noted "that, of course, it cannot be exercised without raising violent objections from Premier Stalin." Churchill said "that aid to Russia must be pushed, and no investment could pay a better military dividend. The United Nations cannot let Russia down." Churchill also asked that sixteen destroyers from the American Navy be assigned to the Russian convoys in order to increase the number of shipments. King main-

6. *U.S. Foreign Relations, Washington and Casablanca Papers,* p. 687.
7. For the minutes of this meeting, see ibid., pp. 707–19.

tained that "the destroyers simply were not available. The escort vessel situation is so tight as to make it necessary to eliminate the Russian convoys starting about June 14 in order to take care of the needs of Operation Husky."[8]

This was news not contained in the Combined Chiefs' report, and neither Churchill nor Roosevelt liked it. Churchill believed "it would be a great thing if we could continue the Russian convoys throughout the Husky Operation." Roosevelt said: "Stopping the convoys in July and August would occur just at the time when the Russians would be engaged in their most severe fighting." Professional opinion, however, remained adamant. According to Pound, "if we were committed to continuing these convoys, the Royal Navy could not play its part in Operation Husky." King was "definitely committed to mounting Operation Husky . . . everything must be done to insure its success, including the elimination of the Russian convoys if that be necessary." Roosevelt and Churchill were equally adamant. It was King who proposed the compromise. He "suggested that before deciding on discontinuing the convoys, the situation should be reviewed as of the first of May."

This same division occurred in the discussion of operations in the Mediterranean. About Husky, Churchill announced that he "wished to set the target date as the period of the favorable June moon rather than that of July." Marshall explained: "The subject of the target date had been quite exhaustively studied, and it is going to be difficult to mount Operation Husky with properly trained forces even in July." Roosevelt wanted to know if the target date was chosen "on the assumption that the Axis forces would be driven from Tunisia by the end of April." What, he asked, would be the effect "if they were eliminated from Africa by the end of March?" Marshall said that "the limiting factor was on the naval side with respect to organizing crews and

8. Ibid., p. 709.

assembling landing craft." Churchill "suggested the possibility of combing the Navy, particularly the 'R' class battleships, with the purpose of setting up a special group of navigators." Sir Dudley Pound replied "that skilled navigators could not be taken from the Navy without serious effects." Roosevelt believed "the present proposals were based on a large number of factors which might well prove correct, but which were estimates." Brooke and Marshall surrendered. It was agreed that "without prejudice to the July date, there should be an intense effort made to try and achieve the favorable June moon as the date of the operation."

Churchill and Roosevelt next considered Bolero and the cross-channel attack. Churchill was disappointed that "there would be only 4 U.S. divisions equipped in the U.K. by August 15th." He wondered if by using the *Queen Mary* and *Queen Elizabeth*, the number could not be increased. Brigadier General Brehon B. Somervell, U.S. Assistant Chief of Staff, explained that "the Queens were all fully employed in various parts of the world." Churchill suggested that the amount of space devoted to supplies and equipment be reduced. He said: "For the type of operations which would be undertaken in France in 1943, a big advance was not likely. Fighting men for the beaches were the prime essential." Somervell indicated that "everything would be done to reduce any unnecessary volume." The Combined Chiefs' report listed "three types of operations for which plans and preparations must now be made: (1) Raids with the primary object of provoking air battles and causing enemy losses. (2) Operations with the object of seizing and holding a bridgehead and, if the state of German morale and resources permit, of exploiting success. (3) A return to the Continent to take advantage of German disintegration." Referring to the second option, Churchill asked that "the word 'vigorously' should be inserted before the word 'exploiting'. . . ."

It was Lord Louis Mountbatten, British Chief of Combined Operations, and Admiral King who brought the discussion back to reality.[9] Mountbatten said: ". . . landing craft resources would only permit of an initial assault by 2 brigade groups with an immediate follow-up of one brigade group and some armor. This could only be increased with U.S. help." King stated: "All available U.S. resources would be devoted to Operation Husky." He might have added, but did not, that all British landing-craft resources, except for the two brigade lifts, were also tied up in Husky. Unless Germany collapsed, the only operation that could be mounted in 1943, and Mountbatten mentioned it, was a raid on the Channel Islands. Roosevelt and Churchill did not dispute the figures. Instead they confirmed the decision of the Combined Chiefs to establish a planning staff in London. Roosevelt, however, reduced its duties. The last sentence of the Combined Chiefs' report on channel operations read: "The directive [to the London planners] will also make provision for the planning of an invasion of the Continent in force in 1944."[1] Roosevelt "suggested that the last sentence of this section should be omitted. This was agreed to." On January 23 the Americans felt they had been planning that particular operation far too long.

The last item discussed was the Combined Chiefs' report on operations in the Pacific and Far East. As he had during the January 18 meeting, Roosevelt felt the Combined Chiefs were slighting China. He also showed himself to be a good strategist. Roosevelt said: "An island-to-island advance across the Pacific would take too long to reduce the Japanese power. Some other method of striking at Japan must be found." The President believed the right combination might be the submarine and U.S. air forces based in China. Roosevelt noted that Japan began the war with 6,000,000 tons of merchant shipping. During 1942, 1,000,000 tons had been sunk, leaving her with 5,000,000 tons. Roosevelt said:

9. Mountbatten was a member of the British Chiefs of Staff Committee and, therefore, of the Combined Chiefs of Staff from March, 1942, to August, 1943. Only 43 years old, he was, at Churchill's insistence, an admiral, a general, and an air marshal.

1. Ibid., note 22, p. 796.

"When this was reduced to 4,000,000, Japan would be hard pressed to maintain her garrison in the chain of islands stretching all the way from Burma to New Guinea and would have to start pulling in her lines. The most effective weapon against shipping was the submarine, and U.S. submarines were achieving notable results. There was another method of striking at the Japanese shipping, and that was by attacking the routes running close to the Asiatic shore from Korea down to Siam. This could be done by aircraft operating from China."[2]

This was an excellent statement of the principle of blockade. The only thing wrong with it was that it didn't go far enough. Japan could not only be forced to pull back, she could be defeated by it. The person who should have answered the President was Admiral King, but he kept silent. Instead General Arnold said that he "was fully aware of the need for reinforcing the U.S. Air Force in China. One group of aircraft was just preparing to leave the U.S.A.; and he would examine . . . the best method of operating the aircraft. He hoped that effective operations would start in April." Marshall also "felt it was vital to step up the effort in China, and this would be done." The Prime Minister "expressed his agreement with the President's proposals." The meeting ended with the President and Prime Minister congratulating the Combined Chiefs on the results they had achieved.

The Combined Chiefs met for the last time at Casablanca at 9:30 that night.[3] Their work was to revise their paper in accordance with the wishes of the President and Prime Minister. The task was quickly done. The only major change was in the section dealing with the Far East. New paragraphs were added entitled "Support of China." The Combined Chiefs agreed "to build up the U.S. Air Forces now operating in China to the maximum extent that logistical limitations and other important claims will permit."

2. Ibid., p. 718.
3. For minutes of this meeting, see ibid., pp. 719-22.

There was no mention of blockades. When the meeting ended, Marshall "expressed his appreciation of the readiness of the British Chiefs of Staff to understand the U.S. point of view and of the fine spirit of cooperation which they had shown during the discussions." Brooke in turn "thanked General Marshall for his words and said that he reciprocated most whole-heartedly General Marshall's expression of the great benefit which had accrued from the Conference."

The British were well satisfied; Ian Jacob, Assistant Secretary to the War Cabinet, wrote in his diary that night: "Our ideas had prevailed almost throughout."[4] On February 2, 1943, Admiral Leahy, who was Chairman of the Joint Chiefs and who had missed the meeting because of sickness, was briefed on the results of the Casablanca Conference by Marshall and King. He felt: "Their comment led me to believe that little of value toward ending the war was accomplished." Marshall went to Casablanca hoping for a plan to invade France in 1943; he returned with a plan to invade the islands of Sicily, Jersey, and Guernsey.

On January 27 Stalin received a vague and carefully expurgated version of the Casablanca decisions. Concerning the issue that interested him most—the defunct Roundup—the Soviet Premier learned nothing. The Allies were going "to launch large-scale amphibious operations in the Mediterranean." They were increasing "the Allied bomber offensive" and preparing to reenter the Continent "as soon as practicable," but no date or place was given.[5] Stalin, however, was adept at reading between the lines. On January 30 he asked his Anglo-American partners for particulars on "the concrete operations planned . . . [to open] . . . a second front in Europe in 1943," since Russian troops were "tired" and "hardly able to carry on."[6]

Roosevelt left the matter for Churchill to reply. The Prime Minister, after consulting "the President and the

4. Quoted in Bryant, *Turn of the Tide*, p. 459 and note 19, p. 459.
5. *Stalin's Correspondence*, I, No. 104, 86–8.
6. Ibid., I, No. 107, 89.

Staffs on both sides of the ocean," informed Stalin that the
sequence of operations in 1943 would be as follows: in April,
clearance of North Africa; in July, seizure of Sicily; and
finally, in August, a cross-channnel attack. Indeed, Churchill
went so far as to say that "if the [cross-channel] operation is
delayed by weather or other reasons, it will be prepared with
stronger forces for September."[7] What the Prime Minister
had done, aside from postponing the inevitable explosion in
Moscow, was to substitute the very problematic emergency
return to the Continent for the dead Roundup. As in the
case of the June, 1942, *aide-mémoire*, Churchill's message
included the necessary escape clause. "The timing of this
attack," he said, "must . . . be dependent upon the condition of German defensive possibilities." Stalin was not informed that this meant Germany's collapse.

Even this half-truth, with its mention of August and
September, raised tempers in Russia. Stalin on February 16
sent almost identical messages to London and Washington
protesting the "undesirable miscalculations" of delay and
calling for "the blow from the West . . . in spring or early
summer of 1943 as Churchill had promised at Moscow."[8]
Roosevelt gave a brief and guarded reply on February 22 in
which he spoke of the American war effort being projected
on the "European Continent" at as early a date as possible
"subsequent to success in North Africa." Stalin's reaction
was to omit all references to the United States and Great
Britain from his Red Army Day speech. He even hinted in
the speech that his sole object in the war was to drive the
German invaders from Russian soil.[9] Churchill did not
answer Stalin until March 11. Unfortunately, his lengthy
reply purporting to explain why a largely fictitious operation

7. Ibid., I, No. 112, 93–4. This message was sent on February 9 and received on February 12, 1943. The only consultation with Washington consisted of cables to Hopkins from Churchill proposing a speedup of Sicilian
operations. See Sherwood, *Roosevelt and Hopkins*, p. 701.

8. *Stalin's Correspondence*, I, No. 114, 94–6; II, No. 75, 55–6.

9. *U.S. Foreign Relations*, 1943, III, 506–7.

could not take place at an earlier date included a repetition of his pledge that the cross-channel attack would come in August, 1943. It was not in fact until June 4, seven months after the Casablanca Conference, that Stalin learned in a message from Roosevelt that there would be no cross-channel assault in 1943.

During the spring, Soviet relations with her cobelligerents had vacillated between such growls as the recall of Ambassador Litvinov from Washington and Ambassador Maisky from London and the smiles of the dissolution of the Comintern and a qualified promise by Stalin to meet Roosevelt in Alaska. The news of June 4, however, brought forth an angry and bitter catalog of what the Soviet Premier regarded, with some justification, as the broken promises of the past two years. He condemned the cancellation of Roundup, stated that his confidence in his Allies was shaken, and called the efforts of Anglo-American arms insignificant.[1] The meeting with Roosevelt was canceled.

Ironically, the President's June 4 message, which provoked Stalin's outburst and brought Anglo-American relations with Russia to a new low, was occasioned by what turned out to be the definitive agreement on the cross-channel attack. Roosevelt had cabled Stalin not to say that Roundup was dead, but that Overlord, the plan for a cross-channel attack in 1944, had been born. On April 29 Churchill had cabled Roosevelt requesting a May meeting in Washington to "settle together . . . , first Sicily and then exploitation thereof, and secondly, the future of the Burma campaign."[2] This request resulted in the Trident Conference, which lasted from May 12 to 25. Although the Prime Minister wanted to continue to close the ring in the Mediterranean, the principal result of the conference was the decision to

1. See Stalin's message to Roosevelt dated June 11, 1943, and an even harsher one to Churchill dated June 24, 1943. *Stalin's Correspondence*, I, No. 162, 131–2; II, No. 65, 136–8.
2. Churchill, Second World War, IV, 783.

build up a force of thirty Anglo-American divisions in England by the spring of 1944 for a cross-channel attack on or about May 1.

After Casablanca, Marshall had worked ceaselessly to get the war back on what he regarded as the proper course, which despite some pessimism at Casablanca now meant the invasion of France in 1944. He strengthened the planning division of the Joint Chiefs and gave maximum publicity to King's Pacific ambitions, which had the intended effect of making his British counterparts fear that America would abandon the European war. He, Stimson, and Hopkins led Roosevelt away from Churchill's all-too-appealing Mediterranean adventures. On May 8, four days before the arrival of Churchill, the President agreed to give his full support to the cross-channel attack; and Marshall was ready to meet the British.[3]

During the Trident Conference, there were twenty meetings of the Combined Chiefs of Staff—twelve working sessions and six plenary meetings, the latter including Roosevelt and Churchill.[4] Of the twelve working sessions, two were "off the record," a procedure now utilized for the first time whereby secretaries and aides were excused from the room and no records were kept. This device was used when discussion became too acrimonious or when one of the delegations wished to retreat in private from a stand previously taken lest its staff think it was lacking in determination.[5]

Brooke and Marshall agreed in principle that a cross-channel assault should be launched in 1944. Where they disagreed was on the relationship of the Mediterranean to that operation. Brooke was convinced that only through

3. Leahy, *I Was There*, pp. 157–8.

4. For minutes and editorial notes concerning meetings during the Trident Conference, see U.S. Department of State, *Foreign Relations of the United States. Diplomatic Papers. The Conferences at Washington and Quebec, 1943* (Washington, D.C.: Government Printing Office, 1970), pp. 24–221. Cited hereafter as *U.S. Foreign Relations, Washington and Quebec Papers, 1943*.

5. Bryant, *The Turn of the Tide*, pp. 509–10.

continued pressure in the Mediterranean would sufficient German strength be drawn away from northern France to make an invasion possible. Marshall was equally convinced that Mediterranean attacks, by drawing men and supplies away from the Bolero buildup, would render the invasion impossible. This purely military argument was compounded by a crisis of confidence. Marshall, having seen the supposed agreements of 1942 dissolve, simply did not trust Brooke and wanted a foolproof, binding contract. He was convinced that the British were fighting a political war in the Mediterranean which was designed to maintain traditional interests. He also felt that they had been so crippled by their experiences in the First World War as to be unable to face major battles in France.[6] Brooke, while admiring Marshall's administrative talents, regarded him as a poor tactician whose plans might lead to disaster. He had the following conversation with Marshall during the Trident Conference, a conversation which was typical of both Brooke's attitude and his rather sharp tongue: "Marshall said to me, 'I find it hard even now not to look on your North African strategy with a jaundiced eye.' I replied, 'What strategy would you have preferred?' To which he answered, 'Cross-channel operations for the liberation of France and the advance on Germany; we would finish the war quicker.' I remember replying, 'Yes, probably, but not the way we hope to finish it.' "[7]

Fortunately, both men believed above all in unity of the Alliance. Fortunately, also, both men had associates, of whom Dill and Hopkins were the most important, who could pour oil on troubled waters. Compromise was inevitable. Indeed, the American planners themselves, before Trident began, indicated that some operation beyond Husky (the invasion of Sicily) would have to take place in the Mediterranean in 1943; the only question was to keep the scale sufficiently low so as not to interfere with Bolero.

6. These attitudes were shared by almost everyone on the American side. See Stimson and Bundy, *On Active Service*, pp. 436–8.
7. Bryant, *The Turn of the Tide*, p. 508.

However, Roosevelt's consistent support of Marshall and the
unity of the American Joint Chiefs—both of which were
lacking at Casablanca—gave the Trident compromise a dis-
tinctly American flavor. Aside from Overlord in May, 1944,
Marshall also won grudging British approval for an immediate manpower freeze in the Mediterranean and the transfer,
from November, 1943, onwards, of three British and four
American divisions out of the Mediterranean and into England to provide a seasoned core for the cross-channel
assault.[8]

On the other hand, the Combined Chiefs did confirm the
Casablanca decision to force Italy out of the war, which was
the primary British objective at Trident, and Marshall
agreed to join Churchill and Brooke in a flying visit to Eisenhower's Mediterranean headquarters to examine ways and
means. The British also secured their secondary objective, a
damping down of the Burma campaign, although this was
probably due more to the simultaneous presence in Washington of Generals Stilwell, Chennault, and Wavell, the
Allied Commanders in China and India. These three men
presented such wildly divergent appraisals of the situation in
the China-Burma-India theater that it was impossible for the
Combined Chiefs to reach any decisions.

Chennault, who directed American Air Force operations
in China, was a close friend of Chiang Kai-shek and represented the "victory through air power" approach. Stilwell,
Chief of the American Military Mission to China, sought a
ground war in Asia, hated Chiang and the British about
equally, and thought that the only good fighters were the
Chinese Communists. Wavell, Commander in Chief, India,
had nothing but contempt for the strategic ability of the
Americans and took the position that the best offense was a
good defense. He was shaken by the Prime Minister's open
condemnation of him as incompetent. Churchill, if not the

8. *U.S. Foreign Relations, Washington and Quebec Papers,* 1943, pp.
121–2, 282.

President, must have been amused at Stilwell's constant reference to Chiang as "Peanuts."[9]

Thus when the conference ended on the 25th, both parties felt reasonably satisfied: Marshall had got his Overlord contract; Brooke had kept the Mediterranean open. True, there were loose ends such as the nature and direction of the Mediterranean attack. Overlord itself was just a sketch whose details would have to be filled in by the planning staff in London under the direction of British General Frederick Morgan. But to the Americans it appeared that the major strategic decision of the Second World War had been reached. As Leahy expressed it: "Led by our respective Commanders-in-Chief, Franklin Roosevelt and Winston Churchill, the Combined Chiefs of Staff achieved at this conference a successful demonstration of planning for coalition warfare."[1] Head-on assault had replaced closing the ring. As for the tidying up of loose ends, provision was made for yet another meeting of the Combined Chiefs in the near future. Since Washington had been the host in May, the next session was initially scheduled for London and given the code name of Quadrant.

During the twelve weeks that separated Trident and Quadrant, however, Washington decided the British had no intention of abiding by the new agreements. Thus when the Quadrant Conference opened on August 14, the Americans were in a fighting mood despite the fact that the intervening period saw the most brilliant successes of Anglo-American arms in the war to date. Shipping losses in June dropped to 120,000 tons, the lowest since the outbreak of the war and a sure indication that the battle upon which all others depended, the Battle of the Atlantic, had been won. Operation Husky, the conquest of Sicily, which started on July 10, was what everyone had hoped Torch would be: a lightning affair of thirty-eight days and a near-perfect demonstration of the

9. Bryant, *The Turn of the Tide*, pp. 504–5.
1. Leahy, *I Was There*, p. 164.

integrated cooperation of the Allied armies in the field. Moreover, on the evening of Sunday, July 25, Rome radio broadcast to the world the news that Mussolini had fallen and that the King was entrusting the formation of a new government to Marshal Pietro Badoglio, a known critic of Fascism. It seemed Italy might soon collapse.

The question of how to exploit these successes brought the Anglo-American alliance, in Marshall's words, "to the crossroads."[2] During their flying visit to the Mediterranean after the Trident Conference, Churchill, Marshall, and Brooke had placed the decision on post-Husky operations in the hands of Eisenhower, subject to the consent of the Combined Chiefs. Marshall himself favored a small-scale assault on Corsica or Sardinia with the obvious intent of a rapid close-off in the Mediterranean. Contradicting their words at Casablanca, Churchill and Brooke, however, painted in glowing colors the advantages of an Italian campaign.[3] Italy, they said, was reeling and could offer no significant resistance. If the Germans chose to fight, it would draw divisions away from France. If they retreated, the whole southern half of Germany would be exposed to a bomber offensive based in Italy. Besides, the invasion of Italy was the only significant operation the Anglo-Americans could undertake in Europe during the next ten months, and the lack of implementation might have grave effects upon Russia. All the arguments were carefully tuned to American ears. With Soviet-American relations at their lowest point of the war, the latter reason was particularly effective.

On May 29 it was agreed that Eisenhower should develop plans for both Italy and Sardinia and let the events of Husky determine the decision. If Husky went well, Italy might follow in late August; if Husky went badly, it would have to be Corsica and Sardinia. In either event, the Trident contract on Overlord was to be maintained. Eisenhower was

2. Matloff, *Strategic Planning, 1943–1944*, p. 161.
3. Churchill, *Second World War*, IV, 812–31.

limited to the forces presently in the Mediterranean and had to prepare also for the transfer of seven divisions and most of his assault shipping to England in the fall. The British, who had few doubts about the condition of the Italian garrison in Sicily, returned happily to London. Husky was launched on July 10 and resistance was negligible. On July 16, without waiting to hear from Eisenhower, Marshall cabled Brooke that he now favored an Italian campaign.[4] Moreover, much to Brooke's surprise and Churchill's delight, Marshall, with King and Leahy's approval, felt that the time had come to take some risks. Eisenhower had been planning a safe attack across the Strait of Messina, Operation Baytown. Marshall now called for a calculated risk—an assault in the Naples area, Operation Avalanche—which, although at the extreme limit of the range of fighter support, might lead to the quick capture of Rome.

Churchill was enthusiastic: "Why crawl up the leg like a harvest bug from the ankle upwards?" he asked Brooke. "Let us rather strike at the knee."[5] But he was also indiscreet. On July 17 he told Henry Stimson, who was visiting London, that he regarded the Marshall proposal as a vindication of his whole Mediterranean strategy.[6] No man in Washington was a more fervent believer in cross-channel attack than Stimson, and few were as suspicious of British pledges on the operation. Indeed, his visit to England was, in part, designed to see if these suspicions were justified. On Thursday, July 15, Stimson had called on General Morgan, who was in charge of the planning for Overlord. Morgan frankly expressed his "fear" of the Italian campaign and its possible effects on Overlord. Stimson found this same fear among most of the Overlord planners, particularly the Americans. Thus when Churchill claimed "with evident delight" that Avalanche constituted an "endorsement by Marshall" of

4. Matloff, *Strategic Planning, 1943–1944,* p. 157.
5. Bryant, *The Turn of the Tide,* p. 550.
6. Stimson and Bundy, *On Active Service,* p. 431.

British Mediterranean strategy, Stimson promptly denied it. Avalanche, said the American Secretary, was intended solely to achieve a rapid end to Mediterranean operations.

On Monday, July 19, Stimson phoned Marshall, who promptly seconded the Secretary's interpretation. Stimson repeated this to Churchill on the 22nd; what followed, according to Brooke, was a "disaster."[7] The Prime Minister launched himself into a full-throated "rivers of blood" attack on Overlord. What made the affair even worse was that on the previous day, July 21, Brooke himself had asked Marshall that nothing be moved out of the Mediterranean until Eisenhower had detailed his requirements for Italy. On his own authority, Brooke issued a British "stand fast" order, thus violating the Trident agreement and breaking Combined Chiefs procedure. Marshall became both angry with Brooke and convinced that Stimson's warnings were justified.

From London Stimson flew to Algiers and there subjected Eisenhower to a high-pressure inquisition aimed against the exploitation of the Sicilian victory.[8] Eisenhower told the Secretary that Brooke had criticized Overlord during his May visit to the Mediterranean. In Stimson's eyes the case was proved: both the Prime Minister and his chief strategist were out to substitute Italy for the cross-channel attack, despite the fact that they had approved Overlord only two months earlier and that the decision had been communicated to the Soviet Union, with whom relations were presently at their nadir. On August 4 Stimson told Roosevelt that Overlord was in danger and that British views on Italy differed widely from those of Washington. Marshall, after the fall of Mussolini, regarded a limited campaign in Italy built around Avalanche as "conservative and orthodox."[9] He

7. Bryant, *The Turn of the Tide*, p. 552.
8. Harry C. Butcher: *My Three Years with Eisenhower: The Personal Diary of Captain Harry C. Butcher, USNR, Naval Aide to General Eisenhower, 1942 to 1945* (New York: Simon and Schuster; 1946), pp. 373–4. Cited hereafter as *Years with Eisenhower*.
9. Matloff, *Strategic Planning, 1943–1944*, p. 160.

ordered Eisenhower to speed its preparation as much as possible, but he was not going to give final approval until he had won from Brooke full, complete, and lasting commitments on Overlord. London could have Italy only in exchange for a lawyer's contract on the cross-channel attack. The Quadrant Conference, which had been shifted from London to Quebec at Roosevelt's request, would see the bargain sealed.

PART TWO

THE QUADRANT
CONFERENCE

PART TWO

V

OVERLORD AND ITALY
August 14-17, 1943

A merican suspicions were evident during
the first session of the Combined Chiefs
at Quebec.[1] The meeting began at 10:30 A.M. on Saturday,
August 14, in the Chateau Frontenac, with Brooke serving as
chairman. It was brief, informal, and devoted to setting up
an agenda. Marshall did propose, however, that Overlord be
given "overriding priority" and that a statement to this
effect be issued by the Combined Chiefs of Staff. Brooke
agreed that Overlord should be the major offensive of 1944
but felt overriding priority might be "too binding."[2] "Overriding priority" and "too binding" became the major themes

1. For minutes and editorial notes concerning meetings during the
Quadrant Conference, see *U.S. Foreign Relations, Washington and Quebec
Papers, 1943,* pp. 849–967.
2. Matloff, *Strategic Planning, 1943–1944,* pp. 220–1.

in the military discussions of the next three days. Leahy also detected a difference of opinion on Italy.

After a brief lunch the first subject discussed by the Combined Chiefs was the war against Japan. Admiral King as usual wanted a speedup in the Pacific attack plus additional resources. His argument was mathematical: "If some 15 per cent of resources of the United Nations were now deployed against Japan, then an increase of only five per cent would increase by one-third the resources available whereas a decrease of five per cent of the forces deployed against the Axis in Europe would only mean a reduction of six per cent."[3] No decision was taken about increased resources, but the Combined Chiefs did approve King's plans for a three-pronged sea offensive involving simultaneous attacks in the South, Central, and North Pacific. It was further agreed to study the proposed schedule of operations with a view to the defeat of Japan twelve months after the collapse of German resistance. Marshall also pointed out that Brooke's "stand fast" order in the Mediterranean would have to be lifted in the next few days if operations in Burma were not to be delayed, since some of the vessels involved had been allocated to the Indian Ocean. This statement, together with King's evasiveness as to the role of the British fleet in the Pacific, constituted the only awkward moments in the meeting. Brooke and Marshall agreed on the Pacific, which was why Brooke had made it the first item on the agenda; therefore, Quadrant opened quietly.

General Brooke, however, described Sunday, August 15, as "a gloomy and unpleasant day."[4] This was a considerable understatement for, on Sunday, Brooke lost the greatest opportunity afforded to any Anglo-American officer in the Second World War: command of Overlord. From the beginning it had been assumed that the leader of the cross-channel attack would be British, as the operation would be

3. U.S. Foreign Relations, Washington and Quebec Papers, 1943, pp. 856–7.
4. Bryant, The Turn of the Tide, p. 577.

launched from England and in the opening phases Britain would supply the majority of the troops. Moreover, Churchill had accepted Eisenhower for Torch with the understanding that an English officer would hold the command in France. Brooke was Churchill's choice; on the evening of July 7, 1943, Churchill told Brooke that "he was the only man he had sufficient confidence in to take over the job."[5] Brooke told no one, but Leahy heard rumors. Shortly before noon on Sunday, August 15, however, Churchill asked Brooke to call upon him at Government House, where the Prime Minister stayed during the Quadrant Conference. There, while walking up and down on the terrace overlooking the St. Lawrence, Churchill told Brooke that, at the President's insistence, Marshall would get Overlord, Eisenhower would replace Marshall in Washington, and British General Sir Harold Alexander would replace Eisenhower in the Mediterranean. The Prime Minister stated that Brooke took the disappointment with "soldierly dignity."[6] Brooke called it a "crushing blow" and wondered if he had been told the whole truth; he had not.

Churchill had just arrived at Quebec after a two-day visit with Roosevelt and Hopkins at Hyde Park. This private gathering, August 12 through 14, of the President and the great diversionist occasioned considerable alarm in Washington. Preparatory to it, Roosevelt met with Stimson and the Joint Chiefs on August 10. During the meeting Stimson and Marshall issued dire warnings about Italy, the Mediterranean in general, and British pessimism on Overlord.[7] Stimson presented Roosevelt with a memorandum on the necessity of compelling Churchill to give the Overlord command to Marshall. The British were described as overcome by their experience in the First World War and by the "shadows of Passchendaele." Roosevelt was to assert his

5. Bryant, *The Turn of the Tide*, p. 542.
6. Churchill, *Second World War*, V, 85.
7. *U.S. Foreign Relations, Washington and Quebec Papers, 1943*, pp. 434–5, 498–503.

leadership. The pledge to Stalin must be kept. Stimson even called up the memory of President Lincoln's support of General Grant during the Virginia Campaign of 1864.

The effort was wasted, for in August, 1943, Churchill was no longer interested in the Mediterranean. In fact, much to the anxiety of the British Chiefs of Staff, he was no longer interested in the European war. He had a new enthusiasm: the Allied conquest of the northern tip of Sumatra. This operation, code name Culverin, Churchill maintained would be the "Torch of the Pacific."[8] Brooke considered it an impossible scheme and one which threatened his own plans.

Culverin had been conceived by the Prime Minister during his trip across the Atlantic. He was irritated by Wavell, whom he blamed for Britain's poor showing in Burma. He still felt humiliated by Singapore and had a great liking for Mountbatten, which he judged was not shared by Brooke. From these diverse elements the Prime Minister molded the plan for Culverin—an amphibious assault across the Indian Ocean to seize northern Sumatra and provide bases for air attacks on Singapore. Such an operation would restore the luster of British arms in the Pacific, and Mountbatten would be its leader. Churchill decided to offer Roosevelt the command of Overlord in exchange for Mountbatten as Allied Supreme Commander in Southeast Asia.

At Hyde Park a surprised Roosevelt was noncommittal on Culverin, but when Churchill "took the initiative of proposing to the President that an American commander should be appointed for the expedition to France, [the President] . . . was gratified."[9] Roosevelt further "cordially agreed" to the new title for Mountbatten. Ignorant of the Stimson memorandum, Churchill was surprised by the ease with which the President accommodated himself to the new arrangements. Brooke, who soon discovered what had happened, was deeply hurt. He rightly felt the Prime Minister had given away the Overlord command so that Churchill's

8. Churchill, *Second World War*, V, 88.
9. Ibid., 85.

protégé Mountbatten might direct Culverin, an operation with little prospect of approval by the Combined Chiefs of Staff. Nor was the loss of Overlord Brooke's only misfortune on Sunday, August 15. After hearing about Mountbatten's new title and Marshall's appointment, Brooke left Churchill and returned to the Chateau Frontenac for a 2:30 P.M. meeting of the Combined Chiefs of Staff. There Brooke discovered just how strongly the Americans were opposed to any further Mediterranean campaign.

The British Chiefs of Staff intended to make Sunday's meeting the decisive encounter where Marshall, Leahy, King, and Arnold would be brought to see the necessity of continuing the campaign in the Mediterranean. Just as the Americans had been preparing for weeks for the Quadrant Conference, the British Chiefs, too, when not distracted by Churchill's Sumatra scheme, had spent long hours studying the best way to present their case for continuing operations in the Mediterranean. The method they adopted was basically simple. Since the Americans wanted Overlord above all else, Italy must be shown to be a prerequisite for the cross-channel attack.

General Morgan had set three limiting conditions for Overlord which must be overcome or the operation would have to be abandoned: first, there must be a substantial reduction in German fighter aircraft in northwestern Europe; second, the Germans could have no more than twelve mobile divisions in northern France at the time of the initial assault and German reinforcement capacity during the succeeding sixty days must not exceed fifteen first-line divisions; and, finally, the Allies must be able to construct at least two effective artificial harbors.[1]

The first of these limiting conditions was a simple call for aerial supremacy in the Channel. The second derived from manpower and lift ceilings set at Trident which provided for thirty divisions, five in assault, for the cross-channel attack in

1. Gordon A. Harrison: *Cross-Channel Attack* (Washington, D.C.: U.S. Government Printing Office; 1951), pp. 71–9.

May of 1944. American mobilization was now swinging into full stride, and the Trident allocations reflected, not a shortage of soldiers, but of shipping, and also reflected problems of balance between various theaters. Artificial harbors were necessary because of the strength of German defenses at Le Havre, Dieppe, and along the Pas-de-Calais. This led Morgan to recommend Normandy as the invasion site which, in turn, meant that Overlord would have to be sustained across the beaches until the port of Cherbourg could be isolated and captured.

Brooke intended to open Sunday's meeting with a general description of Overlord, followed by emphasis on the so-called limiting conditions. The last, artificial harbors, was simply a technical problem, albeit a major one. The first two, however, German troop and aircraft distribution in Europe, could be influenced by Allied strategy through commando operations in the eastern Mediterranean and the invasion of Italy. This would compel Germany to disperse her defensive capabilities throughout southern Europe and so weaken her position in France. Brooke hoped that it would also lead Marshall to confirm Brooke's "stand fast" order and proceed with Avalanche, the invasion of Italy.

The American Joint Chiefs had also been discussing negotiating techniques on Sunday morning. They too agreed the meeting might be decisive; however, their approach was less complex than that of the British. As Marshall told his colleagues: "We must go into this argument in the spirit of winning."[2] Overlord would receive overriding priority, and the British would be overcome by an effort of will. Marshall added, however, that if the President and the Prime Minister decided on the Mediterranean, the Joint Chiefs must support the operation.

The Sunday afternoon meeting lasted, according to Brooke, "three very unpleasant hours."[3] Brooke presented his case. Marshall in reply again asked for overriding priority

2. Matloff, *Strategic Planning, 1943–1944*, p. 220.
3. Bryant, *The Turn of the Tide*, p. 578.

for Overlord, cancellation of Brooke's stand-fast order, and the maintenance of the Trident decision to shift seven divisions and the landing craft from the Mediterranean to England. Unless the seven divisions were returned, Marshall felt that Overlord would become a subsidiary operation. Any change in Trident plans would, according to Marshall, upset supply arrangements as far back as the Mississippi River. Without an agreement on priority, Marshall threatened that the Americans might reduce their forces in England to a single corps for use in an opportunistic attack and concentrate instead on the Pacific.[4] After listening to Marshall, Brooke was of the opinion the Americans had not even read Morgan's plan. Discussion was lengthy, occasionally acrimonious, and wholly unproductive. With the delegations deadlocked, the meeting was adjourned. Late in the evening Dill, who had talked with Marshall privately, informed Brooke that Marshall was now threatening to resign if the British pressed their point.

However, the following day, August 16, Marshall began to show signs of weakening, and before an additional twenty-four hours had passed Brooke got his Italian campaign. There were three reasons for this: first, Marshall had believed in a limited Italian campaign all along; second, he received the most solemn assurances from Brooke and Churchill that Italy was not going to be expanded into a replacement for Overlord; and finally, on the 16th Brooke told Marshall that the Italians were willing to change sides in the war provided the Allies landed on the peninsula. That despite this last reason Marshall still held out for twenty-four hours against any Italian operations speaks much for American determination to get an Overlord contract.

The news about Italy, which as Brooke noted arrived at a most dramatic moment, resulted from the fact that on August 15, while Brooke and Marshall were arguing at Quebec over whether to go into Italy, a representative of the

4. For the minutes of this meeting, see *U.S. Foreign Relations, Washington and Quebec Papers, 1943*, pp. 862–9.

Italian Army, General Giuseppe Castellano, called on Sir Samuel Hoare, the British Ambassador in Madrid. Castellano told Sir Samuel in what must rank as one of the more curious expressions in the history of diplomacy: "We [Italians] are not in a position to make any terms. We will unconditionally surrender, provided we can join as Allies in fighting the Germans."[5]

Churchill was informed of Castellano's offer in a series of telegrams from Anthony Eden which arrived in Quebec on Monday morning, August 16. Eden, together with Alexander Cadogan, Permanent Under Secretary in the Foreign Office, said he intended to fly over from London. The Foreign Secretary's plane, however, was delayed by bad weather. He reached Quebec on August 18, too late to influence decisions on Italy but soon enough to force Roosevelt to ask Cordell Hull to come up from Washington.

Italian capitulation came as no surprise to either Washington or London. Peace feelers had been received from Italian Army and Royalist circles as early as December, 1942. By February, 1943, both governments knew that Marshal Badoglio was preparing an anti-Fascist coup and had passed the information along to Moscow. When Badoglio made his move in July, Eden commented to Winant that the Italian Government could now be expected to pursue "a mixture of the policies adopted by Prince Max von Baden and Pétain."[6] Eden, with considerable foresight, also told Winant that it would be advisable to include Moscow in any Italian negotiations because when the Russian armies advanced into Eastern Europe, the Anglo-Americans might well want to influence Soviet terms of capitulation and occupancy in the areas they conquered. To exclude the Russians from Italy would set a precedent for Anglo-American exclusion from Poland.

<hr/>

5. These sentences are quoted as Castellano's own words in a telegram from Churchill to Roosevelt of August 16. Churchill, *Second World War*, V, 103–4.

6. *U.S. Foreign Relations, 1943*, II, 335.

Eden's recommendation, echoed by Clark Kerr and Maxwell Hamilton, the British Ambassador and American Chargé in Moscow, was largely disregarded. It was not until July 30 that Arkady Sobolev, Counselor of the Soviet Embassy in London and the highest-ranking Russian diplomat in Great Britain after Maisky's recall, was given "for his government's information" a summary of what Britain and America regarded as proper peace terms in case Italy surrendered. The terms themselves had been drafted in the American War Department two months earlier. Indeed, the State Department felt there was a lack of consultation in Washington, much less Moscow.

By the first week of August, with German troops poised on the borders of their country, the Italian Government was in contact with Anglo-American diplomats in Madrid, Lisbon, Tangier, Switzerland, and the Vatican. Everywhere the Italians pleaded for time to deceive the Germans; and at Tangier their representative, Signor Alberto Berio, said that he was empowered by Badoglio to open peace negotiations.[7] Churchill, aboard the *Queen Mary*, noted in red ink on a telegram from Eden, who advised answering Berio with a flat demand for unconditional surrender: "Don't miss the bus."[8] It was obvious that only fear of Germany kept Italy in the struggle.

On August 6, the same day Berio appeared in Tangier, this last restraint snapped. General Vittorio Ambrosio, Chief of the Italian Supreme Command, had a most unsatisfactory interview with Field Marshal Wilhelm Keitel, Chief of the German High Command. Keitel refused permission for the return of Italian divisions presently garrisoning France and the Balkans. Further, the Germans dispatched five infantry and two panzer divisions under Rommel to northern Italy. Badoglio was convinced that this so-called Army Group B, far from being a strategic reserve in

7. *U.S. Foreign Relations, Washington and Quebec Papers*, 1943, pp. 566–7.

8. Churchill, *Second World War*, V, 101.

case the Allies attacked Italy, constituted an occupation force.[9] He ordered General Castellano to Madrid to say that Italy wanted both to surrender and to change sides and to ask that American and British forces be immediately landed in Italy.

From the standpoint of the debate at Quebec, as Brooke noted, Castellano's approach "arrived at a most dramatic moment."[1] On Monday morning, August 16, he and the British Chiefs of Staff were called to Churchill's bedroom at Government House, where they were told what had happened in Madrid and discussed "how to make best use of [the Italian] . . . offer." At the same time, Marshall and the American Joint Chiefs, meeting at the Chateau Frontenac and knowing nothing of Castellano, voted to reject British "indirection" and to demand "priority" for Overlord. They decided to insist that the seven divisions be returned to England and even to deny the validity of Morgan's "limiting conditions."[2] Brooke's arguments of the previous day had not merely failed to move Marshall, they had stiffened his resistance. Marshall ordered General Handy, head of the Joint Chiefs Planning Division, to fly to Washington, where Roosevelt had gone after leaving Hyde Park. Handy was instructed to tell the President that the British were out to torpedo Overlord. Handy saw Harry Hopkins that night and found the President entraining for Quebec. Hopkins asked Handy to join the Presidential party, and Roosevelt received from him a full briefing on Marshall's problems. Handy also discovered that Marshall had not been the only person to appeal to a higher authority.

When Brooke entered Churchill's bedroom on Monday morning, he found the Prime Minister dictating a telegram to Roosevelt concerning the Castellano offer. The telegram recounted the advantages to be gained from having the Ital-

9. Greenfield, *Command Decisions*, p. 233.
1. Bryant, *The Turn of the Tide*, p. 580.
2. Matloff, *Strategic Planning, 1943–1944*, p. 222.

ians fight the Germans.[3] These advantages ranged from
Italian troops giving armed resistance to "patriot" forces in
the Balkans to their "undoubted ability . . . to paralyse
German communications" in the peninsula. He asked
Roosevelt to come to Quebec immediately and ended by
saying: "The Chiefs of Staff are considering practical steps
and timings to make an Italian turnover effective."

The telegram brought Roosevelt to Quebec sooner than
he had planned to come. But that afternoon the Combined
Chiefs, despite Churchill's optimistic prediction, did not
consider practical steps on Italy. The Monday meeting
lasted four hours and, in the face of Brooke's news that
Badoglio was offering the Allies the Italian Army, Navy, and
Air Force, Marshall stood firm. Brooke finally called for a
"closed session." After all the secretaries and planners had
left the room, discussion "was pretty frank." Brooke rightly
stated that the cause of the impasse was not the operation
itself but the lack of trust between the Americans and the
British. Marshall doubted whether the English would put
their "full hearts" into Overlord. Brooke feared Marshall's
efforts to force him into a straitjacket "irrespective of changed
strategic conditions."[4] Brooke now delivered his solemn
promise on Overlord, again detailing his arguments on the
relationship between Overlord and Italy. Marshall would
not commit himself, but Brooke noted in his diary that
night: "In the end I think our arguments did have some
effect." It was also significant that the Combined Chiefs
agreed that their meeting the following day would be
"closed" from the start, an accepted signal that one or both
delegations were willing to modify their stands.

The next afternoon, August 17, members of the Combined Chiefs of Staff made their compromise. Marshall

3. For the text of Churchill's message of August 16, 1943, see *U.S.
Foreign Relations, Washington and Quebec Papers, 1943*, pp. 588–94.
4. Brooke diary, August 16, 1943, quoted in Bryant, *The Turn of the
Tide*, pp. 579–80.

agreed to the invasion of Italy. Brooke, in turn, accepted the following statement for presentation to Roosevelt and Churchill as a decision of the Combined Chiefs: "This [Overlord] operation will be the primary United States–British ground and air effort against the Axis in Europe."[5] Morgan's Overlord plan, complete with limiting conditions, was also approved. In the Mediterranean, Eisenhower was ordered to have two divisions of General Montgomery's Eighth Army cross the Strait of Messina during the first week of September. Two American and two British divisions under General Mark Clark were to land at Salerno one week later. Eisenhower was also authorized to enter into negotiations with Castellano in Lisbon, where Castellano had gone in accordance with his cover story that he was part of a welcome-home mission for the returning Italian Ambassador to Chile. The Combined Chiefs recommended General Walter Bedell Smith, Eisenhower's Chief of Staff, and General Kenneth Strong, head of Eisenhower's Intelligence Section, to serve as the negotiators. Robert Murphy, Eisenhower's American Political Adviser, maintained later that the Generals were used so that Roosevelt and Churchill would not be charged with "making a deal with the Fascists." Actually, since the War Department drew up the terms and the Combined Chiefs approved them, the use of G-2 (military intelligence officers) for the negotiations followed quite naturally.[6]

But if Brooke had now got Italy, he got it within the Trident framework. The Combined Chiefs agreed that, "as between Operation 'Overlord' and operations in the Mediterranean, where there is a shortage of resources, available resources will be distributed and employed with the main object of insuring the success of Overlord."[7] The much-

5. For minutes of this meeting, but not, of course, of the closed session, see U.S. Foreign Relations, Washington and Quebec Papers, 1943, pp. 875–80.

6. Robert Murphy: Diplomat Among Warriors, p. 188.

7. U.S. Foreign Relations, Washington and Quebec Papers, 1943, p. 1025.

contested seven divisions were to be diverted to England in the winter together with the major portion of Eisenhower's assault shipping. Even the dispatch of Mediterranean landing craft to the Indian Ocean was reaffirmed. Marshall wanted to make these points binding, but Brooke succeeded in preserving some freedom of maneuver. The final report read: "Operations in the Mediterranean Theatre will be carried out with the forces allotted at Trident, except in so far as these may be varied by decision of the Combined Chiefs of Staff."[8]

Italian decisions taken, Brooke proceeded to create a more relaxed atmosphere by producing Brigadier Wingate, who gave a talk on Burma and the exploits of his air-supported, deep-penetration columns. Tuesday's session ended in a spirit of friendliness, and Brooke wrote in his diary that night: "To my great relief, they [the Joint Chiefs of Staff] accepted our proposals for the European Theatre, so that all our arguing has borne fruit and we have obtained quite fair results."[9] This was too sanguine; Marshall and Stimson were never really persuaded on the Mediterranean. The fall of Mussolini and the Castellano offer forced the fruit of the North African campaign upon unwilling hands.

8. *U.S. Foreign Relations, Washington and Quebec Papers, 1943,* p. 1025.

9. Bryant, *The Turn of the Tide,* p. 581.

VI

ITALY, CHINA, AND
IMPERIAL REVENGE
August 17–19, 1943

Roosevelt's train arrived at Quebec on Tuesday evening, August 17. The Earl of Athlone, Governor General of Canada, had planned a cocktail party reception. However, introductions were barely over before the Prime Minister, the President, Hopkins, Leahy, and Brooke left the room to prepare a message for Eisenhower. In light of the Castellano approach, the decision to invade Italy involved more than the Baytown and Avalanche campaigns. The Italians were offering to change sides, and Eisenhower needed political instructions.

At Casablanca Roosevelt and Churchill had agreed to demand the unconditional surrender of Germany, Italy, and Japan. The Italian surrender terms had been drafted with this in mind. They envisaged nothing less than the dissolution of the Italian Government, which would be replaced by an Allied Military Government patterned, according to Secretary of War Stimson, on "American experience in the Philippines, Cuba, and Puerto Rico."[1] It was believed Italian Fascism would fight to the last man and foot of territory. The surrender terms provided the legal basis for the administration of a state that had ceased to exist. After the Badoglio coup, it was obvious such thinking was outmoded. Late in July Roosevelt and Churchill pulled out of the surrender terms all articles relevant to a military armistice. These became known as the "short terms." The remaining economic and political articles were brought together in a second document called the "long terms."[2]

At Quebec Tuesday evening, Roosevelt and Churchill quickly agreed that Castellano's offer to fight the Germans rendered even the short terms obsolete. As nothing else was immediately available, however, they ordered Eisenhower to present Castellano with the short terms. At the same time, Castellano was to be told that the armistice would be modified in Italy's favor commensurate with the assistance she rendered the Allies.[3] True, Eisenhower was to warn Castellano that the political and economic terms would be communicated later, but the warning was muted. Instead, Castellano was to be assured without reservation that wherever Italian forces engaged the Germans, "they will be given all possible support. . . ." Even Allied bombing in Italy would as far as possible be directed exclusively on German troops, whereas Italian formations in the Balkans were promised immediate repatriation. The Italian Navy must sail to Allied ports, but nothing was said about its future. According to his political adviser, Robert Murphy, Eisen-

1. Stimson and Bundy, *On Active Service*, p. 556.
2. For the text of both the "short" and "long" terms, see U.S. Department of State: *Treaties and Other International Acts Series 1604, Armistice with Italy, 1943* (Washington: Government Printing Office; 1947).
3. For the text of the dispatch to Eisenhower, see *U.S. Foreign Relations, Washington and Quebec Papers, 1943*, pp. 1060–1.

hower seems to have felt that his orders constituted "a crooked deal" for the Italians.[4] Murphy, too, disliked the deception involved. Roosevelt and Churchill, however, were determined to bag the Italians, and they did instruct Eisenhower to tell Castellano that acceptance of the armistice meant Italy's unconditional surrender. Their work completed, Roosevelt and Churchill returned to Lord Athlone's party.

With the questions of Overlord and Italy out of the way, Wednesday, August 18, was a day of ceremony and sightseeing for the principals at Quebec. The Combined Chiefs did, however, establish Mountbatten's Southeast Asia Command. They also made General Stilwell, who disliked the British, Deputy Supreme Allied Commander. Roosevelt and Churchill passed the day resting and preparing speeches for a state dinner to be held that night by the Canadian Prime Minister, Mackenzie King. The Combined Chiefs, after a formal lunch with Lord Athlone, decided to visit the Plains of Abraham and study the famous battle between Wolf and Montcalm in which England won Canada. The battlefield was poorly marked, and their guide had a patter suitable, according to Leahy, only "for the entertainment of tourists."[5] Soon the Combined Chiefs and other distinguished visitors were scattered over the field trying to recall their military history. In the process they met an elderly French-Canadian priest who knew the battle thoroughly. He spoke no English but Brooke offered to translate. The priest insisted that Montcalm was the better general and would have won had his dispositions not been interfered with by the French Governor-General. He concluded with the statement: "So, by an accident the French General Montcalm with his defenders of Canada lost the battle, which accident made me a British subject, but my heart is still with France." Despite the slight on British military prowess, Brooke found the priest far more interesting than the din-

4. Murphy, *Diplomat Among Warriors*, p. 190.
5. Leahy, *I Was There*, p. 176.

ner, speeches, group photographs, and dull films which followed.

If the 18th was quiet, the next day was not. Indeed, shots rang out during the meeting of the Combined Chiefs. The shooting, though entirely incidental, could be taken as a symbol for dissension between the Combined Chiefs and the Prime Minister. The dissension involved neither Overlord nor the Mediterranean. Instead during the first plenary conference of Quadrant, Churchill spoke at length on the merits of Culverin before a less than enthusiastic audience. Brooke, who by now had learned how he had been sacrificed for Mountbatten, querulously wrote in his diary that night that in his opinion Churchill was no longer at Quebec but, instead, "revolving somewhere around the northern tip of Sumatra."[6]

The sound of shots and blows which echoed from the meeting room of the Combined Chiefs, however, had nothing to do with Culverin. It stemmed from Project Habakkuk. According to Brooke, Habakkuk was born "during the small hours of the morning" at a Chequers weekend between "Winston and Dickie" (Mountbatten). The project was to make aircraft carriers out of icebergs. As originally conceived, one simply cut the top off the berg, smoothed out a landing deck, and inserted engines. Such a vessel, displacing about two million tons, would be unsinkable because when it was bombed or torpedoed, the resulting damage would simply be filled with water and refrozen. Icebergs, according to Brooke, were soon found "not so handy." Ice itself proved too refractory. The project might have languished, but a Mr. Pyke, on Mountbatten's staff, developed a mixture of ice and sawdust. It was christened "Pykrete." It was less brittle and had a lower melting point than ordinary ice.

Mountbatten asked permission to demonstrate Pykrete. Two blocks—one, ordinary ice, the other, Pykrete—were

6. Bryant, *The Turn of the Tide*, p. 583.

wheeled into the room. General Arnold was voted the
strongest man present and was asked to attack the blocks
with a chopper. The ice splintered satisfactorily, but the
chopper rebounded from the Pykrete causing Arnold to cry
out with pain. Mountbatten then pulled out a revolver and
fired at the blocks. The Combined Chiefs were first subjected to a hail of ice and then a ricochet which narrowly
missed Air Chief Marshal Portal.[7] Some officers waiting
outside had heard blows, a cry of pain, and shots. This led
some wag to remark: "My God! They've now started shooting!" The meeting ended in laughter. For one reason or
another, the Habakkuks were never built.

The first plenary session of the Quebec Conference
opened at 5:30 Thursday afternoon, August 19. The President and Prime Minister quickly approved the Overlord
plan, including General Morgan's limiting conditions. It was
assigned a target date of May 1, 1944. Having gotten Italy,
Churchill said he "strongly favored" Overlord. He even
asked Marshall if it would not be possible to increase the
assault force by a quarter. The President agreed and called
for a speedup in sending American troops and supplies to
England (Bolero). Marshall and Brooke, after pointing out
that the limiting factors were not men but landing craft,
agreed to try to satisfy both requests.[8] Discussion of Italy
and the Mediterranean was equally easy. Both Baytown and
Avalanche were accepted. On the delicate question of how
far to go in Italy, the Prime Minister assured Roosevelt that
although in the past he had frequently spoken of the Po
River or the Alps as desirable objectives, he was now willing
to accept a halt at the narrow line between Pisa and Rimini.
This could be held with a minimum of troops and so permit
the movement of men and landing craft back to England in

7. *U.S. Foreign Relations, Washington and Quebec Papers*, 1943, pp.
890–1, note 3, p. 891.
8. For the minutes of this meeting, see *U.S. Foreign Relations, Washington and Quebec Papers*, 1943, pp. 894–903.

the fall. As for additional Mediterranean operations, Churchill believed none should be undertaken which threatened
the integrity of Overlord. In the Balkans, it was decided to
limit Allied activity to the supply of guerrillas and small-
scale commando attacks. The Trident allocations for the
Mediterranean were approved with Brooke's proviso that
these could be changed by the Combined Chiefs of Staff.

When the discussion turned to the Pacific, however, the
smooth forward progress of the meeting came to an end.
There were no objections to Mountbatten's appointment or
to Admiral King's plans. But when it came to Southeast
Asia, the Prime Minister, standing alone, expounded Culverin at length. During the debate which followed, he challenged the whole Burma campaign. To the familiar claim of
northern Sumatra as the "Torch of the Pacific," Churchill
now added the assertion that not since the Dardanelles in
1915 had a single operation afforded such great strategic
possibilities. This statement generated, according to Churchill, "a spirited argument." As Brooke well knew and Marshall now learned, opposition to a Churchill project, far
from leading to compromise, had just the opposite effect.
Marshall entered the room certain that Mountbatten's appointment would achieve British cooperation in a Burma
campaign. When he left it was gone. The Americans wanted
North Burma as the first step in the establishment of a satisfactory supply route to China. By mid-1943 this route was
desired not merely to make the Chinese Army an effective
fighting force but also to obtain bases for the new B-29
Super-Fortresses. According to General Arnold, the B-29s
based in China might bring about Japan's defeat by air
power alone. The Burma attack required the use of Chinese
troops. Chiang was reluctant to grant permission unless the
British demonstrated a sincere interest in the offensive. The
demonstration Chiang wanted was a British amphibious
assault across the Bay of Bengal against the Burmese port
city of Akyab. Even when this had been promised, Chiang

dragged his feet. Without Akyab it seemed certain the Chinese would never move.[9]

When Marshall objected to Culverin on the grounds that the resources were needed for Akyab, the result was inevitable. Churchill denounced the whole Burma plan as the "waste of an entire year with nothing to show for it but Akyab and the future right to toil through the swamps and jungles of Burma, about the suggested reconquest of which [he] was very dubious." The capture of Akyab would be an "act of waste and folly." Operations in Burma should be limited to General Wingate's raiding columns. Culverin had far better prospects. There was more to the Prime Minister's objections than just enthusiasm for Sumatra. Churchill feared Marshall would drag him into a land war in Asia. If he gave in on Burma, he might be led into China and "the presence of very strong Japanese forces . . . operating on interior lines of communication." He suspected "political motivation" in those who supported Marshall's plans, and he much preferred Admiral King's Pacific advance with its reliance on sea power.[1]

Roosevelt said he "saw the advantages of an attack on Sumatra [but] he doubted whether there were sufficient resources to allow of both Sumatra and the opening of the Burma Road." Between the two, the President preferred Burma. It represented "the shortest line through China to Japan"—a short line which in Churchill's opinion would entail tremendous losses and from which the only real gainer would be Chiang Kai-shek. Churchill refused to give way, and when the plenary session ended, the Burma-Sumatra debate was referred back to the Combined Chiefs for further study.

The Prime Minister was less irritated by American enthusiasm for China than by the British Chiefs of Staff's

9. Joseph W. Stilwell: *The Stilwell Papers*. Arranged and edited by Theodore H. White (New York: William Sloane; 1948), pp. 209–12. Cited hereafter as *The Stilwell Papers*.
1. Churchill, *Second World War*, V, 87.

obvious lack of interest in Culverin. This lack of interest
occasioned an angry exchange with Brooke later in the day
with Churchill at one point shaking his fist at Brooke and
shouting: "I do not want any of your long-term projects,
they cripple initiative."[2]

Brooke, upon whom the wrath had fallen, was up until
midnight exploring with Marshall the possibility of doing
both Burma and Culverin. He was equally angry at the
Prime Minister's "hare chasing." He noted in his diary that
he felt "cooked and unable to face another day." Brooke,
however, was being unduly pessimistic. Except for Culverin
and Burma, the plenary session had been a success. Indeed,
from the viewpoint of the Combined Chiefs, Quadrant,
although it lasted four more days, was largely over. Brooke
had Italy; Marshall, Overlord. All that remained was resolution of the Burma and Culverin problems and adjustment of
the timing and scale of all operations so as to assure the
fulfillment of Bolero.

2. Bryant, *The Turn of the Tide*, p. 583.

VII

FRANCE, GREECE,
THE FOUR-POWER
DECLARATION, AND AN
INVITATION FROM RUSSIA
August 20–23, 1943

If, after August 19, the tempo of the military discussions at the Quadrant Conference slowed, the reverse was true on the political level. This was caused by the arrival in Quebec of Anthony Eden and Cordell Hull on August 20. Neither man had expected to come to Quadrant, nor were they entirely welcome. Churchill in the spring of 1943 was angry with Eden, and he spent a good deal of time in April and May in unsuccessful attempts to convince his Foreign Secretary to become Viceroy of India, a position of much ceremony and little responsibility. As for Hull, his relationship with Roosevelt was at a low ebb in August as a result of Hull's dismissal of the President's friend, Sumner Welles, the Assistant Secretary of State.

Eden came to Quebec to consult with the Prime Minister

about the Castellano offer of Italian surrender. Hull came because Eden was there. Eden's plane had been delayed for two days in Ireland by bad weather. Absent also, to his considerable annoyance, had been the American Secretary of State. In 1943 Roosevelt shared Hopkins's opinion that the State Department "was full of leaks as well as creaks."[1] The President kept Hull waiting in Washington until the fog lifted in Ireland.

Although Eden arrived at Quebec too late to effect decisions on Italy, the Foreign Secretary was not greatly disturbed. He and Churchill would have preferred giving Italy the complete surrender terms, but they both regarded the short terms solution as sensible. If the Italians were deceived, they deserved nothing better. Even without Italy there were a number of topics that required discussion with Hull. These included the newly created French Committee of National Liberation and recent signs that the Russians were interested in some sort of political meeting with the British and Americans. The Foreign Secretary was, however, irritated that on the day he and Hull held their first talks, Roosevelt and Churchill went fishing. The President and Prime Minister did not return until nightfall, forcing their subordinates to report at "unpleasantly late" hours.

Eden and Hull met at noon on August 20.[2] After a brief mention of the futility of invitations to Stalin and of Chinese unhappiness with the Anglo-American decision-making process, they engaged in a lengthy discussion over General Charles de Gaulle and the French Committee of National Liberation. No other subject, aside from the Soviet frontier question, was more likely to produce an argument. Eden was one of the few people on either side of the Atlantic who liked the "dynamic personality" of General de Gaulle. Hull fully shared the prevalent view in Washington that de Gaulle was an ambitious politician whose "poisonous propa-

1. Sherwood, *Roosevelt and Hopkins,* p. 756.
2. For minutes of this meeting, see *U.S. Foreign Relations, Washington and Quebec Papers,* 1943, pp. 912–17.

ganda" threatened the alliance of Great Britain and the
United States.[3] What was at issue at Quebec was whether
or not the Anglo-Americans should extend formal recognition to the French Committee. The British favored this; the
Americans were opposed. Eden in his diary noted that "old
Hull . . . got quite heated." Hull in his memoirs more
politely remarked that "the conversation became a trifle
sharp."

At the Casablanca Conference in January, 1943, Roosevelt and Churchill had tried to unite General Charles de
Gaulle's Free French Movement and those officers and civil
servants in North Africa loyal to General Giraud. Though
the initial effort failed, Giraud and de Gaulle had agreed to
continue negotiations at Algiers. On June 3, 1943, Giraud
and de Gaulle announced they had compromised their
differences. The result was the creation of the French Committee of National Liberation. On paper it represented a
union of the North Africans and the Free French. In fact, as
Robert Murphy warned Hull and Roosevelt, it represented
victory for de Gaulle. Under the guise of negotiation, the
Free French had penetrated North Africa and Giraud had
been outwitted. The committee was dominated by Gaullists.
This fact was recognized in Algiers where the anti-Gaullist
Governor General, Marcel Peyrouton, immediately resigned.[4]
It was also recognized in London. On June 4 Churchill
warned de Gaulle against swallowing Giraud "in a single
gulp." De Gaulle took the advice; Giraud himself was un-
touched, but de Gaulle's enemies, including Boisson, were
purged.

This produced tension between London and Washington
and tension between Churchill and Eden. Faced with the
North African purges, Hull and Roosevelt became convinced de Gaulle intended to force a dictatorship on France.
In the summer of 1943, Roosevelt took the position that

3. Hull, *Memoirs*, II, 1219, 1222–3.
4. For Murphy's report on Peyrouton's resignation, see *U.S. Foreign
Relations, 1943*, II, 131.

when Vichy broke relations with the United States after Torch and Germany violated the armistice by occupying all of France, the French State had ceased to exist. For Roosevelt, Washington became France's trustee. When the war ended, America would hold elections and the resulting government would be recognized. Until then no group could speak for France.[5] This was anathema to de Gaulle. By the end of June, de Gaulle, now styled "the President of the French Government," was visiting Eisenhower to see what the Allied Commander was doing with the armies de Gaulle had "imparted to him." Roosevelt in turn was practically urging Eisenhower to overthrow the French Committee by force.

This development was most unwelcome in London. Eden believed the British alliance of 1941 with the Soviet Union "needs to be balanced by an understanding with a powerful France in the west."[6] If he stood for nothing else, de Gaulle did stand for a strong France. Eden also felt de Gaulle's success in North Africa should be encouraged, and the best possible gesture would be the recognition of the new committee as a Provisional French Government. As for Washington's opposition, according to Eden there were "limits beyond which we ought not to allow our policy to be governed by others."

Churchill, though no enthusiast of de Gaulle's, agreed with all of Eden's premises but the last. He would risk no major troubles with America for the sake of the French Committee. He warned Eden they might be coming to a break. It was this conflict that produced Churchill's suggestion that his Foreign Secretary might be happier as Viceroy of India. Eden, however, had the full support of the Foreign Office. America might or might not stay in Europe when the war ended, and Eden maintained that a strong France was

5. Roosevelt informed Churchill on June 17, 1943, that "the time has arrived when we must break with him [de Gaulle]." In this same cable he expressed his ideas about trusteeship. *U.S. Foreign Relations, 1943*, II, 155–7.
6. Eden, *Memoirs*, II, 461–2.

"indispensable for [British] security."[7] At Quebec Churchill compromised and agreed that Eden should make as
strong a case as possible before Hull in the hopes of achieving a coordinated Anglo-American policy. If this failed,
Eden might sound Hull out on the question of separate
British and American statements on the French Committee.

During the meeting of August 20, Eden rapidly discovered
that a coordinated policy was out of the question. In the
course of presenting a good case for the French Committee,
the Foreign Secretary made the mistake of remarking "that
in 1940 de Gaulle had been their [Britain's] only friend."[8]
An irritated Hull immediately chronicled the assistance
given by the United States. Since the year mentioned was
1940 when, in the opinion of the American Secretary, he
himself had almost singlehandedly immobilized the French
fleet, Hull proceeded to defend his Vichy policy at length.
He then moved on to Torch and North Africa. Hull pointed
out, first, that if the landings had had a Gaullist flavor the
French in North Africa would have fought, and second, that
the whole policy had been approved by Eden.

Hull was also sensitive to press criticism of the years of
Vichy recognition. He regarded this criticism as having its
source in de Gaulle. Since de Gaulle was financed by London, the Secretary now implied that British money had been
used to criticize the State Department. A heated exchange
followed. It was quite clear that Hull was sticking with
Giraud and nonrecognition. If anything, there had been a
retreat from Casablanca. At that time Roosevelt had found
de Gaulle amusing; now he no longer did.

When Hull calmed down, Eden raised the question of
separate statements. To his surprise, Hull did not attempt to
exercise a veto. The American Secretary merely pointed out
"that such a procedure, even if done by both governments
simultaneously, would mean an obvious divergence of

7. Ibid., II, 461.
8. Hull, *Memoirs*, II, 1232.

views." The divergence would be "regrettable."[9] Hull and Eden agreed to make another effort, but neither was hopeful. In fact, from a British viewpoint, separate statements would have the advantage of demonstrating to de Gaulle that his sole support was London. When Churchill returned from fishing, Eden told him what had happened and the Prime Minister agreed with Eden's stand.

Friday night the President and Prime Minister dined with Hull, Hopkins, and Eden until after midnight. It ended when an exhausted Hull asked to be excused. Churchill, who delighted in dusk-to-dawn conversation, protested: "Why, man, we are at war!"[1] Roosevelt, who never shared the Prime Minister's enthusiasm for the small hours, probably approved Hull's action. According to Eden, the main subject discussed was the Soviet Union.

On June 19 Churchill had asked Stalin to attend the Quadrant Conference. In his letter he included a defense of the Roundup cancellation.[2] Stalin's first reply, sent on June 24 to both London and Washington, was another harshly worded, if not unwarranted, chronicle of Anglo-American broken promises over the second front. He again described his allies' contribution to the winning of the war as "insignificant," and he felt that the Alliance itself was "being subjected to severe stress."[3] On August 8 Stalin told Roosevelt he would not be able to meet with the President in the fall. On August 9 Stalin informed Churchill that he could not attend Quadrant. As in the earlier exchange over Casablanca, Stalin said he was "unable . . . to lose touch with the front even for one week."[4]

However, in both of the August messages, Stalin for the first time since the outbreak of the war deemed it "advisable

9. Hull, *Memoirs*, II, 1232. *U.S. Foreign Relations, Washington and Quebec Papers*, 1943, p. 917.
1. Eden, *Memoirs*, II, 467.
2. *Stalin's Correspondence*, I, No. 163, 133–5.
3. Ibid., I, No. 165, 136–8.
4. Ibid., I, No. 170, 142.

to hold a meeting of authorized representatives of our states
. . . in the near future."[5] That Stalin was serious was
shown by his further request for agreement "beforehand on
the range of problems to be discussed and on the draft proposals to be approved . . . [without which] the meeting
can hardly yield tangible results." Nor was Stalin reticent as
to at least one of the reasons for this change in policy. Both
messages contained one paragraph which was nearly identical. Roosevelt was congratulated on the Anglo-American
"success in Sicily, which has led to the fall of Mussolini and
his gang."[6] Churchill was offered the same congratulations
and for the same reason. Stalin, though ignorant of the
Castellano offer, had drawn the proper conclusions from the
Badoglio coup. With one of the Axis partners about to collapse, Stalin decided the time had come for serious talks
with his cobelligerents.

Washington seems to have paid little attention to the
Soviet overture. Eden was more sensitive. Stalin's message
arrived on August 10, and the Foreign Secretary, then still in
London, immediately cabled the Prime Minister to accept
the idea of a conference "in principle." Churchill, who was
"very glad to hear again from Bruin [Stalin] in the first
person," agreed.[7] On August 11, just before his visit to Hyde
Park, the Prime Minister answered Stalin saying he "understood" the reasons why the Soviet Premier could not leave
Russia and found a "meeting . . . of responsible representatives in the near future . . . desirable."[8] He said he
would discuss it with the President.

On Thursday, August 19, Churchill and Roosevelt sent
two joint messages to Stalin. The first and longer one announced the Castellano offer of four days earlier and contained a copy of their instructions to Eisenhower. If,
however, the President and Prime Minister acted promptly,

5. Ibid., I, No. 170, 142; II, No. 101, 78–9.
6. Ibid., II, No. 101, 78–9.
7. Churchill, *Second World War*, V, 278.
8. *Stalin's Correspondence*, I, No. 171, 142–3.

they did not act discreetly. At no point was Soviet advice solicited. Stalin was just told that "the Combined Chiefs of Staff have prepared, and the President and Prime Minister approved, as a measure of military diplomacy, . . . [these] instructions which have been sent to General Eisenhower for action."[9] The second message dispatched on the 19th concerned Stalin's request for a "lower level" meeting. Roosevelt and Churchill accepted the proposal provided it was of an "exploratory nature" with "final decisions" left to the "respective Governments."[1] Neither Roosevelt nor Churchill was really interested in a meeting of representatives. What they, and particularly Roosevelt, did want was a Big Three Conference. Stalin was told that the Big Three meeting was "very essential." Roosevelt offered Fairbanks, Alaska, as a prospective site, and the time would be "now."

Although the President and Prime Minister wanted Stalin, neither expected to get him. Friday night's discussion at Quebec, therefore, centered on the lower-level meeting—who would go and what should be discussed. Eden had no doubts on either point. He would go, and the most important topic would be the Soviet Union's western frontier. As he told Roosevelt and Hull during the dinner party: "If we meet the Russians saying no on the Second Front in 1943, and no on the territorial question, then any conference was almost certain to do more harm than good."[2] Eden broadly hinted that the policies of 1942 be inverted. At that time the Soviet Union was promised a second front in lieu of territorial concessions. Now the Soviet Union was to be given the territorial concessions in lieu of a second front.

Roosevelt and Hull would have none of it. American policy was just what it had been in 1942—no territorial settlements until the Peace Conference. When Eden continued to express his "anxieties," Roosevelt replied that should the Soviets raise the question of Finland or the Baltic

9. Ibid., I, No. 172, 144.
1. Ibid., I, No. 173, 148.
2. Eden, *Memoirs*, II, 466–7.

States, the American representative would state that he had no plenipotentiary powers and that all such matters must be referred back to Washington. Churchill asked: "What would be the good of that, since the United States Government would not be able to give an answer?" Eden again repeated that a meeting under present circumstances could only make matters worse. Roosevelt and Hull were unmoved.

Roosevelt turned to a new subject. He mentioned a Four-Power Declaration which Hull intended to discuss with Eden the next day. Roosevelt said the international security organization envisaged in the declaration might play a role in problem areas before peace treaties could be signed. Eden and Churchill thought the whole thing rather "sketchy" but agreed to put it before the War Cabinet. It was at this point that Hull ended the conversation by asking to be excused.

On August 21 Eden and Hull had their longest and most productive discussions of the Quebec Conference. There were two meetings: a brief preliminary conversation after lunch and a longer and more formal meeting in the evening. Of the matters touched on in the preliminary session, the most important was what to do about the French National Committee.[3] The deadlock continued. Eden teased Hull with Lloyd George's definition of a statesman as "a politician with whom one happens to agree." Hull commented: "A statesman is a retired politician like myself." Eden insisted that the word *recognition* would have to be included in any British formula concerning the French Committee. Hull disagreed. It was decided to issue separate, simultaneous statements unless the Prime Minister and the President could come up with a satisfactory compromise.

The Foreign Secretary opened the evening meeting by handing Hull a British memorandum concerning the role of the Allied Military Government in liberated, as distinct

3. For minutes of this meeting, see U.S. *Foreign Relations, Washington and Quebec Papers, 1943*, pp. 918–20.

from enemy, territory.[4] In the latter, full authority was vested in the occupying powers. In liberated areas, however, the "locally constituted authorities" would be responsible for "maintaining law and order."[5] Eden said he only wanted to dissipate the fears of certain United Nations governments that the powers exercised by Great Britain and the United States in Sicily would not be carried over into friendly lands when these were freed from the grasp of the Axis. Far more likely, since he used the awkward phrase *constituted authorities*, the Foreign Secretary was attempting to help de Gaulle. If so, for the moment he succeeded. Blinded by the reference to Sicily and the United Nations, Hull agreed to recommend Roosevelt's approval. There was also general agreement "as to the necessity of setting up some definite machinery for discussing . . . these political and civilian aspects of future military operations on the continent."

Hull next circulated the American Four-Power Declaration the President had mentioned during Friday's dinner. The declaration had been prepared by Leo Pasvolsky, Special Assistant to the Secretary of State, under Hull's personal supervision.[6] On August 10, 1943, it had been approved by Roosevelt for presentation at Quebec. Its purpose was threefold: first, to secure the collaboration of the Soviet Union in planning a replacement for the League of Nations; second, to enhance the position of China; and, third, to reduce the fears of smaller nations who were disturbed by rumors of Roosevelt's views on world government by the great powers.

The title alone, which put China on an equal footing with the United States, Great Britain, and the Soviet Union, would secure the second purpose. Article Four recognized "the necessity of establishing at the earliest practicable date

4. For the minutes of this meeting, see *U.S. Foreign Relations, Washington and Quebec Papers, 1943*, pp. 922–8.
5. For the text, see *U.S. Foreign Relations, 1943*, I, 518.
6. For the text, see Notter, *Postwar Foreign Policy Preparation*, Appendix 27, p. 553.

a general international organization . . . for the maintenance of international peace and security." Article Four was
also intended to lessen the fears of smaller powers in that it
pledged the new league would be "based on the principle of
the sovereign equality of all nations, and open to membership by all . . . large or small." However, what was given
with one hand was taken away with the other. Some powers
were more sovereign than others. Article Seven pledged non-
intervention by the Big Four in the affairs of lesser states
"except for the purposes envisaged in this declaration. . . ."
The declaration also stated that the Big Four would "act
together in all matters . . . relating to the . . . occupation
of enemy territory and of territory of other states held by
[the] enemy." It called for the establishment of a "technical commission . . . on military matters." But it was silent
as to the details of the new international organization. Eden
said he liked the draft and suggested that it be sent to
Moscow for Soviet reaction. Both agreed to further discussion with Roosevelt and Churchill.

So far everything had been harmonious; the next two
items, however, produced less happy results. Eden wanted to
send a high-ranking delegation to Washington to discuss
monetary stabilization and commercial policy. Hull rejected
the idea out of hand. He did not want "to give the impression that the United States and Great Britain were coming
to previous agreement on these matters before other governments were brought in. . . ." Existing lower-level conversations with the U.S. Treasury would be continued. Eden said
everything was to be "handled in a way satisfactory to the
Secretary [of State]."

Hull then asked Eden what decision the British Government had taken on the American draft "Declaration by the
United Nations on National Independence." This paper was
based on that clause in the Atlantic Charter which called for
all people to have the right to choose their own form of
government. It had been written under Hull's personal guidance. It expressed the sweeping anticolonialism of the Secre-

tary of State and the President. Among its many provisions it asserted that definite dates should be fixed on which various colonial peoples would be granted independence.[7] Oddly enough, it was the British themselves who had provoked this indictment of empire. On December 9, 1942, the British War Cabinet decided to issue a paper on future colonial policy as a counter to "the President's large though somewhat vague ideas."[8] A draft was submitted to Hull by Lord Halifax, the British Ambassador to Washington, on February 4, 1943. It invested ultimate authority in the existing "parent" of the peoples involved. It was intended to be a unilateral document.

Hull suggested a multilateral document, and he and Leo Pasvolsky set to work. The result was a draft first given to Eden on March 27, 1943. The British, of course, disliked it, and an *aide-mémoire* to the effect was handed by Eden to Ambassador Winant in London on May 26, 1943. Eden's objections centered on two points: the reference to independence was ambiguous given the British Dominion system, and the call for the immediate setting of dates for independence he considered unrealistic. This was the third time Hull had mentioned the subject at Quebec. Earlier Eden had avoided discussion; now the two talked for over an hour. Eden explained the British Dominion system. Hull cited the example of the Philippines. Positions were "absolutely unchanged at the end of the discussion. . . ."[9]

The last topic brought up was the forcible partitioning of Germany, which Stalin had requested in December, 1941. Hull asked for the current British view. Eden "replied that while there were some in the British Government who felt that dismemberment . . . should be imposed . . . , he himself, and he felt that the Cabinet in general were not in favor . . . largely because of the impracticability of carrying

7. For the text of the declaration, see Notter, *Postwar Foreign Policy*, Appendix 12, pp. 470–2.
8. Woodward, *British Foreign Policy*, note 2, p. 440.
9. *U.S. Foreign Relations, Washington and Quebec Papers*, 1943, p. 927.

it out." This must have come as a welcome surprise to Hull—welcome because he never believed in the policy and a surprise because Eden during a spring visit to America had, on March 16, 1943, stated the reverse proposition. Eden then maintained that "the views of the British Government and his own views in particular, were tending towards the dismemberment of Germany."[1] Now, however, not only did Eden oppose forcible German dismemberment; he wanted Austria-Hungary restored.

The latter project was a favorite of Churchill's. During the Trident Conference, the Prime Minister had called for the creation of a new state based on Vienna, which would "fill the gap caused by the disappearance of the Austro-Hungarian Empire."[2] Eden had mentioned a Danubian Confederation to Hull and Sumner Welles in March but expressed little hope for its realization as the Soviet Union would be opposed to it. Now Eden wanted "to restore . . . the separate States of the old Austro-Hungarian Empire and form them as a Danubian group." Hull, although he approved the changed attitude on Germany, was noncommittal on a revived Austria-Hungary. Both agreed that German decentralization should be encouraged, and Hull noted that Fiume and Trieste might be linked to southern Germany. Each found the other's position "helpful."

While the diplomats met at the Citadel, the Combined Chiefs held their regular afternoon discussions at the Chateau Frontenac. With the important decisions already taken, in the opinion of Brooke and Marshall, these meetings dealing primarily with Pacific affairs had an atmosphere of anticlimax. It was not that either man underrated the Far Eastern War. It was just that both had their eyes fixed on Europe. Brooke looked to the Mediterranean; Marshall, to the Channel, but they agreed the next nine months would be decisive.

By Saturday afternoon the Combined Chiefs had reached

1. *U.S. Foreign Relations, 1943*, III, 18–19.
2. Churchill, *Second World War*, IV, 803.

agreement. In the Central Pacific operations were approved against the Gilbert, Marshall, and Caroline Islands.[3] In the South Pacific, MacArthur's plan to bypass the Japanese strong point in his theater, Rabaul, was also approved. As for Burma, operations would be carried out in "Upper Burma . . . to improve the air route and establish overland communications with China." This attack was assigned a target date of "mid-February 1944." However, it was recognized that this date was "dependent upon logistic considerations." China was to be kept in the war and her ground forces equipped, but primary emphasis was placed on the development of Chinese air facilities, and even here nothing specific was recommended. Culverin was formulated as "continuing preparations for an amphibious operation in Southeast Asia in the spring of 1944." Precisely where would be determined at a later date. As for the broad sweep of Pacific strategy, it was hoped to accomplish Japan's defeat within twelve months after the end of the war in Europe. Britain would advance from the west with India as her base; the United States, from the east and southeast with bases in Australia and Pearl Harbor. The Combined Chiefs emphasized air and sea attack. The Combined Chiefs also found time to bring up to date the plan for the emergency return to the Continent. The new code name was Rankin. Should Germany show signs of collapse, Rankin would be put into effect at once with whatever Bolero forces were available.

Saturday evening the Combined Chiefs of Staff, together with some three hundred of their assistants, embarked on an excursion ship provided by the Canadian Government. The night was passed sailing down the St. Lawrence and Saguenay Rivers. At dawn the ship turned around, arriving in Quebec late Sunday afternoon, August 22, 1943. It was a pleasant and relaxing experience for the military.[4] It provided a sort of "breather" before the holding of the second

3. For the decisions of the Combined Chiefs, see *U.S. Foreign Relations, Washington and Quebec Papers,* 1943, pp. 1121–32.
4. Leahy, *I Was There,* p. 177.

and concluding plenary session at Quadrant, which was scheduled for Monday.

Roosevelt, Churchill, Eden, and Hull, however, stayed behind at the Citadel. On both Sunday afternoon and Sunday evening, Eden and Hull met with the President and Prime Minister.[5] Many items were discussed, but two in particular took up most of the time—Greece and the French National Committee. On August 19 King George II of Greece, then in exile in Cairo, cabled Churchill and Roosevelt asking for advice. He had just received a delegation "of certain individuals from Greece who are supposed to represent various guerrilla bands."[6] They asked King George to stay in Cairo until a plebiscite could be held on the future of the Greek Monarchy. George wanted the opinions of his allies as to the answer he should give. The King himself felt "very strongly that I should return to Greece with my troops even if I left my country after a short period . . . should subsequent developments make it politic for me to do so." The King added that any action he took might create a "precedent" for other countries in the Balkans.

Roosevelt was aware, as the King himself admitted, that the royal cause had opponents in Greece. Before the war Greece had been a royalist dictatorship. George II had, however, fought the Germans. His Government-in-Exile was one of the sponsors of the United Nations Declaration, and the dictator, General John Metaxas, had died. Moreover, during his exile George II had strengthened his case in the eyes of Washington. On January 1, 1942, the King had delivered a radio address in which he repudiated the Metaxas years and promised upon his return to rule within the framework of the liberal constitution of 1911. This broadcast was followed by a Constitutional Act, issued February 4, 1942, canceling the decrees of August, 1936, which had provided the legal basis for the Metaxas dictatorship. And on July 4, 1943,

5. For minutes of these meetings, see *U.S. Foreign Relations, Washington and Quebec Papers, 1943*, pp. 930–4.
6. For the text of this message, see ibid., note 8, p. 915.

shortly before Quadrant, the King broadcast a further declaration pledging himself to free elections for a Constituent
Assembly no later than six months after the liberation of his
country. Since George was acting like a constitutional demo-
crat and the British alone had a military mission in Greece,
Roosevelt after a lengthy discussion accepted Churchill's
suggestion that the King be told to stand on his July declaration. The Prime Minister also said he would instruct his
agents to try to steer the Greek resistance movement into
nonpolitical channels.

Actually, neither George II nor Churchill was being entirely candid. The "certain individuals" represented a union
of all the various guerrilla bands in Greece. Also, they were
asking for more than a plebiscite. They wanted three cabinet
posts in the Government-in-Exile. Further, one of the two
largest resistance groups, the National Democratic Peoples
Army (EDES), led by Napoleon Zervas, was Republican,
while the other, the National Peoples Liberation Army
(ELAS), was Communist. The union of the two groups was
extremely fragile, and a civil war appeared imminent.
General Jan Christian Smuts, who was in Cairo, cabled
Churchill that "Bolshevization" of Greece was just around
the corner. He recommended full support for the King and
consultation with Roosevelt.[7] Churchill that Sunday evening at Quebec obtained support for the King, but he did
not reveal the seriousness of the Greek crisis.

On more familiar topics, where Hull and Eden had
agreed, the President and Prime Minister approved; where
Hull and Eden had disagreed, the disagreement was continued at the higher level. The Four-Power Declaration and
Eden's memorandum on Allied Military Government were
accepted and circulated to Moscow and Chungking. Debate,
hot and prolonged, continued over de Gaulle. Churchill at
one point declared: "All the liberal elements in the world,
including the Governments-in-Exile and the Soviet Govern-

7. Churchill, *Second World War*, V, 537.

ment, were . . . demanding full recognition."[8] Roosevelt
"had to think of the future of France herself." Eventually,
Roosevelt said he would try to prepare a draft acceptable to
all. If this failed, separate, simultaneous announcements
would have to be made setting forth the attitude of the
British and American Governments toward the French
Committee.

The next to the last day of the conference, August 23,
went smoothly. Roosevelt's draft on the French Committee
did not please Eden. Roosevelt wagered Eden a dinner at
the President's expense that before many months had passed
he and the Prime Minister would regret their obstinacy.
Surprisingly, when the separate announcements were made
on August 26, 1943, they differed very little. The British
version was warmer in tone and recognized the committee's
authority in the Levant, which the American version did
not. Both, however, stated it would be for the French people
to establish a government through free elections.

The final plenary session of Quadrant opened at 5:30 that
afternoon.[9] After lengthy discussion Roosevelt and Churchill approved all the recommendations of the Combined
Chiefs of Staff. The only change in the report of the Combined Chiefs to the President and Prime Minister was one
proposed by Churchill. He suggested that should circumstances render Overlord impossible, Operation Jupiter, the
invasion of Norway, might be considered as an alternative.
This operation was an old favorite of Churchill's. He had
mentioned it to Stalin as early as July, 1941. By the summer
of 1942, he was bombarding Brooke and Ismay with memorandums querulously asking why it could not be launched at
the same time as Torch. Brooke considered the invasion of
Norway Churchill's first love, as the invasion of Sumatra was
his second; both, in Brooke's opinion, were equally unsound.
But since the Prime Minister was only asking for planning,

8. Hull, *Memoirs*, II, 1239–40.
9. For minutes of this meeting, see *U.S. Foreign Relations, Washington
and Quebec Papers*, 1943, pp. 941–9.

the suggestion was approved. Churchill also continued to have reservations about Burma, which he expressed, but he agreed to the proposals of the Combined Chiefs. At the end of the plenary session, Roosevelt asked the Combined Chiefs to meet with Dr. Tse Vien Soong, the Chinese Minister for Foreign Affairs and Chiang's brother-in-law, on Tuesday, August 24. Soong had just arrived at Quebec, where it was hoped his presence would give an Asian character to the Quadrant Conference and so lessen newspaper comment on the absence of Stalin or any Russian delegation.[1]

The Combined Chiefs met for the last time at Quebec on Tuesday morning.[2] After approving the final report and having a lengthy discussion of Mediterranean operations and future convoy arrangements in the Atlantic, Dr. Soong was invited into the room. Brooke told him about Wingate's raiders; Leahy "pointed out that the success of operations in Burma . . . largely depended on the confident cooperation of the Chinese"; Marshall talked about the "immense undertaking" involved in getting seven thousand tons per month of supplies. So dreadful was the news regarded that Marshall then led Soong out of the room and, in the privacy of the corridor, imparted the news of Mountbatten's appointment. When Marshall, but not Soong, returned he received the "warm approval" of his colleagues. The Combined Chiefs also prepared a summary message to Stalin. The conference communiqué stated that "the military discussions of the Chiefs of Staff turned very largely upon the war against Japan and the bringing of effective aid to China. Mr. T. V. Soong, representing the Generalissimo Chiang Kai-shek, was a party to the discussions."[3] Roosevelt and the Joint Chiefs returned to Washington; Brooke, Eden, and most of the British Chiefs flew to London. Churchill went fishing.

1. Churchill, *Second World War*, V, 92.
2. For minutes of this meeting, see *U.S. Foreign Relations, Washington and Quebec Papers*, 1943, pp. 954–64.
3. For the text of the communiqué, see ibid., pp. 1157–8.

PART THREE

THE MOSCOW CONFERENCE

VIII

THE ROAD TO MOSCOW
August 25–October 18, 1943

Upon his return to Washington on Wednesday, August 25, Roosevelt, received Stalin's answer to his and the Prime Minister's messages of August 19 telling the Soviet Premier of the Castellano offer. In general Stalin's language when addressing the President was considerably more circumspect than that he used with Churchill, but this time Stalin was frank with Roosevelt to the point of rudeness. Stalin accused his allies of excluding him from the Italian negotiations. He held that Roosevelt and Churchill first reached agreement between themselves and then presented the Soviet Union with a *fait accompli*. This, he said, "cannot be tolerated any longer."[1] Roosevelt's immediate reaction was to have Hull return the

1. *Stalin's Correspondence*, II, No. 104, 84.

Premier's cable to the Soviet Embassy as undeliverable. On second thought, as he informed Churchill, he "gave directions [that] . . . the new Soviet Chargé [Andrei Gromyko] was to be told he was away in the country and would not be back for several days."[2] Since Roosevelt was obviously at the White House, Gromyko could not fail to realize that the President was angry.

On August 19 Roosevelt and Churchill had cabled Stalin accepting the idea of a low-level American, British, and Russian meeting and at the same time informing the Soviet Premier of the Castellano approach. Stalin was also given a copy of Roosevelt and Churchill's instructions to Eisenhower. This message was delivered to the Soviet Foreign Office by Clark Kerr on August 20. It was garbled in transmission, and the concluding sentence was missing. To Stalin, however, three points—all contained in the opening section—must have been clear: first, Italy was changing sides; second, Anglo-American armies were prepared to enter the peninsula within days, if not hours; and third, there was every indication that his cobelligerents intended to accept the Italian offer, and none that the Soviet Union would be given a voice in the negotiations. Exclusion from Italian affairs was annoying in itself. Given the general situation in the autumn of 1943, Stalin must have found it both irritating and dangerous, hence the sharpness of his cable to the President.

In the late summer of 1943, the great bulk of the German Army was tied down in Russia and could not disengage as it was struggling to contain Soviet assaults launched after the Kursk Salient Battle.[3] The speed and success of the Anglo-American campaign in Sicily seemed to show that the Germans lacked any strategic reserve. The Italian Army was

---

2. Churchill, *Second World War*, V, 93–4.

3. It was the opinion of Guderian that the failure at Kursk, much more than at Stalingrad, was the decisive defeat of German arms in World War II. See Heinz Guderian: *Panzer Leader*, translated by Constantine Fitzgibbon (New York: E. P. Dutton; 1957), chap. ix; Chester Wilmot: *The Struggle for Europe* (New York: Harper and Bros.; 1952), p. 145.

largely responsible for the garrisoning of Yugoslavia, Albania, Greece, and the islands of the Aegean. In all three countries, but particularly in Yugoslavia, there were large resistance movements. Axis control was shaky and limited to the larger cities.

Turkey was being armed by the British, and her intervention in the war was part of the Casablanca program. Rumania and Hungary were doubtful allies of the Germans and wanted to follow the Italian example. The British Government on April 20, 1943, informed Washington of Hungarian peace feelers in both Berne and Ankara. On August 13, 1943, the American Minister in Sweden, Herschel V. Johnson, received messages from Iulius Maniu, leader of the Rumanian Peasant Party, that the democratic opposition, the Army, and the Head of Government, Marshal Ion Antonescu, awaited only an Anglo-American presence in the Balkans before following in the footsteps of Badoglio and Italy.[4] This was confirmed when on August 26 Clark Kerr told Molotov that his government had received peace feelers in Istanbul from "an individual purporting to represent the Hungarian Army and Prime Minister."[5]

During his August, 1942, visit to Moscow, Churchill had stressed the advantages of attacking the Mediterranean underbelly. In 1942, however, the Mediterranean assault was a paper plan; now in the summer of 1943 it had been translated into successful operations conducted by large Anglo-American armies. A cable from the Prime Minister to Stalin in July said that the Americans and the British in the attack on Sicily used "half a million men . . . sixteen hundred large ships and twelve hundred special landing vessels."[6] Moreover, this was a blooded force, experienced in amphibious assault, whose size, Stalin could only assume, though wrongly, had increased during the intervening weeks.

An effective Italian switch and the end of Italian occupa-

4. *U.S. Foreign Relations, 1943,* I, 490–1, 493–5.
5. Ibid., I, 495–7.
6. *Stalin's Correspondence,* I, No. 168, 141.

tion of Greece and Yugoslavia could put these forces at the line of the Alps or the Danube within weeks. If to this were joined Turkish intervention and the defection from Germany of Rumania and Hungary, the European war might end in October. A rapid conclusion of hostilities would place the Soviet Union at a severe disadvantage. Russia, following its victory at Kursk, launched its first summer offensive of the Second World War. The Red Army in August, however, was still four hundred miles from the 1939 frontier and six hundred miles from its boundary of June, 1941. The fact that the 1941 boundary was still only a claim in the eyes of her allies must have increased Soviet anxieties. London was, as usual, sympathetic but maintained that its hands were bound by Washington. As for Washington, on the evening of August 10, 1943, the American Ambassador Standley, in a meeting with Clark Kerr, Molotov, and Stalin, made it clear that Roosevelt's position was unchanged. The meeting itself was made necessary by one of the most dangerous problems in the Alliance, the severance of relations by Moscow with the Polish Government-in-Exile in London.

The cause of this open split within the ranks of the United Nations was the announcement by the German Government during April, 1943, of the discovery of mass graves of Polish officers in that part of Poland which had been occupied by the Soviet Union in 1939.[7] With a virtuous show of horror, the Germans had alleged the Soviet Union was responsible and had called for an international investigation. The Polish Government-in-Exile in London had long been disturbed by the disparity between the number of enlisted men and the number of officers that it had found in the Soviet Union when the two nations became allies in the common struggle against Germany. Although Churchill bluntly warned against it and asked the Poles whether they could bring the dead back to life, General

7. For the text of the German announcement, see General Sikorski Historical Institute: *Documents on Polish-Soviet Relations, 1939–1945* (London: Heinemann; 1961), Vol. I, Doc. No. 305, pp. 523–4.

Wladyslaw Sikorski, Prime Minister of the Government-in-Exile, requested the International Red Cross to conduct an inquiry into the German charges on April 17, 1943. Because of the frontier question, relations between Poland and the Soviet Union had long been strained, and Churchill feared Stalin might use Sikorski's action to justify a complete break with the London Poles.

Churchill's anxieties were soon confirmed. In identical messages to the President and Prime Minister on April 21, Stalin said the Polish call for an investigation was "indubitable evidence of contact and collusion between Hitler . . . and the Sikorski Government." Stalin said he had decided, therefore, to "interrupt relations with that Government."[8] By April 21 the Germans had disinterred 14,500 corpses. Churchill did not doubt the Soviet Union was responsible for the massacre, and the British Government "in strictest confidence" informed Washington that "the Soviet Government had broken with the Poles . . . to cover up their guilt."[9] Nevertheless, Churchill wanted no split between Stalin and Sikorski. Churchill lectured Sikorski on the stupidity of seeming to align himself with Hitler. The Prime Minister also cabled Roosevelt asking for American support. Churchill answered Stalin with a plea that the Soviet Premier's decision to interrupt relations with Poland was "to be read in the sense of a final warning rather than of a break."[1]

Stalin himself may have intended his message of April 21 to serve as a sort of trial balloon to see how the Anglo-Americans would react. Certainly, as Churchill pointed out, the word *interrupt* was subject to a variety of interpretations, and when Molotov first talked to the Polish Ambassador in

8. For the text of these messages, see *Stalin's Correspondence*, I, No. 150, 120–1; II, No. 80, 60–1.

9. *U.S. Foreign Relations*, 1943, III, 396. Roosevelt also received a report from the War Department indicating the Russians were probably guilty.. Janusz K. Zawodny: *Death in the Forest: The Story of the Katyn Forest Massacre* (Notre Dame, Indiana: University of Notre Dame Press; 1962), pp. 178–9.

1. *Stalin's Correspondence*, I, No. 151, 121–2.

Moscow, he referred only to a "suspension of relations" between Poland and the Soviet Union.[2] Unfortunately, Roosevelt was away from Washington on an inspection trip when the crisis broke, and this delayed the American response. Moreover, upon his return to Washington, Roosevelt did not give Churchill the sort of firm support the Prime Minister had requested. Instead, Roosevelt cabled Stalin that he "fully understood [the Soviet Premier's] problem" and "hoped" Russia would not sever relations with Poland.[3] Whether firmer language would have had any effect on events in Moscow was debatable, but on April 25 Stalin broke with the London Poles.

After the severance of relations, the Government-in-Exile became increasingly disturbed about the fate of their compatriots in Russia. In August the American and British Governments agreed to make a joint *démarche*. It was this agreement that occasioned the August 10 meeting of Stalin, Molotov, Standley, and Clark Kerr in the Kremlin. Clark Kerr, in accordance with Foreign Office policy, referred only to the evacuation of "certain Poles."[4] Hull and Roosevelt, however, decided to use the *démarche* to reiterate their fundamental position on the Soviet frontiers and also to give some belated support to the London Poles. Against his own advice, Standley was instructed to tell Stalin the United States desired that "all racial Poles in the Union of Soviet Socialist Republics who were domiciled in Poland on September 1, 1939, were to be immediately recognized by the Soviet Government as Polish citizens."[5]

The meeting was friendly. Stalin said that he would take the matter under advisement; but the essential point— American intransigence on the Polish and territorial questions—could hardly have been more strongly made, nor

2. *U.S. Foreign Relations, 1943*, III, 395–8.
3. *Stalin's Correspondence*, II, No. 81, 61.
4. *U.S. Foreign Relations, 1943*, III, 451–2.
5. Ibid., III, 445.

could the Soviet Premier have had any illusions as to the real attitude of a British Government headed by Winston Churchill.

Exclusion from the Italian negotiations, a fluid and potentially adverse military position, the lack of any territorial understandings with his allies—all led Stalin to step up the pace of his diplomatic offensive. His message to Roosevelt of August 22 was blunt.[6] The Soviet Premier had begun by protesting the lack of consultation on Italian affairs. He complained of delay in receiving the full text of Roosevelt and Churchill's cable of August 19. He even voiced the suspicion that Washington and London had arranged the delay deliberately. After this introduction Stalin proposed the creation of a tripartite commission "for consideration of problems related to negotiations with various Governments falling away from Germany." The suggestion was couched in accusatory language: "To date it has been like this: the U.S.A. and Britain reach agreement between themselves while the U.S.S.R. is informed of the agreement between the two Powers as a third party looking passively on. I must say that this situation cannot be tolerated any longer."

The President deeply resented Stalin's allegations. He gave instructions as to what should be told to Gromyko, complained to Churchill, and did not reply.

On August 23 Stalin received the full text of the dispatch concerning Italy and the President and Prime Minister's second cable of the 19th calling for a Big Three meeting or, if this proved impossible, a gathering "of Foreign Office level representatives" to undertake "exploratory" talks. Stalin's answer, sent the following day, was considerably more conciliatory in tone. The Soviet Premier still considered the information on Italy insufficient and urged the formation of a tripartite military-political commission to deal with Italian affairs after her surrender. However, he also said, "The in-

6. *Stalin's Correspondence*, II, No. 104, 84.

structions given to General Eisenhower follow entirely from the thesis on Italy's unconditional surrender and hence cannot give rise to any objections."[7]

As Roosevelt and Churchill expected, an immediate Big Three meeting was rejected for the usual reason—the Soviet Premier had to direct his troops at the front—and with the usual complaint—Hitler's moving of fresh divisions to the east had created a critical situation. But if the Big Three meeting was impossible, this was not true of the meeting of representatives which Stalin now raised to the level of a Foreign Ministers Conference. The time was to be in the near future; the scope, not "restricted to . . . narrow . . . investigation [but] practical preparations so that after the conference our Governments might take specific decisions."[8] Stalin also asked that the agenda be fixed and proposals circulated beforehand.

On August 26 the Soviet Premier received Roosevelt and Churchill's message concerning the military decisions of Quadrant. He learned, probably with astonishment, that despite other obvious opportunities, Overlord remained the principal military objective of his allies. In the Mediterranean, aside from Italy, whose offer to surrender could not very well be ignored, Great Britain and the United States planned to do nothing more than seize Corsica and Sardinia. In the Balkans they would limit themselves to "minor commando raids."

The mood in Moscow now became almost friendly. In his first message Stalin had held that the Italian situation "could not be tolerated." August 23 found Clark Kerr "perturbed."[9] On August 27, however, Molotov sent a note to Kerr stating that the Italian terms were wholly acceptable. He empowered Eisenhower to sign the surrender on Russia's behalf. Even the presence of a Soviet representative was not required. The following day Standley cabled Washington

7. Ibid., II, No. 105, 85.
8. Ibid., II, No. 175, 149–50.
9. U.S. Foreign Relations, 1943, II, 354.

that reports of a decline in Soviet-American relations were "all wrong."[1] The second front remained a more or less virulent cause of friction, but Standley said he for the first time detected an intent on the part of the Soviet Government to engage in postwar discussions with the United States. He recommended that Stalin's proposals for a Foreign Ministers Conference and the establishment of a political-military commission, particularly the latter, "be accepted and motivated at once."

Although the Ambassador's advice arrived too late to affect events in Washington, Roosevelt agreed. The Italians were serious and Soviet participation in the surrender a necessity. Besides, except for the initial growl, Stalin now was being both cooperative and conciliatory; he was even promoting the political discussions which the President so greatly desired. On August 29 Stalin received a cable from Roosevelt and Churchill saying that they were "almost certain . . . plans can be made both for a meeting of representatives of the Foreign Ministers and for setting up a tripartite commission."[2] The following day Churchill asked Stalin if the Soviet Premier would support him in getting Roosevelt to permit participation of the French Committee in the political commission. Stalin, acting with unusual speed, replied on August 31: "If you consider it advisable, you may say so on behalf of our two governments."[3]

On September 2, 1943, with Italian surrender less than twenty-four hours away, Churchill and Roosevelt cabled for confirmation that Eisenhower could sign on Russia's behalf. Again, although the cable arrived too late to influence developments in Sicily, the site of the surrender negotiations, the Soviet Premier agreed. However, despite his cooperative attitude and Churchill's and Roosevelt's optimistic words, Stalin heard nothing more about the political-military commission and the Foreign Ministers' meeting for several days.

1. Ibid., III, 568.
2. *Stalin's Correspondence*, II, No. 107, 87.
3. Ibid., I, No. 179, 152.

Then he received conflicting replies, the reason being that Roosevelt and Churchill differed on what answer to give.

After his Canadian vacation, Churchill traveled to Washington, arriving on September 1 and staying the next eleven days. During this period there were two meetings of the Combined Chiefs of Staff, with Ismay and Dill filling in for the absent Brooke, Portal, and Pound. Dill wrote Brooke that the Prime Minister's conduct was exemplary, and everyone stuck to Quadrant.[4] On the military level, with one exception, this was true. The one exception was in the Aegean where Churchill, on September 9, ordered General Wilson, the British Commander in the Middle East, to seize the Italian-occupied islands. Wilson failed at Rhodes, where the Italians surrendered to a much smaller German force. He succeeded in taking the three little islands of Cos, Leros, and Samos. This action, involving only one brigade, was to have most serious consequences; but at the time, with two Allied Army Corps landing at Naples, it passed unnoticed.

However, if there was unanimity on military policy, Roosevelt and Churchill differed on the political-military commission and the Foreign Ministers' meeting. Roosevelt on September 4 cabled Stalin that he and the Prime Minister favored the Foreign Ministers' Conference but disagreed on its setting. Roosevelt wanted Casablanca or Tunis, where there would be greater freedom from the prying eyes of reporters; the Prime Minister wanted the meeting held in London.

London aside, the President thought September 25 a good opening date. He told Stalin he would have liked to send Hull but, because of the Secretary's age, Sumner Welles and Harriman would represent the United States. As for the political-military commission on Italian affairs, Roosevelt regarded it as unnecessary, asking Stalin, "Why

4. Arthur Bryant: A *History of the War Years Based on the Diaries of Field Marshal Lord Alanbrooke, Chief of the Imperial General Staff*, Vol. II: *Triumph in the West* (New York: Doubleday; 1959), pp. 24–5. Cited hereafter as *Triumph in the West*.

not send an [Soviet] officer to General Eisenhower's headquarters in connection with further settlements with the
Italians?"[5] The President was also hesitant about bringing in
de Gaulle as "the Italians dislike the French greatly."
Finally, Roosevelt again requested a Big Three meeting. He
proposed Africa as the place; the time, late November. He
informed Stalin of the constitutional limitation, the pocket
veto, which prevented his absence from Washington for a
period longer than twenty days.

Churchill sent Stalin two messages, both dated September
5. The first concerned the Italian military-political commission "from which he hoped the President would not dis-
sent."[6] The commission, in Churchill's view, should be
established either in Tunis or in Algiers. Its role would be
strictly advisory both in relationship to the parent governments and to the military functions of the Allied Commander in Chief. Churchill favored French participation
from the start. He also thought it might be necessary to
consult with others, notably the Greeks and the Yugoslavs.
On the Conference of Foreign Ministers, Churchill in his
second message suggested London as the site and early
October as the date. He was silent on a Big Three meeting
but offered to go alone to Moscow. The Prime Minister
further noted, although in diplomatic language, that if
Stalin desired to quarrel about the second front, it might be
better to send a separate and wholly military mission to
London or Washington.

Having received separate answers, Stalin on September 8
dispatched separate replies. They were identical in substance
although, interestingly, the one to Churchill was harsher in
tone. Stalin requested that the Foreign Ministers meet in
Moscow sometime in early October and that an agenda be
circulated immediately. Concerning the Italian commission,
French participation was a matter of indifference to him, but
the Soviet Premier wanted it "to direct on-the-spot negotia-

5. *Stalin's Correspondence*, II, No. 109, 89.
6. Ibid., I, No. 181, 153.

tions with Italy and with the Governments of other countries falling away from Germany."[7] He opposed making its
role simply advisory. He also expressed irritation that the
committee was not already in existence. On the question of
a Big Three meeting, Stalin, for the first time in the war,
suggested a place and a date. The date was Roosevelt's, late
November; the place was Stalin's own, Tehran, the capital
of Iran.

Roosevelt and Churchill, although still separately, responded on September 10. Roosevelt "cheerfully" agreed
with and the Prime Minister "deferred to" Stalin's request
that the Foreign Ministers meet in Moscow. Both accepted
the political-military commission, but despite Stalin's wishes
each was careful to so limit the commission's authority as to
deprive it of any real power. The President proposed that the
commission meet in late September at Algiers. Churchill
nominated as his representative Harold Macmillan, who,
together with Robert Murphy, served as a political adviser to
Eisenhower. Evidently the Prime Minister had been exercis-
ing his powers of persuasion as the President now accepted
French participation. Roosevelt and Churchill said they
were pleased that Stalin had agreed to a Big Three meeting
at the end of November, but each asked for a different
setting from Tehran: Roosevelt mentioned Egypt; Churchill
called for Cyprus or the Sudan; neither, however, ruled out
the Iranian capital.

Stalin on September 12, the day Churchill left Washington, sent cables to Roosevelt and Churchill naming Andrei
Vyshinsky, then Deputy People's Commissar for Foreign
Affairs, together with Alexander Bogomolov, the Soviet Ambassador to the Governments-in-Exile in London, as his
representatives on the Algiers Commission. He accepted the
September date for its first meeting. He did not challenge
Roosevelt and Churchill's limitations upon the commission's authority but intimated that this might be modified

7. Ibid., II, No. 111, 90.

by experience. Stalin wanted the Foreign Ministers to meet on October 4. He repeated his call for an agenda. As for the Big Three gathering, Stalin said he preferred Tehran and rejected Egypt, "where the Soviet Union was not yet represented."

Although the question of setting remained unresolved, it appeared that Roosevelt, Churchill, and Stalin would soon meet and that arrangements for the Foreign Ministers Conference were complete. Then, on September 27, Roosevelt asked that the Foreign Ministers Conference be held in London rather than Moscow. His reason was that he wanted to send his Secretary of State rather than Sumner Welles, and Hull would find the long flight to Moscow extremely difficult for physical reasons.

When Hull learned that Roosevelt was thinking of sending Welles to Moscow, the Secretary was outraged. In the fall of 1943, Hull believed that Welles was conducting a campaign of vilification against him and the State Department. One of the charges Hull attributed to Welles was that the State Department desired that Russia be bled white. This so upset the Secretary that he called on Gromyko in Washington to issue a personal denial and instructed Standley to do the same thing in Moscow with Molotov. An angry Hull called upon the President in late September and "strenuously opposed Welles' going to Moscow."[8] He told Roosevelt that Welles had once said there was nothing to be gained by such a trip and offered, "wherever the conference might be held," to go there himself. According to Hull, Roosevelt expressed his gratification and soon after cabled Stalin requesting the change to London.

The Soviet Premier replied immediately. He was happy that Hull could attend; however, he could not agree to a shift to London. He offered two reasons: first, the press announcements had already been made and a change might cause unfavorable comment; and second, Vyshinsky was

8. Hull, *Memoirs*, II, 1255.

shortly leaving for Algiers, and if Molotov also absented himself, Stalin implied that there would be no one to direct the People's Commissariat for Foreign Affairs.

On October 5 Roosevelt told Stalin that his seventy-two-year-old Secretary of State, who, though Stalin didn't know it, had never before flown and who suffered acutely from claustrophobia, would be at the Kremlin within ten days. If, as seems likely, the Soviet Premier had been seeking a success of prestige, he achieved it. In this same cable, Roosevelt announced that Hull would be accompanied by General John Deane, Secretary to the Joint Chiefs of Staff. The General was to discuss fully and completely the first item on the Soviet agenda: "Measures to shorten the war against Germany."[9]

Stalin, throughout the correspondence, had stressed the importance of an agreement on the range of subjects to be discussed by the Foreign Ministers. The first government to circulate a tentative agenda—on September 18—was Great Britain.[1] As might be expected, it was almost entirely political. Its thirteen points covered nearly all the substantive issues dividing Russia and the West. The sole exception, although it, too, was present in a thinly veiled form, was Russia's western frontier. Eden wanted to talk about the Balkans and, in particular, the possibility of Balkan and Danubian Confederations. He asked the powers to express their attitudes toward Poland, Greece, Iran, Yugoslavia, and Turkey. The German and Italian peace settlements, together with the future of France, were to be explored. He was even honest enough in the third item of his agenda to raise the question of whether the Big Three desired joint responsibility or separate spheres of influence in Europe. In

9. Major General John R. Deane was appointed Chief of the United States Military Mission to the Soviet Union. He served in Moscow from October 18, 1943, to October 31, 1945. See John R. Deane: *The Strange Alliance: The Story of Our Efforts at Wartime Co-operation with Russia* (New York: Viking Press; 1957). Cited hereafter as *Strange Alliance*.

1. For the full text, see *U.S. Foreign Relations, 1943*, I, 525–8.

short, Eden, as he had said at Quebec, proposed to empty the closets with a vengeance.

The State Department on the same day, September 18, circulated Hull's version of what was proper subject matter. Where Eden wished to open the doors, Hull with equal vigor was determined to keep them shut. The American agenda contained just four items: first, the Four-Power Declaration; second, the postwar treatment of Germany; third, economic reconstruction, including such disputatious items as the rehabilitation of Russia and the future of the International Labor Organization; and fourth, methods of dealing with current economic and political problems which Washington suggested might best be handled by ambassadors on an *ad hoc* basis.[2]

On September 29 Moscow circulated its own version of an agenda.[3] It contained three points, of which the second and third were really only qualifications. In its second item the Soviet Union objected to the Four-Power Declaration on the grounds that China was not a participant in the Moscow Conference. The third item probably reflected Stalin's perusal of Eden's agenda; at least the Russians now emphasized the preparatory character of the conference. However, the first and only real item on the Soviet agenda jolted Washington and London: Stalin wanted to discuss the possibility of launching Overlord in 1943. In the language of the People's Commissariat of Foreign Affairs, this read:

It [the Soviet Union] has in view such urgent measures on the part of the Governments of Great Britain and the United States in 1943 as will insure the invasion of Western Europe by the Anglo-American armies across the English Channel and which, together with the powerful blows of the Soviet armies against the forces of the German Army on the Soviet-German front, should basically undermine the military strategic position

2. Ibid., I, 521–2.
3. Ibid., I, 534–5.

of Germany and lead to a decisive shortening of the length of the war.

This demand radically changed the character of the Moscow meeting, but Roosevelt and Churchill chose not to argue, so necessary did they consider it. Instead, Ismay and a suitable military staff were added to Eden's delegation. Deane and other officers were added to Hull's; in fact, of the three planes that left Washington at noon on October 7 for Moscow, two were occupied by the military and only one by State Department personnel. Roosevelt and Churchill had decided that Stalin would receive a full briefing on Overlord.

However, if the dispatch of Deane and Ismay satisfied Russian ideas about the agenda, it still left unresolved the widely divergent views of London and Washington. Roosevelt and Hull were determined to leave them unresolved. On October 3 Sir Ronald Campbell, the British Minister in Washington, delivered the following note from Eden to Hull: "So glad we are to do this work together. Delighted to meet you for preliminary talks either in London or Cairo whichever suits you. Please let me know your dates and mode of travel."[4]

The following day Hull replied: "Deeply appreciate your message and while nothing would give me greater pleasure . . . than to spend the day in consultation with you . . . am apprehensive lest such a meeting be misconstrued to the subsequent disadvantage of both our Governments alike."[5]

A similar attitude prevailed during the President's briefing session for Hull on October 5.[6] The President discoursed on his three pet projects, none of which Hull approved: the dismemberment of Germany; the separation of Croatia and Serbia; the creation of a Rhineland "buffer state" by linking Belgium with Luxemburg, Alsace, and Lorraine. These questions, however, were not to be discussed with the Russians.

4. U.S. Foreign Relations, 1943, I, 538.
5. Ibid., I, 539.
6. Hull, Memoirs, II, 1265–6; Leahy, I Was There, p. 187; U.S. Foreign Relations, 1943, I, 541–3.

Instead, Roosevelt wanted the Moscow Conference to approve the Four-Power Declaration and also at least to open up the question of trusteeship. Hull was told that the Four-Power Declaration must include the Chinese as a sponsoring power. Roosevelt believed that any Mediterranean Commission should be limited to an advisory role. The French were to be kept out of Italian affairs. Concerning the real questions—Poland, the Baltic States, boundaries, and the rest—Roosevelt, while mentioning the Curzon Line as Poland's eastern frontier and possible second plebiscites in the Baltic States, kept to the Quebec policy. He himself would appeal to Stalin on these subjects on high moral grounds at the forthcoming Big Three meeting. Hull was to be silent in Moscow.

The real purpose of Hull's trip was to win the Russians to Roosevelt's grand design, a postwar world dominated by America, Britain, and Russia. Murphy, who met Hull at Casablanca and flew with him to Algiers during that leg of the Secretary's trip, was "astounded at how emotional Hull was" and noted his "almost mystical approach" to the conference.[7] Eden was feeling far from mystical. He regarded the American attitude as the height of folly. He wanted concrete agreements. Washington's Wilsonianism and the advance of the Red Army were eroding what bargaining power he possessed. Even the Polish Government-in-Exile was being unhelpful. It demanded recognition of the Soviet-Polish boundary of 1939 while the most Moscow was willing to concede was the Curzon Line, the ethnographically just frontier sponsored by Lord Curzon at the Versailles Conference.

7. Murphy, *Diplomat Among Warriors*, p. 208.

IX

OVERLORD, TURKEY AND THE FOUR-POWER DECLARATION
October 18–23, 1943

Hull, Eden, and their respective parties arrived at Moscow late on the afternoon of Monday, October 18. The Foreign Ministers held what should have been a brief meeting at the Kremlin that night; it was prolonged, as were all tripartite meetings, by the delays of translation. Eden felt that the atmosphere was pleasant. It was agreed that a short press announcement would be released listing the members of the delegations and that formal meetings would be confidential, without speeches, and limited to as few people as possible. The first working session was scheduled for four o'clock the following day at the Spiridonovka Palace.

On October 19 Eden and Molotov paid separate calls on Hull at Spaso House, the American Embassy. Eden arrived first. Both he and Hull were irritated at the vigor of Soviet censorship. Aside from the official communiqué on their arrival, nothing had been passed; even an innocuous report that Hull looked to be in good health was refused. Although neither man wanted any comments on political matters released, both believed human interest items should be made available to the press. They decided to discuss the problem with Molotov. Hull also suggested that Molotov be asked to encourage informal contacts between the Russians and members of the American and British delegations; Eden agreed. There was a brief discussion on the political-military commission. Eden wanted it split into two parts: one would remain in Algiers to deal with Mediterranean affairs; the other, which could handle more general topics, would meet in London; neither would have any real power. Eden also said that, thanks to Churchill, he expected to have difficulties with the Russians over the northern convoys. Both hoped to avoid any military discussions other than a straightforward presentation of the Quadrant decisions.

Molotov came at 2:30 P.M. Like the earlier meeting with Eden, conversation was brief though not quite so informal. Hull spoke on the necessity for unity between the powers; Molotov agreed. Hull called for contact between subordinates; Molotov agreed. When Hull raised the question of censorship, Molotov said that anything the British or American delegations wanted to release would be passed and that the obstructionism of the previous night resulted from stupidity and would not recur. Both Hull and Molotov pledged themselves to a policy of cooperation.

At the beginning of the first plenary meeting that same day, Hull and Eden insisted that Molotov serve as the conference's permanent chairman.[1] Molotov proposed daily sessions from four to seven o'clock; this was accepted. Molotov then inquired as to the powers of his colleagues: Could the conference make binding decisions? Hull replied that he would have to refer everything to Washington. Eden

1. For minutes of this meeting, see *U.S. Foreign Relations, 1943,* I, pp. 577–82.

thought that it depended on the character of the decisions. Molotov attempted to establish categories: some questions to be settled, some to be formulated and presented for approval, and some to be merely an "informational . . . exchange of views"; Eden approved. Hull, however, insisted that the sessions were preparatory to the meeting of the heads of their respective governments. Molotov did not press the point, but it was clear that Hull's hands were tied.

The Soviet Foreign Minister then circulated a sort of combined agenda. It included every point but one in the American, British, and Russian drafts—that being the Four-Power Declaration. Molotov's first item concerned measures to shorten the war against Germany. Molotov suggested a twenty-minute intermission. At the end of this period, without waiting to be asked, Molotov said he was willing to consider the Four-Power Declaration. Hull received the news with thanks and requested that it be made the second item on the agenda. Eden asked that the items immediately following be the political-military commission, an exchange of views on Italy and the Balkans, and methods of dealing with current economic issues. The remaining questions could follow the Soviet sequence.[2] Molotov agreed. Planned or not, the momentary exclusion of the Four-Power Declaration resulted in the military talks coming first.

The Soviet Foreign Minister then circulated a brief paper listing three measures to shorten the war. The first was the cross-channel attack. The next items, however, caused a furor in London and Washington: the Soviet Union proposed that Turkey be brought into the war immediately and that Sweden be compelled to grant air bases to the Allies. Molotov suggested that Eden and Hull might like to discuss the proposals privately and added, not unnaturally, considering past history, that he would like written answers. Eden and Hull said they would have to consult their governments. Eden also stated that presentation of the Quadrant decisions

---

2. For the agreed agenda, see ibid., I, 703–4.

was not quite ready. He asked that the meeting be adjourned to the following day and, since the subjects to be discussed were of a most secret nature, that only heads of delegations and their military advisers be present; Molotov agreed.

The plenary session of October 20 was preceded by a formal banquet whose atmosphere, according to Harriman, was most cordial. This cordiality carried over into the meeting.[3] Molotov spent a full half hour trying to persuade Hull to direct the session on the grounds that since a Soviet proposal was being discussed, it would be unfair for a Russian to act as chairman; Hull refused.

Nor was it only the psychological atmosphere that was warm. Eden found the room stifling and feared he would faint. The weather outside was, according to Harriman, "perfect [for] November football." Hull, however, liked to work in temperatures above ninety degrees. During the previous day's meeting, he had put on his overcoat. His hosts, taking this as a slight upon their arrangements, had now turned the room into a veritable steam bath. "Happily," according to Eden, "the Three Powers were able to agree on a compromise temperature."[4]

Molotov called for discussion of military measures to shorten the war. Hull and Eden referred the question to Generals Deane and Ismay. As General Ismay was both a member of the Combined Chiefs of Staff and Churchill's personal Chief of Staff and so outranked his American colleague General Deane, it was the Britisher who spoke first. Using a prepared text which was circulated, Ismay outlined the European strategy approved at Quebec. He started with the Combined Bomber Offensive, proceeded to General Morgan's Overlord Plan, giving some but not undue emphasis to its limiting conditions, and ended up in the Mediterranean. Concerning the last-named theater, he told Molotov that operations would be limited to a small campaign in

3. Ibid., I, 583–8, 774–81; Eden, *Memoirs*, II, 477; Hull, *Memoirs*, II, 1280.
4. Eden, *Memoirs*, II, 477.

Italy, the taking of Corsica and Sardinia, and a few commando raids. Ismay mentioned the impending reduction of forces.

Deane spoke next, also from a prepared text, which was just as well since, by his own account, he was feeling the effects of the many toasts drunk at lunch.[5] He too started with the Combined Bomber Offensive and proceeded to Overlord. Characteristically, Deane mentioned the Mediterranean not at all and used considerably more facts and figures than Ismay. He ended by saying that the Americans had increased their manufacture of landing craft by 35 percent with a consequent dislocation in overall war production —all of which proved their devotion to Overlord. Deane also circulated memorandums requesting Soviet assistance in setting up "shuttle bombing" of Germany by Anglo-American aircraft based in England, which after striking from the west would refuel and rearm in Russia and then hit the Germans from the east while flying back to their home bases. Deane further wanted an exchange of weather information and improved air transport facilities. More to the point, both Deane and Ismay asked for a Russian offensive coincident with Overlord. The Russians again learned that the Mediterranean was off and cross-channel on. What they had not been told were the location of the landings, the size of the assault force, and the date. Molotov and Voroshilov, after asking some questions about the withdrawal of divisions from the Mediterranean, thanked Ismay and Deane for their presentations.

The Soviet Foreign Minister then turned to his proposals on Turkey and Sweden. Neither Hull nor Eden had received any instructions, nor had they expected the questions to be raised. Their reactions, however, were significant, both as to personal temperament and the positions they enjoyed within their governments. Hull was silent; he would have to wait for word from Washington. Eden was articulate. In the case

5. Deane, *Strange Alliance*, pp. 13–15.

of Turkey, Eden voiced opinions which, he said, reflected current thinking in the British Government; in the case of Sweden, presumably after consulting Kerr and Strang, Eden improvised a position which put Molotov on the defensive.[6] About Turkey, Eden maintained that the previous commitments made to Ankara, if she intervened, could no longer be met. However, if his "Soviet friends" wanted to discuss the matter, Eden would be happy to consider it. After being pressed, Hull "thought the United States Government shared the same opinion." Concerning Sweden, Eden believed Stockholm would be "influenced by the Soviet attitude to Finland."[7] He presumed that the Soviet Government wanted an independent Finland. An irritated Molotov said that the Foreign Ministers were talking about Sweden; he asked for Hull's views. The American Secretary said that he would have to wait overnight (it turned out to be six days) to hear from Washington. Hull could not refrain from remarking that he had views of his own; he just chose not to express them. Molotov closed the meeting by requesting and receiving formal Anglo-American pledges to Overlord.

If Hull kept in the background at Tuesday's and Wednesday's plenary sessions, this was not the case on Thursday, October 21. But then the subject under discussion was American proposals on the Four-Power Declaration. Copies of the declaration had been circulated together with the American draft agenda. It had been tentatively approved by the British at Quebec. On September 28, however, the Foreign Office delivered an *aide-mémoire* to both Washington and Moscow, suggesting minor changes of wording to dampen the feeling of the smaller powers that they might be subject to Big Four dictatorship. The British also raised questions concerning the self-denying eighth article. In its original form this article read: "That they [the Four Powers] will not employ their military forces within the

6. This war Sir William Strang, Assistant Under Secretary for Foreign Affairs.
7. Eden, *Memoirs*, II, 477.

territories of other states except for the purposes envisaged
in this declaration and after joint consultation and agreement." Did this mean, asked London, that Britain and
America could not fight in France, or Russia in Poland,
except after agreement among all the powers? Washington
had just received the British *mémoire* when, on September
29, the Soviet Union raised doubts about the whole project
by criticizing the inclusion of China. Rather than engage in a
trans-Atlantic debate, Hull waited for the Moscow Conference to try to resolve the differences.

Hull on Thursday circulated a redraft of the declaration
and a short paper explaining the changes.[8] Only two of the
changes were substantive. The first article in its original
form, besides calling for the creation of a new international
organization, had pledged the powers to united action in
"the prosecution of the war." In view of Soviet-Japanese
relations, this article was modified by the insertion of the
words *against their respective enemies.* The second change
involved the "self-denying ordinance." In an arcane response
to British criticism, the new version read: "That following
the defeat of the enemy they [the Four Powers] will not
employ their military forces within the territories of other
states except for the purposes envisaged in this declaration
and after joint consultation and agreement."[9] Inclusion of
the phrase *following the defeat of the enemy* insured freedom of action as long as the war continued. Washington did
nothing to mitigate the "Four Policemen" tone of the declaration.

After explaining the changes, Hull delivered a long and
deeply felt exposition of the principles of international collaboration embodied in the declaration. He was supported,
although more briefly, by Eden. Molotov then tried to
change the declaration into a Three-Power document. He
did not directly challenge American enthusiasm for China

8. For the minutes of the meeting, see *U.S. Foreign Relations, 1943,* I,
590–9.
9. Ibid., I, 601.

but merely asked, and kept on asking, how a Three-Power Conference could pass a Four-Power Declaration. His purpose, however, was clear. Hull had received explicit instructions on just this point; Roosevelt had told him to bring home a Four-Power Declaration or none at all. Moreover, Washington cabled the American Secretary on October 19 that Chiang approved the draft and could be expected to approve any minor changes, thus making Hull something of a Chinese plenipotentiary. Though both assiduously avoided the real issue, neither Hull nor Molotov would give way and, after considerable wrangling, the meeting broke for tea. During the intermission, Hull made a personal appeal to Molotov. When the meeting resumed, it was apparent Hull had failed. The most Molotov would concede was to leave the question of Chinese participation open.

The Foreign Ministers then turned to the text itself, and before the session ended, Molotov, with surprisingly little opposition, was able to alter the document in two significant respects. The second article read: "That those of them [the Four Powers] at war with a common enemy will act together in all matters relating to the surrender and disarmament of that enemy, and to any occupation of enemy territory and of territory of other states held by that enemy."[1] Molotov succeeded in striking out the whole clause on occupation. Common action was restricted to surrender and disarmament. His second success concerned the self-denying provision. The Soviet Foreign Minister asked for elimination of the phrase *and after joint consideration and agreement.* The new wording would give each of the signatories the right to intervene in the affairs of its neighbors if in its opinion, and its opinion alone, such intervention was necessary to fulfill what, again, would be its own interpretation of the purposes of the declaration. Molotov got what he wanted; the words *and agreement* were deleted. The great powers would only consult. Molotov adjourned the meeting.

1. Ibid., I, 600.

On Tuesday, October 19, Eden had requested an interview with Stalin concerning the Arctic convoys. This was arranged for Thursday night. Between January, 1942, and the fall of 1943, roughly half of the supplies shipped to Russia were carried in Russian vessels across the Pacific. The remaining half were split almost equally between Iran and the northern convoys.[2] In terms of proximity to the front and transportation facilities the Murmansk-Archangel route possessed great advantages over the other two, and naturally the Soviet Union pressed for its increased use. Its advantages were equally well recognized by the Germans, who in mid-1942 concentrated almost all their surface ships, including the battleship *Tirpitz*, in Norwegian waters, as well as U-boats and torpedo-carrying aircraft. The planes operated in the extreme north along the approaches to the Barents Sea, where the ice pack even in summer forced convoys to pass within easy range. The *Tirpitz* was particularly dreaded as she was more than a match for any single commissioned American or British battleship.

Until July, 1942, the convoys suffered surprisingly little loss; then occurred the disaster of P.Q. 17. Convoy P.Q. 17, consisting of thirty-six merchant ships, sailed from Iceland on June 27. In the midst of grave anxieties in both the Atlantic and Pacific, Washington and London allocated two new battleships, an aircraft carrier, six cruisers, twenty-three destroyers, and eight smaller vessels to its defense. The escort was, however, divided. Corvettes and a few destroyers were with the merchant ships for antiaircraft and antisubmarine protection. The battleships and carrier sailed behind the convoy and then only to the vicinity of Spitzbergen Island.[3] On July 3 P.Q. 17 entered the Barents Sea. That same day British air reconnaissance failed to locate the

---

2. Morison, *U.S. Naval Operations in World War II*, I, 158–9.
3. For the disposition of defending naval forces, see Roskill, *The War at Sea*, II, 136–7. The American Navy built larger battleships than the *Tirpitz* during World War II, but none had been completed in 1942.

Tirpitz or the other German ships; presumably they had sailed to attack the convoy. The following day Admiral Pound ordered P.Q. 17 to scatter and proceed independently to Russia. Three hundred miles separated the merchantmen from the Allied battleships, and the gap could not be closed in time. Pound believed flight and dispersion offered the best hope for safety.[4] It was a mistake. The *Tirpitz* and her consorts had moved from their bases but because of hesitations by Hitler did not sail against P.Q. 17 until July 5. Upon learning the convoy had scattered, they returned to Norway; P.Q. 17 could be dealt with more economically by U-boats and aircraft. Of the thirty-six merchant ships, only eleven reached Archangel.

The effect of this tactical defeat was compounded by Anglo-American strategic decisions. July also saw Washington and London's agreement to invade French North Africa. Torch strained Allied shipping resources to the limit; losses like those of P.Q. 17 could not be tolerated. The British decided to cancel Arctic convoys until winter when the long nights would afford maximum protection; it was their decision to make since they were responsible for convoy protection. Between December, 1942, and February, 1943, three convoys traversed the Murmansk route, but none was large; and after February the combination of the invasion of Sicily and lengthening days caused a second cancellation. The ending of the convoys in 1942 brought bitter reproaches from Moscow.[5] Stalin termed the news of the second cancellation "catastrophic."[6] The convoys joined the second front as a major source of acrimony within the Alliance.

On September 20, 1943, the Soviet Government submitted an *aide-mémoire* to Clark Kerr insisting on the reopening of the northern route. Churchill dispatched a personal reply to Stalin saying that four convoys were

4. Ibid., II, 139.
5. *Stalin's Correspondence*, I, No. 57, 56.
6. Ibid., I, No. 138, 112.

planned for the coming winter but that this was "neither a
contract or a bargain."[7] The Prime Minister also requested
an improvement in conditions for British and American
seamen in Murmansk. Stalin's answer was abusive. Convoys
were an "obligation"; British seamen were described as idlers
and spies; Churchill's words "threatened" the Alliance.[8]
Upon receiving this message, Churchill became enraged.
Convoy losses amounted to a nearly prohibitive 25 percent.
He told the new Soviet Ambassador, Feodor Gusev, that
Stalin's note was *"nul et non avenu"*;[9] thus when the
Moscow Conference opened, two of the Big Three were not
speaking to each other.

Now it was up to Eden to patch up the quarrel. Thursday's meeting was, according to the Foreign Minister,
"sticky," with Stalin at one point exclaiming: "I understand
that Mr. Churchill does not want to correspond further with
me; well, let it be so."[1] The convoys, however, were vital to
the Russians; and Eden was a persuasive speaker. Stalin
accepted the British explanation of the postponements, and
there was no more talk of idlers and spies. He even agreed to
the improvement of conditions at Murmansk, although he
claimed that the cause of the difficulties was the tendency of
British sailors to look down on Russians. Molotov was instructed to handle the details. Clark Kerr, who had accompanied Eden to the Kremlin, "was very pleased with the
talk."[2]

So far, the Moscow Conference had been relatively
amicable; the mood changed at Friday's plenary session.
Molotov wanted a voice in Italian affairs; Eden and Hull had
been instructed to keep the Russians out. Neither London
nor Washington seemed aware of the dangers in such a
precedent. At the start of the meeting, the Foreign Ministers
set up a Drafting Committee consisting of Dunn, Strang,

7. Ibid., I, No. 199, 166–9.
8. Ibid., I, No. 203, 171–3.
9. Eden, *Memoirs*, II, 475–6.
1. Ibid., II, 478.
2. Ibid., II, 479.

and Vyshinsky.[3] They then turned to the third item on the agenda: the political-military commission. Curiously, though it was a Soviet proposal, Great Britain had put the question on the agenda. Molotov, following the procedure whereby the sponsoring government speaks first, called upon Eden.

The Foreign Secretary circulated two papers. The first called for the creation of a European Advisory Commission to be located in London.[4] The second was a redraft of a British memorandum dated October 12, proposing an Italian Advisory Council. Eden, like Hull the previous day, read a lengthy defense of both papers. This defense was necessary as neither met the wishes of the Soviet Union. In his message of August 22, Stalin asked for a political and military commission possessed of broad powers. Churchill and Roosevelt in their replies wanted only an advisory body restricted to political affairs, and an effort by Molotov in late September to assert the power of the Mediterranean Commission over Eisenhower merely hardened their resolve. Consequently, Eden's drafts were designed to block the Russians. The London Commission would discuss and advise their parent governments on "a wide range of European problems arising out of the prosecution of the war"; the Italian Commission "would advise the Commander-in-Chief as Chairman of the Control Commission on all matters pertaining to the putting into effect of the armistice terms." Neither commission would have any real authority.

Although the agreements were obviously meant to limit Soviet influence, Molotov did not challenge them directly. Instead, he asked Eden how they related to a British *aide-mémoire* of July 1, 1943, calling for the establishment of a "steering Committee for Europe."[5] The committee as conceived in the memorandum was to include the United

3. For the minutes of the meeting, see *U.S. Foreign Relations, 1943*, I, 604–13.
4. For the text, see ibid., I, 710–11.
5. For the *aide-mémoire* entitled "Suggested Principles Which Would Govern the Conclusion of Hostilities with the European Members of the Axis," see ibid., I, 708–10.

States, Great Britain, the Soviet Union, and France. It
would direct the affairs of the Continent "under the rule of
unanimity." The earlier paper also contained the suggestion
that the administration of any armistice be conducted by a
Big-Three Commission with rotating chairmanship. Molotov wanted to know the relationship of Eden's proposals to
the *aide-mémoire*.

Although the *aide-mémoire* and the present drafts were
contradictory, Eden replied that the one grew out of the
other and that the principles of July were still valid. Molotov
said he liked the earlier ideas. Molotov asked Hull for an
opinion; Hull refused to be drawn. Molotov then questioned
Hull on the relationship between Eden's papers and the
American State Department's proposal that questions of
interest among the Big Three be resolved on an *ad hoc*
basis. Hull said that they complemented each other and
proceeded to read the American draft aloud. It held "that
matters on which it is found desirable for the Three Governments to consult should be dealt with in Moscow, London,
or Washington . . . by the permanent diplomatic representatives." Since everyone was being exclusive, Molotov
proposed inserting the words *after preliminary agreement
between the Three Governments* in the American paper.
This insertion was accepted, and all three papers were referred to the Drafting Committee for further study, a procedure henceforth used by the Foreign Ministers whenever
agreement proved impossible.

Molotov turned to the next item on the agenda: "an
exchange of views on Italy and the Balkans." This also was a
British proposal, and he again called on Eden. Eden replied
disingenuously that since Italy was now a cobelligerent, he
had nothing to say but would be happy to answer any questions. Molotov immediately launched himself into an attack
on Soviet exclusion from Italian affairs and read out two
proposals of his own. The first contained seven "urgent
political measures" for Italy, including the widening of
Badoglio's government, a purge of the administration, and

an amnesty for political prisoners.[6] The second called for one Italian battleship, one cruiser, eight destroyers, and four submarines, together with forty thousand tons of merchant shipping, to be "dispatched right away to the Soviet Union."[7] Eden and Hull defended Anglo-American policies and said that they would consult London and Washington on the Russian requests. The session ended with nothing accomplished.

The following day, October 23, Hull and Molotov had an hour's private conversation.[8] Hull, who had requested the meeting, was disturbed by the tendency of the conference "to get submerged in details" and the suspicion of Anglo-American intentions evidenced by Molotov in the discussion of Italy. The American Secretary found the talk difficult. He asked Molotov how he felt about the progress of the conference. Molotov said that he was satisfied. Hull mentioned a joint note just circulated by Eden and himself which detailed the actions of the Allied Military Government in Italy and was designed to clear up any "misunderstandings." Molotov replied that the misunderstandings resulted from the inability of the Soviet Government to obtain firsthand information.

Hull moved from the particular to the general and delivered a short speech on the importance of Soviet-American friendship. He talked of the coming meeting of the heads of state and maintained that no problem existed that could not be resolved by good will. The American and Russian people were declared to have many things in common. "They shared," said Hull, "in large measure the same tastes, the same jokes and in general were very congenial."[9] Russia need have no fears that America would return to isolationism; this time the United States was prepared to play its part in the postwar world.

6. For the full text, see ibid., I, 714–15.
7. For the full text, see ibid., I, 715.
8. Hull, *Memoirs*, II, 1288–9; *U.S. Foreign Relations, 1943*, I, 613–16.
9. Hull, *Memoirs*, II, 1288.

On such a level of high abstraction, Molotov found the Secretary's views "warmly welcome." However, toward the end of the meeting, Hull, "speaking frankly, as must be the case between friends," became more specific as to at least two areas of friction; and Molotov, although smiling, "did not quite understand what the Secretary had in mind." Hull asked the Soviet Union to stop promoting Communism in the United States and to grant religious freedom at home. When understanding was achieved, Molotov, on the first point, doubted that the United States would become Communist and, on the second, felt that the true attitude of his government was hidden by prejudice. Shortly thereafter both men left for the Spiridonovka Palace. Hull wondered if the translators were at fault.

Molotov opened Saturday's plenary session by asking for answers on his Italian proposals.[1] Hull and Eden replied that they were without instructions. Molotov then turned to the second half of the British proposal—an exchange of views on the Balkans. Again he called on Eden.

Although it was a separate item on the agenda, Eden read a statement on resistance movements in Yugoslavia. He said that the policy of the British Government was to preserve the freedom and unity of Yugoslavia. The British were described as being in touch with both General Draza Mikailovic's Chetniks and Tito's Partisans, and as all knew, the two groups fought each other. Eden asked Hull and Molotov to help end the civil war and further stated that the British Government was considering cutting off supplies to Mikailovic if the General did not agree to cooperate. The Foreign Secretary added that he had asked King Peter of Yugoslavia to instruct his Defense Minister in absentia, General Mikailovic, to undertake two specific acts of sabotage as proof of good behavior. Hull and Molotov were evasive in their replies. The American Secretary had "nothing to add . . . at this time." Molotov would "consider the question" but

1. *U.S. Foreign Relations*, 1943, I, 617–21; Eden, *Memoirs*, II, 480; Hull, *Memoirs*, II, 1285–8.

pointed out that the subject under discussion was a general exchange of views on the Balkans, not the Yugoslav resistance.

Actually, by October, 1943, though none was aware of it, the bitter struggle between Chetniks and Partisans was largely over, and Tito had won. Ironically, it was the British strategy of Mediterranean attack which produced this result. The Chetniks and Partisans were essentially regional, not ideological, organizations. Despite his claim of a force of 200,000, Mikailovic's Chetniks were the smaller of the two and were based in Serbia. Far from being a product of World War II, the Chetniks could trace their lineage back to the fighting between Serbs and Turks in the nineteenth century. In the interwar years, they supported the pan-Serb Government of Belgrade. Colonel Draza Mikailovic was one of the leaders of the organization at the time of the Yugoslav collapse. Unfortunately for the Chetniks, Serbia was under German occupation.

Brigadier Fitzroy Maclean, who in September, 1943, was sent by Churchill to head the British Mission to the Partisans, estimated that Tito had a force of 100,000.[2] Although Tito, Josip Broz, was one of the founders and the current Secretary General of the Yugoslav Communist Party, his movement was essentially Croatian. Fortunately for the Partisans, Croatia was under Italian occupation. When Italy surrendered on September 8, Tito, within fifteen days, disarmed six Italian divisions and was joined by two others; no such booty fell to Mikailovic. By the end of September, Tito had control of all the Italian occupied areas of Yugoslavia, or roughly half the country; he even seized Istria. The very scale of his success almost proved his undoing, for Berlin reacted strongly. Fifteen German and Bulgarian divisions moved against the Partisans. By November, Tito was back in the Bosnian hills from which he had emerged, but with forces which were larger, more experienced, and armed. They could

2. Ehrman, *Grand Strategy*, V, 86; Churchill, *Second World War*, V, 465.

not defeat the Germans; but, barring outside intervention, the Chetnik cause was rendered hopeless. Some of the Chetniks further compromised their movement by collaborating with the Germans, and the leadership of Yugoslav resistance passed to Tito.

Since he had been asked by Molotov to speak in general terms about the Balkans, Eden said that it was the universal aim of British policy to promote guerrilla resistance and at the same time to prevent the various bands from fighting each other. Turning away from Yugoslavia, Eden, in quick succession and without giving any details, mentioned the collapse of the United Bands Agreement in Greece and the existence of Rumanian peace feelers. About the latter, which he knew interested Molotov, Eden remarked that it, of course, came under the thirteenth item of the agenda: "Peace Feelers from Enemy States." He concluded by asking Molotov to give him information on Bulgaria, whose divisions had intervened in Yugoslavia and seemed to be fulfilling tasks previously performed by the Italian occupation troops. He noted that Russia, unlike Great Britain, was not at war with Bulgaria.

Eden's talk of guerrillas, with its emphasis on British liaison, led General Deane to say that the American Joint Chiefs also believed there were great opportunities in the Balkans and had directed the Office of Strategic Services to undertake operations there. He hastened to add that American interest was entirely nonpolitical and hoped that the action would be agreeable to the Soviet Union. Molotov asked for details but Deane could not supply any; he never interrupted the proceedings again. The Foreign Ministers decided to pass over the Balkans for the time being. Eden's not-very-subtle inquiry as to what the Russians could do about Tito if he curbed Mikailovic was ignored. Actually Eden acted under a false premise; much to Stalin's irritation the Russians had little control over Tito.

The Soviet Foreign Minister returned to the question of the European and Italian Commissions which had been discussed the previous day. He asked that the drafts be separated; this was agreed. Surprisingly, he now indicated a willingness to accept the Italian Commission, provided it was established immediately and its name was changed to the Politico-Military Commission; this was also agreed. On the London Commission, Molotov still argued that its terms of reference should be the British memorandum of July 1. Eden, who must by now have regretted ever allowing this document to leave the Foreign Office, pointed out that the July paper referred only to postwar conditions. The new draft dealt with such immediate problems as peace feelers from satellite states.

Molotov, who was not lacking in humor, remarked that his colleagues must seek to improve, not worsen, the earlier paper; moreover, if the powers of the London Commission were made too large, the Foreign Ministers would be left with nothing to do. Everything went back to the Drafting Committee. Molotov, however, won his point that the principles of July were not to be ignored. Molotov closed the meeting by mentioning an American paper on Germany which Hull had handed out. He suggested that it be considered at the next session.

X

PROBLEMS OF A BIG THREE MEETING, ITALY, AND IRAN
October 24–27, 1943

The most interesting feature of the Balkan discussions on Saturday had been what was not said, as Churchill was now in full cry for the eastern Mediterranean. The change had been sudden. On October 1, 1943, the Prime Minister was still enamored of Culverin-Sumatra; that day, in a British Chiefs of Staff meeting, Churchill talked of closing down the Mediterranean and diverting its resources elsewhere.[1] The location he had in mind, as at Quebec, was the Indian Ocean. Indeed, so great was his enthusiasm that he declared himself willing to scrap the Arcadia decision and go for Japan first. Brooke, while sympathizing with Churchill's concern over British prestige in Asia, stood out against the Prime Minister. In his opinion,

---

1. Bryant, *Triumph in the West*, p. 26.

and in Eisenhower's as well, there was no surplus in the Mediterranean either for Overlord or Culverin.

The crossing at Messina, launched September 3, had been a simple operation. The Italians offered only token resistance. Montgomery had written Brooke on this date, the fourth anniversary of the war, that he was thrilled to be back on the mainland of Europe. The only fighting at Messina involved a puma and a monkey who, in the confusion, had escaped from a local zoo. Badoglio, after last-minute hesitations because of the presence of Germans in Rome, announced Italy's surrender on September 8. At 3:30 A.M. the following day, the first elements of General Mark Clark's Fifth Army landed at Salerno, and Operation Avalanche was under way. It ran head on into Hitler's Operation Axis, the German plan for defense of Italy.

Italy's armed forces reacted to the surrender announcement with unintended literalness. They gave up their arms with equal willingness to Americans, British, Greeks, Yugoslavs, and Germans. By September 12 the position at Salerno had become critical. The Americans and British found themselves engaged in a buildup race with the Germans while the Italians looked passively on. The passivity continued even after Italy declared war on Germany on October 13. For it, and for Badoglio's failure to prepare militarily for his change of sides—an oversight not made up by Berlin—the Italians were to pay a terrible price.

Churchill, on October 1, was out of touch with events. Then on October 3, German paratroopers landed on the small island of Cos in the Aegean. In the golden days of early September, Churchill had ordered General Wilson, Commander in Chief in the Middle East, to "improvise and dare."[2] Operation Accolade, the capture of Rhodes and other islands in the Aegean garrisoned by the Italians, was set in motion. The Germans got to Rhodes, which was the only important prize, first. The British established them-

2. Churchill, *Second World War*, V, 205.

selves on Leros, Cos, and Samos. As at Salerno, although on a smaller scale, there was a race for buildup. Unlike Salerno, where Mark Clark had won, Wilson lost this race.

In the first week of October, Churchill appealed to Washington and Eisenhower for help. Everywhere, from Marshall and Eisenhower, from Montgomery and Cunningham, came a grim "not possible."[3] No men and no landing craft were available even for the rescue, much less the reinforcement, of Accolade. The Italian situation was too critical. Churchill now forgot Culverin. To him the implications were obvious. If the Americans and British had this much trouble in Italy and the Aegean, then Overlord, only seven months away, and against prepared defenses backed by a superb transport net, would be a disaster.

It was the First World War all over again. Marshall was another Haig; Brooke, another Robertson. Churchill, however, was determined not to be another Lloyd George. On October 20, he wired Eden: "To find out what the Russians really feel about the Balkans. Would they be attracted by the idea of our acting through the Aegean, involving Turkey in the war, and opening the Dardanelles and Bosphorus so that British naval forces and shipping could aid the Russian advance and so that we could ultimately give them our right hand along the Danube?"[4] He frankly admitted that for political reasons the Russians might be opposed. Eden, however, was to do his best. Churchill was starting to bid for Soviet support for an expanded Mediterranean campaign. As for Overlord, the Prime Minister showed he was again thinking of it as a force to exploit German collapse. Overlord was shading into Rankin, the occupation of Western Europe after the deterioration of Germany's position. Despite the urging, Eden, on Saturday and with Balkan operations under consideration, remained silent. Washington's opinions were too well known. Moreover, Eden seems to have felt Churchill was making a mistake.

3. Matloff, *Strategic Planning, 1943–1944*, pp. 253–9.
4. Churchill, *Second World War*, V, 286.

Churchill, however, that same Saturday, October 23, began his own campaign. Ostensibly, it took the form of a cable to Eden with a copy for Roosevelt. Actually, it was a cable to Roosevelt, with a copy for Eden. In it the Prime Minister, although with muted phrases, favored "giving Russia the right hand." Eden was being instructed to tell Molotov the British Government approved bringing Turkey and Sweden into the war.

These developments, however, were in the background. At Moscow during the plenary session of October 24, Molotov won reluctant British approval for the Treaty of Friendship, Mutual Assistance, and Postwar Cooperation between the U.S.S.R. and Czechoslovakia.[5] In the evening Vyshinsky, in a private conversation with Deane, Bohlen, and Geoffrey Wilson, the latter a member of the Eastern Division of the Foreign Office, broadly hinted that the Soviet Union, after the defeat of Germany, would join the war on Japan. However, neither the Czech Treaty nor the Asiatic War was on the conference agenda. On the topics that were on the agenda, no progress was made because of Hull's persistent refusal to deal with substantive issues. His attitude was made abundantly clear both in a private exchange between Eden and Hull at noon in Spaso House and during the plenary session at four.

The Foreign Secretary called upon Hull to obtain his assistance in reestablishing Polish-Russian relations. He met a blank wall. Hull insisted this was a British problem. He would sit in on discussions, which must be kept as small as possible, and he would state that the United States enjoyed excellent relations with Poland, as it did with Russia. He might even mention the role of the Polish vote in American

5. For the text of the treaty, see *U.S. Foreign Relations*, 1943, I, 744–6. The treaty contained, in Article Three, a guarantee of Czech territory against any renewal of German aggression and, in Article Five, a pledge by the Czechs that they would not participate in any revival of the *cordon sanitaire*. No boundaries were defined, nor were there any other specific political or economic clauses. It was signed in Moscow on December 12, 1943. A separate protocol provided for other powers to adhere to the pact.

politics. Beyond this he could not go. Eden would have to fight alone.

The American Secretary was equally unhelpful during the plenary session.[6] He came expecting to discuss the relatively safe topic of the postwar treatment of Germany. Molotov was not ready and suggested moving on to the next item on the agenda—Questions of Agreement Between Major and Minor Allies on postwar problems. In the ensuing discussion, despite pressure from both Eden and Molotov, the American Secretary refused to express an opinion. Nor would he help Eden with the Czech Treaty. The result was a Russian success.

Questions of Agreement Between Major and Minor Allies on postwar problems was a long-winded euphemism for the treaty. The treaty itself was a relatively innocuous document pledging friendship and mutual assistance between Czechoslovakia and the Soviet Union. The Foreign Office, however, disliked it for two reasons, both involving Poland. First was the question of timing. The Soviet Union severed relations with Poland in April. This action was disturbing enough in itself. It became even more alarming when, in June, Moscow held a Congress of the Union of Polish Patriots. If Czechoslovakia only a few months later signed a treaty of alliance with Russia, it would appear that she condoned Russia's action. The second reason for British opposition involved broader issues. London was trying to repair the East European power vacuum created by Versailles. She was sponsoring a scheme of federative union between Warsaw and Prague. It was felt the Soviet treaty would jeopardize the plan.

None of this, of course, was mentioned in the correspondence between London and Moscow. Instead, when the Czechs, ignoring British wishes, went ahead with the negotiations, Eden and Molotov exchanged *aides-mémoire* on whether it was proper for great powers to sign pacts with

6. Ibid., I, 624–8.

little powers involving postwar settlements. The British maintained it was not; Molotov maintained it was. During the meeting of October 24, each introduced drafts supporting his own position. Each asked for Hull's views. The American Secretary first alleged he knew nothing about the subject. Eden and Molotov offered to make their files available. Hull replied that since his colleagues disagreed, there was no need for him to say anything. Eden and Molotov then agreed to form a bilateral subcommittee charged with the impossible task of reconciling their differences. Molotov now produced the text of the proposed Soviet-Czech Treaty. Hull had no comment. Unsupported, Eden thought it a very good draft, and it was approved.

Molotov turned to item ten on the agenda—Common Policy towards Iran. He believed that according to the terms of the Anglo-Soviet Iranian Treaty of March 21, 1942, it was necessary for a representative of Iran to be present whenever the British and Russians discussed her affairs. Eden drew a distinction between discussion and decision. He proposed the fullest possible exchange of views. Hull differed; he thought it would save time if Iranian questions were referred to a subcommittee. Molotov agreed and a subcommittee was appointed.

Eden asked for consideration of agenda items twelve and seventeen. The first dealt with Poland, Danubian, and Balkan countries, including the question of confederation. The second asked whether the powers preferred separate spheres of influence in Europe or some form of joint responsibility. Eden said he was against spheres of influence and in favor of confederations. He insisted the most important point was that the powers refrain from interference in the internal affairs of smaller states. Hull asked that consideration be postponed to some future meeting. Molotov agreed and adjourned the plenary session. Hull had kept the closet doors locked.

On Monday morning, October 25, Hull asked Molotov to arrange a meeting with Stalin. Moving with surprising speed—Eden found his requests took about two days—the interview was set up for three that afternoon. Hull wanted to deliver personally a telegram from Roosevelt which had arrived four days earlier. The subject was Eureka—Churchill's sarcastic code name for the proposed Big Three meeting.

Roosevelt had cabled Stalin on October 14, repeating his earlier suggestion that the meeting date be November 20 or 25. But whereas in September the President had some hesitation concerning Tehran, in October he regarded it as out of the question. His reasons were the pocket veto and the frequent bad weather in the mountains around Tehran which might interrupt courier flights. He offered as alternative sites Cairo; Asmara, the former Italian capital of Eritrea; Baghdad, with three camps nearby; or any eastern Mediterranean port, where the President would place a ship at Stalin's disposal.

Stalin replied on October 19.[7] He insisted on Tehran; his reason was the existence of telephone and telegraph lines from Tehran to Moscow which would enable him to direct the winter offensive. Roosevelt, who suspected he was engaged in a struggle of prestige, which was debatable, and that Stalin failed to understand the workings of the pocket veto, which was true, instructed Hull to deliver his answer and make a personal appeal.

Hull approached Stalin as if he were a colleague in the Senate. He first talked about the depth at which wheat should be planted and how rafts were constructed when he was a boy in Tennessee; then, with the proper mood established, he handed over Roosevelt's note.[8] The President explained his objections to Tehran in greater detail and suggested two new locations: Basra and Ankara; and, in the case of the former, he offered to lay special lines from Tehran. He included the sentence "Future generations would look upon it as a

7. *Stalin's Correspondence*, II, No. 130, 101.
8. For Hull's record of this meeting, see *U.S. Foreign Relations, Tehran Papers*, p. 45; Hull, *Memoirs*, II, 1292–6.

tragedy if a few hundred miles caused yourself, Mr. Churchill, and me to fail."[9]

Stalin gave the note to Molotov, who was present, for an opinion. Molotov believed even the trip to Tehran was opposed by military authorities. Stalin then suggested to Hull that everything be postponed to the spring, when he could meet the President in Fairbanks, Alaska.

The American Secretary was shocked. He discoursed on the pocket veto, the quality of the security and communications which could be established at Basra, the importance of the decisions that needed to be taken, and the impact on world opinion if there was no meeting. Stalin in turn could not understand why the delay of a few days in the delivery of a state paper was of any consequence. He believed the present campaign might afford an opportunity to destroy the German Army. Prestige was not involved, but he could go only to Tehran. With either that place or the spring date, Hull must be satisfied. He had enjoyed meeting the Secretary. Hull had failed in his mission.

At the plenary session that day, the first subject discussed was Hull's paper on Germany.[1] The draft was a product of the State Department's Interdivisional Country Committee on Germany established in September, with David Harris as chairman. Hull had taken a personal hand in the work and had also discussed the draft with Stimson. It was considerably more lenient in its approach to Germany than the course advocated by Roosevelt and Sumner Welles.

German authorities, either *de facto* or *de jure*, were to sign an instrument of unconditional surrender that included an admission of total defeat. The entire country would be placed under military occupation, and the American draft set no limits to the length of occupation. The National Socialist Party would be dissolved. During the armistice

9. *Stalin's Correspondence*, II, No. 132, 102–3.
1. For the discussion at the seventh session, see *U.S. Foreign Relations, 1943*, I, 629–34. For the draft itself, see ibid., I, 720–3.

period, the functions of a central government would be exercised by an Allied Control Commission, which would implement the agreed policies of Great Britain, Russia, and the United States. No mention was made of any veto power or of participation by other states. After being purged, local government, although subject to the power of the Control Commission and other occupation authorities, would be allowed to operate with a minimum of interference. Germany was to be disarmed under a system of permanent inspection, and she would pay reparations, the amount, form, and distribution to be determined by a Reparations Commission. Like the Control Commission, initial membership would be limited to the Big Three, but provision might subsequently be made for representation of others.

Long-range goals included the development of a broadly based German democracy operating under a bill of rights. The Americans favored a federal form of government and encouraged the breaking up of Prussia. Early political steps should include granting freedom of speech, religion, press, and association. Later there would be elections for a central German Government to which the Control Commission would gradually transfer its authority. Despite references to a federal system, the State Department said it was still studying this question. There was no mention of dismemberment. German frontiers would be determined at "the general settlement."

Lengthy, awkwardly worded, largely confined to general principles, the draft was considered by Eden a "useful contribution." Molotov added "that to the United States Government and to Mr. Hull in particular belongs the honor of setting forth the first definite expression of an attitude toward Germany."[2] The discussion which followed was dominated by Molotov.

Largely ignoring the draft, which was referred to the proposed London Commission for study, the Soviet Foreign

2. Ibid., I, 632.

Minister concentrated on three points. First, he wanted a minimum of publicity on the treatment to be accorded Germany, since to do otherwise would play into the hands of Hitler and unite the German people in their war effort. This was agreed. Second, despite Hull's later comments on the adulatory response of the Soviet Government to his program, Molotov clearly indicated the proposals were not harsh enough. He regarded them as minimal. Finally, Molotov was surprised that the Americans made no mention of dismemberment, which was favored by Soviet public opinion. Molotov, however, did not put forward any program of his own; even dismemberment would require study. Eden also was cautious; the British Government favored partition but was divided on the use of force. Hull thought there were good arguments for and against this position. He described his own paper as a tentative first step. The Foreign Ministers broke for tea.

During the intermission Molotov asked Hull about the American attitude on Turkish intervention.[3] He said the Soviet Union favored a preemptory suggestion to Ankara. Hull, aware of the Quebec decision, refused to be drawn out. He knew nothing of military matters, and besides, Turkey was a British responsibility. Hull then repeated all his arguments for a Big Three meeting. It was Molotov's turn to be evasive, and he chided Hull about American isolationism between the wars. This struck a sensitive spot. Hull said that isolationism had nearly destroyed Russia as well as the United States. He hoped the Soviet Union did not intend to act like a bully and gobble up all its neighbors. Molotov denied the charge. The talk moved into safer channels, but this was the first sharp exchange between the two men and reflected Hull's disappointment over Eureka.

When the meeting resumed, Molotov pointed out that the American paper was silent on Germany's frontiers. Hull, supported by Eden, favored those of 1938. Hull also said

3. Ibid., I, 634–5; Hull, *Memoirs*, II, 1296–7.

there was "unanimity about East Prussia."[4] Molotov was
vaguer and thought Germany should disgorge her conquests.
Surprisingly, Hull's remark about East Prussia passed without comment. Molotov then turned to a British paper on
Austria. It called for the restoration of the Republic and also
mentioned Austria's right of association with other Danubian powers. With no discussion the paper was referred to
the drafting committee. The powers seemed united on two
of the most important questions before the conference:
German frontiers and Austria.

The last item considered on Monday was a British proposal for exchanging information on enemy peace feelers.
Molotov attempted to draw Eden out on approaches from
Hungary and Rumania. Eden said he had nothing to add to
what had already been communicated, whereupon Molotov
issued a warning about maintaining the principle of unconditional surrender. The paper was sent to the drafting committee, and the meeting was adjourned.

The following day, October 26, Washington began to
react to events at Moscow. Except for Roosevelt's message to
Stalin, the only news Hull had received was that Eisenhower
and Murphy wanted to stop the Italian Commission from
having any contact with the Italian Government, and this
merely confirmed existing policy. Now in a series of cables,
all sent over the President's signature, Hull learned Washington's views on Turkey, Sweden, and Molotov's Italian proposals. Although Hull knew little about the military situation
in the Mediterranean, he could anticipate Marshall's response
to any scheme for forcing Turkey and Sweden into the war.
The answer would be no. He was correct. Roosevelt and the
Joint Chiefs of Staff did not "deem it advisable" that either
country be brought in because of possible adverse effects upon
Overlord. However, as Washington knew that Eden had been
instructed to give a favorable response, Hull was to present
the bad news in the best possible way. In the case of Turkey,

4. *U.S. Foreign Relations*, 1943, I, 632.

the Allies could ask for the immediate lease of transport facilities and air bases. In the case of Sweden, a similar procedure might be followed later.

Roosevelt's cable on Molotov's Italian political proposals also contained no surprises for the Secretary. Hull had suggested approval provided a paragraph was inserted placing implementation firmly in Eisenhower's hands. The President agreed. About the Italian naval and merchant vessels, however, Hull was disappointed. He had recommended that the Soviet request be met. Roosevelt said the ships should be used "wherever it may promise the best service to the common Allied cause . . . , without any final transfer of title to any Nation at the present time."[5]

Hull assumed this meant no and proceeded to give evasive replies whenever Molotov raised the question. Actually, the White House believed it had left the decision up to Hull, with the reservation that transfer of title would have to await signing of an Italian Peace Treaty. Until the confusion was cleared up—and despite the sugarcoating on Turkey—Hull felt himself to be in the unhappy position of saying no on three of the four Soviet proposals, whereas on the fourth the Secretary was sponsoring a limiting amendment. By contrast, as Hull was painfully aware, Eden seemed to possess plenary powers to approve everything "in principle."

On October 26 Molotov opened the eighth plenary session of the conference by proposing a restricted meeting for the following day during which his proposals on Sweden and Turkey would be discussed.[6] He then returned to the question of joint responsibility versus separate spheres of influence in Europe. The topic was not entirely theoretical but was linked with the question of East European confederations. The British wanted some sort of union between Czechoslovakia and Poland. Their Austrian paper mentioned an association of Danubian states. The Russians were

5. Ibid., I, 643.
6. Hull, *Memoirs,* II, 1298–1301; *U.S. Foreign Relations,* 1943, I, 637–42.

opposed to both. As for Hull, this was yet another topic he hoped to avoid.

Molotov asked Eden to speak first. Eden said he had nothing to add to his paper. It called for collective responsibility and affirmed the right of smaller states to choose their form of government and to join in confederations. Molotov then asked for Hull's opinion. The Secretary, in what amounted to a speech, replied that the American Government felt the first step should be the formulation of general principles in international relations. The principles should have worldwide application and should be designed to secure a stable and lasting peace. When the principles were established, they would provide guidelines for the solution of specific issues, of which this was one. Until the general principles were formulated, however, he could not speak on specific issues.

Molotov gave way to temptation. He said he was confused. He asked, "Was the question general as against separate areas of responsibility to be discussed or was it not?" Hull again retreated into the worldwide principles, although this time his stay was not so prolonged. An exasperated Molotov hinted that he and Eden might settle the question between themselves. Hull immediately spoke in favor of joint responsibility.

Molotov then guaranteed that there "was no disposition on the part of the Soviet Government to partition Europe." He thought, however, that questions of cooperation between the powers and the noninterference pledge were covered by the Four-Power Declaration and that any additional statement was unnecessary. Eden and Hull agreed. This limited present discussion to confederations. The Soviet Foreign Minister proceeded to read a lengthy paper that protested against the Danubian and Polish-Czech projects. Concerning the first, Molotov doubted the propriety of sponsoring associations between Axis satellites and the victims of aggression. Concerning the second, Molotov, substituting the words *émigré governments* for *governments-in-exile*, argued that these were insufficiently representative to make binding arrangements. The Soviet paper concluded by saying such projects were reminiscent of the *cordon sanitaire.*

Eden denied the charge but admitted "there was great force in Molotov's arguments." Hull upheld the right of small governments to take such action as they considered desirable. Neither attempted to rebut the Soviet paper, and, at least for the time being, Eden withdrew his paper on confederations.

Molotov then turned to the Four-Power Declaration. Hull had requested a report from the Drafting Committee as to its status at the end of Sunday's and Monday's sessions. Now Hackworth, speaking for the committee, said the text was the same as that submitted the previous Thursday, but the committee had been unable to agree on a title. Molotov stated that although the Soviet Union had no objection to the inclusion of China as an original signatory, he wished the declaration to be published before the conference ended and doubted that the Chinese Ambassador could receive the necessary powers in time. Hull replied he would undertake to communicate the text to the Chinese Government and was certain authorization would be immediately forthcoming.

On October 21, it had been possible for Molotov to postpone the issue because there was no agreed text. Now with the text before him, the Soviet Foreign Minister had to either come out in the open or retreat. He chose to retreat. Molotov "authorized the Secretary to submit the text to the Chinese Government on behalf of the Conference."[7] During the remainder of the meeting, Molotov sought and received vague assurances that the so-called self-denying ordinance would not prevent the establishment of military bases within the territory of other states. He also proposed setting up a Tripartite Commission to prepare detailed plans for the future world organization. Eden and Hull thought

7. Ibid., I, 640.

the suggestion excellent. When the session ended, Hull immediately contacted the Chinese Ambassador Foo Ping-Sheung. He also instructed Washington to forward the agreed text to Chungking directly, "as the Ambassador's communications with his capital were slow." The Secretary asked Roosevelt's "authorization to sign . . . on behalf of the United States."

The following day, October 27, the Iranian Subcommittee held its first working session.[8] An exchange of views on Iran was included in the British draft agenda of September 18. On October 6 the Foreign Office circulated an *aide-mémoire* setting forth its own views. At Moscow on October 23, Eden sent Hull and Molotov a second memorandum on the subject, while the following day Hull blocked Eden's efforts at discussion in the plenary sessions by proposing a subcommittee.

The subcommittee was composed of men experienced in Iranian affairs. The American representatives were George Allen, Assistant Chief, Division of Near Eastern Affairs, and John Jernegan, Third Secretary of the Tehran Legation; the British representatives were Adrian Holman and William Iliff, respectively the Political and Financial Secretaries at Tehran; the Russian representatives were Sergey Kavtaradze, Vice Commissar for Foreign Affairs, and Andrei Smirnov, formerly the Soviet Ambassador to Iran.

Nor was it lacking materials. To the original British memorandums of October 6 and 23, Eden had added two more, and Hull one, by Wednesday. Despite the proliferation, however, only two main points were involved. The British and Americans wanted public renewal of the pledge contained in the Anglo-Soviet Iranian Treaty of January 29, 1942—that all foreign troops would be withdrawn from the country six months after the end of hostilities. They also sought a commitment to treat Iran as an economic unit.

By September, 1943, it was apparent that the first experi-

8. Ibid., I, 645-9.

ment in tripartite occupation, Iran, was in difficulty. The Russians resented the preeminence of American advisers in Tehran, particularly the Economic Mission, headed by Dr. A. C. Millspaugh, and refused them entrance into the Soviet zone.[9] Washington and London, in turn, suspected Moscow was encouraging separatist movements in the area under Russian control.[1]

Although Molotov had not objected to the formation of the subcommittee, it rapidly became apparent that the Russians had no intentions of engaging in any serious discussions, much less of approving the various Anglo-American drafts. Kavtaradze, the senior Soviet delegate, was elected the subcommittee's permanent chairman. Repeating Molotov's argument, Kavtaradze proceeded to open the meeting by challenging the competence of his own committee on grounds that no Iranian was present. Allen and Holman had been expecting this. Allen pointed out that Molotov would hardly have approved the creation of an illegal committee. Holman argued that the relevant article of the Anglo-Soviet Iranian Treaty most definitely did not enjoin an exchange of views. Both agreed to submit any declarations to Tehran for approval.

Kavtaradze tried a different approach. The various drafts before the committee, he said, merely repeated pledges contained in the treaty. They were therefore unnecessary. As he also refused either to discuss the drafts themselves or to submit any counterproposals, the session became a: exercise in futility. Even a broad hint by Allen that the American Government might act unilaterally brought no reaction. The most Kavtaradze would do was to agree to a second meeting of the subcommittee, which under the circumstances hardly seemed promising.

A similar atmosphere of frustration and no progress obtained during Wednesday's plenary session. It had been

9. The Soviet Government had specifically warned Tehran against American advisers. Woodward, *British Foreign Policy*, note 1, p. 315.
1. Hull, *Memoirs*, II, 1503–4.

agreed the previous day that the meeting would begin with a discussion of Turkey and Sweden, but Eden requested a change. Just before the meeting opened, Molotov told Eden that an interview had been arranged for the Foreign Secretary with Stalin that night.[2] Churchill had cabled Eden on October 25 to request a second private conversation with the Soviet Premier, the subjects to be British reaction on Sweden and Turkey as well as a general review of the military situation in Italy and its possible effects on Overlord. Eden, who had no desire to expose his hand to Molotov, asked for a day's postponement so that, as he put it, he might have the benefit of hearing Stalin's views first. Molotov asked Hull's opinion. The American Secretary, with Roosevelt's negative responses in his pocket, was in no particular hurry. He supported Eden and the postponement was arranged.

Elimination of Sweden and Turkey did not, however, increase the tempo of the Foreign Ministers' deliberations. Instead, they used a procedure that by now was almost habitual—a brief exchange of views followed by referral to the drafting committee or to the proposed London Commission. Molotov opened the ninth session by asking for answers on his Italian political proposal.[3] Hull and Eden said they were still without instructions. Eden mentioned the Anglo-American note on Italy which had been circulated on Saturday. Molotov suggested that both papers go to the drafting committee in the hope that some agreed declaration might result. Hull and Eden approved. Hull, following Roosevelt's orders, also said that the views of the Commander in Chief would have to be taken into account.

Molotov then inquired whether any action had been taken on the Soviet request for a share in the Italian Navy and Merchant Marine. Again Hull and Eden replied that they had heard nothing, a statement which was true for Eden but

2. Eden, *Memoirs*, II, 481.
3. For proceedings of the ninth session, see *U.S. Foreign Relations, 1943,* I, 650–3; Hull, *Memoirs*, II, 1301.

not for Hull. Molotov protested the delay and circulated a brief memorandum answering Eden's request for information on Bulgaria. It declared Bulgaria's war against the United States and England to be purely symbolic, which was true. However, on the more important question of Bulgarian troop movements in Yugoslavia, the paper was silent. There was no discussion. Instead the Foreign Secretaries turned to a British proposal on common policy in liberated areas.

This was the latest version of Eden's Declaration on Liberated Areas which had been introduced at Quebec. As originally planned, it was to be a brief, bilateral statement that in enemy territories the United States and Great Britain would be the governing authority, whereas in liberated countries the Government-in-Exile or some other constituted authority would assume power. Eden now asked that the declaration be released simultaneously in London and Washington in mid-September. He anticipated having some difficulties.

On September 4, 1943, Hull had sent a copy of the Quebec memorandum to Standley with instructions to show it to the Soviet Government. He was to see if they desired to subscribe. On September 15, 1943, the date originally chosen for its release, Standley was notified the declaration had been canceled. This cable crossed a dispatch of Standley's to Hull informing the State Department that Moscow had serious reservations about the declaration. Eden, in August, had kept the declaration separate from the question of recognition for the French Committee. Washington, in the first weeks of September, began, nevertheless, to wonder who the constituted authorities were. As Hull now pointed out, the Americans "saw a connection between the question of liberated areas and . . . the French Committee."[4]

Possible advantages for the French were not the source of Moscow's reservations. Indeed, Molotov told Clark Kerr as

4. Hull, *Memoirs*, II, 1301.

early as June 20 that the Soviet Union desired to extend
formal recognition to the Gaullists.[5] What disturbed Moscow was that the first part of the declaration kept the Italian
door locked, whereas the second part, on liberated areas,
threatened Soviet aspirations in Poland, Yugoslavia, and
Greece. By September, with their own attack gathering
momentum, Russia was beginning to have second thoughts
on the role of the Commander in Chief in liberated territories. As Molotov told Standley September 14, his government recognized the principle of the commander's authority,
although it also believed the military should "draw into the
administration on a wide scale personnel who are sympathetic to the Allies."[6] This recruitment of local personnel
would, according to Molotov, prove even more useful in
liberated areas. The Soviet Union, however, "cannot subscribe to the Declaration." Molotov in September suggested
referral to the political-military commission. Hull replied on
September 23, and with his eyes focused on North Africa,
the American Secretary stressed the authority of the Commander in Chief in both conquered and liberated areas. Hull
also had no doubts as to who the sympathetic persons were.
He thought "the decision as to the time and degree of such
participation must be left to the Allied Command."

By the time of the Moscow meeting, the Foreign Office
had radically altered the original declaration. In the new
draft presently before the Foreign Ministers, all reference to
enemy territory was stricken. Although not so titled, it was a
Declaration on Liberated Europe. It stated that it was the
policy of the powers to "facilitate the resumption of authority by . . . Allied Government; or, where no such government exists, by an appropriate authority . . . pending the

5. This, as Murphy points out, was probably simply a fishing expedition
in what were obviously troubled waters. Ironically, at the time of Torch,
de Gaulle, in his only personal appeal to Roosevelt of the entire war, por-
trayed himself as the man who would save France from the Communists.
De Gaulle, *War Memoirs*, V, 66–71; Murphy, *Diplomat Among Warriors*,
pp. 206–7.

6. *U.S. Foreign Relations*, 1943, I, 524.

formation of a freely elected constitutional government."
During the period of active military operations, however,
London believed "supreme responsibility in civil as well as
military affairs should de facto be concentrated in the hands
of the Allied Commander in Chief."[7] Anticipating opposition from both sides, Eden tried to avoid discussion. After
stating that a common policy was necessary, the Foreign
Secretary proposed referral to the London Commission. Surprisingly, Hull took the opportunity to issue a warning. He
said, "Increasingly . . . the question [will arise] as to how
far the Allied Governments are prepared to go in setting up
the kind of governments they desire and in using force to
maintain them."[8] He agreed to submit the paper to the
London Commission. He hoped the commission would review each case individually, but no one was "to directly and
inflexibly impose one form of government." When asked for
his opinion, Molotov found the question complicated and
accepted study by the London Commission. The Foreign
Ministers adjourned for the familiar tea and cakes.

Hull's words about those who would impose a form of
government in liberated areas indicated a new attitude on
the part of the American Secretary. He was still unwilling to
join Eden and Molotov in open debate of substantive issues,
but his negative passivity of the previous nine days was over.
There were two reasons for the change. Hull was deeply
disturbed by the collapse of Eureka; to him Tehran represented prestige. Hull was also irritated by the snaillike pace
of the conference. According to Eden, on this day the
American Secretary, angrily waving his pince-nez, asked
Eden to make a personal appeal to Stalin to get things
going.[9] Perhaps because he suspected Stalin of being the
cause of the slowdown, Hull, during intermission, now took
matters into his own hands. He told Molotov that although
the conference was one of the most enjoyable in his experi-

7. Ibid., I, 738.
8. Ibid., I, 652.
9. Eden, *Memoirs*, II, 480–1.

ence, he would have to leave Moscow four days hence, on
Sunday. Molotov offered no objections. The Foreign Minis-
ters agreed that Hackworth, Strang, and Vyshinsky should in
Hull's words, "whip together all the odds and ends."[1]

When the meeting resumed, the only topic discussed was
an American paper titled "Civil Affairs for France."[2] Complicated and probably unworkable, it represented yet another
stage in Washington's prolonged struggle against General de
Gaulle. Having welcomed the creation of the French
National Committee in North Africa on August 26, Washington in October sought to keep it out of France. According
to the American draft, after the invasion the Supreme Allied
Commander would exercise authority in liberated France for
as long as he judged necessary. He would strive to balance
the scales among all political and resistance groups until
elections could be held. In the interim French civil administration would be under the direction of a French officer
chosen by the Supreme Commander. The National Committee would have a military and civil mission at Allied
headquarters, but the Allied Commander in Chief was
specifically forbidden to deal with them as they were a
political body. The draft concluded with a condemnation of
the Vichy regime. Molotov applauded the section on Vichy;
asked some questions about the complex relationship among
the French National Committee, the French Military Mission on Civil Affairs, and the Supreme Allied Commander;
and suggested the draft be sent to London. This was agreed.
At the conclusion of the meeting it was decided that the
drafting committee would determine what documents might
be published at the end of the conference.

1. *U.S. Foreign Relations, 1943,* I, 653–4.
2. For the text, see ibid., I, 760–1.

XI

PROBLEMS OF PATIENCE, AND THE EUROPEAN AND ITALIAN ADVISORY COUNCILS

October 27–30, 1943

Because his Wednesday, October 27, meeting with Stalin was to be essentially a military one, the Foreign Secretary was accompanied not only by Clark Kerr but also by General Ismay when he went to the Kremlin. By the 27th Eden had received a series of cables from Churchill on Turkey and the Balkans, each evidencing progressively less enthusiasm for large-scale operations. On October 20 the Prime Minister thought Overlord "open to very grave defects" and was "attracted by the idea of our operating through the Aegean, involving Turkey in the war, and opening the Dardanelles and Bosphorus so that . . . we could ultimately give them [the Russians] our right hand along the Danube." To provide the necessary forces, the Italian theater would be closed down. On the 23rd, after talking with Brooke and Cadogan, the

Prime Minister again cabled his Foreign Secretary. This dispatch was the one seconded to Washington. Accordingly, it was more measured in tone. Churchill wrote:

> If we force Turkey to enter the war, she will insist on air support, etc., which could not be provided without detriment to our main operations in Italy. If, however, Turkey enters on her own initiative, perhaps moving through a phase of nonbelligerency, we should not have the same obligation, and yet great advantages might be reaped. . . . The prize would be to get into the Black Sea with supplies for Russia, warships, and other forces. . . . Such a movement by Turkey is not impossible, especially if the Germans should begin to cut their losses in the Balkans and withdraw toward the Danube and the Save.[1]

Omission of the doubts on Overlord can be explained by the necessity to propitiate Roosevelt and Marshall, but the general attitude of hesitancy reflected divided counsel in London. The Foreign Office, although not the Foreign Secretary, was in favor of bringing the Turks in. Tito's triumph in Bosnia and Herzegovina, the outbreak of fighting in Greece between ELAS and EDES, the emergence of the Polish National Committee, the Soviet Union's suspicious, even unreceptive, attitude toward Rumanian and Hungarian peace feelers—these pointed to a Russian effort at dominating Eastern Europe. Turkish intervention was felt to be the best available counter.[2]

The British Chiefs of Staff were sympathetic to "swinging the strategy back to the Mediterranean at the expense of the Channel."[3] But the military were also deeply upset by a pessimistic report from Alexander on the 21st concerning the German buildup in Italy. Churchill, on the 20th, talked of closing down operations in Italy in favor of Turkey once Rome had been taken and the narrow portion of the boot

1. Churchill, *The Second World War*, V, 288–9.
2. Woodward, *British Foreign Policy*, note 1, p. 326.
3. Bryant, *Triumph in the West*, p. 35.

had been reached. He would not "debouch into the valley of
the Po." In the light of Alexander's report, Brooke regarded
talk of Rome and the Po, much less the Danube, as fan-
tastic. The Italian theater might indeed be closed down,
but it would be the Wehrmacht which did the closing. As
Brooke wrote in his diary on October 25:

> Our operations in Italy are coming to a standstill, and . . .
> owing to lack of resources, we shall not only come to a stand-
> still, but also find ourselves in a very dangerous position unless
> the Russians go on from one success to another. . . . We are
> now beginning to see the full beauty of the Marshall strategy!
> It is quite heartbreaking when we see what we might have done
> this year if our strategy had not been distorted by the Ameri-
> cans.[4]

In April, before Trident and at a time when the Casablanca decision on Turkey was still in effect, the British had
held detailed staff talks at Ankara. The Turks were promised
upon entry into the war a four-phase program of reinforcement including fifty fighter squadrons, four antiaircraft regiments, two antitank regiments, and two armored divisions.
The operation's code name was Hardihood.[5] Hardihood was
to be preceded by a step-up in the pace of so-called normal
arms deliveries to the Turks. From January to May, 1943,
some $48 million worth of equipment was shipped.

At Trident the cross-channel operation was restored. At
Quadrant Hardihood was canceled. By the time of the
Moscow Conference, the Italian campaign seemed endangered. Brooke had to tell Churchill there was not a surplus
but rather a shortage in Italy, in fact a shortage everywhere
in the Mediterranean. The British could not help the Turks.
Instead, the British were the beggars. They needed Turkish
assistance in the form of air bases if they were to supply or
evacuate the garrison on Leros. The Foreign Office might
find Turkish intervention desirable. The British Chiefs of

4. Ibid., p. 36.
5. Ehrman, *Grand Strategy*, V, 90.

Staff, lacking the men and supplies for Hardihood, did not. Churchill, on the 23rd, was ambivalent. He hoped the Germans would simply go away so the Turks could come in on their own without Hardihood, perhaps passing through a phase of nonbelligerency, namely the establishment of air bases, so that the situation in the Aegean could be salvaged.

On October 25 and 26, after more gloomy talks with Brooke, Churchill sent a third message to Eden concerning the proper answer to the Soviet proposal on Turkey.[6] Eden was to request a second interview with Stalin. He was provided with a copy of Alexander's appreciation of the battle in Italy and told to show it to the Soviet Premier. The Prime Minister informed Eden:

> The reason why we are getting into this jeopardy is because we are moving some of our best divisions and a large proportion of of vital landing craft from the Mediterranean in order to build up for Overlord, seven months hence. This is what happens when battles are governed by lawyers' agreements made in all good faith months before, and persisted in without regard to the ever changing fortunes of war. . . . We will do our very best for Overlord, but it is no use planning for defeat in the field in order to give temporary political satisfaction.

The Foreign Secretary was to make it clear to Stalin that Overlord must be deferred because of the deteriorating conditions in Italy. As for Turkey, the Prime Minister in a separate cable instructed Eden to "agree in principle and let the difficulties manifest themselves, as they will certainly do, in the discussions of ways and means."[7]

In a sense, Churchill had moved full circle, from Turkey in, to Turkey out, in less than a week. On a more fundamental level, however, the Prime Minister's position was becoming increasingly firm. He intended to reopen the whole question of Anglo-American strategy for 1944 which had supposedly been settled at Quebec. The Aegean crisis of

6. Churchill, *Second World War*, V, 289–90.
7. Ibid., V, 289.

the first week of October revealed weakness in the eastern Mediterranean. Alexander's appreciation extended the area of weakness to Italy. Churchill's response to the situation in the Aegean, aside from ending the Prime Minister's enthusiasm for Southeast Asia, had been to question withdrawing troops from Italy for use in Overlord. Alexander's message confirmed his doubts on the withdrawals and, since the two were related, extended them to the timing of Overlord. Cross-channel in the spring of 1944 was, in his eyes, rapidly joining its predecessors Sledgehammer and Roundup. It was to be Eden's unhappy duty to explain to Stalin that because of German reinforcements in Italy, the pledge of Overlord in the spring, only seven days old, must now be modified. Eden found his task surprisingly easy.

Eden opened Wednesday's meeting by handing Stalin a Russian translation of Alexander's report.[8] News of Anglo-American weakness in the Mediterranean failed to disturb the Soviet Premier. He said Alexander's appreciation did not tally with Soviet intelligence but admitted that the man on the scene should have the best information. Stalin was of the opinion that the Anglo-Americans had a choice between two strategies: assaulting Germany through Italy or by means of Overlord. He himself favored Overlord and a cutoff in the Mediterranean once suitable defensive positions north of Rome had been achieved. Eden assured him this was the British view too and read aloud that portion of Churchill's cable which contained the pledge of doing "our very best for Overlord." Stalin was almost cordial. Even the Prime Minister's desire to nourish Italy at the cost of a delay in Overlord failed to provoke the usual flow of accusations. Stalin merely asked if the postponement would be for one month or two. Eden said he could not possibly know, and Stalin did not press the point.

On Hull's request for a speedup in the Foreign Ministers'

8. For accounts of the Stalin-Eden meeting of Wednesday, October 27, 1943, see ibid., V, 291–3; Eden, *Memoirs*, II, 481–2; Ismay, *Memoirs*, pp. 326–7.

meeting, Stalin was equally cooperative. He asked what was wanted; Eden replied that it was decisions on topics under discussion for more than a week. Stalin said he would speak to Molotov. As the Foreign Secretary cabled Churchill, "the whole talk went off surprisingly well."[9] This does not mean there were no differences. Stalin expressed disappointment at the coolness of the British reply on Turkey. Semibelligerence, the leasing of air bases, and transportation facilities, all of which the British proposed, were in Stalin's opinion no substitutes for an immediate declaration of war. This would draw off ten German divisions from the Russian front. Eden, who shared Ankara's fears that belligerency would mean yet another country on Russia's frontier left militarily exhausted at the end of the war, pointed out that the British were weak in the eastern Mediterranean. Istanbul was vulnerable, and the promises of Hardihood could not now be kept. An equally suspicious Stalin asked why the Turks were being armed if not to fight Germans.

Nor was the Foreign Secretary any more successful than Hull in luring Stalin away from Tehran. Eden did not subscribe to Hull's opinion that what was involved was a battle of prestige. He accepted Stalin's personal leadership of the Red Army as a fact.[1] The Foreign Office also believed Stalin would stay only at a Soviet Embassy because of his fear of hidden microphones.[2] Nevertheless, Eden proceeded to suggest Lake Habbaniya, in Iraq, as a possible site. He baited his proposal by mention of the strategic decisions to be taken, particularly with regard to Italy. Stalin, after observing that a gathering of the heads of government could not create divisions, insisted on Tehran. If this site were not possible, he offered to send Molotov elsewhere as his deputy. Eden replied that the Prime Minister and President could hardly be expected to travel long distances except to see Stalin himself. Mutual suspicion over Turkey and continu-

9. Churchill, *Second World War*, V, 293.
1. Eden, *Memoirs*, II, 481.
2. Woodward, *British Foreign Policy*, note 1, p. 244.

ing difficulties on the Big Three meeting, however, failed to alter the prevailing atmosphere of friendliness. Indeed, to Eden's pleasure, Stalin admitted a good deal of the Red Army's present success was due to the forty divisions the Germans were compelled to keep in Western Europe by the mere threat of a cross-channel attack; while the following day, for the first time in many years, Molotov dined at the British Embassy.

The Foreign Secretary, however, was well aware of the relationship between current warmth and the Overlord promise. Equally, he could see the direction in which Churchill was moving. The Prime Minister, in his Balkan message of October 20, had ended with the words "all the above is simply for your inner thoughts." The Italian telegram of October 26, although more peremptory, also left Eden free as to how much or how little to say. Eden's decision was to keep as close as possible to Ismay's exposition of the previous Wednesday. He ended his report to Churchill with this warning: "It is clear . . . that he [Stalin] expects us to make every effort to stage Overlord at the earliest possible moment, and the confidence he is placing in our word is to me most striking."[3] The Soviet Premier had been warned that conditions in Italy might delay Overlord. He was not told about the Prime Minister's renewed interest in the Balkans. On the other hand, Stalin now had a clear appreciation of Anglo-American strength in the Mediterranean. Henceforward, Soviet enthusiasm for Turkish intervention, at least as expressed in deeds rather than words, constantly diminished. Unfortunately, London saw only the words.

Eden noted a change in atmosphere at the plenary session on October 28. The Foreign Secretary informed Churchill "though he [Molotov] was obviously disappointed . . . at our failure wholly to endorse Soviet proposals about Turkey and Sweden, he conducted our business with an evident desire to avoid embarrassment."[4] Indeed, the second mili-

3. Churchill, *The Second World War*, V, p. 293.
4. Ibid., V, 294.

tary meeting was one of the shortest of the Moscow Conference. The time before tea was devoted to Overlord; after, to
Turkey and Sweden.

On Overlord Voroshilov asked for a more precise definition of the limiting conditions. He wanted to know how the
figure of twelve mobile divisions had been determined and
what would be the effect on the invasion if the Germans had
thirteen or fourteen available. Ismay, speaking for the
British and American delegations, indicated that the figure
twelve was only approximate. The difficulty was that the
Germans would blow up harbor facilities in northern France.
This, in turn, meant an estimated sixty days of across-the-
beach supply for the attacking forces. Ismay believed air
power and pressure on other fronts would prevent any significant German buildup until a port was cleared. Voroshilov remarked: "May God see it so."[5]

Molotov inquired whether the Quebec decision on an
early spring attack was still valid. Eden assured him it was
with the qualification that this should not be regarded as a
legal contract. Molotov, who wanted just that, proposed that
the earlier statements of Deane and Ismay be incorporated
in the protocol of the conference. To avoid future controversy, the Soviet Foreign Minister suggested a two-column
format with Anglo-American views in one and Russian comments in the other. Hull was hesitant and referred to the Big
Three meeting. Eden, however, was more forthcoming, and
after Molotov guaranteed to the American Secretary that
nothing beyond the original presentation would be included,
the Russian proposal was adopted.

After tea Molotov turned to Turkey and Sweden. Hull
circulated his version of Roosevelt's dispatch of October 26.
It was sympathetically worded and mentioned the immediate leasing of air bases and transportation facilities from
Turkey with similar policies to be pursued in Sweden at a

5. *U.S. Foreign Relations*, 1943, I, pp. 656–62.

later date. On the central issue of intervention, however, Hull said no. His reasons were adverse effects on Italy and Overlord.[6] Eden, too, distributed a memorandum. London and Washington were agreed on Sweden, but on Turkey the British called first for air bases and the opening of the straits, and then, provided it was voluntary so as to avoid sending the promised military supplies which were no longer available, a declaration of war.

Molotov noted that the three governments held widely divergent views concerning Ankara. The Soviet Union, he said, wanted the Turks in; the Americans wanted them out; the British put forth so many suggestions it would take another two conferences to discuss them all. Molotov believed intervention would hurt the Germans more than the Allies. He would like to see a three-power *démarche* with a threat to cut off aid providing the teeth. Eden doubted threats would work. Hull underlined American opposition because of a shortage of resources. It was decided that the question of Turkish intervention should be referred to the heads of government. Similar action was taken on Sweden. With some justification an irritated Molotov asked if the Soviet Union was the only power interested in shortening the war. He admitted his proposals might not be sufficiently worked out and called for other suggestions. Hull repeated Deane's proposals on shuttle bombing and closer cooperation between the Soviet General Staff and the Combined Chiefs of Staff. Molotov pointed out that these were not new and adjourned the meeting.

The sessions on October 29 and 30, the last of the conference thanks to Hull's deadline, were long, exhausting, and focused on those proposals over which differences had developed within the Drafting Committee. This did not totally exclude new business. On the 29th Eden brought up Poland, and Hull introduced papers on economic coopera-

6. For the text, see ibid., I, 655–6.

tion, German reparations, and colonialism. On the 30th, although outside the formal meetings, there occurred what the American Secretary regarded as the most significant event of the conference—Stalin's pledge to enter the war against Japan.

During the plenary sessions themselves, however, lack of time meant abbreviated discussion, and wherever there was disagreement, a topic simply had to be dropped without any exploration of the causes or significance of the dispute. If this resulted, as Eden later put it, in the conference's ending "at the top,"[7] it also meant that a number of things were swept under the rug. The first half of Friday's meeting was devoted to the Mediterranean and London Commissions.[8] The Soviet Union had reservations about both. On the Mediterranean Commission, the Russians objected to including Greece and Yugoslavia. Molotov said he was also confused by the American attitude toward membership for the French Committee. On the London Commission, Molotov reversed himself. He now called for the inclusion of other members of the United Nations when their interests were involved. The Mediterranean Commission was discussed first.

Russian confusion about Washington's attitude toward the French was understandable. The day before the conference opened, October 18, Stalin received a message from Roosevelt expressive of the President's usual feelings about de Gaulle. It was addressed to just this question of French participation in the Mediterranean Commission and ended with this sentence: "It was never my intention that the . . . Committee . . . should function on the same plane as the Governments of the Soviet Union, Great Britain, and the United States or enter into its [the Commission's] delibera-

7. Eden, *Memoirs*, II, 484.
8. *U.S. Foreign Relations, 1943*, I, 662–70; Eden, *Memoirs*, II, 482–3; Hull, *Memoirs*, II, 1303–6.

tions on all subjects."[9] Yet in the Drafting Committee, Hackworth, the American representative, supported Eden's paper which made France one of the original members of the Italian Council. Molotov asked for clarification.

·Actually, there was no conflict. Once the advisory nature of the commission was accepted, Washington had little interest in matters of membership. As early as October 13, Hull instructed Winant to tell Strang that the State Department favored enlarged representation and had already received applications from Brazil, China, Greece, and Yugoslavia. Roosevelt's message did not mark a change in policy. The advantages of receiving the advice of the many and weak as against the few and powerful were obvious. The President's cable was in reaction to Russia's continuing efforts to increase the authority of the Italian Council. What Roosevelt was saying was that France or any other member of the United Nations was welcome in a debating society but not in any substantive body. Naturally, neither Hull nor Eden expressed themselves in quite these terms. Instead Hull maintained that the President's message referred only to the London Commission, where he felt it inadvisable for any other nation to be given voting power. As for the Italian Commission, Hull and Eden pointed out that Eisenhower had already agreed to representation for the French Committee.[1] Molotov accepted the explanation.

In the case of Greece and Yugoslavia, Eden simply cut off discussion before it could begin. Churchill had mentioned possible membership for both governments in his replies to Stalin's call for a political-military commission. Support for the unknown King Peter and the unpopular King George, if not in the form of armed intervention, seemed advisable on the diplomatic level. However, Hull's disinterest in the Balkans together with Molotov's challenge to the authority of emigré governments now led Eden to abandon the effort.

9. *Stalin's Correspondence,* II, No. 129, 100–1.
1. *U.S. Foreign Relations,* 1943, I, 663–4.

He proposed making participation by Greece and Yugoslavia depend upon the consent of the powers. Molotov appeared satisfied. The matter of the Italian Council was sent back to the Drafting Committee supposedly for final touches.

If British hopes were frustrated in the case of Greece and Yugoslavia, the Russians were equally unhappy about the terms of reference for the London Commission. But Molotov, like Eden, had given up trying to persuade his colleagues to assign the commission substantive powers. Instead he asked, first, that other members of the United Nations be allowed to participate in discussions when their interests were involved, and, second, that the commission restrict itself to questions related to the conclusion of hostilities and the drawing up of armistice terms.

Eden pointed out that the Foreign Ministers had already referred such general subjects as the postwar treatment of Germany to the commission. He proposed a meaningless amendment that would limit the commission's terms of reference to European issues connected with ending the war. He could not agree to any increase in membership, as once the door was opened everyone would want to come in. Molotov remarked that such had not been the British position in July and withdrew his suggestions. The agreement was returned to the drafting committee. Great Britain and the United States had preserved their freedom of action in Italy and France. They also extended similar rights to the Soviet Union in Eastern Europe.

After tea, American proposals on postwar economic co-operation, a subject dear to Hull, were considered by the Foreign Ministers.[2] Distributed a few days earlier, they were four in number. The first, which was accepted without discussion, pledged American aid to the Soviet Union and suggested preliminary conversations between Russian representatives and the United States Mission in Moscow. The

---

2. Hull, *Memoirs*, II, 1303–4; *U.S. Foreign Relations, 1943*, I, 665–6.

second called for the powers to channel aid to smaller states through the United Nations Relief and Rehabilitation Administration. It also suggested setting up an international lending agency. Hull asked if everyone approved of a cooperative approach. Molotov said he did but asked that it be made clear that economic assistance would be given primarily to members of the United Nations. Hull agreed and added that the reason he was introducing these questions now was in view of the experience of Versailles, where insufficient preparation on economic matters had wrought incalculable harm. He wished to ensure that this time the subject received full and early consideration.

The third memorandum outlined an American program for postwar economic cooperation. Essentially it was a call for free trade. Hull mentioned conversations just ended in Washington between the British and American governments on this topic. He regretted the inability of the Soviet Union to attend but included a summary in his paper.[3] He asked for opinions. Eden and Molotov avoided discussion. Both thought the general principles excellent. When the Foreign Ministers took up the fourth paper, however, this happy unanimity came to an end. Its subject was German reparations.[4] The paper embodied the supposed lessons of the 1920's. It was also intended to dampen any undue Soviet enthusiasm for the subject. Reparations, it stated, were not to so affect Germany's living standards and productive plant as to create serious economic and political problems. They were not to be used as an instrument of control over her military power. The total obligation would be expressed in terms of goods and services. Claimant countries would share in proportion to their losses of nonmilitary property. The program was to be completed as rapidly as possible. The

3. For the full text of the memorandum, see Notter, *Postwar Foreign Policy Preparation*, Appendix 30, pp. 560–4. For the Washington meeting, see *U.S. Foreign Relations*, 1943, I, 1099ff.
4. For the text, see ibid., I, 740–1.

paper concluded with a call for the creation of a Three-Power Reparations Commission.

Although in favor of free trade, Molotov had some doubts about American views on reparations. There were, he said, "certain objections from the Soviet point of view to the purposes . . . of the draft." He did not, however, detail their nature. He did think creation of a commission was premature. Eden, while certain his government would go along with the American proposals in general, agreed that "the subject would require very close and detailed study." Hull did not press the issue because of lack of time, so the subject of reparations was dropped.

Hull then asked if there was any reaction to his draft on dependent peoples. He realized it was too late for the conference to consider the question, but he was interested in any views. The views were predictable. The Soviet Government attached great importance to the question, whereas the British Government was not in agreement with the opinion set forth. Colonialism joined German reparations. Hull was paying a high price for his speedup.

Eden now asked for an exchange of views on Poland. Privately Eden regarded the situation as critical, particularly if the Red Army maintained its present rate of advance. The London Poles themselves were worried and had addressed identical pleas for support to both London and Washington shortly before Hull and Eden left for Moscow.[5] Critical or not, Eden had no illusions as to the weakness of his hand. The fault, in his opinion, rested with his friends. Hull placed a strict interpretation upon Roosevelt's instructions. The President intended a personal appeal to Stalin. The Secretary, therefore, could only speak in the most vague way about neighborliness. Frontiers were wholly beyond the pale.

The Polish Premier, Stanislaw Mikolajczyk, was equally unhelpful. He feared that the appearance of the Red Army on Polish soil would see the establishment of a Russian

5. For the text, see *U.S. Foreign Relations, 1943*, III, 468–71.

puppet government.[6] He asked America and Britain for political guarantees and the use of their good offices in restoring relations with Moscow. The London Poles, however, refused the territorial concessions which might make this possible. Nor were they discreet about their refusal. Instead, to London's disgust, they seemed determined to justify Molotov's policy. It was not just Katyn, though even here Churchill had bluntly asked the Poles if they could bring the dead back to life.[7] It was the general attitude. The London Poles appeared to be living in the 1920's. President Eduard Beneš of Czechoslovakia, for his effort at intelligent accommodation, was denounced by them as a tool of the Soviets. The Riga frontier was not negotiable, but German cessions were just. The Russians must be kept out of Rumania and Hungary, and the *cordon sanitaire* should be revived. American and British troops ought to be sent to Poland. Warsaw had interests in Slovakia which was described as an enemy state. She even had interests in the Mediterranean. All this interspersed, presumably for American ears, with protestations of friendship for Russia.

On October 5, Mikolajczyk had called upon Eden before the latter left for Moscow. He provided the Foreign Secretary with but one card to play in negotiating with the Russians—a mass Polish uprising against the Germans. He expressly forbade mention of the frontiers. Eden, who felt only the territorial concession afforded much chance of success, and, to be effective, should be made before the Red Army gained possession, was pessimistic.[8] Washington and

6. Edward J. Rozek: *Allied Wartime Diplomacy: A Pattern in Poland* (New York: John Wiley & Sons; 1958), p. 142. Cited hereafter as *Allied Wartime Diplomacy*.

7. "Early in April, 1943, Sikorski came to luncheon at No. 10. He told me that he had proofs that the Soviet Government had murdered the 15,000 Polish officers and other prisoners in their hands, and that they had been buried in vast graves in the forests, mainly around Katyn. He had a wealth of evidence. I said, if they are dead, nothing you can do will bring them back." Churchill, *Second World War,* IV, 759.

8. For the October meeting, see Rozek, *Allied Wartime Diplomacy,* p. 143.

the London Poles both undercut his efforts to save something from the wreck, whose approach he saw only too
clearly. It was this knowledge, perhaps, which gave Eden's
defense of Poland on the 29th an almost perfunctory quality. As he himself later put it, he "spoke his piece." He asked
for restoration of relations and offered Britain's good offices.
He mentioned the fact that the Polish Government had
requested additional arms from the Combined Chiefs of
Staff in order to step up resistance activities. What was the
Soviet view?

Mikolajczyk's inducement of a mass uprising had the
opposite effect from that intended. Molotov said he was not
a military man, but even a layman knew it was important
into whose hands arms fell. The Soviet Union desired a free,
independent, and friendly Poland. The Government-in-Exile
was unfriendly; therefore, the arms should not be sent. As
for Hull, he delivered a short speech to the effect that "when
two neighbors fell out the other neighbors, without going
into the causes or merits of the dispute, were entitled to
express the hope that these differences could be patched
up."[9] Eden pointed out that Great Britain was in the position of having treaties of alliance with both Russia and
Poland. He said Mikolajczyk had asked him to tell Molotov
of his desire to establish relations.

The Soviet Foreign Minister remained noncommittal.
There followed a brief discussion between himself and Eden
as to which Poles, the Russian-supported or those loyal to
the Government-in-Exile, were the better fighters. As General Wladyslaw Anders' British-sponsored Second Polish
Army Corps was still training in the Middle East, Eden
sounded apologetic.[1] Molotov also scored when he noted
that General Sosnkowski, Mikolajczyk's new Army Commander in Chief, had resigned from Sikorski's government

9. *U.S. Foreign Relations, 1943*, I, 668.
1. The Polish Army Corps did not go into action until March 3, 1944.
General W. Anders: *An Army in Exile: The Story of the Second Polish
Corps* (London: Macmillan; 1949), p. 161.

because of the dead Premier's friendship for the Soviet Union.[2] With this, Poland was dropped.

The last two topics mentioned were Soviet proposals concerned with a Three-Power Commission on the United Nations Organization and her request for a share in the Italian fleet. On the first, Hull favored the commission provided its existence was kept secret. Molotov and Eden agreed. On the second, Molotov remarked that the American reply was unsatisfactory. He asked if Eden had heard from London. Eden had, just that day. As might be expected, Churchill had expressed himself at some length on the subject.[3] The Russians should be offered their choice of three battleships launched between 1911 and 1913, as those of more recent vintage would be useful in the Japanese war. Even this bounty, the Prime Minister thought, might best be withheld until Eureka. The Foreign Secretary was discreet. He answered with a claim of ignorance. Molotov angrily asked why it was so hard to get replies on such a simple matter and adjourned the meeting.

Saturday, October 30, was the last formal session of the conference. In the early afternoon there were meetings of the Iranian and drafting committees. Later, Eden, Hull, and Molotov assembled at the Spiridonovka Palace for the twelfth and final plenary session. The principal feature was to be the public signing of the Four-Power Declaration.

The Iranian meeting, as might be expected, wasted everyone's time.[4] Kavtaradze had received no new instructions. He was unwilling to discuss anything. He was even less forthcoming than he had been on the 27th. His colleague Smirnov, however, possessed some of Molotov's talent for saying no in a number of different ways. Even he, though, at

2. *U.S. Foreign Relations, 1943,* I, 668, and note 28, 668. Premier Wladyslaw Sikorski was killed in a plane crash at Gibraltar during July, 1943. Stalin once said that Churchill had ordered him murdered for being pro-Russian. Milovan Djilas, *Conversations with Stalin* (New York: Harcourt, Brace & World; 1962), p. 73.
3. Churchill, *Second World War,* V, 294–6.
4. See *U.S. Foreign Relations,* 1943, I, 674–9.

one point ran out of excuses for inaction and was forced to take refuge in the allegation that the Soviet Foreign Ministry hadn't yet translated the Anglo-American proposals. After hours of fruitless struggle, the committee unanimously adopted a draft report prepared by Iliff of the British delegation. Its first sentence was a masterpiece of irony. It noted that "after an exchange of views they [the committee] detect no fundamental difference in the policy towards Iran of any of the three Governments." Although there were no differences, there would be no declaration either. In fact, the one thing Holman, Iliff, Allen, and Jernegan could show for all their work was a statement that the discussions "might be continued at Tehran." Eden, during the plenary session, was able to transform the "might" into a "would," but no one could have been sanguine about the prospects.

As this was expected to be the last day of the conference, it might be assumed that Hackworth, Strang, and Vyshinsky, who together formed the Drafting Committee, the Protocol Committee, and Hull's odds and ends group, would be concerned only with niceties of language, itself no small task. Of the original seventeen items on the agenda, only one was in finished form—the Four-Power Declaration. True, a number had been dropped entirely. These included such major questions as Hull's papers on German reparations and dependent peoples as well as Eden's draft on spheres of influence, though here the Foreign Secretary intended one last effort at resuscitation. Others, like the treatment of Germany and joint policy toward liberated France, had been referred to the London Commission for further study and, consequently, needed no special attention. But many, including the important enabling acts for the Italian and European Advisory Commissions, while approved by the Foreign Ministers, needed final touches. These they now received. Indeed, Vyshinsky reported to the Foreign Ministers in the afternoon that, with two exceptions, agreement had been reached on all documents submitted.

The two exceptions were the paper on peace feelers from

enemy states and the various proposals attempting to define political guidelines for the Italian Advisory Commission. Before the Foreign Ministers, Vyshinsky described the differences in the committee as involving only minor points. Actually, they raised major questions of policy. Probably because real rather than theoretical issues were at stake, more papers had been circulated on Italy than on any other item on the conference agenda. By the 30th, without counting either the British enabling act for an Italian Advisory Commission or the Soviet proposal on the Italian fleet, the Drafting Committee had before it no fewer than five separate drafts and memorandums dealing with the political prin-ciples of Italian occupation. These included the Soviet paper of October 22, with its accusation that the Anglo-Americans condoned the existence of Fascist organizations. It also included the various replies distributed by Hull and Eden defending military government and outlining the Combined Chiefs of Staff directives governing its acts.

On October 27 Molotov had suggested that all documents be turned over to the Drafting Committee with instructions to produce a common paper which would include a modified version of the Soviet proposal. This proved impossible. Not only did Vyshinsky refuse to remove what Hackworth and Strang regarded as censure of Eisenhower's policies from the Soviet draft, but, with the acceptance of the Anglo-American version of the Italian Advisory Commission, Vyshinsky tried to use the political directive as an instrument whereby the Soviet Union might yet obtain a significant voice in Italian affairs. He proposed an amendment to the effect that the Commander in Chief could act in the political sphere only after consultation among the three governments. As this would give the Soviet Union veto powers, Hackworth and Strang insisted that everything be referred back to the Foreign Secretaries.

The disagreement over the British draft on peace feelers from enemy states brought on Eden's last-minute efforts to revive his paper on spheres of influence. Curiously it also saw

Hackworth expressing reservations about the principle of unconditional surrender and Vyshinsky defending the Casablanca policy, with Strang taking a neutral position. On October 25 Eden had briefly mentioned peace feelers from Hungary and Rumania. With seeming casualness, he agreed to leave the Rumanian matter in Soviet hands. He also circulated a short paper calling for an exchange of information between the three governments on any future approaches.

After Castellano and the Italian surrender, Molotov was feeling far from casual. He criticized Maniu, the sponsor of the Rumanian feeler. He asked the British to refrain from any further contact, much less negotiations, with either the Rumanians or the Hungarians. The Soviet Union, he declared, supported the principle of unconditional surrender for all the smaller Axis states, including Finland, and could agree to no half measures. On Monday Hull had had no opinion. Unconditional surrender was an American policy, albeit one the Secretary disliked. Soviet approval was officially welcome. The Foreign Ministers referred Eden's paper on peace feelers to the Drafting Committee.

By Saturday, however, the Americans had changed their minds. Hackworth maintained his government could not be put in the position of recommending unconditional surrender to countries with which it was not at war.[5] Since only Finland fell into this category, Hackworth's reservations were a polite way of informing the Soviet Union of America's continuing support for that unhappy country. The British were in sympathy with the Americans on Finland. The legal niceties of unconditional surrender, however, interested them not at all. When faced with reality, as in the case of Italy, Roosevelt had been gratifyingly prompt to abandon the principle. Presumably this would be true in the future. What did disturb them was the assertion by Molotov and Vyshinsky that the Soviet Union had exclusive rights in

5. Ibid., I, 681.

Eastern Europe. Eden decided to raise again the question of joint responsibility versus separate spheres of influence.

The last plenary session began late in the afternoon of October 30.[6] Molotov wanted the first order of business to be the report of the Drafting Committee. Eden asked for reconsideration of his paper on spheres of influence instead. He was willing to drop those sections supporting confederations which had provoked the cry of *cordon sanitaire*. Eden hoped, however, that the conference would publish the opening and concluding paragraphs of his paper pledging the powers not to create separate areas of responsibility in Europe or to obstruct the right of smaller states to choose their form of government. The answer was no. Molotov questioned the raising of an issue once it had been withdrawn. Litvinov, speaking for the first and only time during the conference, believed the points were fully covered by the Atlantic Charter. He also thought the making of a special declaration would only arouse fears among the smaller powers that one or more of the Big Three intended to violate their rights. Thinking of British possessions in Asia and Africa, Litvinov delivered a final twist by asking why the draft was limited to Europe. Russian opposition was to be expected, but when it was seconded by Hull, Eden's effort became hopeless. The American Secretary said he "was agreeably disposed toward Mr. Eden's suggestion but . . . wondered whether there was sufficient time at this closing session . . . to consider the question." It was agreed that Eden's paper would be considered at some unspecified future occasion. It was not referred to London.

Molotov then called upon Vyshinsky to present the report of the Drafting Committee. Vyshinsky detailed the major point of conflict on the Italian paper, the desire of the Soviet Union to insert a statement that "the Commander in Chief would only take action in this sphere [the political] . . . on the basis of instructions from the Combined Chiefs

6. Ibid., I, 679–83; Hull, *Memoirs*, II, 1306–7.

of Staff after consultation between the three governments."[7]
Hull immediately proposed that a period be inserted after the
words *Combined Chiefs of Staff* and that the following
sentence be added: "The Three Government parties to this
declaration will at the request of any one of them consult on
this matter." It was a solid, economical piece of work, and
Molotov, whose hopes were probably few in the first place,
gave way. He was equally amiable when Eden requested that
Soviet strictures on Allied Military Government be toned
down. The papers were sent back to the Drafting Committee.
It, in turn, produced a paper in which the opening and closing paragraphs derived from the Anglo-American memorandums while the middle contained a softened version of
the Russian political proposal. The authority of the Commander in Chief was unimpaired and meaningful Soviet
participation blocked.

Hull was equally adamant on the unconditional surrender
issue. Even when Molotov went so far as to say his government would interpret the phrase to mean that the United
States would only morally support the Soviet Union against
Finland, Hull would not budge. The American Government
would not recommend unconditional surrender to Helsinki.
The Drafting Committee was instructed to make one last
effort, but if this proved unsuccessful, all reference to unconditional surrender would be stricken from the agreement,
leaving it a simple pledge that the powers would inform each
other of any contacts from their respective enemies. Unlike
Eden, Hull seemed unaware of the larger issues. He was only
preserving his government's freedom of action in Finland.
He had, in fact, blocked a Russian effort to interpose unconditional surrender between London and Budapest. Having
thwarted Eden only a few minutes earlier, Hull now had
retrieved some of the substance of the British position.

Just before tea the Foreign Ministers briefly touched on
Churchill's Declaration on German Atrocities. Molotov

7. *U.S. Foreign Relations*, 1943, I, 680.

asked if it was to be issued carrying the names of Roosevelt, Churchill, and Stalin. Hull said that this was his understanding and that the role of the Foreign Ministers was simply to make it public. These brief questions and answers, together with a short exchange on October 23, constitute the only occasions on which Hull, Eden, and Molotov considered the paper that resulted in the Nuremburg Trials. Churchill had proposed the declaration and provided the text in identical cables to Roosevelt and Stalin on October 12, 1943.[8] He hoped the threat of punishment might act as a deterrent. He suggested the Big Three meeting as the place and time of publication. With Hull en route to Moscow, Roosevelt, on October 13, sent a copy of the Prime Minister's message to Edward Stettinius, the Under Secretary of State, for comment and recommendation. Stettinius replied the same day; he was "in hearty accord" with Churchill but thought the declaration "might best be issued at the end of the Moscow Conference."[9] Roosevelt agreed, as did Churchill and Stalin when they were consulted. Thus the declaration was decided on over the heads of the Foreign Ministers. The declaration warned that there would be no repetition of the Leipzig Trials, where Germans tried and acquitted themselves for crimes committed in World War I. This time Germans guilty of war crimes would either be extradited to the countries in which the crimes took place or, in the case of so-called major criminals, they would be punished by the "joint decision of the governments of the Allies."[1] As a deterrent it failed.

Following tea the Four-Power Declaration was signed. Foo Ping-sheung, the Chinese Ambassador, had received his instructions in time. Russian and English texts were carefully compared. Klieg lights and still and motion picture equipment were set up. At 6:30 P.M. on October 30, the

8. *Stalin's Correspondence*, I, No. 204, 173–5.
9. *U.S. Foreign Relations*, 1943, I, Note 75, 557.
1. For the text released to the press November 1, 1943, see ibid., I, 768–9.

three Foreign Secretaries and the Ambassador affixed their
signatures. Hull later wrote he was truly thrilled at the his-
toric event and, as he signed, recalled "his long personal
battles on behalf of the old League of Nations."[2] Eden in
his memoirs does not mention the ceremony.

After Foo Ping-sheung and the cameramen had left, Hull,
Molotov, and Eden took up the last formal business of the
conference—the negative report of the Iranian Committee.
Eden won Molotov's approval for the continuation of discussion through normal diplomatic channels; his further
efforts to make the channels ambassadors Harriman and
Clark Kerr in Moscow failed. Hull and Molotov preferred
discussion in Tehran. It was agreed the conversations would
be kept secret. The meeting ended with an exchange of com-
pliments. Molotov thanked Eden and Hull, and Eden and
Hull engaged in a brief competition as to who could say the
nicest things about Molotov. Eden won when he proposed
Molotov as the permanent chairman of all future meetings.
Eden and Hull do not seem to have thanked each other.

2. Hull, *Memoirs*, II, 1307.

XII

RUSSIA AGAINST JAPAN,
AND THE ANGLO-SOVIET
TURKISH AGREEMENT
October 30–November 7, 1943

With the conference formally concluded, the Catherine the Great Hall of the Kremlin was the scene of a banquet given to the delegations by Marshal Stalin on Saturday night.[1] About sixty persons were present, which made the gathering intimate by Kremlin standards and greatly pleased Harriman, who took it as a sign of special favor. The display was extraordinary. Deane found the halls and table, the glitter of candles, crystal, and mirrors beautiful beyond description. Indeed, so splendid was the occasion that Deane felt it made the reception of October 20, where the service was solid gold, seem shabby by

1. For reports and descriptions of the banquet, see *U.S. Foreign Relations, 1943*, I, 685–7, 690–2; *U.S. Foreign Relations, Tehran Papers*, p. 147; Deane, *Strange Alliance*, pp. 23–5; Hull, *Memoirs*, II, 1308–11; Ismay, *Memoirs*, p. 328.

comparison. The Russians went out of their way to flatter the Americans. Hull was seated at Stalin's right, and when Deane delivered the familiar toast to the meeting of the Allied Armies in the streets of Berlin, the Soviet Premier, acting as if he had never heard it before, left his chair and passed around the entire table to clink glasses. Even Hull, although unfamiliar with the etiquette of Stalin's court, reported the Premier to be "in a most agreeable state of mind and no matter what subject was discussed, he seemed to overlook nothing that might make more clear my understanding of his situation present and prospective."[2]

Toasts and agreeable state of mind or no, Hull had to report failure in what he regarded as his principal mission for the night—persuading Stalin to go elsewhere than Tehran for Eureka. He cabled Roosevelt that he spent two hours in the effort and rehearsed all possible arguments. Stalin was unmoved; it would have to be Tehran or nothing as far as he was concerned. Stalin did repeat his offer made earlier to Eden to send Molotov to Cairo or Casablanca as his deputy. In public Hull, still hoping for Stalin, was not overly enthusiastic; in private Hull advised Roosevelt that it was most important that the invitation to Molotov be sent as otherwise the matter could become delicate. Reluctantly the Secretary decided to press the subject no further, although he remained skeptical of Stalin's arguments of military necessity. In his eyes, Stalin, for unknown reasons, simply did not want the meeting. The subject of listening devices, which Eden occasionally used as an irregular bargaining instrument when in Moscow, seems never to have occurred to Hull.

If, however, the American Secretary was unsuccessful on Eureka, he did hear news from Stalin, to use his own words, of such "transcendent importance" as to justify in itself his long trip to Moscow. Stalin promised unequivocally that as soon as Germany was defeated, the Soviet Union would join

2. *U.S. Foreign Relations, 1943,* I, 685.

in the war against Japan. Hull, who had carefully refrained from raising the subject, was astonished and delighted. Moreover, to underline his point, Stalin had arranged that the evening's entertainment include a film dealing with Japanese intervention in Manchuria in 1918. The promise was given without any mention of territorial or other compensation. It was confidential and for the President alone. Eden, although he guessed what had happened, was told nothing either by Hull or Stalin. Nor was the news about Japan the only pleasant surprise or mark of special favor Hull received. During dinner Stalin told Hull of his whole-hearted support for the Four-Power Declaration and the policy of international cooperation which it embodied. He pledged himself to the new League of Nations and a world order under law. He favored the most intimate relations between the United States and the Soviet Union. With the exception of Eureka, Hull discovered Stalin's views to be similar to his own whether the subject was political, military, or economic.

The courtship was unremitting. After dinner and before the film, Hull found himself alone with Stalin and a few others in a small anteroom. The Soviet Premier, again with no prompting from the Secretary, proceeded to allay Washington's greatest fear, the possibility of a separate Russo-German peace.[3] Using the most sarcastic terms, Stalin ridiculed all who spread such rumors. He repeated himself several times, and when Hull seconded his views, the Soviet Premier responded with enthusiasm as if to dispose of the reports effectively once and for all. Even Hull's leave-taking was made the occasion for a special display of Soviet-American amity. After the usual expressions of farewell, Stalin shook hands with the Secretary and began to walk away. Then he turned, came back, took Hull's hand, and held it

3. London was considerably more skeptical about the possibilities of a separate Russo-German peace than Washington. As Churchill told Ismay: "The hatreds between the two races have become a sanitary cordon in themselves." Ismay, *Memoirs*, p. 260.

for several minutes without saying a word.[4] For Hull, who after Pearl Harbor had not been invited to attend a single meeting of Roosevelt's War Cabinet despite many pleas on his part, it was a most impressive experience.[5] As he told a joint session of Congress on November 18: "I found in Marshal Stalin a remarkable personality, one of the great statesmen and leaders of this age."[6] It must have appeared to the American Secretary that he was better appreciated in Moscow than in Washington.

When Hull returned to Spaso House Saturday night he was in a most optimistic mood. Despite the lateness of the hour, he sent three messages to Roosevelt and also prepared a lengthy memorandum summarizing the evening's events. The news about Soviet participation in the war against Japan was handled with the greatest secrecy. Neither Harriman nor Deane was informed. The cable to Washington was kept as short as possible and went directly to the Map Room at the White House. Moreover, it was sent in two parts, each unintelligible without the other. As a final precaution against its falling into indiscreet hands, the first part went out in Navy code via Navy channels, while the Army performed the same functions for the second part. As a result, five days elapsed before Roosevelt learned of Stalin's promise.

Brevity made these messages cold and formal. However, in the third cable to Roosevelt, which dealt with the political discussions with Stalin, Hull gave expression to his real feelings, which were ones of intense satisfaction. Stalin was described as being "one hundred percent in favor of our new general forward movement of international cooperation."[7] Hull admitted failure on Eureka, but, without going so far as to recommend it, he did suggest that the President might fly to Tehran for a day or two. If this were not possible, then it

4. Hull, *Memoirs*, II, 1311.
5. Hull records that he was deeply disturbed by the almost total lack of any coordination between military and diplomatic policy in Washington. He envied Eden his position in London.
6. Ibid., II, 1315.
7. *U.S. Foreign Relations*, 1943, I, 691.

was essential Molotov be invited. In either case, collaboration with the Russians was well launched. It would be cemented by increasing military and diplomatic contact, and Hull mentioned in this regard the agreement for tripartite discussions on the form of the future United Nations organization. In due course a Big Three meeting would take place unless, as Hull put it, Stalin's "entire sincerity, including both words and acts here are false and this is incredible." The fact that except for the Japanese pledge this sincerity of words and acts was limited to declarations of general principle disturbed Hull not at all. In fact, although he did not say so to Roosevelt, Hull regarded Soviet failure to raise the boundary question as a personal compliment.[8] The conference was a success. The Russians were not "isolationists," which in the Secretary's terminology meant they did not intend to pursue unilateral policies. They were pledged by the Four-Power Declaration, by Stalin's promises, to Wilsonianism.

Eden was less enthusiastic. The Four-Power Declaration, except insofar as it meant the Americans were in Europe to stay, interested him very little. Wilsonianism frankly disturbed him.[9] No progress had been made on Iran, Poland, or Yugoslavia. Soviet views on the Balkans remained those first expressed by Stalin in December, 1941. The Premier had been personally friendly but, except for his willingness to laugh, Eden found meetings with him "a creepy, even sinister experience."[1] On the other hand, Molotov's Italian ambitions had been dampened. The Russians were reasonable about possible delays in Overlord. The European Advisory Commission, about which Eden felt nearly as warm as

8. Hull, *Memoirs*, II, 1313.
9. Eden disliked the sweeping generalizations of the Americans. He particularly feared the "academic" and "feckless" opinions of Roosevelt, whose knowledge of the geography and history of Europe in the Foreign Minister's eyes derived partly from the President's hobby of stamp collecting. Eden, *Memoirs*, II, 432–3.
1. Ibid., II, 479. The quote is from a diary entry of October 21, 1943. Eden did like Stalin's laugh and thought he looked like a bear.

Hull did toward the Four-Power Declaration, was accepted. Nor, although he learned nothing definite, was he unaware of the implications of the Soviet film on Japan. As Eden cabled Churchill: "When I came here I had no conception of how much they [the Russians] wanted this Conference to succeed. There were, of course, checks and setbacks, but general progress was cumulative and we ended at the top."[2] Eden's sense of achievement, much to the concern of Washington, was increased by events occurring after the conference had formally ended. He and Molotov signed an agreement, separate from the protocols, reversing the Quadrant decision and calling for Turkish intervention.

Eden and Hull both expected to fly out of Moscow Sunday morning, leaving final details to Clark Kerr and Harriman. The weather turned bad, however, and their trip had to be postponed. Shortly after four that afternoon, Eden called upon Hull at Spaso House.[3] There was a brief discussion of Eureka, which both men hoped somehow might be brought off, and Hull showed Eden his cable to Roosevelt summarizing the political conversation with Stalin the previous night, although he was silent about the Japanese pledge. Eden then brought up the main purpose of his visit. He had been instructed by Churchill to reopen the Turkish question and was going to see Molotov at the Foreign Ministry in a few minutes. Churchill wanted Turkish air bases and he wanted them now. Further, Eden was to meet the Turkish Foreign Minister at Cairo on November 5 because the situation in Leros had become critical.

On October 27 British Intelligence reported the presence of four thousand German Alpine troops and many landing craft in the Piraeus. Their apparent destinations were the British-held islands of Leros and Samos. London enjoyed naval supremacy in the Aegean but unfortunately was not master of the air. On the night of October 3, the Germans recaptured the island of Cos, depriving the RAF of its only

2. Ibid., II, 484.
3. U.S. Foreign Relations, 1943, I, 688–9.

forward landing strip. Churchill's pleas for support were turned down by Washington. The most he could wring from a reluctant Eisenhower were two squadrons of very long-range fighters, and even these were withdrawn on October 11. Churchill later admitted that the loss of the fighters sealed the fate of the other islands, but, at the time, he rejected the possibility of defeat. Instead of discreet withdrawal, the defending garrison was built up to four full battalions, and the Admiralty ordered in naval reinforcements, including five cruisers from Malta. Despite this effort, the lessons of Norway and Crete remained valid. The ships could operate only at night. Losses were high. The British Chiefs of Staff, meeting on the 28th, correctly judged the significance of the Alpine troops and, with the Luftwaffe unopposed, Middle East Command could neither get its men out nor hope for a successful fight. As Brooke wrote in his diary Thursday night: "Our only hope would be assistance from Turkey . . . from which air cover could be provided."[4] Eden was asked to seek immediate Soviet support in putting pressure on Ankara.

Eden tackled Hull first.[5] In light of Washington's well-publicized attitude toward the eastern Mediterranean, the Foreign Secretary feared an American effort to veto the whole project. Certainly he went out of his way to stress the limited nature of his proposals. All the British wanted was to lease a few air bases and to pass some submarines and merchant ships through the Dardanelles. Both measures had been included in the American Turkish memorandum circulated on Thursday and so could be expected to arouse a minimum of anxiety. Both were described as mild steps. No mention was made of bringing Turkey into the war. It was simply a question of retrieving the position in the Aegean. Eden asked for and received Hull's approval before talking to Molotov. Indeed, Eden cabled Churchill Sunday night

4. Bryant, *Triumph in the West*, p. 37.
5. For Eden and Hull's discussion of October 31, 1943, see *U.S. Foreign Relations*, 1943, I, 688–9.

that the American Secretary "was in favor of the line I proposed to take with the Russians."[6]

The line with Molotov that afternoon, however, involved much more than a few leased air bases and some submarines. As he also informed Churchill, Eden at one point declared to Molotov: "Our Government was in complete agreement that before the end of the year Turkey should enter the war, and that I was prepared to sign at once . . . [an Anglo-Soviet Agreement] to that effect." The change in part reflected Molotov's skill as a negotiator, but it was also true that Eden had been less than honest with Hull. Churchill was determined to reorient grand strategy. He had empowered his Foreign Secretary to say that the grant of air bases was a first step only, and if Turkish acquiescence itself did not involve Ankara in a war with Germany, Great Britain would be prepared together with the Soviet Union to demand Turkish belligerency.

For two weeks Molotov had been asking for this. In the same period Hull and Eden had remained loyal to the policies of Quadrant. Now the British Foreign Secretary adopted the Soviet view. Eden nevertheless found his task difficult. The trouble was the first step. Molotov declared that the Soviet Union could not support the British request because it was insufficient, even trivial. The powers should not waste their time with such minor matters as air bases. Turkey must be ordered to war. The failure of the British and Americans to agree to this constituted a bitter disappointment to Russia. Eden, to use his own expression, "wanted two nibbles at the Turkish cherry, first, the air bases then, the declaration of war." Eventually both compromised; Eden got his staged approach, but Molotov insisted on a formal agreement, free of equivocations, that the Soviet Union and Great Britain would bring Turkey into the

6. For Eden's report to Churchill of October 31, which covered both the meeting with Hull and the one with Molotov, see *U.S. Foreign Relations, Tehran Papers*, pp. 144–6.

war before the end of the year. Aside from political pressure, the big stick would be a cutoff of all arms and supplies for Ankara. Molotov also asked Eden if he thought Hull would be willing to make the agreement tripartite. Eden discreetly replied that he could not say for sure, and he offered to sound out the Americans.

In the evening Eden dispatched his cable to Churchill. Ostensibly, it was a report from the Foreign Secretary to the Prime Minister. A copy, however, went to Spaso House and was meant as much for American as British eyes. Hull learned: "It had been a bitter disappointment [to Molotov] that not one suggestion presented by the Russian delegation for shortening the war had been approved."[7] The Soviet Foreign Minister was quoted as describing the Turkish question as "a sore which might fester once the good effects of the Conference had worn off" and as being "pleased" upon learning the British "shared fully the Russian view." Eden even went so far as to call a satisfactory resolution of the problem "a coping stone on the Conference's work."

If not exactly subtle, the gambit was most successful. The last thing Hull wanted was a festering sore in Moscow. Far from accusing Eden of sharp practice, the American Secretary took the most moderate line compatible with his instructions while at the same time urging Washington to reverse its Turkish policy. On November 1 Hull sent Eden a brief and hurriedly written note thanking the Foreign Secretary for the copy of the cable to Churchill. It contained no words of recrimination. More significantly, Hull failed to mention the effect of Turkish intervention on operations in Italy and on the cross-channel attack, two points stressed in the American memorandum of October 28. Instead, after noting that his hands were bound, Hull said he would be "glad" to inform Washington of the "expeditious steps" now being taken by his colleagues. The American Secretary

7. Ibid., p. 145.

was equally mild when Eden called upon him Monday
afternoon to say the new agreement was nearly complete and
would, together with the conference protocol, be signed by
himself and Molotov in the evening.[8] Hull offered no objections. All he asked was for Eden to explain to the Russians
that the American delegation was not empowered to take
decisions of a military nature.

As in the case of Stalin's pledge on Japan, Hull regarded
the news about Turkey so important as to necessitate bypass-
ing his own department. The message to Roosevelt went out
in Navy code and via Navy channels.[9] The President received a copy of Eden's cable to Churchill, complete with
reference to bitter disappointments and festering sores. Hull
also included his note to Eden putting full responsibility in
Washington's hands. The Secretary of State summarized his
two conversations with Eden. He concluded with a recommendation to bring Turkey into the war and, since he was
leaving Moscow, suggested that Roosevelt empower Harriman to sign the Eden-Molotov agreement on the President's
behalf, his reason being that the British and Russians were
going ahead regardless of America's attitude.

Shortly before midnight Harriman arrived at the Soviet
Foreign Ministry carrying the protocol of the Moscow Conference, which Hull had signed earlier in the day. He was
present when Eden and Molotov agreed on the exact wording of their Turkish document. In the first two paragraphs
the United Kingdom and the Soviet Union pledged themselves to suggest to Ankara "at the earliest possible date
. . . that before the end of 1943 Turkey should enter the
war." In the third and final paragraph, the two powers
decided "a request should immediately be made of Turkey
to place at the disposal of the Allied Forces Turkish air bases

---

8. For Harriman's minutes of the November 1 meeting, see *U.S. Foreign
Relations, 1943*, I, 693–4.
9. For the full text of Hull's report, see *U.S. Foreign Relations, Tehran
Papers*, pp. 144–6.

and such other facilities as may be agreed upon as desirable by the two Governments." Molotov and Eden initialed their own paper first and then the protocol. Harriman received a copy of the Turkish agreement. Molotov hoped the Americans would make it tripartite. He was unimpressed by Washington's arguments against it and delighted that the British had seen the light. According to Harriman, the labor of two weeks, the Moscow Conference protocol with its sweeping declaration, was mentioned not at all. Harriman, making use of personal relationship with the President and the familiar Navy channels, now added his voice to Hull's. He cabled Roosevelt: "There is no doubt they [the Russians] place great importance on Turkey's entry into the war."[1]

By November 3 the weather had cleared sufficiently so that Eden and Hull were able to leave Moscow. The American Secretary was bound for Washington, where, as he proudly recorded, he shortly became the first holder of his office to address a joint session of Congress.[2] Eden's immediate destination was Cairo and a slightly more difficult audience, the Turkish Foreign Minister. Eden reached Cairo on the evening of November 4, and his troubles began immediately. A meeting was arranged with General Sir Henry Wilson, Commander in Chief, British Forces in the Middle East; Air Chief Marshal Sir Sholto Douglas, Commanding Officer, Royal Air Force in the Middle East; Richard Casey, Minister of State for the Middle East; and Sir Hughe Knatchbull-Hugessen, the British Ambassador to Turkey who himself had just flown in from Ankara.[3] The news Eden received was all bad. The most Wilson and Douglas could provide for the Turks was ten squadrons of fighters and some antiaircraft units. Knatchbull-Hugessen frankly doubted they would come in under any circum-

---

1. For Harriman's message to Roosevelt, which included the text of the Molotov-Eden agreement, see *ibid.*, pp. 147–9.
2. Hull, *Memoirs*, II, 1314–15.
3. Eden, *Memoirs*, II, 485.

stances but certainly not if this was the best their allies had to offer. Nevertheless, Eden decided to go ahead and try to push Ankara into the war.

The Turkish delegation arrived Friday afternoon, November 5. It consisted of the Foreign Minister, Numan Menemencioglu, his secretary and son, Torgut Menemencioglu, and Cvar Acikalin, Turkish Undersecretary for Foreign Affairs. The conversations extended, according to Eden, through "three days of ding-dong argument." The situation was not improved by a curious and contagious disease in the Turkish ranks—deafness. This struck the elder Menemencioglu on the first day, spread to his colleague, Acikalin on the second, and even affected the younger Menemencioglu before the meetings ended. As Eden later wrote: "No one can be so deaf as a Turk who does not wish to be persuaded."[4]

Deaf or not, the Turks presented some effective arguments. They were greatly concerned about possible Russian penetration in the Balkans, and the failure of the Moscow Conference to take any concrete decisions on the future treatment of Iran and southeast Europe made it difficult to meet the British views. Why was the Rumanian peace offer not being pursued? Eden's talk of two stages on the road to belligerency was described as nonsense. The Germans would react immediately and violently to the grant of air bases, and Turkey was weak. Did Britain want her militarily exhausted at the end of the war? Numan even voiced the suspicion Great Britain had traded Russia a free hand in the Balkans to be released from the promised cross-channel attack.

Eden denied any such bargain and declared that the lack of political guarantees was due to America's refusal to discuss frontiers until the end of the war. Turkey's best hope for the future lay in assistance to the Allied powers. Britain's need in the Aegean was urgent. Revelation of weakness did not help Eden's case, but on November 7 Hugessen delivered the threat about supplies, and the atmosphere, from

4. Ibid., II, 485.

a British perspective, slightly improved. When Numan left Cairo the following day, he promised Eden his government would give sympathetic consideration to the British proposals. He added, though, that if the Turkish response was negative, he hoped it would be received with understanding. Eden considered the outcome a draw, which was a success for the Turks.

PART FOUR

THE SEXTANT CONFERENCE

XIII

CHURCHILL TURNS TO STALIN
November 1–20, 1943

While the Foreign Secretary argued in Cairo, the Anglo-Soviet Turkish Agreement was having a serious effect in London and Washington. The prospect of Soviet support for the Mediterranean attack, more than anything else, was what brought Churchill and Roosevelt to Tehran. It reopened the old arguments on European strategy; in the end it made Stalin the arbiter of that strategy.

Prior to November 1, Churchill's enthusiasm for a Big Three meeting was nearly indiscernible. The first item on the Soviet agenda for the Moscow Conference, cross-channel attack, had seen to that. In the fall of 1943, the last thing Churchill wanted to hear was a chorus of Roosevelt, Stalin, and Marshall, all singing praises of the French coast. On the other hand, his willingness to fly to Fairbanks after Quebec

showed he would try to prevent a private gathering of his
partners. When Stalin proposed Iran and November as the
time and place for a Big Three meeting, Churchill accepted.
But after suggesting that the code name for the conference
be Eureka, the Prime Minister addressed not a single line to
Stalin on the subject. During October Churchill simply
watched Roosevelt's struggle to get Eureka's setting
changed. The Prime Minister offered Roosevelt, though not
Stalin, various alternatives to Tehran. He himself, however,
made no appeals to the Soviet Premier but waited to see
whether the President would succeed, even seeing some
humor in the situation. On October 14 he proposed to the
President that Eureka be held in Iraq and included in the
message an ironic reference to "three tabernacles in the
desert."[1] What Churchill wanted in mid-October was not
an assembly of the Big Three but a meeting of the Combined Chiefs of Staff to revise Quadrant.

Churchill first suggested a Combined Chiefs meeting, if
not its subject matter, in a message to Roosevelt on October
20. The date would be the first or second week of November, preferably no later than the 10th. The setting would be
somewhere in North Africa. The War Cabinet asked for the
conference "irrespective of whether Eureka takes place or
not."[2] Should Eureka be agreed on, Churchill desired that
the Combined Chiefs of Staff meeting precede it. Roosevelt
and Marshall had little doubt as to what was on Churchill's
mind. Within forty-eight hours the Joint Chiefs of Staff
produced a paper rejecting the Prime Minister's request and
proclaiming the sanctity of Overlord. Roosevelt, however,
was less concerned with military questions than with the
effect of an Anglo-American conference upon Soviet sensibilities. He wanted to see Stalin and would allow nothing to
jeopardize the prospect. It was Churchill's call for the Combined Chiefs of Staff conference that sent Hull to the

1. Churchill, *Second World War*, V, 307.
2. *U.S. Foreign Relations, Tehran Papers*, p. 34.

Kremlin to deliver Roosevelt's near-frantic appeal for a Big Three meeting.

The appeal went out on October 21, and Churchill received a copy. Whole generations would think it a tragedy should the Big Three fail to meet. Hull was to offer every site proposed by the Prime Minister, including the camps in the desert. The message ended with these words: "Please do not fail me in this crisis."[3] The next day, October 22, Roosevelt answered Churchill. Relations with Russia were of paramount importance. He would be happy to meet with the Prime Minister but only after Eureka. Besides, the Pentagon was busy drawing up ways and means for the defeat of Japan, and the American Joint Chiefs would need an opportunity to consider these proposals before holding a combined meeting. As Churchill later noted: "The President thus appeared to favor the idea but not the timing."[4]

The Prime Minister's answer was immediate. On October 23 he cabled Roosevelt that the Russians ought not be vexed if Americans and Britishers concerted their own joint operations. Nor would he want to see Stalin, if Eureka could ever be arranged, until this had been done. Having, at least to his own satisfaction, disposed of the question of Soviet sensibilities, Churchill proceeded to confirm Washington's worst suspicions. Present plans for 1944, according to Churchill, were open to grave defects; and German General von Thoma, currently a British prisoner, had been heard hinting that the one thing that might save Germany was a cross-channel attack. Churchill declared that he was loyal to Overlord and had the greatest confidence in Marshall, who was expected to be the operation's commander.[5] Morgan's limit-

3. *Stalin's Correspondence,* II, No. 132, 103.
4. Churchill, *Second World War,* V, 311.
5. In late September the news of Marshall's prospective appointment had been leaked to the press. Reaction was largely unfavorable. Roosevelt was even accused of giving Marshall a "Dutch" promotion. The President, who had been intending to make the announcement, pulled back. Delay and uncertainty provoked controversy within the administration and military circles. Hopkins and Stimson wanted Marshall in London as the man most

ing conditions, however, must be satisfied. Churchill wondered if this were possible within the rigid framework of Quadrant. What was needed, in his opinion, was to keep up the Mediterranean assault. The matter was urgent and should not be delayed by any Japanese studies. The Prime Minister would be available for a Combined Chiefs meeting any time after the first week of November. A copy of his "giving Russia the right hand" cable to Eden was enclosed.[6]

Hoping Hull would solve his problem for him by getting Stalin to attend Eureka, Roosevelt remained silent for the next two days; then, on October 25, London learned his decision. The President would go to Cairo, which was close to his proposed site for Eureka. The date, too, was that previously accepted by the Soviet Premier—November 20. However, Roosevelt also prepared for the collapse of Eureka. Churchill might have his Combined Chiefs of Staff meeting, but its participants, the President thought, should include Molotov throughout and, toward the close of the talks, Chiang Kai-shek. Actually, by October 25 pressure for some sort of strategic review was becoming irresistible. It was then that Roosevelt received Alexander's long and gloomy appraisal of the Italian situation. Nevertheless, as long as there was any chance, no matter how slim, of seeing Stalin, Washington wanted to avoid private talks with the British. Molotov and Chiang would serve as chaperones.

The next day, October 26, Roosevelt got Hull's pessimistic summary of his first interview with the Soviet Premier. Future generations or no, it seemed unlikely that Stalin would go beyond Tehran. Roosevelt sent Hull instructions to oppose Turkish intervention, and he cabled to

---

likely to keep Churchill on a straight course. Leahy and King argued against breaking up a winning team. Throughout October, despite some urging from Churchill, Roosevelt sniffed the wind. Marshall himself kept out of the fight, which at one point even included General Pershing at Walter Reed Hospital. For both sides, see Sherwood, *Roosevelt and Hopkins*, pp. 758–65; and Leahy, *I Was There*, pp. 190–4.

6. The State Department, for unknown reasons, has printed this cable in three separate parts. See *U.S. Foreign Relations, Tehran Papers*, pp. 38–9, 110–12; and *U.S. Foreign Relations, 1943*, I, 621–2.

London a request that the role of the Soviet delegation at Cairo be greatly increased. He asked Churchill to allow Russian military representatives to sit in on all sessions of the Combined Chiefs of Staff with full freedom not only to comment but also to make proposals of their own. This, he said, "would increase the confidence of Stalin in the sincerity of our intentions."[7]

Churchill now found himself in a most awkward position. Neither he nor Brooke had any doubts as to the reasons behind Washington's maneuvers. The Russians, although the latest signs from Moscow were confusing, could be expected to demand Overlord and nothing but Overlord. Chiang's presence meant Burma and the specter of a land war in Asia. For the moment, at least until he learned exactly where Stalin stood, Churchill considered the Russians the greater danger. On the 26th the Prime Minister cabled Roosevelt that he would be delighted to meet the President anywhere in North Africa. He hoped for a date earlier than November 20. Perhaps they and the Combined Chiefs of Staff could gather at Casablanca first, moving on to Egypt, as Churchill put it, if and when convenient. Chiang as well as Molotov might come, presumably to the Egyptian meeting. Although Roosevelt had spoken of Pacific planning, Churchill again issued a warning as to what the British wanted to discuss. He called attention to the Alexander report. The Italian battle, said Churchill, must not be allowed to degenerate into deadlock "no matter what effect is produced on subsequent operations."[8]

On October 27 Churchill addressed himself to the question of a Soviet voice in the Combined Chiefs of Staff. He deprecated the idea. The Russians would be bound by his instructions. He would, according to the Prime Minister, "simply bay for an earlier second front and block all other discussions."[9] As he had four days earlier, Churchill asked

7. Churchill, *Second World War*, V, 314.
8. Ibid., V, 247.
9. *U.S. Foreign Relations, Tehran Papers*, p. 48.

why the Soviet Union need have any say in purely Anglo-American operations. He also reiterated his fears for 1944. The one thing that mitigated these fears, according to Churchill, was the intimacy and friendship established between himself and the President and between the respective staffs. If that were broken, he should "despair of the immediate future." The right of the British and Americans to sit together was "fundamental and vital."

Although it might be fundamental and vital, the British could hardly look forward to Marshall's lectures on the sanctity of Overlord. As Brooke wrote in his diary on the 25th: "We shall have to have an almighty row with the Americans . . . with their insistence to abandon the Mediterranean for the very problematical cross-channel operations."[1] The Chief of the Imperial General Staff fully shared the Prime Minister's apprehensions, in addition to feeling a sense of personal failure. He had lacked sufficient force of character to sway the Pentagon. Proper strategy would by now have had the whole Balkans ablaze. The war, he felt, might have been ended in 1943. He regarded the coming Chiefs of Staff meeting with a sense of foreboding, even despair.

If, however, Washington remained rooted to Quadrant, Molotov in Moscow was demanding that Turkey be forced into the war. To Roosevelt, Churchill protested against allowing the Russians any role in Anglo-American planning. To Eden in Moscow went the cables complaining of Quadrant and its "lawyers' bargain." The first of these was sent October 20, the date of the Prime Minister's initial appeal to Roosevelt for a Combined Chiefs of Staff meeting. By October 27, while the President was learning how "fundamental and vital" was the relationship between Brooke and Marshall, Eden had also been given a copy of Alexander's report and been asked to tell Stalin that a delay in Overlord might be inevitable. With the Americans in their present

1. Bryant, *Triumph in the West*, p. 36.

mood, Soviet support for continued action in the Mediterranean might, and indeed probably would, be decisive.

Eden could hardly have been ignorant of the Prime Minister's purpose. He could also see that the Prime Minister was uncertain about the new course, hence the on, off, and on again messages over Turkey. The Foreign Secretary seems to have felt that Churchill was making a mistake. After his second interview with Stalin on October 27, he had warned the Prime Minister that Stalin expected his Allies to bend every effort to stage Overlord at the earliest possible date and had included the words "the confidence he is placing in our word is to me most striking." Nevertheless, he also informed Churchill that the news of a possible delay in the cross-channel attack had gone over surprisingly well. It was just at this point that the situation in the Aegean became critical. Churchill decided to go for the Russians. On October 27, while Eden was meeting with Stalin, Churchill and Smuts gave a long discourse before Beaverbrook, the one influential member of the War Cabinet who supported cross-channel operations, on the relative merits of the Mediterranean theater as opposed to Overlord. Brooke, who was present, believed it was intended to educate Beaverbrook. He also felt it succeeded. On the 28th the British Chiefs of Staff made its recommendation for Turkish air bases. By October 31 it was clear that the Moscow Conference would end with an Anglo-Soviet agreement to bring Turkey into the war before the end of the year. Churchill now became an enthusiastic supporter of Eureka.

Since it was clear that Stalin would not go beyond Tehran, Churchill had somehow to get Roosevelt to the Iranian capital. This meant he had to overcome the pocket veto problem. On November 1 the Prime Minister instructed Ismay, then still in Moscow, to go to Tehran and conduct an on-the-spot investigation.[2] Ismay was to find out exactly what the weather was like in November. Was it true

2. The cable to Ismay is quoted in Churchill, *Second World War*, V, 317.

that flying conditions between Cairo and Tehran might interrupt the transmission of documents? Churchill also wanted to know if there was a road from Tehran to Syria and how long a car would take to travel it carrying dispatches. This was important because once the transportation difficulty was solved, Churchill could convince Roosevelt of the feasibility of Eureka and bring Russian pressure to bear on the Americans.

But what if time and distance proved intractable? Churchill prepared for this eventuality as well. Indeed, he did so before hearing from Ismay. The Prime Minister sent a long cable to Roosevelt on November 2. Churchill unblushingly declared: ". . . notwithstanding what I have previously written, we [the British] ask for a triple conference with a proper Russian military delegation."[3] He still favored preliminary Anglo-American meetings; in fact, he proposed a whole series of them strung across the length of the Mediterranean. He would see Roosevelt first at Oran or Gibraltar on the 15th or 16th to discuss the general situation and the results of the Moscow Conference. The staffs would assemble at Malta on the 17th for four days of conversations with some unnamed generals, presumably Eisenhower and Alexander, who could be expected to plead the cause of Italy. Churchill and the President would join the Combined Chiefs of Staff on the 21st and then, two days later, fly to Cairo.

But it was Cairo and the Russians, not the Combined Chiefs of Staff, which Churchill now described as the main conference. Before the proper Soviet military delegation, the Combined Chiefs of Staff would lay out the whole war situation frankly and fully. It was at Cairo that "final decisions can be taken." According to Churchill, Chiang could come at the end of the Cairo Conference, on the 27th or 28th. As for Uncle Joe, Churchill hoped to wheedle him to Lake Habbaniya, or, if this failed and the weather was good, the Prime Minister and the President might fly to Tehran for a

3. *U.S. Foreign Relations, Tehran Papers*, pp. 60-1.

day. Lacking Stalin, Molotov ought to be at Cairo. Churchill closed with a glowing reference to the Moscow communiqué, which he thought presaged an eventual, even near, breach between Russia and Japan. It was clear that Churchill regarded the Russians as his allies whose "final decision" would help him overcome Marshall's opposition and nourish the Mediterranean attack. Unmentioned was that fundamental and vital right of the Anglo-Americans to determine their military policy alone.

While Churchill was making his bid for Russian support, Roosevelt continued with his own preparations. On October 27, having received the Prime Minister's approval, Roosevelt sent out the invitation to Chiang Kai-shek.[4] Like most important messages, it went via military channels and its delivery was entrusted to Stilwell rather than to the American Ambassador, Clarence E. Gauss. The Generalissimo was asked to meet with Roosevelt and Churchill in Egypt sometime between the 20th and 25th of November. The President expected the conference to last two or three days. He did not know whether Stalin would be there, but in any case the President, in his own words, intended to press "for the full-blown partnership of China, Great Britain, Russia, and the United States."

Chiang replied on October 30. The Generalissimo had little enthusiasm for a full-blown partnership with the Soviet Union. As he told Hurley, who was in Chungking trying to unravel the Stilwell-Chennault feud, he suspected that the Russians hoped either to communize all of China or to gobble up Manchuria.[5] Chiang did not include this particular piece of news in his cable to Roosevelt, but he did say he wanted to see the President before the latter met Stalin. If a meeting could not be arranged, Chiang would wait until some other time more convenient to him and Roosevelt. The Generalissimo, of course, had no objection to a private meeting with the President, nor did he oppose joint sessions

4. *U.S. Foreign Relations, China,* 1943, p. 154.
5. Ibid., pp. 163–6.

with Churchill. Here, he would willingly accept the guidance of Washington. For Roosevelt the message raised problems of its own, but at least Chiang was available.

It was not, however, the Chinese that Roosevelt really wanted to see; it was Stalin. He had received no formal reply to his plea of October 21, although Hull had informed him that its reception was chilly, and the President could not very well make a second personal appeal while the first remained under consideration. He did, though, on the 28th, instruct Hull to keep up the pressure. If Cairo or any of the other sites proved unacceptable, the Secretary should ask Stalin to fly to Basra. This, said Roosevelt, was of "supreme importance." Even a single day would do. The rest of the time Molotov could sit with Churchill and him. Indeed, so anxious was the President that on the 29th he seriously proposed to Churchill, should Stalin remain adamant, that he and the Prime Minister, together with a small staff, ought to fly to Basra themselves, meet Molotov, whose coming was assumed, and "plead with UJ to come there if only for one day."[6] Churchill, with his Moscow arrangements incomplete, replied that he was game for Basra, but since Stalin showed no signs of moving beyond Tehran, he thought Molotov might just as well come directly to Cairo.

On October 31 Roosevelt received Hull's panegyric, which was generated by Stalin's favors during the final dinner party of the Moscow Conference. The next day, November 1, he learned that the British and Russians hoped to push Turkey into the war and that the lack of this arrangement might create a festering sore in Soviet-American relations. Churchill asked for a triple conference with a Russian military delegation on November 2. That same day Roosevelt learned of Stalin's pledge to enter the war against Japan. November 3 saw a request by London for a Supreme Commander in the Mediterranean. This appointment would end the exist-

6. Churchill, *Second World War*, V, 315–16.

ing division of authority between the British in the Middle East and Eisenhower in Italy and would make Eisenhower's resources available for use elsewhere. Nor were the British the least bashful about spelling out where was "elsewhere." The new commander, in their opinion, should assume responsibility for operations in Italy and in "Greece, Albania, Yugoslavia, Bulgaria, Rumania, Hungary, Crete, the Aegean islands and Turkey."[7] Unmentioned, although very much in everyone's mind, was the expectation that when Marshall took over Overlord, Eisenhower would replace him in Washington. This meant that the new commander would be either Wilson, Alexander, or Montgomery. The Balkans would be opened up, and the man directing the campaign would be British. On November 4 Eden arrived in Cairo for his talks with the Turks. In Washington's eyes the pattern appeared complete. London, evidently with Russian support, intended to press for large-scale Mediterranean operations which would undercut Overlord.

To Roosevelt, the Four-Power Declaration, Stalin's pledge on Japan, and the general tenor of Hull's reports seemed to indicate that a turning point had been reached in Soviet-American relations. Nothing must be permitted to jeopardize this, even if it meant a major change in American military strategy. At the same time, Roosevelt was convinced that Overlord remained the surest and quickest way to end the European war. This, the Pentagon believed, meant limiting, not expanding, the Mediterranean attack. Increased operations might divert so much in the way of men and material into the Mediterranean as to transform Overlord into a problematical Rankin. Stalin had to be weaned away from his seeming enthusiasm for the Balkans. Roosevelt also wanted to establish a relationship with Stalin similar to that which he enjoyed with Churchill. There was the further necessity for an exchange of views, prohibited to

7. *U.S. Foreign Relations, Tehran Papers*, pp. 150–1.

Hull, on the touchy subject of Soviet territorial aspirations. Everything pointed to a personal meeting with the Soviet Premier.

On November 4 Harriman was instructed to dampen any Russian-American tension over Turkey. He was to sign the Anglo-Soviet agreement for an immediate grant of Turkish air bases to be followed by pressure for belligerency. This action, however, was so arranged as to remind the Russians of the interdependence of the various military theaters and of Washington's continued preference for a cross-channel assault. America's signature would be subject to the following proviso: "No . . . resources will be committed to the Eastern Mediterranean area which in the opinion of the commanders responsible are necessary for Overlord or for operations in Italy."[8]

The next day, November 5, Roosevelt addressed himself to Churchill's continuing, although much altered, request for preliminary consultation between the Americans and the British before the decisive get-together with the Russians. He wanted none of it. Churchill had spoken of meeting as early as November 15. Hull's delay in leaving Moscow enabled Roosevelt to block this meeting; he cabled Churchill on November 2 that "for many reasons it is advisable that Cordell be back in Washington while I am away."[9] Hence the earliest Roosevelt could get to Cairo, and then only "by going straight through," would be November 22 or 23.

The President hoped he would be met at the airport both by Churchill and a smiling Molotov, but, despite London's new line, the latter's presence remained problematical. Roosevelt now arranged for the attendance of at least one chaperone. He informed the Prime Minister on the 5th that he wanted to ask Chiang to get to Cairo the same day the American delegation arrived. The reason given was that General Somervell, who had just returned from an inspection trip to Chungking, believed the President and Prime

8. U.S. *Foreign Relations*, 1943, I, 698.
9. U.S. *Foreign Relations*, *Tehran Papers*, p. 62.

Minister ought to see the Chinese before the Russians. The fact that Chiang had made this a condition for coming to Cairo was unmentioned. As to any preliminary meeting between himself and the Prime Minister, the best Roosevelt could suggest was that Churchill be at Oran when the President's ship docked on the 20th, and the two of them could then fly across the desert together.

A week earlier Churchill's reaction would probably have been one of irritation. By the 5th, however, Churchill was less interested in the Combined Chiefs of Staff than in Eureka. He replied the following day accepting Roosevelt's arrangements, including Chiang's presence from the beginning of the Cairo Conference. The Prime Minister still talked of Anglo-American discussions coming first, although how Chiang was to be ignored he did not say. More significantly, Roosevelt also received a copy of Ismay's on-the-spot survey of flying conditions at Tehran. Ismay held that reports of interruptions in communications between Cairo and Tehran were exaggerated. Roosevelt's attention was also drawn to the railroad from Basra to Tehran. Churchill suggested that the President wait until he got to Cairo to shape his plans finally.

While Churchill broadly hinted that the President might yet be able to get to Tehran, Roosevelt, also on November 6, learned that Stalin would go nowhere else. Despite Hull's persistent advocacy and Roosevelt's personal appeal, the Soviet Premier, in his long delayed answer to the President's message of October 21, still found no other city more suitable. The decision as to whether Roosevelt might be able to come, said Stalin, rested entirely with the President. As usual it was his duties as Supreme Commander which prevented Stalin from going farther afield. If Roosevelt's going to the Iranian capital proved impossible, Stalin would be willing to send Molotov to any Roosevelt-Churchill meeting.[1]

On November 7 Harriman, who had been told of Stalin's

1. *Stalin's Correspondence*, II, No. 133, 104.

decision, added, probably unknowingly, his voice to those of
Churchill and Ismay. Like them, he cabled Roosevelt that
reports of adverse flying weather in and out of Tehran were
unduly pessimistic. During November, 1941, and November,
1942, only two flights had been delayed and neither for more
than twenty-four hours. He suggested that Molotov and a
Russian military delegation be invited to Cairo, with the
question of Eureka left open. Then, when the President
arrived at Cairo and if the weather was good, he and Churchill could fly on to Tehran for a brief conference with Stalin.
If the weather was bad, he could issue a public statement
that this and this alone had prevented the long-expected
gathering of the Big Three.[2]

In an earlier cable dated November 4, but apparently not
forwarded to Roosevelt until the 7th, Harriman also gave
some of the reasons why he considered a Roosevelt-Stalin
meeting, however brief, to be important.[3] The problem of
Poland, he reported, was much tougher than Washington
had previously believed. The Russians interpreted Hull's
silence on the territorial question as a tacit acceptance of
their demands. Their attitude on Finland was harsh and
uncompromising. On the whole, however, Harriman
thought prospects for Soviet-American relations were good.
Harriman described the Free Germany Committee, whose
creation had so disturbed the State Department in the
summer, as purely a propaganda device. Their German
policy, if anything, was harder than Washington's. The
flirtation with the French Committee seemed over. True,
they wanted Turkey in the war, but unlike Deane, who in
his cables to the Pentagon placed great emphasis upon
Soviet desires for immediate military assistance, Harriman
believed the cross-channel attack still came first in Moscow's
eyes. If the good effects of the Moscow Conference, which
Harriman described as a Soviet experiment in international
cooperation, were not to be vitiated, they must be brought

2. U.S. Foreign Relations, Tehran Papers, pp. 70–1.
3. Ibid., pp. 152–5.

into Anglo-American planning at the consultative stage. He believed that Molotov ought to meet with the Combined Chiefs of Staff and that Roosevelt should make every effort to see Stalin in the near future.

Perhaps Roosevelt had been merely waiting for the official reply from Stalin. Perhaps he was influenced by the news on transportation from Churchill or Harriman's estimate of the mood in Moscow. In any case, on November 8 Roosevelt cabled Stalin that he would be in Tehran by the 26th and would stay as long as the Soviet Premier wished. He also asked Molotov and a Russian military delegation to be at Cairo on the 22nd. The constitutional difficulty had been overcome and the President said: "The whole world is watching for this meeting of the three of us."[4] He "looked forward to a good talk."

Roosevelt, also on the 8th, issued the formal invitation to Chiang. The Generalissimo, like Molotov, was asked to reach Cairo by the 22nd. Chiang also learned that Churchill and Roosevelt expected to meet Stalin in Iran about the 26th. Roosevelt also preferred that the conference with Churchill and the Generalissimo precede his seeing the Russians. The President would provide accommodations and a guard for the Chinese.[5] Curiously, considering their importance, neither the message to Stalin nor the one to Chiang was seconded to London.

Chiang answered Roosevelt on November 9, saying that Madame Chiang had dysentery which might cause some delay, but if she recovered he would leave Chungking on the 18th and be with the President before his departure for Iran. Otherwise, despite his earlier pronouncements, Chiang indicated he would meet with the President and the Prime Minister after their return from Tehran. Stalin's reply to the President went out on November 10. He accepted Roosevelt's date for Eureka. He agreed to send Molotov and a military representative to Cairo by the 22nd. The cable was

4. *Stalin's Correspondence*, II, No. 134, 104–5.
5. *U.S. Foreign Relations, China*, 1943, p. 160.

short, almost curt, and contained none of the glowing phrases of the President's message.[6]

On November 11, just as Roosevelt and his party were about to leave the White House on the first leg of their long sea and air trip to Cairo and Tehran, Roosevelt received what, under the circumstances, was only a mildly expostulatory cable from Churchill. The Prime Minister had just learned from Clark Kerr in Moscow that the President intended to go to Tehran and had invited Molotov and the Soviet military advisers to appear at Cairo on the 22nd. Churchill was very glad to hear about Tehran, though, as he put it, "I rather wish you had been able to let me know direct."[7] He found the news about Molotov less pleasing. He pointed out that on the 5th Roosevelt had spoken of many meetings between the British and American staffs before they were joined by other parties. Now it appeared that not merely the Chinese but the Russians as well would be at Cairo from the start. He asked that Molotov's arrival be postponed until the 25th at the earliest.

Roosevelt delayed his departure in order to dictate a reply. He claimed that as far as his going to Tehran was concerned, he had not informed the Prime Minister solely because of his uncertainty as to whether Stalin really wanted Eureka. With regard to Cairo, the President expressed himself fully and openly. He told Churchill:

> I have held all along—as I know you have—that it would be a terrible mistake if UJ thought we had ganged up on him on military action. During the preliminary meetings in Cairo the Combined Staffs will, as you know, be in the planning stage. That is all. It will not hurt you or me if Molotov and a Russian military representative are in Cairo, too. They will not feel they are being given the "run-around"![8]

The President, too, though for different reasons, was making the Soviet Union the arbiter of Anglo-American strategy.

6. *Stalin's Correspondence*, II, No. 135, 105.
7. Churchill, *Second World War*, V, 317–18.
8. *U.S. Foreign Relations, Tehran Papers*, pp. 79–80.

Churchill could hardly have been surprised by Roosevelt's answer. In fact, Churchill anticipated it and had already devised and set in motion an effective counter. While the President was being asked to do the obviously impossible—withdraw the invitation to Molotov—Churchill for the first time in over a month sent a personal message to Stalin. Feigning partial ignorance of Roosevelt's arrangements, Churchill informed Stalin that the Combined Chiefs of Staff would meet in Cairo on the 22nd for, as he put it, "domestic and Far East discussions," and that among the participants would be "Chiang Kai-shek himself and a Chinese military delegation."[9] He hoped Molotov could come to Cairo on the 25th. He was happy to learn the President was willing to fly to Tehran, which Churchill claimed to have pressed him to do for a long time.

The effect was immediate. Until the arrival of Churchill's cable, Stalin had no idea Chiang would be at Cairo. Neither, for that matter, did Harriman. When Molotov pressed for a Cairo agenda, the best the American Ambassador could say was that he thought it would involve Turkey and the Dodecanese. Harriman asked Roosevelt for more information, but the President remained discreetly silent. He wanted both Chiang and Molotov even though he was aware of the danger involved for the Russians in attending an Asian conference with Chiang. Perhaps Roosevelt intended to jeopardize Soviet-Japanese relations. Perhaps he thought Tokyo would overlook the affront. In any case, Moscow, as Churchill probably anticipated, hastily backed away from Cairo. The one thing, aside from the Anglo-Americans' dropping out of the war, that might bring about Russian defeat was a Japanese attack in Manchuria. Nor need the Japanese go so far to injure seriously the Soviet war effort; 50 percent of the lend-lease aid the U.S.S.R. received crossed the Pacific in Russian bottoms unmolested by the Japanese fleet.

Considering the provocation, Stalin's reaction was surpris-

9. *Stalin's Correspondence*, I, No. 205, 175.

ingly mild. He cabled Roosevelt and Churchill "that due to some reasons, which are of a serious character, Mr. Molotov, unfortunately, cannot come to Cairo." He added: "It goes without saying that in Tehran a meeting of only three heads of Governments is to take place. . . . And the participation of representatives of any other countries must be absolutely excluded."[1] Churchill's and Roosevelt's answers were delayed, Churchill having left Plymouth with his staff aboard the battle cruiser *Renown*, while Roosevelt was at sea in the battleship *Iowa*. Both were observing radio silence, but it was clear that Roosevelt had overreached himself. Churchill, in a cable which arrived in Moscow November 15, said he understood Stalin's position. Roosevelt, on November 20, wished Molotov a speedy recovery from an illness that had never been mentioned.

1. *Stalin's Correspondence*, I, No. 207, 176; II, No. 136, 106, No. 137, 106.

XIV

THE CHINESE STORY
November 22–27, 1943

Despite the intense maneuvering which preceded it, the Cairo Conference itself was indecisive. During the five days it lasted, Roosevelt, who looked forward to the coming meeting with Stalin with all the enthusiasm of a small boy, tried to avoid Churchill. He conferred repeatedly and at length with the Chiangs. He closeted himself with all available non-British notables, including Vyshinsky, who was on his way to join the Mediterranean Commission and refused to be drawn into any substantive discussions. He received state visits from King George of Greece, King Peter of Yugoslavia, and, since Farouk was incapacitated by an automobile accident, Sir Ahmad Mohammed Hassenein Pasha, Chief of the Egyptian Royal Cabinet. It was the President and not, as Churchill had hoped, the Generalissimo who went out to see

sunset on the pyramids and listened to a native guide detail
their history. Twice he dined alone with such intimates as
Leahy and "Pop" Watson. Only once during the five days
did Churchill see the President more or less alone. This was
at a luncheon Tuesday, November 23, and even then Roosevelt contrived to have Sara Oliver, Churchill's daughter,
included among the guests. "Winston," as Eden dryly
noted, "had to play the role of courtier and seize opportunities [for serious discussion with Roosevelt] as and when
they arose."[1] The President saw to it that the opportunities
were few indeed.

But if Churchill watched his success in keeping Molotov
away being negated by Roosevelt's charming country gentle-
man style and the distractions of the Chinese story which, as
the Prime Minister later expressed it, "was lengthy, complicated, and minor," it was also true that Brooke and the other
members of the British Chiefs of Staff, presumably acting
under the Prime Minister's instructions, did remarkably
little about it.

The Americans came to Cairo in their usual fighting
mood. They had no doubts the British were out to torpedo
Overlord or, rather, to reduce it to the status of Rankin and
then make the latter operation possible by dissipating and
exhausting German strength through attacks in Italy and the
Balkans. This was not just a question of ancient history or
the Prime Minister's reiteration of familiar fears. The Anglo-
Russian agreement of November 2 was a flagrant violation of
the Quadrant accords. The British proposal of November 3
concerning unity of command in the Mediterranean also
contradicted Quadrant by naming Rumania, Bulgaria, and
Hungary as sites for future operations. The day before the
American delegation left Washington Stimson addressed a
memorandum to Hopkins literally praying that Hopkins
would keep Roosevelt steadfast for Overlord.[2] Even Marshall, who was inclined to give the British the benefit of the

1. Eden, *Memoirs*, II, 491.
2. Sherwood, *Roosevelt and Hopkins*, p. 766.

doubt, announced during a meeting with Roosevelt while crossing the Atlantic that if Brooke insisted on the Balkans, the Americans, as King had long argued, should pull out of Europe and go for Japan. Roosevelt in reply asked the key question: What about the Russians? They might demand a Danubian attack. Marshall became equivocal and talked of air support for any Soviet offensive in Rumania, but he did insist the time had come to see what he called the "Balkan matter" settled once and for all.[3]

The American agenda for Cairo was prepared in this spirit of belligerency. It began with a reaffirmation of the overall strategic concept of the war—Germany first, then Japan. The second item, presented in nine sections, boiled down to Overlord versus the Mediterranean. The Far East, Chiang's presence or no, ranked third on the list. Much to the Americans' surprise, however, Brooke at the opening meeting of the Combined Chiefs of Staff in Cairo suggested a change in sequence.[4] He believed plans for Southeast Asia ought to come first. Later the Combined Chiefs of Staff could turn to Europe so that, as Brooke put it, "if possible, operations there might be considered before meeting with the Russians."

War Office interest in matters Chinese constituted a revolution. Moreover, as Brooke well knew, the Combined Chiefs of Staff was no instant calculating machine. Conclusions came through slow, if sometimes heated, deliberation. The Americans were offering just the sort of strategic review the British claimed they wanted. Brooke, with the Russians only four days away, proposed instead to lead his colleagues into the muddy waters of the Irrawaddy River. Without consulting Marshall, Admiral King, who was always ready to talk about the Far East, accepted the British suggestion on behalf of the Joint Chiefs of Staff. Chiang's presence required an examination of the Chinese theater, but it was Brooke who made it the Combined Chiefs of Staff's first

3. *U.S. Foreign Relations, Tehran Papers*, pp. 259–60.
4. For the minutes of the meeting, see ibid., pp. 304–7.

order of business. Having put it first and considering the complexities of the issues and the nature of the personalities involved, Brooke could scarcely have been surprised when the Hump, Burma, and the Indian Ocean dominated the conference. Indeed, out of the four working days for the Combined Chiefs of Staff at Cairo, two were spent arguing about Burma. It seemed the British had brought Marshall to Egypt to prepare instructions for Mountbatten.

The two Chinese days, as Brooke called them, were November 23 and 24. The 23rd began with a plenary session;[5] Roosevelt acted as chairman. Present aside from the President, Prime Minister, and the Generalissimo were the Combined Chiefs of Staff, Madame Chiang and three Chinese generals, Mountbatten together with his ill-assorted colleagues Stilwell and Chennault, and Roosevelt's Special Assistant, Harry Hopkins. After welcoming Chiang, Roosevelt explained that the purpose of the meeting was to hear Mountbatten's plans for reopening the Burma Road. Mountbatten's plan, worked up in the previous four weeks, called for the conquest of North Burma before the May, 1944, monsoon. It involved a four-pronged offensive starting in February. There were to be three attacks across the India-Burma frontier: one in the south based on Chittagong, one in the center at Imphal, and one in the far north from Ledo. At the same time, Chiang was to commit his Yunnan Army to an advance down the Burma Road. Two of the columns, the Chittagong and the Imphal, were Anglo-Indian. One, the Ledo force, was mixed and included Britishers, Indians, Chinese, and a small number of Americans. The Yunnan Army was Chinese with American advisers. Hopefully, before the monsoon ended the campaigning season, there would be a linkup of the Ledo and Yunnan forces.

This in itself would not restore land communications with China. Subsequent operations might be directed to gaining the railway from Rangoon to Lashio; this railway had served

5. For the minutes of the plenary meeting, see ibid., pp. 311–5.

as a feeder to the Burma Road until its capture by the Japanese in March of 1942. Alternately, American engineers could push a new road through the mountains and jungle of North Burma linking Ledo to Lashio. Until either or both were accomplished, China, as she had for over a year, remained dependent upon the trickle of supplies flown in over the Hump—a trickle which for all the efforts put into it amounted to less goods per month than could be transported by a single freighter. But these decisions lay in the future. Mountbatten addressed himself solely to the immediate operation—code name Champion. He asked for Chiang's approval. The Generalissimo said he would have to see the plan illustrated on a map before answering, whereupon Mountbatten concluded his part of the meeting by repeating the pledge first given at Trident and reaffirmed at Quadrant to do everything possible to get ten thousand tons a month into Chungking by air. He hoped to achieve this figure in March or April.

It was now Churchill's turn to speak. Chiang had always refused to commit himself to any campaign in Burma unless his allies could guarantee Japan's inability to reinforce the theater. This, in turn, meant the Allies must secure naval supremacy in the Bay of Bengal and be able to interdict by air Japanese communications extending northward up the Irrawaddy River. The symbol of supremacy, the base for the bombers, was to be an amphibious operation somewhere in the Bay of Bengal. This operation had been discussed at Trident and Quadrant. To this end, though they were the horseshoe nails for the Allies in 1943, Mountbatten had been supplied with six attack transports and eighteen Landing Ship Tanks (LSTs).[6]

Though there was seeming agreement that an attack should be made, no decision had yet been taken as to where. Churchill at Quadrant had been all for his "Torch of the Pacific," Culverin, the invasion of northern Sumatra. Al-

6. The figures are given in Greenfield, *Command Decisions*, p. 193.

though it had never been ruled out. Culverin evoked no particular enthusiasm in either the Pentagon or on Great George Street. Brooke felt it called for more resources than were available. Washington suspected Culverin would be followed by Singapore and imperial revenge rather than by Rangoon and supplies for China.[7] Combined Chiefs of Staff planners had come up with two smaller operations. One was a landing on the Burmese coast at Akyab, which was not far from Chittagong and was capable of fairly rapid reinforcement. On the other hand, it would not put bombers much closer to the vital Rangoon-Mandalay railroad than they were already. The second operation, an attack on Ramree Island, reversed the situation. It was far from Chittagong and near Rangoon. Its capture would provoke a strong Japanese response, and, unfortunately, Ramree was so close inshore it could be reached by lighters. Ramree might become a trap for the Allies if relieving columns became mired in the jungle.

In November Mountbatten put forth a new suggestion, the taking of the Andaman Islands—Operation Buccaneer. From the Andamans it would be possible to strike at Rangoon and attack Japanese naval traffic through the Malacca Strait. Moreover, since the islands were two hundred miles from the nearest coast, they could be defended by air and sea power alone. The Japanese garrison was estimated at five thousand men. Ordinarily this was just the sort of plan to appeal to Churchill. It involved the intelligent application of sea power. No options were closed because the Andamans could be used as much against Malaya as against Burma. Buccaneer was also the handiwork of a man Churchill patronized. In its dash it rivaled American Pacific operations, of which the Prime Minister was more than a little jealous. But these were not ordinary times. On November 17, while traveling to Cairo, Churchill learned that the British garrison on Leros had been overwhelmed. Two days earlier, when

---

7. Sherwood, *Roosevelt and Hopkins*, p. 773.

it was apparent the British were going to lose their gambler's bid, Ankara had formally rejected Eden's proposals.[8] What was needed was a show of force. Middle East Command had the men; what it lacked was the shipping. On October 23 the British Chiefs of Staff had urged Mountbatten to make good use of his amphibious circus. When Mountbatten arrived at Cairo, he found that Churchill and the British Chiefs of Staff wanted his circus for the Mediterranean.

If Chiang learned of this, he might pull out of Champion. Chinese nonparticipation would reduce the operation to a series of meaningless raids, and that in turn would produce explosions in Washington. Churchill's solution, not a very happy one, was to tell Chiang that some amphibious operation was being planned and at the same time have Brooke oppose Buccaneer in the Combined Chiefs of Staff. It speaks volumes for the importance of landing craft in the fall of 1943 that, with much greater issues at stake, Churchill was willing to provoke the Americans for the sake of eighteen vessels; but then it was just possible that the eighteen might bring Turkey into the war.

Churchill, in what amounted to a speech at the plenary session, now stressed to Chiang the magnitude of Champion and particularly the India-based portion of the offensive, which involved more than 320,000 men. He was optimistic as the Allies enjoyed qualitative and numerical superiority, but, in obvious reference to Chungking's reputation as a leaking sieve, the Prime Minister called for the utmost secrecy. After this introduction Churchill turned to the heart of the matter, at least in Chiang's eyes—the naval situation in the Bay of Bengal and the promised amphibious attack. According to Churchill, preparations for the latter were going ahead full speed, although final plans were yet to be decided. Reticence about Buccaneer, however, was compensated for by glowing references to the future of the British fleet in Indian waters. At Arcadia this theater was assigned

8. Eden, *Memoirs*, II, 490.

to London. Past performance had been poor. Since 1942 Japan had ruled the Burmese seas with a small force of cruisers. A roughly equal British squadron based in Ceylon never met the challenge because it was always dispersed in convoy duty. Churchill said this would be changed. The Admiralty intended to concentrate in the Bay of Bengal a force of no less than five battleships, four armored carriers, and twelve auxiliary carriers, together with escorting cruisers and destroyers. Considering the pressure being exerted by the Americans in the Pacific, the Prime Minister felt the fleet sufficient to assure naval supremacy.

Chiang was experienced enough at negotiation to wonder why a subordinate presented the land campaign while the Prime Minister himself talked about naval matters. A little questioning elicited the reason. Churchill's armada would not arrive until late spring or early summer, whereas Champion was scheduled for early February. With a nominal strength of 320 divisions, China possessed the largest army of any of the United Nations. Unfortunately, this was largely a paper army, which in the polite language of the Joint Chiefs of Staff "had deteriorated considerably since 1938."[9] The divisions at Ledo and the Yunnan Army were the only real force Chiang possessed. Not unnaturally, he was fearful for his troops. Chiang insisted that success in Burma depended upon simultaneous land and sea operations. Churchill denied this and maintained that the Japanese supply routes for Burma were the road and rail systems of the Malay peninsula. As neither would give way, Roosevelt ended the plenary session by suggesting that the question be referred to the Combined Chiefs of Staff. He invited the Generalissimo to attend.

The Combined Chiefs of Staff met at 2:30, and although the first paper considered was entitled "The Role of China in the Defeat of Japan," Chiang was not present.[1] The Generalissimo, after several changes of mind, elected to stay

9. *U.S. Foreign Relations, Tehran Papers*, p. 242.
1. For minutes of the meeting, see ibid., pp. 316–22.

away. Instead, he sent a military delegation headed by Shang Chen, Director of the Foreign Affairs Bureau of the Chinese General Staff. The Combined Chiefs of Staff were pleased by Chiang's absence as it gave them the opportunity to review the Chinese and Burmese theaters in private while Shang Chen waited outside—a procedure which could never have been followed had Chiang himself been present.

The paper on China had been prepared by Stilwell, acting in his capacity as the Generalissimo's Chief of Staff. It was then, in theory, a Chinese paper. It had been circulated the previous day, and in the present discussion it was quickly apparent that nobody except its author liked it. The opening paragraphs, which dealt with Champion, the training and equipping of the Chinese Army, and the B-29 bomber program, caused no dissension. All of this had been agreed at Quadrant. However, after discussing the launching of B-29 attacks, Stilwell went on to recommend the recapture of Canton, Hong Kong, Shanghai, and Formosa. This constituted a ground war in Asia, and Brooke rejected it out of hand. He was supported not only by Cunningham and Portal but also by Leahy, who was worried about logistics. Arnold believed air power could defeat Japan alone. Marshall and King hoped to encourage Chiang's new interest in fighting the Japanese, but no one favored a ground war. Stilwell later wrote that he was disgusted with war by committee.[2] The Combined Chiefs agreed to reaffirm the Quadrant decisions but also agreed that China's future role required further study.

The Combined Chiefs of Staff next turned to Buccaneer and immediately found themselves involved in a quarrel which was to dominate the Cairo Conference. Stilwell voiced the opinion, unfortunately not listened to, that Chiang would be satisfied with Allied naval supremacy in the Bay of Bengal alone and that the amphibious attack could be dropped. Mountbatten, although in a muted voice,

2. White, *Stilwell Papers*, p. 247.

defended Buccaneer. King became its enthusiastic champion. He also maintained that if Buccaneer were abandoned, Mountbatten's LSTs ought to go to the Pacific. Here was the real issue, and Brooke dug in. He would accept neither Buccaneer nor the Pacific reallocation because Mountbatten's ships might bring Turkey into the war. The Combined Chiefs of Staff divided along national lines. King and Brooke had a row, and compromise proved impossible.[3] It was agreed to postpone any decision. From a British viewpoint, the whole affair was most unfortunate as Buccaneer now became a fighting issue blown up out of all proportion. What was worse was that it was unnecessary. Stilwell, who was in the best position to know, said Chiang would go along with naval reinforcements alone. Brooke had blundered badly; instead of arguing with King, he should have supported Stilwell. Unfortunately, Brooke appears to have expected a fight and so provoked one; moreover, Brooke was contemptuous of Stilwell's abilities.

Perhaps aware he had made a mistake, Brooke turned his colleagues' attention to the calmer waters of an American proposal for a United Chiefs of Staff. Impressed by the success of Moscow, Roosevelt had suggested that the Russians be admitted as regular members of the Combined Chiefs of Staff. Neither Marshall nor Brooke liked the idea. The Britisher was inclined to let sleeping dogs lie. Marshall, however, wanted to have a fall-back position in case, as he put it, "pressure was exerted."[4] This was to be the United Chiefs of Staff. Everyone thought it a good idea to keep in mind and all hoped it would not prove necessary.

With the proper atmosphere restored and a further agreement that as far as tonnages over the Hump were concerned, a little bit of realism was required, Brooke invited the Chinese delegation into the room. They were supposed to be bringing Chiang's reaction to Champion. What ensued,

3. Bryant, *Triumph in the West*, pp. 51–2; White, *Stilwell Papers*, p. 245.
4. *U.S. Foreign Relations, Tehran Papers*, p. 320.

even in Stilwell's opinion, was a fiasco.[5] Brooke made a short speech of welcome and asked for Shang's views. There followed a long silence punctuated by whisperings in Chinese. Finally, General Chu, Military Attaché from Washington, rose to his feet and said his colleagues were unprepared.[6] He asked for a second meeting the following day. Mountbatten, Stilwell, Chennault, and Stratemeyer, united for once, came to the aid of their Chinese colleagues and proceeded to fire questions and answers at each other, but there was no disguising the poor impression made. Stilwell subsequently produced a prompter's list, regrettably anti-British, for Shang Chen. Brooke, however, was confirmed in his opinions as to the quality of the Chinese Army, and even Marshall was shaken. If this was the best of the Chinese General Staff, little could be expected in their theater.

Wednesday, November 24, also began with a plenary session.[7] This one was exclusively Anglo-American, and with Eureka only seventy-two hours away, Roosevelt and Churchill began to face up to the real issues. Roosevelt opened the meeting with the frank statement that although he favored preliminary consideration of operations in Europe and the Mediterranean, all final decisions must be made at the conference with Stalin. Without naming names—although since both Harriman and Deane were present their identity was no secret—Roosevelt admitted he had received conflicting advice as to what the Russians really wanted and, evidently, were going to get. Some argued that Stalin desired only Overlord. Others held he wanted both Overlord and the Mediterranean. Roosevelt felt it was almost certain Stalin favored the second course. If so, there then arose the very real problem of whether Overlord could retain its integrity while the Mediterranean attack was pursued. Roosevelt was equally frank about Turkey. The Germans, he held,

5. White, *Stilwell Papers*, p. 245.
6. Bryant, *Triumph in the West*, pp. 54–5; Ismay, *Memoirs*, p. 336.
7. For the minutes of the meeting, see *U.S. Foreign Relations, Tehran Papers*, pp. 329–34.

could go nowhere from the Dodecanese. On the other hand, if Turkey entered the war the whole situation would be changed. Again Roosevelt implied that it was for Stalin to say what should be done. It was a fair expression of the President's stand. Certainly he would defend Overlord and was against any new ventures in the Mediterranean, particularly the eastern Mediterranean; but Stalin's voice would be decisive.

Churchill was equally candid. He spoke briefly about the golden days of Torch and Alamein, of Sicily's capture and Mussolini's fall, but this was followed by a long and gloomy survey of the events of the last two months as viewed in London.[8] Although he specifically denied the charge, the Americans were convinced they were hearing the demise of Overlord and the substitution of a problematical Rankin. Churchill said he had agreed to the troop withdrawals from Italy with a heavy heart, and the result was that the Allies had bogged down and failed to take Rome. This failure, in turn, discredited the Badoglio government, for the master of Rome was the master of Italy. It also meant no north Italian airfields and therefore hindered Pointblank, the combined bomber offensive. According to Churchill, a brilliant campaign was wasting away.

Passing across the Adriatic to Yugoslavia, Churchill lavished praise on Tito's Partisans. They were described as holding down as many Germans as Eisenhower. On the other hand, the Germans had recently regained the initiative. The Partisans lacked supplies, and here Churchill put in a brief plea for unity of Mediterranean command. Eisenhower, he said, had the forces but not the responsibility to assist the Yugoslavs. It was, in the Prime Minister's opinion, another case of opportunities being lost. The Dodecanese situation was also a sad story, but Churchill hoped to retrieve it through Turkish intervention. He thought the Russians would share his views. Turkey at war meant the

8. Churchill, *Second World War*, V, 333–4.

opening of the straits. It would have an immediate and profound effect on Hungary, Rumania, and Bulgaria. The price, according to Churchill, would be two divisions and a few landing craft. Although the words were not unexpected, Hopkins became alarmed.[9] The Americans saw the Eden-Molotov agreement, on the one hand, and their troops fighting in the Transylvanian Alps, on the other. Churchill's combination of two divisions as the sole price for gaining Turkey, Hungary, Rumania, and Bulgaria only added insult to injury.

Turning to Asia, Churchill did not even mention Buccaneer, nor did he make any reference to Champion. Instead, he noted that resources were insufficient for Culverin (operations against Sumatra). It might be best, therefore, to divert Mountbatten's landing craft to the Mediterranean for use in an assault on Rhodes. He summed up his program as "Rome in January, Rhodes in February, supplies to the Yugoslavs, a settlement of the [Mediterranean] Command arrangements and the opening of the Aegean, subject to the outcome of an approach to Turkey."[1] All this Churchill called preparatory to the knockout blow—Overlord. As for Overlord, the Prime Minister urged the buildup go forward, but he reminded his audience that the timing of the cross-channel attack depended more on "the state of the enemy than on the set perfection of our preparations."[2] To the Americans it sounded like Rankin. The British would cross the Channel only when there were no Germans on the other side.

If this were truly the British program, then it should have been presented at Quadrant. By November, unless Brooke performed miracles of persuasion, only one man could give it substance—Stalin. In his reply Roosevelt plainly showed this was what he feared would happen. The President pointed out that at their present rate of advance the Russians would

9. Sherwood, *Roosevelt and Hopkins,* pp. 775–6.
1. Churchill, *Second World War,* V, 334.
2. *U.S. Foreign Relations, Tehran Papers,* p. 333.

soon arrive at Rumania. Stealing Churchill's phrase, Roosevelt asked the Combined Chiefs of Staff to consider what answer it would give if Stalin suggested "a junction of our right in the Mediterranean with their left in Rumania." He also thought it possible that the Russians might desire an amphibious operation at the top of the Adriatic to aid Tito.[3]

Roosevelt expressed no opinion on Rhodes. He did, however, read some figures which showed the numerical superiority in land, sea, and air which the Americans would enjoy over the British in 1944.[4] The unspoken implication was that the side contributing the most men should determine their employment. The Joint Chiefs of Staff had also devised a counter to the British proposal for unity in the Mediterranean. They proposed to enlarge the authority of the American cross-channel general to include supervision of all operations against Germany. Roosevelt was silent on the proposal itself, but he dropped some hints. He called for a single commander for American bomber forces from London to Ankara, and he mentioned the magic name of Foch.

Either Churchill was remarkably sensitive, or he had received advance warning from Dill. About statistics the Prime Minister could do nothing, although he was painfully aware that the British had passed their peak in mobilization and were slipping into the role of junior partner vis-à-vis the United States and the Soviet Union, but he was certainly not going to permit Marshall to run the European war more or less on his own. He was, however, as indirect as the President. He merely noted that the Combined Chiefs of Staff worked quite well under existing arrangements.[5] With this exchange, if anything so ephemeral can be called an exchange, the meeting petered out. Roosevelt remarked that

3. Ibid., pp. 333–4.

4. The exact numbers are not given in the Combined Chiefs of Staff minutes, but in a meeting on November 19, aboard the *Iowa*, the Joint Chiefs of Staff told Roosevelt the United States would by January of 1944 have a military establishment of 11 million men, compared with Britain's 4.5 million. Ibid., p. 249.

5. Ibid., p. 334.

Chiang had territorial ambitions which included both Man-churia and Korea. Churchill repeated his often-made pledge to the war against Japan. He also complimented Roosevelt on the performance of the American daylight bombers over Germany. Both invited the Combined Chiefs of Staff, if possible, to come up with some agreed views on Europe before Eureka. The request was not entirely a formality, but Eureka was only three days away, and the Combined Chiefs of Staff were still mired in Burma. Nor were any additional plenary sessions scheduled for Cairo. The next time Churchill and Roosevelt sat together with the Combined Chiefs of Staff, it would be in the presence of Stalin.

Despite the injunction to turn their attention to matters European, the 129th meeting of the Combined Chiefs of Staff Wednesday afternoon was, with two exceptions, an-other Chinese day.[6] The two exceptions, coming at the very beginning, involved Marshall's proposal for a United Chiefs of Staff and a military agenda for Eureka. Brooke had recon-sidered the United Chiefs of Staff idea and decided to oppose it. He felt it better simply to invite Russian and Chinese representatives to all future meetings of the Sextant variety. He feared that even in a watered-down form the United Chiefs might attempt to usurp the authority of the Combined Chiefs of Staff. King and Leahy again warned of political pressure, but, since nobody wanted the Chinese and Russians in anyway, it was agreed to drop the plan.

Consideration of a Eureka agenda should have brought Anglo-American differences about European strategy out into the open, but not the way Brooke handled it. He described Eureka as primarily a political meeting, and, there-fore, a formal military agenda would be unnecessary. The Combined Chiefs of Staff would just deal with what was referred to them by the Big Three. For the Americans the idea of no agenda at all was too vague. Leahy agreed that Eureka would be primarily political, but he felt it might be

6. For minutes of the meeting, see ibid., pp. 335–45.

wise for the Combined Chiefs of Staff to have a few things
in mind for discussion with the Russians. He mentioned
shuttle bombing. It was decided to leave the agenda question open, but certain broad topics were defined, including
coordination of operations, Turkey, and supply problems.

The Combined Chiefs of Staff now returned to Southeast
Asia. Marshall had had lunch with Chiang. He reported that
the Generalissimo wanted Champion widened to include
the capture of Mandalay. Chiang also demanded that the
Burmese attack be coordinated with Buccaneer. Without
Buccaneer, Chinese forces would be withdrawn from Champion. Even with Buccaneer, the Chinese could not advance
beyond Lashio. In short, Mountbatten was to take North
Burma, Mandalay, and the Andamans within the next six
months. Nor was this all. Chiang regarded the ten thousand
tons per month over the Hump as sacrosanct.[7] The program
was too preposterous for discussion. Marshall suggested that
Mountbatten call on Chiang and explain that his own plans
represented a safe and conservative first step.

The fact that it was a first step, however, worried Mountbatten. He pointed out that Champion was not a complete
operation. When the monsoons broke in October, 1944,
Mountbatten would have to either advance against Mandalay and South Burma or pull back to India. He asked the
Combined Chiefs of Staff to consider as soon as possible
how to provide the necessary forces. Since both Brooke and
Marshall believed the fall of 1944 would find the Anglo-
Americans involved in an all-out war in Europe, though they
differed as to where, the most the Combined Chiefs of Staff
would do was to take note of Mountbatten's apprehensions.
Having described the military aspirations of Chungking,
Marshall turned to one of Chiang's political desires. Chiang
wanted the frontiers of Southeast Asia Command redrawn
so as to put Thailand and Indochina under his control.
Mountbatten expressed the blunt opinion that the peoples

7. White, *Stilwell Papers*, pp. 245–6.

involved were considerably more suspicious of Chinese than of Anglo-American intentions. It was agreed to defer action on Chiang's request.

The Combined Chiefs of Staff were now joined by the Chinese military delegation and their American advisers. Having spent most of the previous evening being coached by Stilwell, General Shang was no longer inarticulate.[8] He asked detailed questions about Mountbatten's dispositions; the questions, however, dealt entirely with Anglo-Indian operations, and after answering a few of them, Mountbatten inquired whether Shang was trying to impugn the fighting qualities of British troops. Shang was also insistent on the ten thousand tons, which provoked the ire of Marshall. He told Shang that what the Chinese ought to be concerned with was the struggle for Burma. Brooke considered the whole business an utter waste of time. Shang was asked to arrange a meeting between Mountbatten and the Generalissimo. In the words of the Secretariat, "the Combined Chiefs of Staff noted with interest the Chinese views," and with this Brooke adjourned the meeting.

It was not until Thursday, November 25, that the British and Americans finally got down to the supposed purpose of Sextant—discussion of European strategy. This was during the 130th meeting of the Combined Chiefs of Staff, the fourth of the Cairo Conference and the last one before Eureka.[9] Even so, nearly a third of the session was again taken up by Southeast Asia, despite the fact that the Combined Chiefs eschewed the controversial issue of Buccaneer.

Brooke opened the meeting by asking Mountbatten to report on the results of his conversations with Chiang. Mountbatten, who had been accompanied by the Prime Minister and the Foreign Secretary, said the Generalissimo appeared to be willing to go ahead with Champion.[1]

8. White, *Stilwell Papers*, p. 245.
9. For minutes of the 130th meeting, see *U.S. Foreign Relations, Tehran Papers*, pp. 346–9.
1. Eden, *Memoirs*, II, 491.

Mountbatten admitted that Chiang had started out demanding Mandalay, but when he had been told this was impossible because of the shortage of men and supplies, Chiang had been reasonable. The Generalissimo also expressed pleasure at the size of the British naval concentration in the Bay of Bengal. This did not mean, however, that everything had gone smoothly. Chiang wanted formal notice from the Combined Chiefs of Staff that his plans for Burma called for more resources than the Allies could provide, and he was still insisting that the ten thousand tons per month be flown into Chungking over the Hump. More important, despite Churchill's contrary arguments, Chiang held out for the amphibious operation. When the talks ended, however, Mountbatten felt Chiang would support a limited offensive in North Burma. He suggested, however, that, in view of past behavior, the Combined Chiefs of Staff put everything in writing and get Chiang to sign it.

Brooke foreclosed debate on Buccaneer by saying that any decision must await Eureka. Without Buccaneer, discussion was amiable. Only once was there any friction. Mountbatten asked to be given control over any additional aircraft assigned to Burma. Marshall said he would have to refer the question to Roosevelt. The Combined Chiefs of Staff then agreed to hand Chiang a formal no on his plan, and Mountbatten's suggestion about putting everything in writing was also adopted. Mountbatten was asked to get the Generalissimo's signature. With Burma disposed of, at least for the moment, the Combined Chiefs of Staff held a "closed session" on Overlord and the Mediterranean.[2] The British submitted two papers. The first dealt with general strategy.[3] The second involved the effect of weather on the timing of Overlord.

Concerning general strategy, the British felt that the defeat of Italy and the possibility of Turkish intervention required modification of Quadrant plans. Brooke insisted he had no wish to sidetrack Overlord, but he believed the surest

2. Bryant, *Triumph in the West*, p. 57.
3. For the text see *U.S. Foreign Relations, Tehran Papers*, pp. 409–11.

and quickest way to win the war was to attack the Germans remorselessly on every possible front. The front the British had in mind was, of course, the Mediterranean. For the Mediterranean Brooke detailed a six-point program. First, he called for unity of command; second, he asked that the offensive in Italy be maintained until the securing of the Pisa-Rimini line; and third, he wanted guerrilla forces in Yugoslavia, Greece, and Albania to be "nourished . . . on a regular military basis"—a statement which could mean anything from increased supplies to an amphibious attack in the Adriatic. So far the British had stayed within the letter, if not the spirit, of Quadrant. Brooke's next three proposals, however, involved a radical shift in strategy. First, Turkey was to be brought into the war within the next four weeks; second, the Dardanelles were to be opened; finally, the Allies were to "do everything possible to promote a state of chaos and disruption in the satellite Balkan countries."

Where were the resources to come from? Brooke called for the delay of Overlord. The British did not "attach vital importance to any particular date or to any particular number of divisions in the [cross-channel] assault and follow-up." If the new program handicapped the concentration in England, this would just have to be accepted. Brooke claimed that everything he proposed was preparatory to Overlord, but this claim rang hollow in American ears. Were not the British substituting Rankin for the larger attack? Indeed, paragraph five of their strategy paper opened with this sentence: "If we pursue the above policy, we firmly believe that Overlord, perhaps in the form of Rankin, will take place next summer."[4] The memory of Flanders was in Washington's opinion still London's incubus. The British would cross the Channel only if the Germans were at the point of collapse. The second British paper formed a sort of extended footnote to the first. It argued that cross-channel operations could take place as late as mid-July, a three-

4. Ibid., p. 410.

month postponement of the date agreed at Quadrant, without jeopardizing General Morgan's plans.

Brooke must have expected an explosion, but he didn't get one. Instead, Marshall circulated the American draft calling for a single Allied commander who, under the general supervision of the Combined Chiefs of Staff, would direct the whole European war. This draft had been prepared earlier by Joint Chiefs of Staff planners. It had Roosevelt's enthusiastic support and was based on the assumption, not explicit in the text, that since the majority of forces were American, the new Foch would be a Washington appointee. The obvious choice was George Marshall. With Marshall in charge, Overlord would be safe and British diversions checked. It would also put an end to rumors that Marshall's expected command over Overlord constituted a kick upstairs. Brooke found the American paper impractical.[5] Leahy thought the British proposals alarming.[6] There was no discussion. The great strategic review turned out to be a set piece battle. The session ended with the Combined Chiefs of Staff going to a special Thanksgiving service in All Saints Cathedral in Cairo.

The last and longest meeting of the Combined Chiefs of Staff before their flight to Tehran was held Friday afternoon, November 26.[7] It opened with formal approval of Mountbatten's paper for Chiang. Champion was reaffirmed and the Generalissimo's plan rejected. Mountbatten could divert one hundred tons per month from the amount going over the Hump for the requirements of Champion, but Chiang was also to be assured the Trident figure of ten thousand tons would soon be achieved. Chiang's call for an amphibious operation would be considered after Eureka. Mountbatten was again asked to get Chiang's signature without delay—a task the Supreme Commander could scarcely have

5. Bryant, *Triumph in the West*, p. 58.
6. Leahy, *I Was There*, p. 201.
7. For minutes of the meeting, see *U.S. Foreign Relations, Tehran Papers*, pp. 358–65.

relished as Stilwell had told him in the morning that Chiang was again demanding all of Burma.

Turning from Southeast Asia, Brooke asked the Mediterranean Commanders, Eisenhower and Wilson, to express their views on future strategy. Both men had been present at Cairo from the start, but this was the first time they had met with the Combined Chiefs of Staff. As might be expected, Eisenhower and Wilson mirrored their superiors' attitudes. Speaking first, Eisenhower favored an end to the split in Mediterranean command. He then presented two alternative lines of action depending upon whether or not the Mediterranean attack was to be pursued. If the pressure were to be kept up, Eisenhower wanted to advance into the Po valley, from which the Allies could simultaneously threaten France, the Balkans, and Germany. Aside from the buildup presently scheduled, all he needed was additional landing craft. The seven divisions recently dispatched to England could stay there. If the pressure were relieved and, as planned, his landing craft diverted to Overlord, then the best Eisenhower felt he could do would be to establish a line north of Rome. There might be strong local offensives, but the strategic position must be defensive. In his opinion any Balkan attack should be limited to the islands of the Aegean. This could be undertaken only after he had either driven into the Po valley or secured the line north of Rome. Action in the Aegean, in his opinion, presupposed Turkish entrance into the war.

Brooke asked for Eisenhower's views on Yugoslavia. Eisenhower felt aid to Yugoslavia depended on whether he received permission for the Po campaign. If he got to the Po, then he would establish small garrisons in the islands of the Adriatic to supply the guerrillas. Should he be ordered to stand on the defensive, then he could do little to aid the guerrillas. Eisenhower also believed all supplies should go to Tito, as in his judgment Mikailovic was useless. Eisenhower ended his appraisal by stressing the delay involved in establishing any new theater. The implication was that even if forced to continue the Mediterranean attack, the Americans wanted to confine it to Italy and keep out of the Balkans.

Whereas Eisenhower's eyes were focused on Italy, Wilson's were centered on the Aegean. Wilson said it was essential to cut the German ring running through Rhodes, Crete, and Greece. Rhodes and Turkish intervention were the twin keys. Aside from an amphibious lift and perhaps one division, which could be returned after taking Rhodes, Wilson, like Eisenhower, felt that he had the resources to do the job. Unlike Eisenhower, however, who put Turkish intervention somewhere in the distant future, Wilson talked as if the Turks were coming in immediately. The air component of Hardihood was described as ready. Even now, according to Wilson, Ankara was laying steel mats on two airstrips in the vicinity of Rhodes to receive the planes. If Wilson was specific about Rhodes and Turkey, he was vague as to where the Allies went from there. He did, however, mention convoys through the straits and a wireless station in Bucharest. When asked about Yugoslavia, Wilson stated that he thought assistance to the guerrillas should be given as far north as possible. Islands in the Adriatic were named stepping stones to the mainland, and an attack near Trieste was described as a serious threat to the German rear—the rear to a front which presumably started at Istanbul.

With their presentations completed, Eisenhower, Wilson, and their staffs left the room. Brooke asked for the views of the Americans. Leahy, as chairman of the Joint Chiefs, replied that the United States tentatively accepted the British proposals for action in the Mediterranean as a basis for discussion with the Soviet staff. It was his understanding that the British desired to take Rhodes and open the Dardanelles. Until this was done, the sixty-eight landing craft presently scheduled to leave for England would instead remain in the Mediterranean. He asked for assurance that the new operations would not interfere with Buccaneer.

Brooke could not believe his ears. He asked Marshall if

the Americans understood that the mounting of Buccaneer and the capture of Rhodes and Rome meant postponement of Overlord. Marshall was evasive; he repeated that the Joint Chiefs tentatively accepted the new program as a basis for negotiation at Eureka. In Italy the attack would be pushed to the Pisa-Rimini line, Rhodes would be taken, and the landing craft would be retained. Like Leahy, Marshall asked that Buccaneer go ahead. Brooke repeated his question. Did the Americans accept the delay of Overlord? Marshall said they did. He also said it was essential to go ahead with Buccaneer. He gave three reasons: the forces were available; it was vital to Pacific operations; and, for political reasons, it could not be interfered with.

By now Brooke must have grasped what had happened. Roosevelt either had promised or was about to promise Chiang the amphibious attack—this despite British opposition and the much talked about strategic review to follow Eureka. Although he did not charge Marshall with sharp practice and probably had some sympathy for him, Brooke lost his temper. Taking up what was traditionally the American refrain, Brooke asked the Joint Chiefs to consider the overall strategic picture. Europe ought to come first; resources must be concentrated; the road to Tokyo ran through Berlin; elimination of Buccaneer might shorten the war. Portal was even more telling. He wondered what the American Joint Chiefs of Staff would do if Stalin asked for both the Mediterranean attack and an early Overlord. However good the arguments, the Joint Chiefs of Staff's hands were tied. King, who was completely opposed to a ground war in Asia, talked about the usefulness of China's manpower. Leahy wanted it clearly understood that the Joint Chiefs were not in a position to abandon Buccaneer. Marshall believed that Brooke's words about shortening the war were an overstatement. He also implied that since he had given in to the British, the British ought to give in to him.

Brooke asked the secretaries to leave the room, and then,

in his own words, he and Marshall had "the father and mother of a row."[8] Thus the Combined Chiefs of Staff, with Eureka only hours away, spent their last session at Cairo as they spent their first—quarreling over the Andaman Islands. Brooke also discovered that the Americans had reservations about his proposals. Assistance to Turkey must not jeopardize other operations. The words "everything possible" were taken out of that part of the British memorandum concerning fomenting trouble in the Balkans. But it was Buccaneer which started the argument and provided most of the heat. When the secretaries were recalled, no progress had been made. Buccaneer would have to be decided by Roosevelt and Churchill.

Concerning Europe, however, the British, at least on paper, had won. Brooke's memorandums, subject to the reservations on Turkey and the Balkans, were accepted. The Joint Chiefs of Staff also approved unity of Mediterranean command, although consideration of their own paper on the European Generalissimo was postponed. Both sides agreed that Leahy's earlier suggestion that something specific be asked of the Russians was a good one. The topics chosen, however, were not very adventurous. They included shuttle bombing, air routes to Moscow, and an exchange of weather information. Finally, Brooke and Marshall pledged to consult together before answering any Soviet proposals.

Brooke left the meeting well satisfied. Angry words or no, had he not secured most of the points he was after? The Americans were committed to Rhodes, Turkey, and the straits. Actually, he was wrong. The Americans gave way because they expected the Russians would demand more and as an inducement to support Buccaneer. Brooke could do nothing about the Russians, but he might have done something about the Americans. November 26 was Brooke's last chance to explain British strategy before Eureka. Perhaps nothing could have changed Marshall's mind. Brooke, how-

8. Bryant, *Triumph in the West*, p. 57.

ever, did not try. With sixty-eight landing craft in his grasp, he chose to fight for Mountbatten's eighteen. The British counted too much on Russian support. They dropped hints about Rumania and Bulgaria but, when the Americans bristled, they backed hastily away. Having failed to put forward any coherent alternate strategy to cross-channel attack and instead wasted hours on Burma, London would be at a great disadvantage should Stalin call for Overlord and nothing else.

A good case militarily could have been made for a Balkan campaign in the winter of 1943 and a delayed Overlord. The Germans certainly thought so, hence their response to Leros and Samos. Brooke believed the war might have been ended in 1943 or early 1944. Unfortunately, he did not explain how to Marshall, and the fault was not entirely Chiang Kai-shek's or Roosevelt's enthusiasm for China. Washington thought in terms of massive plans and disliked improvisation. Marshall came to Cairo expecting a plan for the Balkans from Brooke. Instead, Brooke presented an outline. Moreover, by accepting American limitations on aid to Turkey, even the outline became fuzzy. What was left Winant properly described as "bush league tactics," and bush league tactics carried no weight with the Pentagon.[9]

The Chinese story which dominated the military meetings at Cairo also monopolized almost all the political discussions, but this was as Roosevelt intended. The Anglo-Americans would present no common front, either military or diplomatic, before Stalin. Where Churchill had to court, Chiang was invited. Chiang was asked to a private dinner and an equally intimate tea. Churchill also had dinner with the President, but on Thanksgiving Day with a large party and an orchestra in attendance. Eden recalled some desultory political talk, but for the most part he was deafened by the band.[1]

9. *U.S. Foreign Relations, Tehran Papers,* p. 303.
1. Eden, *Memoirs,* II, 492.

Roosevelt, of course, was not uninterested in the Chinese story. He had never met Chiang. He was sincere in his belief in China's future as a great power. He was aware of the military, political, and economic problems which faced the Chinese. He feared their collapse and a resultant freeing of the Japanese garrison in China which might result in a prolongation of the Pacific war. But it was also true that Roosevelt wanted to avoid discussion of European affairs, and by closeting himself with Chiang, he thwarted Churchill. The result was a triumph for the Chinese. On November 24 Chunghui Wang, Secretary-General to the Chinese War Cabinet, handed Harry Hopkins a long memorandum detailing what Chiang hoped to achieve at Cairo. The Generalissimo asked for the creation of a special council, meeting in Washington, to implement the Four-Power Declaration. He called for an Asiatic version of the European Advisory Commission. The Combined Chiefs of Staff was to be widened to include Chinese representatives, or, alternately, a new body might be created to direct the Far Eastern war and the authority of the Combined Chiefs of Staff be limited to European affairs.

The memorandum also detailed some of Chiang's political aspirations. China asked for Manchuria, Dairen, Port Arthur, Formosa, and the Pescadores. Korea was to be made an independent state. China was also to have a voice in the disposition of Japanese mandates. All Japanese property in China, together with the Japanese merchant fleet, was to be turned over to Chungking. Finally, the Allies were to issue a Declaration on Atrocities for Japan similar to the one against Germany. These, together with the military demands, constituted Chiang's official position. Wang asked that some be included in the conference communiqué.

Unofficially, as expressed in private conversations with Roosevelt, Chiang wanted still more. He sought a one-billion-dollar gold loan to check inflation. He wanted Japan's industrial plant and rolling stock transferred to China as reparations. Chinese sovereignty was to be recognized in Tibet and Mongolia. He requested Roosevelt's support of China's opposition to British imperialism and Soviet pressures. No major decisions on either European or Asiatic affairs were to be taken without Chiang's consent.

In return Chiang would assist with Champion and the long-range bomber program. Eventually, when his army was properly equipped and trained, he would conduct offensive operations in central China and Manchuria. Chiang seems to have been almost effusive concerning the postwar world. He pledged personal allegiance to Roosevelt, the principles of democracy, and Washington's anticolonial policies. He was favorably impressed by Roosevelt's proposal for an alliance of China and the United States to maintain peace in Asia. He was less pleased with a suggestion that China assume primary responsibility for the occupation of Japan, but he promised assistance. Perhaps most important of all, given Roosevelt's state of mind, Chiang muted his anti-communism. When Hopkins mentioned Dairen and Outer Mongolia as the possible price of Russian intervention against Japan, Chiang, although unhappy, was reasonable. Mongolia could be the subject of negotiation. For Dairen he preferred a Sino-American garrison, but he did not rule out the idea of a free port, particularly if similar arrangements applied in Hong Kong. He favored Soviet participation in the Asiatic Advisory Council. Indeed, according to Elliott Roosevelt, the Generalissimo went so far as to agree to an accommodation with the Chinese Communists.[2] In short, Chiang asked much, but he was also a pro-American and cooperative member of the Big Four.

Judging by results, the Generalissimo's tactics were a success. On the afternoon of November 25, Roosevelt, to insure Chinese participation in Champion, promised Chiang the amphibious operation in the Bay of Bengal, despite Church-

2. Elliott Roosevelt: *As He Saw It* (New York: Duell, Sloan and Pearce; 1946), p. 164. Cited hereafter as *As He Saw It*.

ill's vigorous denial of a few hours earlier that there was
any connection between North Burma and Buccaneer. Also
on the 25th, Roosevelt personally revised a Joint Chiefs of
Staff memorandum dealing with tonnages over the Hump.
Both the interim figures and the date for achieving the full
ten thousand tons were advanced. The following morning—
although he opposed a policy of promises—Arnold called
upon Chiang and said that even with the diversion for
Mountbatten, it might be possible to meet or exceed the
Trident figures on tonnages to be flown into China over the
Hump in the near future. Apparently Chiang did not get the
one billion dollars in gold. At least, such is the implication
of his suggestion, made when Buccaneer was canceled, that
the one billion dollars might serve as an adequate substitute.[3] However, on December 5 Madame Chiang cabled
Roosevelt her thanks for his "promise to speak to the Treasury about the two hundred million gold bar arrangement."[4]
She also noted that Chiang deeply appreciated Roosevelt's
proposal for buying an unspecified amount of yuan with
dollars. The faltering Chinese economy, which Chiang represented as a greater danger than the armies of Japan, would
be buttressed.

Chiang's most important gains, however, were not military
or financial. They were formal British and American recognition, subject to Soviet approval, of Chiang's territorial
aspirations. At the same time, and also subject to Soviet approval, Great Britain and the United States committed
themselves to reducing Japan to a second-class power. China
would assume the role of the leading Asiatic state. Both
decisions were expressed in the conference communiqué.
The draft of the communiqué was prepared by Harry Hopkins shortly after he received the Wang memorandum,
November 24. The following day Roosevelt and Churchill
made minor changes of wording. Approval of the communiqué and of Mountbatten's plan for Champion consti-

3. *U.S. Foreign Relations, China, 1943*, pp. 180–2.
4. Ibid., pp. 178–80.

tuted the last act of the Cairo Conference. Release of the communiqué was withheld until it had been agreed to by Stalin.

In the communiqué China was awarded Manchuria, Formosa, and the Pescadores. Eventual freedom and independence were pledged to Korea. Japan was to be stripped of all islands in the Pacific which she had held since 1914. She was also to lose "all other territories taken by violence and greed." Under the circumstances, this could only refer to the southern half of Sakhalin. Territorially, Japan would be forced back to the start of the Meiji era. The principle of unconditional surrender was reaffirmed. China was named one of the "three great Allies" who "covet no gain . . . and have no thought of territorial expansion."[5] Washington, unlike Tokyo, never considered a negotiated end to the Pacific war. Even so, the Cairo Declaration was a mistake because Japan now had no alternative but to fight to the end. As for Chiang, according to his wife, when he said goodbye to Roosevelt that afternoon, "he could not find words adequately expressive to convey his emotions and feelings, nor to thank you sufficiently for your friendship."

Although Chinese affairs, the ambiguous debate within the Combined Chiefs of Staff, and Roosevelt's refusal to shape a common political strategy with Churchill were the salient features of the conference, the President also took certain steps at Cairo which affected the arrangements for Eureka. Roosevelt was a believer in personal diplomacy. He wanted to establish an intimate relationship with Stalin. How better to accomplish this than by living in the same building with the Soviet leader? Here topography played into Roosevelt's hands. The British and Russian embassies at Tehran faced each other. The American Legation was located nearly a mile away in a different quarter of the city. It had been planned that each of the Big Three would stay at his country's embassy and that meetings would be held in

5. *U.S. Foreign Relations, Tehran Papers,* pp. 448–9.

a round-robin manner. On November 22, immediately after his arrival in Cairo, Roosevelt cabled Stalin a broad hint that other arrangements might be made. He wondered if driving back and forth from the meetings did not constitute an unnecessary risk, and he asked Stalin where he should live.[6] The following day Hurley was dispatched to Tehran. Ostensibly, Hurley's mission was to improve cooperation between the various British, American, and Russian agencies operating in Iran, but, in a memorandum dated the 23rd, Roosevelt ordered Hurley to carry out certain unnamed additional duties. The nature of these duties was to see that the hint of the 22nd received proper attention. It did; on November 26 Hurley cabled that he had inspected Roosevelt's quarters at the Soviet Embassy and that they were suitable. In fact, aside from two rooms occupied by Russian communication experts, Roosevelt would have a whole wing of the embassy to himself.

Sometime between the 22nd and the 23rd, however, Churchill invited Roosevelt to stay with him. Roosevelt would not commit himself. He gave Churchill a copy of his message to Stalin but was silent about the Hurley mission. In separate cables sent on the 25th, Stalin informed Roosevelt and Churchill he would be at Tehran on Sunday, November 28.[7] Although he mentioned Roosevelt's message, no invitation was included. The President became piqued. He refused Churchill's offer and wired Hurley that he would stay at the American Legation. Actually, Stalin wanted Roosevelt. The difficulty was Churchill. The Prime Minister had told Stalin of his own invitation to Roosevelt. Rather than be put in the position of bidding against Churchill, Stalin adopted a more novel procedure. By the 27th the Russians at Tehran were uncovering a German plot to assassinate the Big Three. It was convenient and diplomatic; Roosevelt and Stalin would share quarters to confound Berlin.

The American and British delegations left Cairo early on

6. Stalin's Correspondence, II, No. 140, 107–8.
7. Stalin's Correspondence, I, No. 211, 177; II, No. 141, 108.

the morning of Saturday, November 27. Marshall and the Joint Chiefs were worried. The British, as always, were pledged to the cross-channel attack. As always, too, they demanded immediate operations in the Mediterranean. With the Overlord buildup finally getting into full swing, London was starting fresh hares. In the summer it had been Italy; now it was Turkey. Marshall believed he could hold the British in line, but not if they were joined by Stalin, and on the subject of what the Russians wanted, the advice of the American experts on Soviet affairs was conflicting. Harriman held that Moscow still put Overlord first but desired Turkey as well, whereas Deane maintained they wanted Turkey and the Mediterranean.[8] Three things, however, all discouraging from the Pentagon's viewpoint, were clear. Churchill talked as if Soviet support for his plans was a foregone conclusion; the opening of a Turkish theater was a Russian proposal; and, finally, Roosevelt had not traveled six thousand miles to quarrel with Stalin.

The apprehension of the military was not shared by Roosevelt. According to Hull, Roosevelt was exuberant at the thought of meeting Stalin.[9] Murphy, who was present at Cairo, received the same impression.[1] Hull and Roosevelt were elated at the success of the Moscow Conference. Roosevelt was going to Tehran to cement Soviet-American partnership. For both men belief in this partnership was an act of faith, not reason. Where they differed was on the nature of the cement. Hull used paper agreements, whereas Roosevelt intended to rely on territorial concessions.

As for European strategy, Roosevelt, though uncertain, hoped Harriman's view that Marshall might find Stalin his ally was correct. Recent news from Ankara was confusing as to whether the Russians really desired Turkish intervention.

8. Deane blames himself for the anxiety his cables and words caused Marshall during November, 1943. He feels he was deliberately misled by Molotov as to Soviet intentions in order to throw the Anglo-Americans off balance at Eureka. Deane, *Strange Alliance,* pp. 44–5.

9. Hull, *Memoirs,* II, 1313.

1. Murphy, *Diplomat Among Warriors,* pp. 236–7.

At Cairo Roosevelt interviewed Laurence Steinhardt, the American Ambassador to Turkey. Probably Steinhardt repeated and amplified the news contained in his recent cables to Washington. If so, Roosevelt learned that the Turks were resisting British pressure and, even more significantly, that the Soviet Ambassador, Sergei Vinogradov, was doing nothing to implement the Moscow Agreement. Lacking instructions, Steinhardt himself played the role of an observer. Only Knatchbull-Hugessen and the German Ambassador, Franz von Papen, were active, and of the two von Papen was the more successful. He warned the Turks that granting a single air base would bring an immediate German declaration of war in which Bulgaria would join. He painted a vivid picture of what destruction the Luftwaffe would wreak on Istanbul. German threats combined with Soviet-American passivity were producing a Turkish no, and this would block any Balkan war. Roosevelt, of course, could not be sure that Vinogradov's silence meant a Russian change of mind. Harriman, indeed, sided with Deane as far as Turkey was concerned. But at least the signs were mixed, and although Roosevelt shared Marshall's anxieties that the Russians would demand some operations in the eastern Mediterranean, the President intended to try and keep the scale sufficiently small to preserve Overlord.

If the Americans were of two minds about Eureka, this was not true of the British. Had not Stalin taken Eden's news of a possible delay in Overlord calmly? All three powers were pledged to bring Turkey into the war before the year was out, and the initiative had come from the Soviet Union. The Americans had reservations, but they would give way before Stalin. After the war the British regarded Sextant as a disaster, with Roosevelt to blame.[2] Eden in 1965 described it as the most difficult conference he ever attended. Brooke in 1959 was acid about what he termed "the Chinese farce."[3] But much of this seems to be *ex post facto* argu-

2. Churchill, *Second World War*, V, 328.
3. Bryant, *Triumph in the West*, p. 51.

ment. Brooke's diary entry for the 26th, after mentioning his row with Marshall, contains this satisfied comment: "In the end, we had secured most of the points we were after." Eden, quoting from his diary for the same day, mentions a dinner party with Churchill. The Prime Minister was described as "being in tremendous form" and "keeping everybody up till two in the morning." This does not sound like disaster. Brooke had gotten one of Marshall's feet into the Mediterranean; Stalin would get the other. Even on Buccaneer, the British were covered because Churchill had told Chiang he would not be bound by the President's promise. The only worrier in British ranks appears to have been Eden. At Moscow the Foreign Secretary had called attention to Stalin's faith in Britain's pledge to Overlord. At Cairo he warned Churchill: "If we alone cannot get what we want out of the Turks, will a tripartite approach really do the trick?"[4] He never seems to have doubted, however, that the approach would be made. He was irritated by American efforts to downgrade the European Advisory Commission simply because it was located in London, and he wondered whether Roosevelt would face up to the Polish problem. But even Eden enjoyed the "pleasant and easy journey" to Tehran.

4. See Eden, *Memoirs*, II, 491.

PART FIVE

THE EUREKA CONFERENCE

XV

STALIN CHOOSES OVERLORD
November 27–29, 1943

The President, the Prime Minister, and their advisors landed at Gale Morghe airport outside Tehran on Saturday afternoon, November 27. Stalin had arrived in the morning. Although the Joint Intelligence and Planning Committees of the Combined Chiefs of Staff had been left behind in Cairo, the American and British delegations, not counting guards or communications personnel, still numbered over two hundred. In contrast, Stalin brought with him just four men—Foreign Minister Molotov, Defense Minister Marshal Voroshilov, and two translators, Vladimir Pavlov and Valentin Barezhkov.

Still lacking an invitation from the Russians, Roosevelt, together with Harry Hopkins, Admiral Leahy, and Major John Boettiger, the President's son-in-law, drove to the American Legation where they spent the night as guests of the Minister, Louis Dreyfus. The American Legation was a little over two miles from the British Legation and the Soviet Embassy. It was too small to accommodate more of the Presidential party, so everybody else, including Marshall, Arnold, and King, was quartered some five miles northwest of Tehran at Camp Parker, the headquarters of the Persian Gulf Command, United States Army. This split, together with tight security arrangements, meant that some Americans arrived late or not at all at conference meetings. The British were better situated. Their Embassy was across the street from the Soviet Embassy. A large ramshackle house, it was built by the Indian Public Works Department in the days when the British Minister required an escort of cavalry for protection. Consequently, Churchill and his principal advisers were able to stay together in one place.

Although the Big Three were finally together, they did not meet on Saturday. Churchill was feeling ill and had lost his voice on the flight from Cairo. Eden believed the trouble was too much talk the previous night.[1] Lord Moran, Churchill's personal physician, was, however, taking no chances. The Prime Minister was ordered to bed and told to stay there until the next day. Eden regretted this as it ruled out preliminary discussions with Roosevelt. In light of the President's behavior at Cairo, Eden's regrets were probably wasted because Anglo-American preliminary discussions were out of the question regardless of the state of Churchill's health.

Shortly after his arrival, Roosevelt decided to ask Stalin to dinner. He also wanted to clear up the confusion over his quarters in the Soviet Embassy. The message was delivered to the embassy by Rear Admiral Wilson Brown, the President's Naval Aide, and Minister Dreyfus. The dinner invitation was refused. Brown and Dreyfus were told by the Soviet Chargé, Mikhail Maximov, that Stalin would be unable to come as he had had a very strenuous day. In reply to a

1. Eden, *Memoirs*, II, 494.

question of Dreyfus, Maximov said he had no instructions with regard to Roosevelt's staying at the Soviet Embassy, but since Stalin was now at Tehran he was certain everything could be arranged.

The Russians were true to their word. Around midnight Saturday, Molotov requested an emergency meeting with Eden. He also called in the American and British Ambassadors to the Soviet Union, Averell Harriman and Sir Archibald Clark Kerr. When all had gathered, Molotov announced the discovery by Russian agents of the German plot to assassinate the Big Three. He believed security was good in the Soviet and British compounds, which were surrounded by troops. What he feared were the long trips back and forth to the American Legation through the narrow and twisting streets of Tehran. He suggested that Roosevelt move to the Soviet Embassy as otherwise there might be a "scandal." Eden offered the President accommodations in the British Legation. Harriman said he would take the matter up with Roosevelt. Ismay, when he learned what had happened, believed the only plot was a Russian one. He also wondered "if the microphones had already been installed in anticipation."[2] Ismay was partially wrong. There had been a real plot, but when Molotov called his meeting all the conspirators were dead or in jail. Sunday morning, November 28, after receiving appeals from both Stalin and Churchill, Roosevelt made his decision. He, Leahy, and Hopkins would move to a suite in the Soviet Embassy, which adjoined the main conference room. It also adjoined a room filled with Soviet communications machines. Much to the nervousness of Michael Reilly, Chief of the White House Secret Service, Roosevelt entrusted his personal protection to the NKVD— the Russian secret police. Stalin was to have no doubt as to whether the Americans trusted him.

Before leaving the American Legation, Roosevelt and Hopkins met briefly with the Joint Chiefs of Staff. The con-

2. Ismay, *Memoirs*, p. 337.

versation was far from cheerful as everyone was convinced they would shortly be faced with a united Soviet-British front for a stepped-up Mediterranean campaign. As Leahy put it: "We can do either of two things: undertake Overlord; or go after Italy and Rhodes, and then Overlord would . . . revert . . . to Rankin." Marshall believed "the Soviets want a more immediate operation than Overlord." Roosevelt, too, felt "Marshal Stalin will ask just how many German divisions could be taken off the Soviet Western Front immediately." Nor did the President believe a Mediterranean attack could be limited, though he intended to make every effort to do just this. He pointed out that "the British would probably say after Rhodes was taken, 'Now we will have to take Greece.' "[3] The Americans agreed to try to keep Overlord intact and to offer the Russians guerrilla operations in the Adriatic. Although he was pledged to bring pressure on Ankara, Roosevelt informed the Joint Chiefs that "he did not have the conscience to urge the Turks to go to war." He also instructed Marshall not "to get involved in a discussion as between the relative merits of the Dodecanese and the Andamans." The promise to Chiang was to be kept. Toward the end of the meeting, Marshall asked the President if he thought there would be a conference with Stalin and Churchill in the afternoon. With Churchill sick and the President moving, Roosevelt thought it unlikely. Marshall and Arnold then decided to take a car and drive north into the Russian military zone. The result was that Marshall missed seeing the decisive victory for his plan of cross-channel assault.

The British Chiefs of Staff, too, met Sunday morning. Brooke left Cairo feeling that "we [the British] had secured most of the points we were after." Twenty-four hours later he was not so certain. There was really no basic "agreement with the Americans on the main points for discussion."[4] He

---

3. For the minutes of the meeting, see U.S. Foreign Relations, Tehran Papers, pp. 476–82.
4. Bryant, Triumph in the West, p. 60.

tried to get Churchill to go ahead with Operation Buccaneer in order to win Roosevelt to the Mediterranean. Churchill's throat was no better and his voice was practically gone. Brooke found him "not in the best of moods." The Prime Minister would have nothing to do with the Andamans. Despite his earlier optimism, Brooke now believed "it was evident we were heading for chaos." Having done so much to make Stalin the arbiter of their policy, the British were having second thoughts.

Roosevelt, Leahy, and Hopkins arrived at the Soviet Embassy at three in the afternoon. They learned that Stalin wanted a plenary session at four and that Churchill had agreed. Camp Parker was immediately notified, but Marshall and Arnold had gone out right after lunch. Admiral King, who had stayed behind to write some letters, left at once for the embassy. He was joined by Major General John R. Deane. Deane would have to fill in for Marshall, and Deane knew only the broad outlines of the Overlord plan. The Joint Chiefs were to enter one of the most important meetings of the war lacking their principal strategist. What was worse, the British, who had only to cross the street to get to the Russian Embassy, would be present in force.

Roosevelt was less interested in Overlord than in Stalin. In the President's opinion, Germany had already lost the war. Overlord might accelerate the process, but the end was not in doubt. The question that most concerned Roosevelt was whether the defeat of Germany would bring peace. To Roosevelt the best peace—the grand design—would see the full and friendly cooperation of the Soviet Union, the United States, the British Commonwealth, and China. He recognized that China, even with the elimination of Japan, was more of a potential than a real force. This reduced the Big Four of the future to an existing Big Three. Within the three, Churchill, the Tory, and Stalin, the Communist, were extremes united in Roosevelt's opinion only by a common enemy. It was for him to turn this cobelligerency into real alliance. The Americans could work with the British; they must work with the Russians. Stalin had opened the door of cooperation at the Moscow Conference. It was now up to Roosevelt to keep the door open, allay Soviet suspicions, satisfy Soviet aspirations, and win Stalin, if Stalin could be won, to the President's own belief in a world peace secured by the united action of the great powers.

The two men met for the first time at 3:15 in Roosevelt's new quarters. Charles Bohlen, First Secretary of the American Embassy at Moscow, and Vladimir Pavlov served as translators. No one else was present. Roosevelt greeted Stalin with these words: "I am very glad to see you. I have tried for a long time to bring this about."[5] Stalin welcomed the President, blamed himself for the delay in meeting, and excused it on the grounds of military necessity. Roosevelt asked if the Red Army still had the initiative over the Germans. Stalin said it did but was being hard pressed. Roosevelt replied that the removal of thirty or forty German divisions from the Eastern front by Anglo-American action was one of the purposes of the conference. Stalin "believed it would be of great value if such a transfer . . . could be brought about."[6]

Roosevelt then changed the subject. Perhaps because of the confusion at Moscow over the disposition of the Italian fleet, Roosevelt now offered Stalin "a part of the American-British merchant fleet, which, at the end of the war, would be more than either nation [America and Great Britain] could possibly utilize." Stalin thought "this would be of great value." There was a brief discussion of the possible exchange of American manufactured goods for Soviet raw materials. Roosevelt passed on to the Cairo Conference and discovered that, Four-Power Declaration or no, Stalin had a

5. For the American minutes, see *U.S. Foreign Relations, Tehran Papers,* pp. 483–6. For the Soviet minutes, see "Tehran Conference of the Leaders of the Three Great Powers (November 28, to December 1, 1943), Documents," *International Affairs* (Moscow), July 1961, pp. 134–6. Cited hereafter as "Tehran Conference," *International Affairs* (Moscow), followed by the month.

6. *U.S. Foreign Relations, Tehran Papers,* p. 483.

very low opinion of the Chinese Nationalist Government. Roosevelt mentioned that "he had had an interesting conversation with Chiang Kai-shek . . . on the general subject of China." Without waiting to hear more, Stalin said "that the Chinese have fought very badly . . . [and] . . . it was the fault of the Chinese leaders."[7] Roosevelt avoided a direct reply and instead described Mountbatten's coming Burma campaign and American hopes to train an effective Chinese Army.

But if Stalin was negative about Chiang, he was also, to Roosevelt's pleased surprise, equally opposed to General Charles de Gaulle. At Cairo Robert Murphy told Roosevelt that the Soviet Representative to the French National Committee of Liberation, Alexander Bogomolov, was treating de Gaulle as if he were a chief of state. The news was most unwelcome because after a relatively peaceful September and October, de Gaulle was again an explosive issue with Roosevelt. De Gaulle, who hoped for his committee's recognition as a provisional government, was displeased with the Quebec Declaration. Nevertheless, he pursued a policy of quiet consolidation throughout the fall of 1943. His reward was the French Committee's inclusion in the Italian Advisory Council. Then, on November 10, de Gaulle finally eliminated his rival, General Henri Giraud. Giraud was stripped of his offices as Co-President of the National Committee and Commander in Chief of the French Armed Forces.[8] This could have been done any time in August, but de Gaulle held his hand in the wake of the explosions in Washington following the purge of Pierre Boisson and Marcel Peyrouton in June. Roosevelt had barely started to react to Giraud's fall when, on November 11, rioting broke out in Lebanon. Lebanon was garrisoned by the French Committee. The cause of the rioting was a decree passed by the Lebanese Chamber of Deputies three days earlier calling for an end to the French mandate and immediate indepen-

7. Ibid., p. 485.
8. *U.S. Foreign Relations, 1943*, II, 188–92.

dence. De Gaulle had the deputies arrested and proclaimed martial law. Roosevelt was now wholly convinced that de Gaulle was both a Fascist and an Imperialist. British and American pressure, including the threat of force, caused de Gaulle to retreat in Lebanon, but that Bogomolov and the Russians were playing up to him in Algiers upset Roosevelt.

Stalin now asked the President what the situation was in Beirut. Roosevelt replied that the entire trouble was due to de Gaulle and the French Committee. Stalin then proceeded to describe de Gaulle as unrealistic, his movement as cut off from France, and his power as insignificant. Nor did Stalin stop with de Gaulle. He widened his attack to include the French ruling classes and the French Empire. The real France, according to Stalin, was that of Marshal Pétain and Vichy. It was now decadent and collaborationist. Roosevelt agreed; the President felt that "no Frenchman over 40 . . . should be allowed to return to position [in the French Government] in the future."[9] He believed that Churchill's opinions regarding a strong France were wrong. For Roosevelt "many years of honest labor would be necessary before France would be reestablished." Stalin "did not propose to have the Allies shed blood to restore Indochina, for example, to the old French colonial rule."

Condemnation of the French Empire led to condemnation of colonialism in general. Stalin believed the Allies must offer some counter to the Japanese slogan of Asia for the Asiatics. Roosevelt pointed with pride to the American record in the Philippines. He mentioned Hull's Declaration by the United Nations on National Independence, which had been circulated but not discussed at the Moscow Conference. Stalin saw "merit" in Hull's ideas. Before the conversation ended, Roosevelt, though he asked Stalin not to mention it to Churchill, was calling for "reform [in India] from the bottom, on the Soviet line."[1]

9. *U.S. Foreign Relations, Tehran Papers*, p. 404.
1. Ibid., p. 486.

It was now time for the opening of the first plenary session of the Tehran Conference. Stalin walked and Roosevelt was wheeled to the conference room. Except for the not unexpected strictures on Chiang, Roosevelt was pleased with his initial contact with Stalin. Anticolonialism and Lebanon were, however, the two subjects he had discussed at Cairo with Andrei Vyshinsky, the Soviet Representative to the Italian Advisory Council. Vyshinsky had probably cabled Roosevelt's views to Stalin. Certainly Stalin's opinions mirrored those of the President. Roosevelt, after this first conversation, told his son Elliott that he found Stalin "altogether quite impressive."[2]

The plenary meeting lasted three hours and twenty minutes. Present, aside from the Combined Chiefs less Marshall and Arnold, were Harry Hopkins, Eden, Molotov, and Marshal Voroshilov.[3] Each delegation used its own translator. Thus when Roosevelt spoke, he would pause after a sentence or two and Bohlen would repeat his remarks in Russian. Stalin's interpreter was Vladimir Pavlov; Churchill's was Major Arthur Birse. Brooke found the delays exasperating.

Roosevelt, as the only Chief of State present, Churchill and Stalin being merely heads of government, was made the conference's permanent chairman. The President then opened the meeting with a short speech on the theme of Allied unity. He was seconded at length by Churchill. Stalin replied, "I take pleasure in welcoming those present. I think history will show that this opportunity has been of tremendous import. Now let us get down to business."[4] Whereupon Roosevelt surveyed Anglo-American planning for the Pacific, Chinese, and European theaters. In the Pacific

2. Roosevelt, *As He Saw It*, p. 176.
3. For Bohlen's minutes of this meeting, see *U.S. Foreign Relations, Tehran Papers*, pp. 487–97. For the Soviet minutes, see "Tehran Conference," *International Affairs* (Moscow), July, 1961, pp. 136–9.
4. *U.S. Foreign Relations, Tehran Papers*, p. 497. According to Admiral King, Pavlov was embarrassed by Stalin's abruptness. King and Whitehill, *Admiral King*, p. 516.

Allied strategy was based on the doctrine of attrition, which was proving successful. In China, the President said he hoped to open the Burma Road soon, send Chiang the supplies necessary to keep China in the war, and eventually secure air bases there for the bombing of Japan. Roosevelt emphasized, however, that "the number of ships and men allocated [to the Far East] were being held down to a minimum."

Turning to Europe, Roosevelt named it the most important theater of the war. He said all Anglo-American military planning had revolved around the question of relieving German pressure on the Soviet Union. Until Quebec, and largely because of a severe shortage of naval transport, it had not been possible to set a firm date for the cross-channel operation. Now the shortage had been overcome and the date was set; Overlord was scheduled for May 1, 1944. If, however, Roosevelt continued, Overlord were delayed one, two, or three months, use could be made of Mediterranean forces so as to bring more immediate aid to Russia. Possible operations included attacks in Italy, the Adriatic, the Aegean, and, should Turkey enter the war, the Black Sea. Roosevelt believed the "large cross-channel operation should not be delayed by secondary operations." He asked Stalin's opinion. Brooke considered it "a poor and not very helpful speech."[5]

Stalin's reply might have been written by the absent George Marshall. He promised the Soviet Union would enter the Pacific war as soon as Germany was defeated. The Red Army was described as having a seventy-division superiority over the enemy. Mediterranean prospects were poor. Italy, according to Stalin, presented a hopeless military problem, and although Allied attacks in Turkey or the Balkans might be helpful, both were far from centers of German strength. What his allies must do was concentrate on Overlord. Overlord was vital. Any forces not used for Overlord

5. Bryant, *Triumph in the West,* p. 61.

might assault southern France one or two months before the main blow. They would draw German forces from the Channel and, when Overlord was launched, act as pincers.

It was now Churchill's turn to speak, and, sore throat or no, the meeting became virtually a monologue, with the Prime Minister using every argument he knew to persuade Stalin and Roosevelt to change their minds. Churchill said he was fully committed to Overlord for the late spring or early summer of 1944 but that this was a long way off. Following the capture of Rome, which was expected in January, it would be six months until Overlord. The question was how the six months could best be used. Present plans looked forward to the stabilization of the Italian front on a line between Pisa and Rimini, but penetration into the Po valley was not intended. Stabilizing the Italian front would make available some twenty to twenty-three divisions. Some of these divisions were going to England for use in Overlord, but the majority would remain in the Mediterranean. There were also available roughly twenty divisions in Egypt and the Near East. These troops represented a considerable body of men, and the lack of operations for them was not right.

Unfortunately, any operation would require naval transport—in particular tank landing craft which, said Churchill, were in critically short supply. Such vessels were being concentrated in England for Overlord. The Prime Minister proposed retaining a few in the Mediterranean. If this were done, it might delay Overlord, but the gains would be worth it. One possible operation would be in the Adriatic to support the Yugoslavian Partisans. Others, in the Aegean, might bring Turkey into the war, and if Turkey came in, their entrance would open up the Black Sea and insure an uninterrupted supply route to Russia. It would also have an effect on Rumania, from whom peace feelers had been received. Even Hungary might drop out of the war. Turkish intervention could well start a landslide among the satellite states.

Roosevelt could not resist Churchill's enthusiasm. Much to Harry Hopkins's concern, the President came out for an attack at the head of the Adriatic. It would aid Tito. The Allies might even push northeast into Rumania and thereby link up with the advancing Russians.[6] Stalin, however, remained immune. He asked if the divisions marked for Overlord would be affected in any way by the Prime Minister's plans. Churchill assured him they would not. Stalin then asked what Anglo-American forces would be involved if Turkey entered the war. Churchill replied two or three divisions for the capture of the islands in the Aegean, but, as aid to Turkey proper, it was only proposed to send twenty squadrons of fighters and some antiaircraft units. Stalin questioned the dispersal of forces from Overlord and repeated his earlier suggestion of using Mediterranean troops in a supporting assault on southern France. With regard to Turkey, he now reversed the Soviet stand taken at the Moscow Conference. He said it was his opinion that Turkey would not enter the war.

Churchill admitted that if this were so it would limit the scope of his proposals. He wanted, however, both the Russians and Americans to put pressure on Ankara. Stalin agreed but believed the effort would be wasted. Churchill maintained "it would be an act of supreme unwisdom if the Turks were to refuse an invitation from Russia to join the war on the winning side." He added that "Christmas . . . was a poor season for Turkeys."[7] Roosevelt took the same position as Stalin. He would ask the Turks to come in but expected they would ask for so much in the way of supplies as to make their entry impossible. With this exchange the plenary session adjourned. The only decisions taken were that Marshal Voroshilov was to meet in the morning with the Combined Chiefs to "examine various possibilities" and that the Big Three would meet Monday afternoon.

Sunday night Roosevelt was host at a dinner party for

6. Hopkins scribbled a note to King asking: "Who's promoting that Adriatic business?" King replied, "As far as I know, it is his own idea." Sherwood, *Roosevelt and Hopkins*, p. 780. See also *U.S. Foreign Relations, Tehran Papers*, p. 493.

7. *U.S. Foreign Relations, Tehran Papers*, p. 496.

Churchill and Stalin. Present also were Molotov, Eden, and Hopkins, as well as the two Ambassadors from Moscow, Clark Kerr and Harriman.[8] The first subject discussed was possible locations for the next Three Power Conference; Fairbanks, Alaska, was considered the most likely site. Stalin then raised the question of France and her position in the postwar world. He repeated before Churchill what he had said to Roosevelt earlier. The French ruling class was described as "rotten to the core." They had delivered their country into the hands of the Germans. France was "now actively helping our enemies." She must be punished by the loss of her empire. It would be "not only unjust but dangerous to leave in French hands any important strategic points after the war."[9]

Roosevelt agreed and also repeated his idea of eliminating from the French Government anyone who was over forty years of age. He believed Dakar and New Caledonia should be put under United Nations trusteeship. Churchill was silent about France and denied any desire on the part of Great Britain to acquire new territory, but he, too, thought the Big Four—Russia, Great Britain, America, and China—should enforce the peace by controlling "certain strategic points throughout the world."

Mention of the peace led to a discussion of the treatment to be accorded Germany. Roosevelt called for the destruction of the very concept of German unity. He would eliminate the word *Reich* from the German language. Churchill also favored dismemberment. Stalin thought this insufficient. Germans would always unite; maybe not in the next ten years, but certainly within twenty-five. Stalin felt the best way to handle Germany would be for the Big Three to occupy permanently certain areas from which they could strike out against any revival of militarism or nationalism. In the ensuing conversation, Stalin did not develop his pro-

---

8. Ibid., pp. 509–12; Sherwood, *Roosevelt and Hopkins*, pp. 781–3; Eden, *Memoirs*, II, 495.
9. *U.S. Foreign Relations, Tehran Papers*, p. 509.

posal. Instead, whatever was suggested by Churchill or Roosevelt, Stalin objected to as inadequate. Charles Bohlen, who served as Roosevelt's translator throughout the Tehran Conference, felt Stalin was probing the Americans and British while at the same time refusing to commit the Soviet Union. As for Stalin, he must have wondered why, if Churchill and Roosevelt both favored dismemberment, Eden and Hull had ducked the issue at Moscow.

It was during the German discussion that an incident occurred which showed Roosevelt the difficulties he would face if he approached Stalin on the question of the Soviet Union's western frontier. Roosevelt mentioned the possibility of creating an international zone, in the vicinity of the Kiel Canal, to insure free navigation in the Baltic. Pavlov misinterpreted Roosevelt's remarks so that the impression was given to Stalin that what was being discussed were the Baltic States. In an angry voice Stalin stated categorically that the Baltic peoples had voted to join the Soviet Union. This was not open to question. When the error in translation had been corrected, Stalin calmed down, but Roosevelt had received a vivid demonstration of what any appeal "on high moral grounds" would entail. It was also during this discussion that Stalin questioned the desirability of unconditional surrender as a war measure. Unconditional surrender, according to Stalin, merely served to unite the German people in resistance; whereas specific terms, no matter how harsh, might hasten capitulation. Stalin remained silent as to what the terms might be.

Roosevelt, who was tiring, briefly mentioned his ideas about the future United Nations Organization. He described it as a body which would have sovereign rights and occupy certain areas about the world. It was a "concept which had never been developed in past history." Following this, Roosevelt left the room. Stalin, Churchill, and everyone else remained behind to continue the discussion. Eden felt Roosevelt had been "below par."

Churchill now raised the question of Poland. He had waited until Roosevelt left because of the President's supposed aversion to any mention of the subject. According to Eden, "the opening moves did not go too badly."[1] Churchill pointed out that Britain had gone to war with Germany because of the German invasion of Poland. The British Government was committed to the reestablishment of Poland; it was not, however, committed to any specific frontier. He hoped to reach an agreement at the present conference. Stalin asked if this could be done without Polish participation. Churchill believed it could. After the powers had made their decision, the Poles would be informed. Stalin felt that nothing the British had yet said on the Polish question made him optimistic of a solution. Churchill repeated that he personally had no commitment to any particular frontier between Poland and the Soviet Union. He also stated that the "governing factor" in determining the frontier must be Russian security. Eden asked "if . . . the Soviet Union favored the Polish western frontier on the Oder."[2] Stalin "replied emphatically that he did favor such a frontier and that the Russians were prepared to help the Poles achieve it." Churchill agreed and, using three matchsticks, showed how the Polish-Russian frontier might advance to the west in lockstep with the Polish-German frontier.[3] With this the dinner ended.

The following morning, November 29, Marshal Voroshilov met with the Combined Chiefs of Staff.[4] Although George Marshall had missed the plenary session, he was well satisfied with the report given him by Admiral King. According to General Arnold, King told Marshall: "Uncle Joe had talked straight from the shoulder about how to carry on the war against Germany. Despite earlier fears Stalin's ideas

1. Eden, *Memoirs*, II, 495.
2. *U.S. Foreign Relations, Tehran Papers*, p. 512.
3. Churchill, *Second World War*, V, 362.
4. *U.S. Foreign Relations, Tehran Papers*, pp. 514–28; "Tehran Conference," *International Affairs* (Moscow), July, 1961, pp. 139–43.

. . . were much more in accord with American ideas than were those of the British."[5] Marshall hoped Voroshilov's support would assure the primacy of Overlord and put an end to Mediterranean adventures.

If Marshall was optimistic, Brooke was pessimistic. To Brooke Roosevelt's speech had been "poor." Churchill in reply "was not at his best." Brooke wrote in his diary Sunday night: "We sat for three-and-a-half hours and finished up the conference by confusing plans more than they ever have been before."[6] Brooke had met Voroshilov during Churchill's trip to Moscow in 1942. He thought him a political general, and he expected Voroshilov to parrot Stalin; his expectation proved correct.

As at Cairo, Brooke served as chairman. He welcomed Voroshilov in the name of the Combined Chiefs, and said "he would run through . . . the war as seen by the British at the present moment and then examine the relation of the Overlord operation to other parts of the war effort."[7] He asked Marshall to interrupt at any point if something was said with which the Americans disagreed. Brooke's talk was long and rambling. Since Voroshilov was familiar with the Overlord plan as presented at Moscow, Brooke said nothing about the cross-channel operation itself. Instead, like Churchill, Brooke concentrated on the "five or six months" between Eureka and Overlord. What the British wanted was to stop "the movement to the Russian front . . . [of] . . . all the German divisions it was possible . . . [for the Anglo-American Armies] . . . to hold." The only active Anglo-American front was in the Mediterranean. Brooke therefore "desired to take full advantage of the [Allied] forces now established" there.

Having offered his principal bait, Brooke turned to the familiar opportunities. Italy, Yugoslavia, Turkey, and the Dardanelles were all mentioned. Exploiting these oppor-

5. Arnold, *Global Mission*, p. 465.
6. Bryant, *Triumph in the West*, p. 61.
7. *U.S. Foreign Relations, Tehran Papers*, p. 515.

tunities required landing craft, and the landing craft were already in the Mediterranean. Keeping them there would, unfortunately, "retard the date set for Overlord." Brooke, however, described the delay as a short one that would enable the Allies "to destroy the German forces in the . . . area." He opposed a landing in southern France "two months prior to Overlord . . . that was certain to be defeated." During Overlord, though, he believed "a small attack [against southern France] might be made." At no point did Brooke challenge Overlord. He talked only about "difficulties and dangers" in the buildup after the initial assault. Using an argument that meant as much for Marshall as Voroshilov, Brooke described his Mediterranean program as one that would ensure the success of the cross-channel operation by drawing German reserves away from France. With this description Brooke concluded his presentation. Leahy thought Brooke was simply being "stubborn."[8]

Voroshilov asked for American views. Admiral Leahy, as Chairman of the Joint Chiefs, called on Marshall. If anything, Marshall was more rambling than Brooke. He pointed to the "dilemma" of fighting in the Atlantic and the Pacific. He stressed that there was "no lack of troops and no lack of supplies." Instead, the Americans had "more than fifty divisions in the United States" which it wished to deploy as soon as possible. Voroshilov learned "while this is of course an exaggeration, it might almost be said that we have reached the point of having to ignore strategy in order to advance communications." When it came to specifics, however, Marshall put the same question as Brooke: "What do we do in the next three months, and then in the next six months?" Marshall also agreed that the limiting factor was landing craft. He, too, felt an attack in southern France should come only "two or three weeks . . . in advance of Overlord." But on the decisive issue of what to do between Eureka and Overlord, Marshall was silent. He asked the

8. Leahy, *I Was There*, p. 206.

question and gave no answer. Instead Marshall issued a warning: an attack in the Mediterranean now might endanger Overlord in the spring.

Admiral Leahy asked for Voroshilov's opinion. Voroshilov first put a number of questions concerning the landing craft program, air support for Overlord, and the American buildup in England. He seemed to think Overlord comparable to the crossing of a river on the Russian front. Marshall pointed out that "the failure of a river crossing is a reverse, while the failure of a landing operation from the sea is a catastrophe." Voroshilov "appreciated [Marshall's] frankness." Turning to Brooke, Voroshilov wanted to know "whether . . . [the] Chief of the Imperial General Staff considered Overlord as important an operation as General Marshall had indicated he did." Brooke replied: "As chief of the Imperial General Staff, he considered Operation Overlord as of vital importance, but there was one stipulation that he should like to make. He knew the defenses of northern France and did not wish to see the operation fail. In his opinion, under certain circumstance, it was bound to fail."[9]

Voroshilov then said that Stalin and the Soviet General Staff attached primary importance to Overlord. Other operations in the Mediterranean could only be regarded as auxiliary. The Americans "thoroughly" understood the Soviet position. Voroshilov suggested putting on record the "conclusions" of the meeting. Brooke objected that this was premature, but Soviet-American agreement was complete. When the meeting ended, Brooke felt like "entering a lunatic asylum."[1] Leahy, however, admired the "young and vigorous" Russian who asked such "searching questions."[2]

While the Combined Chiefs and Marshal Voroshilov were meeting in the Soviet Embassy, Churchill was having an unsatisfactory conversation with Averell Harriman in the

9. *U.S. Foreign Relations, Tehran Papers*, p. 524.
1. Bryant, *Triumph in the West*, p. 64.
2. Leahy, *I Was There*, pp. 206–7.

British Legation. The Prime Minister wanted Roosevelt to come to lunch. Harriman was explaining why this was impossible. By Monday morning Churchill must have been regretting his tactics. He had come to Tehran expecting Stalin to break the "lawyers' bargain" of Quebec. Stalin was to put pressure on Roosevelt. Roosevelt, in turn, would overrule Marshall. He, Roosevelt, and Stalin would force an unwilling Turkey into the war; an eastern Mediterranean campaign was to follow. Overlord must then revert to the status of Rankin, and the liberators of at least half the Balkans would be wearing American and British uniforms. This was what Churchill expected and what Roosevelt and Marshall feared. It had not occurred.

Lord Moran, Churchill's physician, saw the Prime Minister shortly after Sunday's plenary session. Churchill looked dispirited. Moran asked if anything had gone wrong. Churchill replied: "A bloody lot has gone wrong."[3] The straws in the Moscow wind had proved unreliable. Eden's warnings were right; the Prime Minister's hopes were wrong. At Moscow Molotov demanded Turkey be pushed in; at Tehran Stalin appeared uninterested. At Moscow Stalin calmly accepted Overlord's delay; at Tehran Voroshilov all but used Marshall's expression about "overriding priority." It was not Roosevelt and Marshall who were being pressured. It was the Prime Minister and General Brooke. Stalin was in full cry for the cross-channel attack; Churchill feared the operation would end in disaster. The Foreign Office believed that only military intervention could prevent Greece and Yugoslavia from going Communist, whereas Roosevelt seemed determined to play Stalin's game.

Nor could the Prime Minister have found much solace in the previous night's political discussions. At Moscow Molotov had insisted Eastern Europe must, except for Soviet territorial aggrandizement, revert to its prewar status. Any other policy was condemned as a revival of the *cordon*

---

3. Wilson, *Churchill*, p. 145.

sanitaire. At Tehran Roosevelt and Stalin were bent on partitioning Germany. From the way both talked, France, too, was to be weakened. Churchill's opening moves on Poland had gone well, but what was Poland? When George Marshall's American Army left Europe to fight Japan, Britain would face the Soviet Union across a power vacuum. Monday morning Churchill asked Roosevelt to lunch.

Roosevelt refused and made Harriman his messenger. The President "did not want Stalin to know" he and Churchill "were meeting separately."[4] There must be no intimations of a common Anglo-American front. Anything that might arouse Soviet suspicions was to be avoided. Churchill pointed out "that Roosevelt was staying in the same building with Stalin." He told Harriman he was surprised at the President's attitude because: "I thought we all three should treat each other with equal confidence." Churchill's words were wasted.

If Roosevelt would not see Churchill, he did talk with Stalin. As on Sunday, the Monday afternoon meeting was private. Only the two interpreters, Bohlen and Berezhkov, were present.[5] Roosevelt began with a gesture of friendship. He handed Stalin a highly laudatory report on Tito, which described the Partisan movement as resembling George Washington's Army at Valley Forge. Stalin said he would read it with interest. Roosevelt then gave Stalin three memorandums prepared by the Combined Chiefs at Cairo. They requested Soviet assistance in shuttle bombing, an exchange of weather information, and permission for an Allied Military Mission to visit Siberia.[6] In explanation of this last request, Roosevelt referred to Stalin's pledge to enter the war against Japan and indicated that the time had come for advance planning. Stalin promised to study the memorandums.

4. Churchill, *Second World War*, V, 363.
5. For the minutes, see *U.S. Foreign Relations, Tehran Papers*, pp. 529–33.
6. For the texts, see *Stalin's Correspondence*, II, Nos. 143, 144, and 145, 109–11.

The President then explained his ideas about the future world organization promised in the Four-Nation Declaration. Roosevelt envisaged a three-part organization: first, a large assembly composed of all members which would meet periodically and make recommendations to a smaller body; second, a smaller body which would be a ten-member executive committee, consisting of America, Britain, Russia, and China, together with two European states, a British Dominion, and one country each from South America and the Near and Far East. The executive committee could deal with nonmilitary matters such as world agriculture and health, and it could also make recommendations for settling international disputes with the hope that the nations concerned would listen. Roosevelt, however, did not believe the Congress of the United States would accept, as binding, proposals from such a body. Roosevelt then turned to the third part of his proposal, which he called "the Four Policemen." The Soviet Union, America, Great Britain, and China must be empowered to deal immediately with any threat to the peace. To illustrate, the President said that if the Four Policemen had been in existence at the time of the Ethiopian crisis, it could have prevented the Italian attack by closing the Suez Canal.

Stalin had two comments: first, he did not think Europe would accept the idea of the Four Policemen; second, he regarded China as weak and of little use. Stalin proceeded briefly to sketch an alternative. He proposed two regional committees: one for Europe and another for Asia. Membership would be strictly limited: in Europe, the Big Three plus one other power; in Asia, the Big Three and China. Roosevelt said this was similar to current British thinking. He then made a statement which must have greatly interested Stalin. The President said he doubted whether Congress would agree to American participation in a strictly European organization, particularly if it had the power to compel the dispatch of American troops. Only a great war could bring his country to take such a step.

Stalin immediately pointed out that any organization to enforce the peace might entail sending American troops to Europe. The President said America would provide air and naval support but that troops would have to come from Great Britain and the Soviet Union. He went on to propose a two-step procedure for dealing with such a crisis: first, the Four Powers should impose a quarantine, closing the frontiers of the offending country and imposing an embargo; second, if embargo failed, the Four Powers should, after issuing an ultimatum, carry out an air attack and invasion.

Conversation turned to the treatment of Germany. Stalin felt the British proposals were ineffective. He stressed the speed with which Germany had recovered after the First World War. Stalin favored permanent occupation of certain strategic points, either within Germany or along the German frontier. He added that a similar method could be used with Japan. Interestingly, the only strategic point Stalin mentioned by name was one proposed by Roosevelt the previous evening—Dakar in French West Africa. The President agreed "100%."

Stalin then began to repeat his doubts about China as a member of the Big Four and, like Churchill before him, discovered the topic was sacrosanct in Washington's eyes. The President admitted that China now was weak, but her future was described as one of great promise. She was a nation of four hundred million, and it was better, according to the President, to have her a friend than a foe. Ending the meeting, Roosevelt expressed his agreement with Stalin on the control of Germany and Japan via strategic points. He added that the areas would be put in the hands of the future international organization.

A "Sword of Stalingrad" ceremony, held at 3:30, preceded the opening of the second plenary session. The ceremony was a colorful one, complete with bands, speeches, and honor guards. The sword was the gift of the King of England to the people of Stalingrad. However, this public expression of friendship was followed in the plenary session by some of the harshest words exchanged at Tehran. Before the day ended, Churchill was "white with anger," and Roosevelt suffered an attack of indigestion so severe his doctors suspected poisoning.

As at the first plenary conference, Roosevelt served as chairman.[7] He opened the meeting by asking Brooke, Voroshilov, and Marshall to summarize their morning discussions. Brooke, speaking first, held that the Staffs had not finished their work but had merely made a preparatory survey of various operations. These included Overlord, the widening of the Italian campaign by going beyond the Pisa-Rimini line into the Lombard Plain, providing assistance to Yugoslavia, and bringing Turkey into the war. Brooke also mentioned an attack in southern France "in connection with Overlord."

Marshall spoke after Brooke and avoided any direct attack on the British. Instead, in a brief speech, he emphasized the shortage of landing craft and the tight schedule of the invasion buildup in England. The implication was that any new operations might affect both adversely. As instructed, he did not mention Roosevelt's pledges to Chiang on Buccaneer. Voroshilov, when his turn came, was even briefer. He said that operations in Yugoslavia and Turkey had not been discussed in any detail. His own questions concerning Overlord had been answered satisfactorily.

There was one question, however, that Voroshilov had not asked and Stalin asked it now. He wanted to know who would command Overlord. What Stalin probably intended was to force the Overlord decision. What he achieved was Roosevelt's embarrassment. Had the British agreed at Cairo to a Supreme Commander for all of Europe, Roosevelt would probably have answered Stalin with the name of George Marshall. The British, however, had rejected the

7. For Bohlen's minutes, see *U.S. Foreign Relations, Tehran Papers,* pp. 533–40. For the Combined Chiefs of Staff minutes, see ibid., pp. 540–52. For the Soviet transcript, see "Tehran Conference," *International Affairs* (Moscow), August, 1961, pp. 110–15.

American proposal, and Roosevelt was being pressed by King and Arnold to keep Marshall in Washington. Their argument was not to break up the Joint Chiefs, which they considered a winning team. They suggested that Overlord go to Eisenhower. Roosevelt, who knew how much Marshall wanted the command, hadn't made up his mind. Under the circumstances Roosevelt refused Stalin a direct answer. He said the Overlord buildup was proceeding satisfactorily under the direction of Deputy Commander General Morgan. He promised Stalin that a decision would be made shortly. Stalin, unaware of the complication, remained dissatisfied. He believed that until someone was selected, the whole operation was only tentative. Morgan, Stalin pointed out, might say all was ready, but the Supreme Commander, when he took over, could disagree. Everything would then be delayed until his wishes were met. Stalin denied he wanted any voice in the selection but recommended that the choice be made as soon as possible.

All this talk of Overlord led Churchill to undertake a second defense of the Mediterranean. As he had the previous day, the Prime Minister noted that men and arms were available but that landing craft were lacking. These could be provided in two ways—one was to hold boats in the Mediterranean which were scheduled to go to Overlord. If that were done, Overlord would be delayed six to eight weeks. Alternately, and this was the first time Stalin heard of Roosevelt's promise to Chiang, landing craft could be drawn from the Indian Ocean. This would cancel Buccaneer, but Overlord could be kept to schedule. His needs, said Churchill, were not large; all he wanted was landing craft for two divisions. The two divisions could be used in any of three places: first, they could help Eisenhower leapfrog up the Italian peninsula; second, they might aid Tito; finally, they might be decisive for Turkish intervention.

On Turkey, Churchill again asked for Russian support. He wanted a Soviet declaration of war on Bulgaria should Bulgaria move against the Turks. He repeated his plea for a

Three-Power *démarche* in Ankara. He added that the British Government would tell the Turks that a refusal to come in would have serious territorial consequences, particularly on the future of the Dardanelles. Churchill also proposed that Eden, Molotov, and some representative of the President discuss the political aspects of Turkish intervention. They could consider all questions involving the Balkans. He insisted Great Britain had no ambitions and merely sought to pin down the twenty German divisions located there—divisions which, if sent to France, would jeopardize Overlord. The Prime Minister concluded by saying that if Turkey declared war, it would be a blow to German morale, would neutralize Bulgaria, and would adversely affect Rumania and Hungary—all this at the price of two divisions and a few fighter squadrons. The conference must explore the Mediterranean, relieve Russia, and "help Overlord."

Hopkins found Churchill's effort "gallant."[8] According to Elliott Roosevelt, Marshall couldn't "believe his ears."[9] Churchill later felt he could move Stalin but not the Americans. It was, however, not Roosevelt who came to the defense of Overlord but the Soviet Premier. Although he started moderately, Stalin was soon involved in an increasingly harsh personal attack on Churchill. Stalin began by repeating his belief that Turkey would not enter the war under any circumstances. He agreed to Churchill's request for a Soviet declaration of war on Bulgaria should she move against Turkey. He also agreed that aid to Tito would be a good thing. But neither Turkey, the Partisans, nor even taking Rome was for Stalin a decisive operation; only Overlord was. Nothing should be done to weaken it. He proposed a three-point directive for the Combined Chiefs: first, set a nonpostponable date for Overlord so a Russian attack might be coordinated with it; second, plan a supporting operation in southern France; and, third, appoint a Supreme Commander immediately. He added that until the commander

8. Sherwood, *Roosevelt and Hopkins*, p. 788.
9. Roosevelt, *As He Saw It*, p. 184.

was chosen the Soviet Government could not consider Overlord more than a promise.

Roosevelt agreed with Stalin; he said that the danger of
any expedition in the eastern Mediterranean was that it
would draw forces away from and delay Overlord. Overlord
must be launched in May, 1944. As for pinning German
divisions in the Balkans, Roosevelt believed this could be
accomplished by commando operations.[1] Churchill tried
again; he spoke of his chagrin at the large British forces in
the Middle East spending the winter in inactivity. He
stressed the necessity of constant pressure on the Germans
in the Mediterranean if they were to be prevented from
reinforcing France so that the necessary preconditions for
Overlord could be fulfilled. He once more waved the bait of
the opening of the Dardanelles. He pleaded that all he
wanted was a small quantity of landing craft. The British
Government was anxious to begin Overlord as soon as possible but not to the neglect of great opportunities merely for
the sake of avoiding a month's delay. He admitted that most
of these opportunities presupposed Turkish intervention,
and if she stayed out, "that was the end of it." He believed
Turkish military needs would be slight. He also believed "all
were agreed on the question of Turkey's entrance into the
war."[2]

The effort failed. Roosevelt proposed a two-point directive
for the Combined Chiefs and Marshal Voroshilov: first,
they should accept Overlord as dominant; second, they
should examine Mediterranean operations but take care that
no delay of Overlord would be involved. Stalin was more
blunt. He said he saw no need for any more low-level meetings. The question should be decided at the present table.
He added that "he wished to ask Mr. Churchill an indiscreet
question, namely, do the British really believe in Overlord or
are they only saying so to reassure the Russians?"[3] The

1. *U.S. Foreign Relations, Tehran Papers*, pp. 537–8.
2. Ibid., p. 538.
3. Ibid., p. 539.

Prime Minister replied that "if the conditions set forth at Moscow were present, it was the duty of the British Government to hurl every scrap of strength across the channel."

Before anything more was said, Roosevelt interrupted to point to the lateness of the hour. He and Churchill were to be Stalin's guests for a dinner that was to begin shortly. He suggested postponing further discussion until the following afternoon. Churchill agreed; he also invited Roosevelt and Stalin to lunch at the British Legation on Tuesday. He further proposed that Molotov, Eden, and Hopkins might meet for "political conversations." Stalin maintained that things were moving too slowly and that conversations between subordinates would only result in further delay. Nevertheless, he accepted Roosevelt's and Churchill's proposals.

The tension between Churchill and Stalin reached its peak during Monday's dinner party. Present, aside from the Big Three, were Hopkins, Harriman, Bohlen, Eden, Clark Kerr, Birse, Molotov, and Berezhkov. Churchill says the party started out with a good deal of gaiety and much toasting. He admits Stalin indulged in some "teasing" at his expense, but the Prime Minister denies the truth of Elliott Roosevelt's description of his "mounting fury" as "highly colored and extremely misleading." Churchill did admit, however, that "I was not then and am not now fully convinced that all was chaff, and there was no serious intent lurking behind."[4] Hopkins also refers to the "teasing," and he, too, wondered "whether it was intended or accepted in a spirit of good humored raillery."[5] Bohlen wrote:

> The most notable feature of the dinner was the attitude of Marshal Stalin toward the Prime Minister. Marshal Stalin lost no opportunity to get in a dig at Mr. Churchill. Almost every remark he addressed to the Prime Minister contained some

4. For Bohlen's minutes and Churchill's description in his memoirs, see *U.S. Foreign Relations, Tehran Papers,* pp. 552–5; Churchill, *Second World War,* V, 373–4.

5. Sherwood, *Roosevelt and Hopkins,* p. 790.

sharp edge, although the Marshal's manner was entirely friendly. He apparently desired to put and keep the Prime Minister on the defensive. At one occasion, he told the Prime Minister that just because the Russians are simple people, it was [a] mistake to believe that they were blind and could not see what was before their eyes.[6]

Churchill was not exactly guarded in his replies. Once, after Stalin had "congratulated" the Prime Minister for never having been a "liberal," Churchill admitted "that after the last war he had done everything in his power to prevent the spread of Bolshevism in Europe and the setting up of Communist regimes." Stalin replied that the Prime Minister need not have worried as he had discovered the process was not an easy one. Roosevelt discoursed at length on the excellence of the champagne.

The quarrel reached its climax when Stalin, who accused Churchill of wanting an easy peace for Germany, called for the summary execution of 50,000 German officers. Churchill took exception to "the cold-blooded execution of soldiers who had fought for their country." Roosevelt tried to pass the matter off as a joke by proposing that not 50,000 but 49,500 be killed. Stalin appealed to Elliott Roosevelt for his opinion, and the latter, who by his own admission was more than a little drunk, made what Churchill regarded as a pro-Russian speech. Churchill replied, "I would rather be taken out into the garden here and now and be shot myself than sully my own and my country's honor by such infamy."[7] The Prime Minister then walked out of the room. Stalin and Molotov followed him, however, and persuaded Churchill to return. The rest of the evening was quieter.

Under the circumstances, there was little real discussion. Stalin spoke proudly of the capabilities of the Red Army but also expressed the fear of a rapid German recovery. He again called for the Allies to seize important points throughout the

6. U.S. Foreign Relations, Tehran Papers, p. 553.
7. Churchill, Second World War, V, 374.

world to enforce the peace. Roosevelt believed such points should be placed under the trusteeship of the United Nations.

Churchill bridled at the word "trusteeship." Britain, he said, desired no new territory but neither would she surrender any except of her own free will. He specifically mentioned Hong Kong. Stalin said that far from taking anything away from Great Britain, he favored an enlargement of the British Empire. The United States and England, he suggested, should install more suitable governments in Spain and Portugal. Churchill asked what territorial interests the Soviet Union had. Stalin refused to be drawn saying only: "There is no need to speak at present, but when the time comes, we will."[8] The dinner ended at midnight. According to Lord Moran who saw Churchill just before he went to bed that night the Prime Minister said he "wanted to sleep for billions of years." Churchill also said: "Europe would be desolate and I may be held responsible."[9] Roosevelt's reaction was physical; he suffered from violent indigestion for the remainder of the night.

8. *U.S. Foreign Relations, Tehran Papers*, p. 553.
9. Wilson, *Churchill*, pp. 149, 151.

XVI

CHURCHILL SURRENDERS
November 30, 1943

Tuesday, November 30, 1943, was Churchill's sixty-ninth birthday. It was also the day the British surrendered. The Tehran Conference was now two days old, and in those two days Churchill and Brooke had used every argument they could muster to preserve the Mediterranean option. They had secured one success. They were also faced with a rising tide of Russian and American irritation.

The success was small. In the future, when the German Ambassador to Turkey, Franz von Papen, threatened Ankara with a Bulgarian declaration of war, the British Ambassador, Sir Hughe Knatchbull-Hugessen, could counter by saying that any Bulgarian move would result in a Soviet declaration of war on Sofia. Considering how terrified the Turks were at having the Russians anywhere in the Balkans, Knatchbull-Hugessen must have considered this addition to his meager armory of arguments for Turkish intervention to be of dubious value. Telling the Turkish Foreign Minister, Numan Menemencioglu, that one of the possible results of Turkey's joining the Allies would be to put the Russians in Bulgaria was not likely to generate much enthusiasm in his listener. In fact, von Papen, when he learned what was going on, could now threaten the Turks first with destruction at the hands of the Germans and then with possible liberation by the Red Army.

By November 30, however, what the Turks, much less the Bulgars, might or might not do was almost inconsequential. Churchill, Brooke, and Eden, on this the Prime Minister's birthday, had only two alternatives before them. They could go back to London or they could accept Overlord. To keep on arguing against Overlord would be worse than useless as it would just increase their isolation. As Brooke said that morning: "Unless we . . . give the Russians a firm date for Overlord, there would be no point in continuing the Conference."[1] He made this remark during a Combined Chiefs meeting; otherwise, he might have bracketed the Russians with the Americans. The British decided to give up. True, as a sort of rear guard action, they continued to press for the Turks, but with the men and supplies committed to Overlord and no real support from Roosevelt or Stalin, they were only playing the game out to the end.

Tuesday morning Churchill called on Stalin at the Soviet Embassy. According to his memoirs, he intended to remove from Stalin's mind the "false idea" that "the British . . . mean to stop 'Overlord' if they can, because they want to invade the Balkans instead."[2] He began by reminding Stalin that he was half American and that the things he "was going

1. *U.S. Foreign Relations, Tehran Papers*, p. 561.
2. "Tehran Conference," *International Affairs* (Moscow), August, 1961, pp. 115–17; Churchill, *Second World War*, V, 375–6.

to say should not be understood as disparaging to the Americans." Churchill then proceeded to be a little disparaging. If there was no commander for Overlord, the fault was Roosevelt's as it was up to the President to make the decision. Roosevelt "had delayed the appointment for domestic reasons connected with high personages." Churchill was pressing Roosevelt to make his choice before leaving Tehran.

Churchill also felt Stalin had been misinformed as to the available options. It was not, said Churchill, a question of keeping to the date for Overlord or pressing on in the Mediterranean; it was a choice between the Bay of Bengal and the date of Overlord. Churchill explained to Stalin the "unfortunate" presence of Chiang Kai-shek at Cairo, the landing craft "bottleneck," and American promise of Buccaneer for which he "was not keen." The Americans had committed themselves to Buccaneer to satisfy Chiang Kai-shek, against the advice of the British Staffs. If the Prime Minister could get these landing craft into the Mediterranean, they would be sufficient for his needs.

Churchill insisted he was serious about Overlord. As proof he mentioned the British divisions withdrawn from Italy and sent to England. Churchill said he was also impressed by Stalin's offer to join the war against Japan. Upon hearing this, he had suggested to the Americans a slowdown in the Pacific and the use of Pacific landing craft to strengthen the Overlord assault. The Prime Minister further believed, and this gave the full measure of his retreat, that of all the operations in the Mediterranean, the most promising was the one suggested by Stalin, the invasion of southern France. Elsewhere he wanted only an "amphibious landing . . . near the Tiber" to nourish the Italian campaign. Churchill promised that the exact date of Overlord would be given to Stalin at lunch. He thought Stalin "would be satisfied." Stalin, though he must have been pleased, issued a warning. He told Churchill: "If there were no operation in May, 1944, the Red Army would think there would be no operations at all that year. . . . If there was no big change in the

European war, . . . it would be very difficult for the Russians to carry on."[3]

While Churchill talked with Stalin, the Combined Chiefs met in the British Legation. Here, too, the British retreated. Brooke, echoing the Prime Minister, now proposed an operation in conjunction with Overlord against southern France.[4] He also thought it important to take Rome, but after Rome had been taken, the Italian front should be stabilized on the Pisa-Rimini line. Help would be given to the Partisans, but there was no more talk of landings in the Adriatic. As far as Rhodes and the Aegean were concerned, Brooke said everything depended upon Turkey. If Turkey came in, operations might be necessary. If Turkey did not, everything would be dropped. Brooke did point out that the cancellation of Buccaneer would make available additional landing craft for the Mediterranean, but the reference was almost casual. Brooke's Mediterranean sequence of operations was first Rome, possibly Rhodes, and then southern France. Both the Italian campaign and the attack on southern France, Operation Anvil, were "completely interlocked with Overlord."

When it came to Overlord, the Combined Chiefs considered not the operation itself but what date should be given the Russians. After a lengthy discussion, remarkable for its lack of acrimony, the date of "not later than 1 June" was agreed on. Initially, Marshall held out for May 1 or May 15. But this meant stripping the Italian theater of its landing craft immediately so that the ships could be prepared for an early Overlord. Without landing craft Eisenhower could not get to the Pisa-Rimini line, and since reaching this line was desired by everyone, Brooke persuaded Marshall to leave sixty-eight landing craft in the Mediterranean until January 15. This in turn meant a June date for Overlord as it would take about four months to get the ships ready for the cross-channel operation. A three-point memorandum embodying

3. Churchill, *Second World War*, V, 380.
4. For the minutes, see *U.S. Foreign Relations, Tehran Papers*, pp. 556–63.

these decisions, Pisa-Rimini, southern France, and a June
Overlord, was drawn up for submission to the President and
the Prime Minister. Leahy believed his "British colleagues"
finally "fell into line" because as military men they were
convinced Marshall's strategy was correct.[5]

At 1:30 in the afternoon, Churchill, Roosevelt, and Stalin
met for lunch in Roosevelt's quarters. The atmosphere was
far different from that of the previous day. Roosevelt read
Stalin the recommendations of the Combined Chiefs of
Staff. Stalin expressed great satisfaction and promised a
Russian offensive at the time of Overlord. He also asked
when Overlord's commander would be named. Roosevelt
said he hoped to make the appointment shortly after returning to Cairo. The President and Prime Minister also announced that they were making the Overlord commander
responsible for the southern France assault; Stalin approved.[6]

Churchill then asked Stalin if he had read the communiqué of the Cairo Conference with Chiang Kai-shek. Stalin
had, and although he could make "no commitments on the
Far East," he "thoroughly approved of the Communique
and all its contents." He favored both an independent Korea
and the transfer of Manchuria to China. However, he added
that "the Chinese must be made to fight." Roosevelt and
Churchill took Stalin's words to mean that the communiqué
could be released without change, which was done the
following day.

During the rest of the lunch, discussion centered on
Russia's need for warm water ports. It was Churchill who
introduced the topic by saying that Russia deserved year-
round access to the ocean and that this would form part of
the peace settlement. The Prime Minister believed all "could
be settled agreeably and as between friends." Stalin was
willing to discuss the question "at the proper time." He

5. Leahy, I Was There, p. 209.
6. U.S. Foreign Relations, Tehran Papers, pp. 555–6; Churchill, Second
World War, V, 381; "Tehran Conference," International Affairs (Moscow),
August, 1961, p. 117.

also wanted Churchill's views "as to the regime of the Dardanelles." Churchill thought it was not advisable to do anything about the Straits until the Turks had reached a decision on entering the war. He regarded the question as "legitimate" and "looked forward to the day when Russian fleets would be seen on all the seas of the world." Stalin pointed out that this was hardly the traditional position of the British Government. The Prime Minister did not "deny that in earlier days Russia and England had disagreed."

Roosevelt called for the internationalization of Bremen, Frankfurt, Lubeck, and the Kiel Canal. Stalin agreed and asked what could be done for Russia in the Far East. Roosevelt believed a "free port" solution could be used. He mentioned Dairen. Stalin doubted "the Chinese would like such a scheme." Roosevelt thought Chiang Kai-shek would go along if the port were under international guarantee. Stalin replied that "the Russians had their views" and would present them when they were "active . . . in the Far Eastern War."

Churchill held that discussions like this were important as the peace of the world rested upon the cooperation of the Soviet Union, the United Kingdom, and the United States. The powers must feel satisfied. "Hungry and ambitious nations" are "dangerous," and the Prime Minister would "like to see the leading nations of the world in the positions of rich and happy men."[7] Churchill's remark provided a pleasant note on which to end the luncheon, but before the guests left the table it was decided that the afternoon plenary session would be the last of the conference. The following day the Big Three would meet informally to discuss political matters.

As had been agreed Monday, Hopkins, Eden, and Molotov had their noon meal together in the British Legation.[8] Each had certain definite topics to explore. Hopkins tried to find out what the Soviet Union meant by "strong points to

7. *U.S. Foreign Relations, Tehran Papers*, p. 568.
8. Ibid., pp. 568–75; Sherwood, *Roosevelt and Hopkins*, p. 792.

keep the peace." Eden questioned Molotov as to whether
the Russians would keep their Bulgarian promise and cooperate in putting pressure on Turkey. Molotov, like Stalin,
was interested in the Dardanelles. There were also brief
references to Yugoslavia and Poland.

Hopkins opened the discussion by asking Molotov to
define "strong points." Molotov was evasive; he mentioned
the same two places Roosevelt had named on Sunday—
Bizerte and Dakar. This reply was followed by a brief
harangue on French decadence, which again parroted Stalin
and Roosevelt. To his credit Hopkins refused to be drawn
into side issues, and he spoke of possible air bases in Belgium. Eden suggested that the leasing of islands in the West
Indies to the United States by Great Britain might serve as
an example of how such arrangements could be made "with
friendly countries." Despite this not-so-subtle probing, the
Russian Foreign Minister refused to go beyond Bizerte and
Dakar, both of which he allocated to the Anglo-Americans.

Molotov did say that occupation of strong points would
affect the countries in which they were located and that the
powers responsible for securing the peace should provide the
forces. Despite Roosevelt's talk of United Nations control,
Hopkins admitted that the United States, too, had no intention of placing its Philippine bases under any international
authority. All agreed, however, that a United Nations approach would be a useful device for dealing with the French.
Hopkins pointed out that the question of "strong points"
was of the utmost importance and must be resolved in a
friendly way; otherwise, Great Britain, Russia, and the
United States might "start arming against [each] other."
Molotov proposed referral to the Big Three.

Eden then took up Turkey. He suggested a joint summons
to the Turks "making clear what consequences would follow" if she refused. President Ismet Inonu of Turkey would
be invited to come to Cairo and meet with Churchill and
Roosevelt. When Molotov rather reluctantly accepted this
procedure, Eden frankly asked whether the Soviet Union

had changed its mind about Turkish intervention. Hopkins, too, wanted to know if there was a shift in the Soviet position. Molotov said no, but that the Soviet Union was discouraged by the lack of success of Eden's November negotiations. Molotov repeated Stalin's pledge about Bulgaria and held this pledge proved the importance Russia attached to Turkish intervention. Molotov then pressed for a clarification of his own. He asked Eden the meaning of Churchill's comment on the Straits. Eden replied: "Frankly, I do not know." He added that Churchill probably had in mind putting pressure on the Turks; he said he would try to find out.

Hopkins did not like the renewed interest in Turkey and proceeded to throw some cold water on the topic. He said Turkish intervention might lead to such large military commitments as to delay Overlord; however, if important political and psychological advantages could be gained through Turkey's entering the war, the Americans might accept the delay. Molotov immediately asked whether the timing of Overlord and Turkish intervention were related. Hopkins said that such was the feeling of Washington, whereupon Molotov reversed his position and maintained that if this were so, Stalin would be opposed to forcing Turkey in. Eden did not, as would surely have been the case the previous day, protest. The British, too, were now tied to Overlord.

Discussion of Turkey was followed by much briefer consideration of Yugoslavia. Eden offered to make available to the Russians an air base in Egypt for the purpose of supplying Tito. Molotov mentioned that the Soviet General Staff planned to send a mission to Tito in Yugoslavia. Since the Russians were pursuing a Popular Front policy which tried to unite all resistance movements against the Germans, Molotov also talked about a possible mission to Mikailovic. Eden felt Mikailovic "would not be good to deal with." This produced an inconclusive discussion of the areas occupied by Tito, the Germans, and Mikailovic. The time was now approaching for the start of the plenary session. But, before leaving, Eden turned to Molotov and referred to what he called Churchill's "indiscreet conversation" on the Polish frontier. He wanted Soviet views on "how large Poland's two steps to the left" were going to be. Molotov agreed to further discussion. Hopkins said the President was shortly going to give Stalin his views on the subject.

With the decisions reached on the primacy of Overlord and the supporting operation in South France, the military part of the Tehran Conference was over. Consequently, the third plenary meeting was a brief affair.[9] Though all were familiar with its contents, Brooke read out the agreement reached by the Combined Chiefs that morning, and Stalin repeated his pledge to launch a massive assault on the eastern front at the same time as Overlord. As a great deal of work remained to be done on the southern France attack, Operation Anvil, which at present was little more than a sketch, Churchill and Roosevelt recommended that the Combined Chiefs return to Cairo in the morning. It was also agreed that Churchill, Roosevelt, and Stalin and their foreign policy advisers would remain in Tehran through December 2 to discuss political questions and to draft a conference communiqué.

Dinner that night was held at the British Legation in celebration of Churchill's birthday; it was a large affair and included the Combined Chiefs. Thanks to Churchill's surrender, the Americans and Russians were happy. Conversation took the form of toasts. Stalin complimented the American industrial machine "without which victory could not be won."[1] Roosevelt toasted the unity of the Big Three with the words "we can see in the sky, for the first time, that traditional symbol of hope, the rainbow." Churchill toasted that "worthy figure: Stalin the Great!" Overtones of

9. For the minutes of this meeting, see *U.S. Foreign Relations, Tehran Papers*, pp. 576–81. "Tehran Conference," *International Affairs* (Moscow), August, 1961, pp. 117–18.
1. *U.S. Foreign Relations, Tehran Papers*, pp. 583–5. Full text of the toast is given in the Log, ibid., p. 469. The Soviet Government has published nothing relating to the banquet.

Anglo-Russian friction, however, were still present. Bohlen heard Stalin mutter after one toast to his "fighting friend Churchill" the further observation "if it is possible for me to consider Churchill my friend." On another occasion, when Churchill had noted that the complexion of Great Britain was becoming "pinker" and Stalin interrupted to state that this was a sign of health, the Prime Minister "agreed provided the process was not carried so far as to induce congestion." It was the most relaxed dinner of the Tehran Conference. Churchill later wrote that he detected a "sense of solidarity."[2]

2. Churchill, *Second World War*, V, 387.

XVII

CROSS-CHANNEL ATTACK AND TERRITORIAL CONCESSIONS
December 1–7, 1943

The political discussions were to have occupied at least two more days; however, on Wednesday morning, December 1, a cold front passed through Cairo and meteorologists predicted cloudy conditions for Iran, particularly in the mountain passes, by Friday. Roosevelt's and Churchill's planes could climb above them, but that would necessitate the use of oxygen, and neither Admiral McIntyre nor Lord Moran, Roosevelt's and Churchill's respective physicians, wanted their charges to fly at high altitudes for any length of time. It was decided to end the conference Wednesday evening so that Churchill and Roosevelt could leave Thursday morning. Discussions began at noon and continued through both lunch and dinner and into the night. The meetings were held in the conference room of the Soviet Embassy. Present, other than the Big

Three, were Hopkins, Eden, and Molotov as well as the two Ambassadors from Moscow, Harriman and Clark Kerr.[1]

The first topic considered was an invitation to Ismet Inonu. It was agreed that the Turkish President would be asked to meet with Roosevelt and Churchill in Cairo on December 4 or 5. Churchill further volunteered that should Inonu say he would be unable to come to Cairo, the Prime Minister would himself go to Ankara. Either way, said Churchill, the Turks would be presented with "the ugly case that would result from their failure to accept the invitation to join the war and the unappetizing picture of what help could be afforded her if she did."[2]

Hopkins now played the role of the absent George Marshall. "Lord Root of the Matter," as Churchill liked to call Hopkins, wanted to pin Churchill down on the amount of military aid to be offered Turkey, which was to be limited to twenty squadrons of fighters and three antiaircraft regiments. Hopkins even tried to get a short handwritten note of his own signed by Roosevelt, Churchill, and Stalin, which read: "Under any circumstances it should be clearly understood that no mention should be made to President Inonu, implied or otherwise, that an amphibious landing could be made on Rhodes."[3] He failed in this attempt, but as Churchill admitted, it was but a small piece of cheese he had to offer the Turks—only a few aircraft and Russia's Bulgarian promise.

Stalin mentioned Eden's suggestion, made at Moscow, of getting the Turks in indirectly by requesting bases for Anglo-American or Russian aircraft but not asking that they declare war on Germany. Roosevelt approved; Eden, however, explained that this approach had been tried during his conversations with the Turkish Foreign Minister, but the Turks

1. For minutes of this meeting, see *U.S. Foreign Relations, Tehran Papers*, pp. 585–93; "Tehran Conference," *International Affairs* (Moscow), August, 1961, pp. 118–22.
2. *U.S. Foreign Relations, Tehran Papers*, p. 587.
3. A photograph of this document is included in Sherwood, *Roosevelt and Hopkins*, pp. 794–5.

maintained that they preferred peace or war, not a middle course. Churchill interjected that this was typical behavior. "If you suggested a small move they said they preferred the big. And if you suggested the big, they said they were not ready." Churchill also commented that he would have preferred to "offer something substantial to the Turks" so that if they refused, the British could "wash their hands of Turkey, both now and at the peace table."

For Molotov the opportunity to question Churchill directly as to what these hints about "the peace table" really meant proved irresistible. He noted that the Prime Minister had earlier said that if Turkey failed to enter the war "her interests in the Straits . . . would be adversely affected." Molotov "wished to know what this meant." Churchill took refuge in the British Constitution. He "personally favored a change" in the Montreux Convention, but he was bound by his Cabinet and they were "far away."

The British Cabinet may have been far away, but Roosevelt was not. The President proposed making the Dardanelles "free to the commerce of the world and fleets of the world, irrespective of whether Turkey entered the war or not." This remarkable suggestion, probably equally repugnant to both Great Britain and the Soviet Union, had the effect of cutting off further talk on the Straits. Instead, attention turned to the manner of Soviet participation in the Inonu meetings. Stalin proposed sending both his Ambassador to Turkey, Sergei Vinogradov, and his Deputy Foreign Minister, Andrei Vyshinsky, to Cairo. This was acceptable to Roosevelt and Churchill.

Roosevelt introduced the next topic, Finland; the President wanted to find out what sorts of terms the Soviet Union was willing to offer Finland should she drop out of the war. Stalin said that the Swedish Foreign Minister, Eric Boheman, had recently contacted the Soviet Ambassador in Stockholm, Mme. Alexandra Kollontay, on behalf of the Finnish Government. Boheman informed Mme. Kollontay that the Finns feared that Russia intended to destroy the

independence of their country and would like an opportunity for direct conversations. Stalin said he had instructed
Mme. Kollontay to reply that the Soviet Union had no
designs on Finnish independence or any objections to conversations, but would like to know under what conditions
the Finns would negotiate. He added that it was only today
that he had received the Finnish reply, the gist of which was
that the Finns desired to take the 1939 frontier as a basis of
negotiation and made no mention of peace with Russia
being followed by a declaration of war on Germany; this, in
his opinion, showed that the Finns had no serious interest in
peace.

Roosevelt and Churchill asked Stalin if Anglo-American
pressure might help; both also said they were pleased by
Stalin's statement regarding Finland's independence. Churchill further suggested that terms should be drawn so as to
give defense in depth to Leningrad and to assure Russian
supremacy in the eastern Baltic.[4] He pressed Stalin for a
concise statement of Russia's demands. Stalin replied these
would involve, first, the restoration of the Treaty of 1940,
with the possible exchange of Petsamo for Hango; second,
compensation for 50 percent of the damage done to the
Soviet Union by the Finns, the exact amount to be discussed; third, a break with Germany; and, finally, reorganiza-
tion of the Finnish Army. He added that Washington and
London had been told all this earlier, and since neither
government had seen fit to pass the information on to
Helsinki, it was obvious that his allies, too, felt the Finns
would not accept these demands.

Churchill was upset by the reference to reparations; he
questioned Finland's ability to pay. Stalin explained he
meant goods and services, such as paper and wood, but the
Soviet Union definitely wanted reparations. The Prime Minister, fully aware that a precedent was being set, said he had
always been impressed by the slogan "no annexation and no

4. Churchill, *Second World War*, V, 398.

indemnity." Stalin laughed and replied that he was "becoming a Conservative." Roosevelt remained silent.

It was now after 3 P.M., and as the President had requested a private conversation with Stalin on the Soviet Union's western frontier, he and Stalin withdrew to the President's quarters, which were immediately adjacent to the conference room. Hopkins had proposed this meeting at the end of the luncheon with Eden and Molotov the previous day. Roosevelt desired to explain to Stalin the facts of American political life. A decisive shift in American foreign policy was also involved; Roosevelt intended to accept Russia's territorial demands with no strings attached. Present, aside from Roosevelt and Stalin, were Harriman, Bohlen, Molotov, and Pavlov.[5] Roosevelt began by saying he had an election coming up in 1944, and while "personally he did not wish to run again, if the war was still in progress, he might have to." The President added that there were in the electorate from six to seven million Americans of Polish extraction and that as a practical politician "he did not wish to lose their vote." He personally accepted the necessity of shifting Poland's eastern frontier to the west and establishing her western frontier on the Oder. He hoped, however, that Stalin would understand that he could not "publicly take part in any such arrangement at the present time." Stalin "understood."[6]

The President went on to say that there were "numbers of persons of Lithuanian, Latvian and Estonian origin . . . in the United States." He "fully realized" that the three Republics had in Czarist times and "again more recently been a part of Russia." He added "jokingly" that when the Red Army "reoccupied these areas, he did not intend to go to war." On the other hand, American opinion would want some expression of the right of self-determination on the part of the peoples involved. This expression might take the

5. For Bohlen's minutes, see U.S. Foreign Relations, Tehran Papers, pp. 594–6.
6. Ibid., p. 594.

form of new plebiscites. Roosevelt hastened to add that the referendum need not take place immediately. "Some day" would be good enough, and he "personally was confident the people would vote to join the Soviet Union."

Roosevelt now rediscovered what was obvious on Sunday. Stalin would not tolerate the slightest hint that the Baltic States were not a part of the Soviet Union. No one had raised the question of public opinion before, and Stalin "did not quite see why it was being raised now." Roosevelt believed "the public neither knew nor understood" the issues involved. Stalin replied that if the public did not understand, they ought to be "informed and some propaganda work should be done." However, he then softened the effect of these words while maintaining the essentials of his position. He said there would be "opportunities" for the "expression of the will of the people," provided it was free from "any form of international control."

Roosevelt tried to pin Stalin down; he asked whether some public statement "in regard to the future elections to which the Marshal had referred" could be made as it would be "helpful to him personally." Stalin, who had said nothing about elections, avoided a direct answer, and the President did not insist. Thus, without even being asked for any concession, Stalin received *de facto* American recognition of Russia's principal territorial claims.[7]

The President then reverted to his proposal for the Four Policemen. He asked Stalin not to raise this issue with Churchill, as he felt it "premature." Stalin agreed and added that after thinking the matter over, he had come to believe with Roosevelt that the future United Nations Organization

7. Hull was not informed of this conversation. Indeed, on December 23, 1943, he instructed Harriman to "tactfully point out to the Soviet Union that any and all boundary questions must necessarily await the termination of the fighting." This does not mean, however, that Stalin had not received *de facto* recognition. As late as July and August of 1946, Washington raised no protest when delegations of the Latvian, Lithuanian, and Estonian Soviet Socialist Republics participated in the debates of the Paris Peace Conference. For Hull's telegram, see *U.S. Foreign Relations*, 1943, III, 611–12, and Note 46, 611.

"should be worldwide and not regional." The President asked what decision had been reached concerning his memorandums on shuttle bombing and military cooperation in the Far East. Stalin replied that he "had not had time to study the documents" and would take the matter up with Harriman on his return to Moscow. With this, the "private exchange" ended.

At six the regular session reconvened.[8] Roosevelt opened the meeting by saying there were two main questions remaining for discussion—Poland and the German settlement. Molotov interrupted to inquire whether it would be possible to obtain any answer on the Soviet Union's request, made at Moscow, for Italian ships. Roosevelt said he favored the use of Italian merchant and naval vessels by all three powers until the end of the war, when a formal division based on title and possession might be made. Churchill inquired where the Soviet Union would like its share delivered. Stalin replied in the Black Sea if Turkey came into the war; if not, then to the northern ports. Roosevelt and Churchill agreed. Churchill further asked that the decision be kept secret as several months would be required to work out the arrangements, and he wanted to avoid any possibility of mutiny in the Italian fleet and the scuttling of the ships. Stalin ignored the several months and proposed delivery by the end of January, 1944. This was accepted; the number and type of vessels were to be those named in the Soviet request of October—one battleship, one cruiser, eight destroyers, four submarines, and forty thousand tons of merchant shipping. Having amicably disposed of the Italian fleet, Roosevelt returned to the first item of his informal agenda, Poland. He asked Stalin if "negotiations could be started for the reestablishment of [diplomatic] relations between the Polish [Government-in-Exile in London] and the Soviet Government." Stalin in reply repeated his April arguments, at the time of the Katyn Forest incident, justifying the break. The

8. For the minutes, see U.S. *Foreign Relations, Tehran Papers*, pp. 597–605.

London Poles were described as being pro-German. He also made the new accusation that their agents in Poland were murdering anyone who sympathized with the Allied cause. Roosevelt, though well aware of what had really happened at Katyn, kept silent. Churchill, however, pointed out that England had gone to war because of Poland and warned Stalin not to underestimate the importance of this question to the British public. The Prime Minister remarked that he had been astounded when Chamberlain, after refusing a guarantee to the Czechs, had guaranteed the Poles. He had been astonished and glad. Churchill requested a resumption of normal relations, adding, almost as an afterthought, that the frontier question might properly be settled along the lines of his "matchsticks" proposal.

Stalin was fully aware of what Churchill meant. Britain would try to force the London Poles to accept the Curzon Line if in return the Soviet Union would restore diplomatic relations. He intended to go along with this proposal, but not before he in turn made the point that the London Government would have to alter both its policies and its personnel. Stalin began by saying that for security reasons Russia, more than any other country, was interested in having friendly relations with Poland. Not merely did he favor the reconstitution of Poland, but also its "expansion at the expense of Germany." On the other hand, Stalin said one must distinguish between Poland and the London Government. The Soviet Union had broken relations not out of whim, but because of the Government-in-Exile's slanderous propaganda attacks and their complicity in the murders of partisans within German-occupied Poland. If relations were restored, what guarantee did he have that such activities would not continue? Russia would welcome relations with a Polish Government that led its people in the common struggle but he "was not sure the Polish Government-in-Exile could be such a government." After this preface, Stalin made the carefully qualified statement that "if the London Poles would go along with the Partisan movement and sever connections with German agents . . ., then Russia would be prepared to negotiate with them."

Churchill in turn became more explicit. If some reasonable territorial formula could be devised, he would recommend it to the Polish Government-in-Exile. This would be done without telling them the Soviet Government had previously accepted the solution. If the Poles refused the frontier, Great Britain would be "through with them . . . and not oppose the Soviet Government . . . at the peace table." Stalin accepted the offer. He asked for the 1941 boundary, which he said restored to the Soviet Union parts of the Ukraine and White Russia taken from them in 1921. Eden commented that this was the Ribbentrop-Molotov line. Stalin replied, "Call it what you will, we consider it just and right." Molotov claimed the new frontier paralleled the Curzon Line. Eden stated there were differences, but Molotov insisted that they were not in essentials.

Throughout these exchanges Roosevelt had remained silent, but now he asked Bohlen to spread out on the conference table a series of maps of eastern Poland which had been prepared by the State Department Advisory Committee on Postwar Foreign Policy. After some consideration of maps showing ethnography, to which Stalin objected as being based on Polish statistics, the Big Three concentrated their attention on map number twelve, which showed the Polish-Soviet boundary of 1939. It showed the Curzon Line, it showed the boundary as of June, 1941, and it also included three hypothetical Polish-Soviet frontiers which in general followed the Curzon Line except that they assigned Lvov and the surrounding area to the Poles.

As the Curzon Line and the 1941 line largely corresponded, and as both Churchill and Roosevelt had separately given Stalin assurances on this question, there was hardly any discussion, much less negotiation. Stalin requested one major deviation from the Curzon Line. He pointed out that in the northern sector around the rail center of Bialystok, the Curzon Line ran approximately a hundred miles to the east of the 1941 line. He picked up a red pencil and, tracing along the Lithuanian-Polish frontier from its meeting with the Curzon Line to the boundary of East Prussia, he continued to draw across Prussia until his pencil met the Baltic at Koenigsberg. Poland, he announced, while making some parallel strokes on the map to indicate the area under consideration, could have Bialystok if the Soviet Union received Koenigsberg, Insterburg, and Tilsit. There were no objections from Roosevelt or Churchill. Poland's eastern frontier would be a modified Curzon Line. Roosevelt requested and Stalin approved a "voluntary transfer" of population from mixed areas.

Roosevelt proceeded to the second item on his agenda—Germany. He said he felt the basic question was whether or not to split up Germany. Stalin replied that he preferred dismemberment. Churchill agreed and suggested that Prussia in particular, as the evil core of German militarism, ought to be detached from the rest of the Reich. Roosevelt, who had been expecting this response, proceeded to introduce his own plan for a five-way division of the Reich. These were to be first, Prussia, made as small as possible; second, Hanover and the Northwest; third, Saxony; fourth, Hesse-Darmstadt, Hesse-Kassel, and a general area south of the Rhine; and, finally, Bavaria, Baden, and Wurttemberg. The parts would be independent and self-governing. The President further suggested that two additional regions be placed under some form of international control. One was the Kiel Canal and Hamburg. The other was the Ruhr and Saar.

Churchill commented, "To use an American expression, the President has said a mouthful."[9] The Prime Minister then introduced a two-way plan, a separate and reduced Prussia with the rest of Germany linked to Austria and Hungary in a Danubian Confederation. Considering the vigor with which Molotov had countered Eden's talk of a Balkan Confederation at Moscow, Stalin's reaction to the

9. Churchill, *Second World War*, V, 401.

resurrection of the Hapsburg Monarchy in an enlarged form was predictable. He liked Roosevelt's plan and disliked Churchill's. According to Stalin, to include Germans within the framework of a large confederation would simply facilitate their revival as a great power. The Soviet Union desired the independence of Austria, Hungary, Rumania, and Bulgaria. Stalin added that Churchill was mistaken in identifying German militarism with Prussia. All Germans, with the exception of the Austrians, fought like devils. He supported the elimination of the Prussian Officer Corps, but as to the mentality of the people, Stalin held there was no "difference between one part of Germany and another."

Roosevelt said he agreed with Stalin. Fifty years ago when the President had lived in Germany there were regional differences, but this was no longer true. Also, like Stalin, Roosevelt would make an exception for the Austrians. Churchill, who could see the Balkanization of Central Europe emerging, interrupted to say he was most emphatically not opposed to dismemberment. He sought a divided Germany, but the division should be so arranged to last for fifty years, and he doubted that Roosevelt's scheme could survive for so long a period. Stalin replied that no matter what plan was adopted, Germany would always seek reunification; therefore, Churchill's idea was more dangerous than Roosevelt's. Stalin further held that prevention of reunification would be one of the tasks of the United Nations Organization. Churchill asked "whether Marshal Stalin contemplated a Europe composed of little states, disjointed, separated and weak."[1]

Stalin denied the charge. He replied that he sought the breakup not of Europe but of Germany. Aside from the increase in the strength of Poland and the elimination of Germany, Stalin anticipated the restoration of prewar conditions. Europe would again be a mixture of major powers like France and Italy and smaller, weaker states such as Rumania and Bulgaria. Churchill attempted to head off any commit-

1. *U.S. Foreign Relations, Tehran Papers*, p. 603.

ment on the partitioning of Germany by turning the discussion back to Poland's new frontiers. He read the following memorandum which he held embodied the decisions taken: "It is thought in principle that the home of the Polish state and nation should be between the so-called Curzon Line and the Line of the Oder, including for Poland East Prussia and the province of Oppeln; but the actual tracing of the frontier line requires careful study, and possibly the disentanglement of the population at some points."[2]

Roosevelt insisted, however, that before the Polish question was decided, some agency ought to be assigned the task of studying German dismemberment. Churchill, after carefully pointing out that the present discussion had been only of the most broad and preliminary nature, accepted the suggestion of further study, whereupon the Big Three agreed to add this to the other duties of the European Advisory Commission.

Churchill again asked for approval of his Polish formula and repeated his earlier pledge that he would present it to Premier Mikolajczyk without informing him that it had already been accepted by the Soviet Union. He also requested that Stalin put a kink in the Curzon Line in the vicinity of Lvov so that this predominantly Polish city could be in the new Poland. Stalin, who had just made a far larger alteration of that line in the north so as to make Koenigsberg a Russian city, bluntly refused. He did, however, say that if Churchill would accept the Koenigsberg transfer, he would approve the British formula. It was now time for dinner. Although no definite answer had been given the Prime Minister, it was assumed that Churchill would open territorial negotiations with Mikolajczyk, the successful completion of which the Anglo-Americans expected would in turn lead to the restoration of diplomatic relations between Moscow and a now friendly Polish Government-in-Exile.

The dinner meeting lasted until 10:30 that night. After

2. "Tehran Conference," *International Affairs* (Moscow) August, 1961, p. 122.

eight straight hours of negotiation, all present were tired and
Bohlen thought Stalin looked particularly exhausted, but the
Big Three continued their work until texts had been agreed
on for the conference communiqué, a Three-Power Declaration on Iran, and a brief memorandum embodying the
military decisions of the conference.[3]

Although Molotov had agreed that the representatives in
Tehran of the United States, Great Britain, and the Soviet
Union should discuss the various proposals put forward by
Hull and Eden during the Moscow Conference dealing with
Iran, no such conversation had taken place. The American
Minister, Louis Dreyfus, and the British Minister, Reader
Bullard, found the Russians in Iran just as uncooperative as
their superiors in Moscow. By November, however, the
proposals on Iran were no longer the exclusive concern of
the Big Three. Hull had stopped in Tehran on his way back
from Moscow and had mentioned the drafts to the Iranian
Government.[4] Later in the month the British Embassy
provided the Iranians with the Moscow texts. When it was
learned the Big Three would meet in Tehran, the Iranians
seized the opportunity to present their case. On the morning
of November 29, acting on instructions of the Shah Mohammed Reza Pahlavi, the Prime Minister of Iran, Ali
Soheily, called on Eden and the American Minister Louis
Dreyfus. He asked the Big Three to issue a statement on
Iran recognizing in specific terms Iran's assistance in the war
against Germany, confirming that the powers would withdraw from Iran when Germany was defeated, and promising
postwar economic aid.

Eden and Dreyfus agreed in principle with Soheily's pro-
posal. Eden further suggested that the next step for the
Iranian Government would be to approach Molotov and win
Soviet approval. Molotov was uninterested. Indeed, the

3. There are no minutes for this final meeting. It is described in a
memorandum written by Charles Bohlen after his return to Moscow. *U.S.
Foreign Relations, Tehran Papers*, pp. 836–8. See also Churchill, *Second
World War*, V, 404; Sherwood, *Roosevelt and Hopkins*, p. 798.
4. Hull, *Memoirs*, II, 1506.

whole matter might have been passed over but for John Jernegan, Third Secretary of the American Legation, and Roosevelt's friend Patrick Hurley, then enjoying the rather cumbersome title of Personal Representative of the President on Mission to the Middle East with the Rank of Ambassador. Dreyfus informed Hurley of Soheily's request, and Hurley immediately went to Roosevelt, who both approved the idea of a "Declaration on Iran" and charged Hurley with the task of its preparation. At this point Jernegan, who had participated in the Moscow discussions, showed Hurley a rough draft he himself had worked up combining the earlier proposals. This draft, shortened and altered so as to cover the three points raised by Soheily, though in the most general way, was approved by Hurley on the night of the 29th and became the basis of the Iranian declaration.[5]

The following day, November 30, the Shah, together with Soheily, called on Churchill, Roosevelt, and Stalin while Hurley saw Eden and Molotov. By the evening of the 30th, the British had approved the draft and the Soviets, although doubtful, had not rejected it. On December 1 the Russians fell into line perhaps because the wording was so vague as to make the declaration almost meaningless. In fact, of the two issues which most concerned the Iranian Government, the treatment of Iran as an economic unit and the early withdrawal of British and Soviet troops, the draft was wholly silent on the first and vaguer than the Anglo-Soviet-Iranian Treaty on the second.

There was no real discussion of the declaration by the Big Three at dinner. The declaration did, however, produce one last exchange between Churchill and Stalin. The Prime Minister desired to substitute the name *Persia* for *Iran* in order to avoid any confusion between Iran and Iraq. Stalin brushed this aside with the remark that the name of the country they were in was Iran and no other. Roosevelt

5. *U.S. Foreign Relations, Tehran Papers*, pp. 646–9.

backed Stalin, and Churchill said he surrendered. When the time came to sign the declaration, Stalin insisted Churchill go first so that the Prime Minister might know "the designation of the country that they were in."[6]

The declaration stated that the three powers would give full consideration to any economic problems confronting Iran at the close of hostilities. It recognized the assistance which Iran had given in the prosecution of the war and concluded with the pledge that "the United States, the Union of Soviet Socialist Republics, and the United Kingdom are at one with the Government of Iran in their desire for the maintenance of the independence, sovereignty and territorial integrity of Iran." The Iranians were disappointed at the vagueness of the wording but pleased that they had received some sort of American commitment. The Iranian Foreign Minister, Mohammed Saed, initialed the declaration that night.

The communiqué entitled a "Declaration of the Three Powers" was a short document intended to serve as no more than a press release. Stalin and Molotov, however, went over it word by word. Harry Hopkins was its main author, although the President had taken a personal hand in the drafting. At one stage it included a sentence which might have engendered some discussion; the sentence drew a distinction between the German people and their political and military leadership and may have reflected Stalin's criticism of the propaganda effectiveness of unconditional surrender. However, it did not appear in the version considered by the Big Three Wednesday night. Instead, the world was informed that Churchill, Roosevelt, and Stalin had met in cordial conferences and were determined that their nations would work together in war and in the peace that followed. As to the war, German forces were promised destruction. As to peace, the Three recognized "fully the supreme responsibil-

6. Ibid., p. 838.

ity resting upon us . . . to make a peace which will command the good will of the overwhelming mass of the peoples of the world." Lesser states, "whose people are dedicated . . . to the elimination of tyranny and slavery, oppression and intolerance" would be allowed to "cooperate."[7] The declaration was not signed.

The last and by far the most important paper approved Wednesday night was one entitled "Military Conclusions of the Tehran Conference." It had been prepared by the military staffs the previous day and read as follows:

The Conference:

(1) Agreed that the partisans in Yugoslavia should be supported by supplies and equipment to the greatest possible extent, and also by Commando operations.

(2) Agreed that, from the military point of view, it was most desirable that Turkey should come into the war on the side of the Allies before the end of the year.

(3) Took note of Marshal Stalin's statement that if Turkey found herself at war with Germany, and as a result Bulgaria declared war on Turkey or attacked her, the Soviet would immediately be at war with Bulgaria. The Conference further took note that this fact would be explicitly stated in the forthcoming negotiations to bring Turkey into the war.

(4) Took note that Operation "Overlord" would be launched during May 1944, in conjunction with an operation against Southern France. The latter operation would be undertaken in as great a strength as availability of landing craft permitted. The Conference further took note of Marshal Stalin's statement that the Soviet forces would launch an offensive at about the same time with the object of preventing the German forces from transferring from the Eastern to the Western Front.

(5) Agreed that the military Staffs of the three Powers should henceforward keep in close touch with each other in regard to

7. For the text as approved Wednesday night, see ibid., pp. 640–1.

the impending operations in Europe. In particular it was agreed that a cover plan to mystify and mislead the enemy as regards these operations should be concerted between the Staffs concerned.[8]

The initialing of this document at 10:30 P.M., Wednesday, December 1, 1943, constituted the last act of the Tehran Conference. The atmosphere was cordial, but Stalin, Roosevelt, and Churchill did not imitate the Foreign Secretaries and indulge in a long round of mutual congratulations. Harry Hopkins believed that this moment, the successful completion of Eureka, represented the supreme peak in Roosevelt's career, with the President convinced he had won Stalin's acceptance of Washington's grand design.[9] The friendly cooperation of the three Policemen had been achieved, and both the winning of the war and the maintenance of the peace were secured. Eden, however, records that at the end of Eureka he was feeling less easy than he had at the close of the Moscow Conference. He was disturbed by the sudden shifts in Soviet policy as exemplified in their attitude toward Turkey. Roosevelt's keeping Churchill at arm's length was also upsetting. Above all, Eden began "to fear greatly for the Poles."[1]

Roosevelt left the Soviet Embassy at the end of the meeting and spent the night at the American Army Camp in Amirabad. On December 2 the President and Prime Minister flew out of Tehran. Their destination was Cairo, where they would rejoin the Combined Chiefs and settle the details of Anglo-American planning in light of the decisions of Eureka. Settling these details kept everyone in Cairo until December 7.

The most important point still unresolved was the question of Turkish intervention. On December 1 Churchill and Roosevelt invited President Ismet Inonu to meet with them

---

8. Ibid., p. 652; Churchill, *Second World War*, V, 404.
9. Sherwood, *Roosevelt and Hopkins*, p. 799.
1. Eden, *Memoirs*, II, 497.

in Cairo on Saturday, December 4.[2] The Turks were anxious
to learn what had happened at Tehran, but they hoped to
avoid any "orders" from the great powers. President Inonu
told the British Ambassador Knatchbull-Hugessen on
Thursday that he was willing to fly to Cairo provided there
would be "free discussion . . . as between equals." Churchill and Roosevelt immediately cabled their assurances, whereupon President Inonu agreed to come to Cairo. Inonu was
accompanied by his Foreign Minister Numan Menemencioglu and a small party which included the American, British,
and Soviet Ambassadors to Ankara: Laurence Steinhardt,
Sir Hughe Knatchbull-Hugessen, and Sergei Vinogradov.
Inonu did not make the mistake of bringing with him any
Turkish military authorities. His delegation was aggressively
civilian.

The Turkish talks, which lasted from December 4 to
December 7, followed the course everyone expected.[3] Churchill argued, threatened, and cajoled. The Turks must come
in now. The United States, Great Britain, and the Soviet
Union were all asking for a proper decision. If Turkey "accepted the invitation . . . Turco-Russian relations would
be put on the best possible footing."[4] She must not miss her
chance. Didn't Turkey want to sit on the bench with the
victorious powers? Did she want the war to end with Turkey
wandering about in court? If Turkey failed in her duty, the
Anglo-Turkish Alliance would cease to have any value. Again
and again Churchill mentioned the Soviet promise about
Bulgaria. He wanted the immediate infiltration of radar and
other specialists to prepare Turkish air bases for the Royal
Air Force. When the bases were ready, the planes would fly
in and Turkey would declare war. Four to six weeks should

2. For the text of the invitation, see *U.S. Foreign Relations, Tehran
Papers*, p. 633.
3. There were three formal meetings of Churchill, Roosevelt, and Inonu
at Cairo. For the minutes, see ibid., pp. 690–8, 711–18, 740–7; see also
Churchill, *Second World War*, V, 415–18; Eden, *Memoirs*, II, 497; Sherwood, *Roosevelt and Hopkins*, pp. 799–800.
4. *U.S. Foreign Relations, Tehran Papers*, p. 691.

provide sufficient time. Churchill's courtship was unremitting. It continued through formal meetings, informal meetings, dinners, and luncheons. The Prime Minister was both unsuccessful and unsupported.

President Inonu learned at the start that the Anglo-Americans intended to launch a second front in 1944 and that consequently the only military hardware his allies could supply would be some twenty fighter squadrons and a few antiaircraft units. From that point on, Churchill's cause was in trouble. Almost regretfully Inonu pointed to what might have been. Inonu said he could contemplate two things: first, a plan of preparation involving supplies, and second, a plan of military collaboration. Turkey wanted to fight side by side with British and American contingents in her own part of the world. This should be done "on a big basis."

As for what Churchill proposed, the Turks would have none of it. Inonu was, of course, diplomatic. According to him, even in the darkest days Turkey had believed in the Allied cause, and she believed in it now. Turkey would enter the war as soon as she was equipped. All Inonu wanted "was a reasonable, practical plan." The Turks felt that infiltration of guns and technicians would bring on a full-scale German attack. Turkey was not prepared to meet such an attack, nor could her allies assist her. As Churchill saw it, things were getting into a difficult circle. The British were "satisfied that no preparation could be effective without the introduction of personnel while the Turks refused the introduction of personnel because of the danger of provoking Germany." Inonu pointed out that twenty fighter squadrons hardly constituted a practical plan; the cheese was too small. Churchill's threats were also meaningless as everyone knew Great Britain would never abandon Turkey to Russia. Having drawn his circle, Inonu stayed in it for the next three days.

If British threats were only gestures, this was not true of American or Soviet threats. Inonu could and did resist Churchill. He might not have been able to stand up to Stalin and Roosevelt. Fortunately, from a Turkish viewpoint, he didn't have to. Nominally Roosevelt supported Churchill. His assistance, however, was of the silent variety, and on the few occasions he did speak, Churchill must have found the intervention far from helpful. Roosevelt would welcome Turkey to the ranks of the United Nations. Beyond that, Roosevelt found Inonu's views reasonable. He "vigorously disclaimed" any intention of forcing Turkey into the war.[5] Roosevelt doubted whether dates could be fixed for Turkish intervention. He advised Inonu that it was very necessary that the Turks have full political talks with the Russians. Roosevelt felt it would "be a mistake to defer the political phase" until the Turks were militarily involved. This last point was particularly telling, for if the Americans gave only limited support to Churchill, the Russians gave none at all.

Upon landing at Cairo, Harry Hopkins was disturbed when he failed to find the Soviet Deputy Foreign Minister Andrei Vyshinsky on the scene. He immediately cabled Harriman, who was still in Tehran and was preparing to return to Moscow, to go and see Molotov at once and make certain the Russian representatives would be in Cairo by the 4th. Harriman replied on December 3 that Molotov had already left Tehran. He suggested that Hopkins himself get hold of Vyshinsky, who as the Soviet delegate on the Italian Commission was supposed to be in Algiers, and offer him air transport to Cairo. Hopkins did and Vyshinsky finally appeared on December 9, two days after the Cairo Conference had ended and full of explanations about delayed messages from Moscow.[6]

Nor was it only with Vyshinsky that Soviet communications broke down. The other Russian representative at the Turkish talks was supposed to be their Ambassador to Ankara, Sergei Vinogradov. Vinogradov, too, had his difficulties. When President Inonu was leaving Turkey, the Russian Ambassador had yet to receive any instructions. The

5. Ibid., p. 696.
6. Ibid., pp. 839, 858–9.

American and British Ambassadors persuaded him to go to
Cairo as President Inonu's guest. They believed instructions
might be awaiting him there. Steinhardt and Knatchbull-
Hugessen were right; when Vinogradov landed, Moscow
informed him that Russia would be represented by Vyshinsky. Ambassador Vinogradov promptly went into seclusion
and refused to attend a single meeting with the Turks even
as an observer. A puzzled Ambassador Steinhardt cabled
Washington that as late as Christmas Eve Vinogradov was
still without word from Moscow. Whether by policy or by
accident, there were, as Roosevelt was quick to point out, no
Russian negotiators at Cairo. Inonu added this to his list of
arguments. He "regretted the Russians were not at the
Conference," and the Turkish Foreign Minister Numan,
too, had lots of points he "would like to discuss" with the
Russians.[7] Roosevelt "thought there was much in this."
Churchill never gave up, but he was defeated. Without men,
without supplies, without a plan, without American and
Russian support, the Turks, as Hopkins noted, became in-
creasingly deaf to Churchill's pleas.[8]

But if Churchill lost the Turks, which was important,
Roosevelt also lost Buccaneer, which was unimportant.
Roosevelt, however, fought almost as long and as hard as
Churchill to keep his promise to Chiang Kai-shek. Like it or
not, when the British returned to Cairo they were pledged to
Overlord and Anvil, and they intended to make both operations work. Brooke in the Combined Chiefs meetings
sounded exactly like George Marshall at Quebec. Overlord
and Anvil must have overriding priority, and nothing could
be undertaken anywhere in the world which might jeopardize either. According to Brooke, Anvil required two or more
divisions in assault and a ten-division drive up the Rhone
River.[9] Overlord, too, must be beefed up, and since Medi-

7. Ibid., p. 713.
8. Sherwood, *Roosevelt and Hopkins*, p. 799.
9. For Brooke's views on Anvil expressed during the first meeting of the
Combined Chiefs at Cairo on December 3, see *U.S. Foreign Relations,
Tehran Papers*, p. 671.

terranean landing craft were being assigned to Overlord, Mountbatten's landing craft must be assigned to Anvil. In short, the Americans could keep either their promise to Chiang or their promise to Stalin, but they could not keep both.

Brooke also had three other arguments against Buccaneer, one of which was embarrassing to the British. First, the Russians were pledged to fight Japan, which pledge greatly reduced the value of Chinese bases. Second, the Combined Planning Staff in Cairo during Eureka had produced an overall plan for Asia, which stressed air and sea power and held the main effort against Japan should be put into a drive straight across the Pacific.[1] The last, embarrassing reason was that Mountbatten, now back in India, cabled that he needed additional resources for Buccaneer. Since Mountbatten's request came at an opportune moment for Brooke, there might have been some suspicion of collusion. This was not the case. Mountbatten wanted to use 58,000 men to assault an island defended by 5,000. Churchill was furious with his protégé, so furious he not merely sent a rocket to Mountbatten asking for an explanation but even told Roosevelt that if odds of ten to one were required to defeat the Japanese, the war was impossible. Embarrassing and impossible, Mountbatten's request was a blow against Buccaneer.

King, Arnold, Leahy, and Marshall were as quick to defend Roosevelt as Brooke and his colleagues were to defend Churchill. The Combined Chiefs deadlocked; closed sessions changed nothing. Buccaneer was declared sacred for political reasons. It was clear, however, that the Joint Chiefs' hearts weren't in it. Roosevelt held out from Thursday to Monday. By Sunday night, though, the President was as completely isolated as Churchill had been at Tehran. Not only were the British against him, but Hopkins, Leahy, Marshall, and King all took turns explaining the advantages of an increased amphibious lift in the Mediterranean. On

1. For the full text, see ibid., pp. 765–73.

Monday Roosevelt surrendered and cabled Chiang that Buccaneer was off.[2] The President said he hoped the Generalissimo would be prepared to go ahead in Burma substituting naval superiority and commando operations in the Bay of Bengal for Buccaneer. If not, Roosevelt asked whether Chiang would prefer to have the Burma campaign delayed. Chiang's answer was to cancel Burma and demand a billion dollars in gold.[3]

With the Turks adamant and Roosevelt's surrender, Sextant-Eureka was over. Monday evening, December 6, Churchill and Roosevelt signed the final report of the Combined Chiefs of Staff. Stalin was also informed that Roosevelt had decided to give the Overlord command to General Dwight Eisenhower.[4] It was George Marshall who drafted the message; Marshall later gave the handwritten original with Roosevelt's signature at the bottom to Eisenhower as a memento.

Churchill had remained loyal to Overlord during the Cairo talks. Only once, on Saturday, did the Prime Minister, like President Inonu, muse aloud before the Americans about what might have been. Eden mentioned that the Rumanians seemed willing to surrender unconditionally. Churchill again pointed to the great advantages that were to be gained in the Mediterranean. He said that "if we could get a grip on the Balkans . . . the next Conference might be held in Budapest."[5] The decisive paragraphs of the Combined Chiefs of Staff report on Monday read:

> Overlord and Anvil are the supreme operations for 1944. They must be carried out during May, 1944. Nothing must be undertaken in any other part of the world which hazards the success of these two operations.

2. For a reproduction of the cable to Chiang Kai-shek, see Sherwood, *Roosevelt and Hopkins,* p. 801.
3. *U.S. Foreign Relations, China, 1943,* pp. 180–2.
4. *Stalin's Correspondence,* II, No. 149, 112.
5. *U.S. Foreign Relations, Tehran Papers,* p. 680.

We have examined the role that Turkey might be called upon to adopt if she agrees to come into the war* and the extent of our commitments that is likely to be involved.

* See [Overlord] paragraph above.[6]

According to Harry Hopkins, when Roosevelt left Cairo on the morning of December 7, 1943, he was a happy man and convinced he had "gotten" Stalin.[7] Earlier Lord Moran had asked, "Tell me, Harry, is the President quite certain about Moscow?"[8] On December 10 General Brooke had lunch with Churchill, who remained behind at Cairo to settle what British general would become Supreme Commander of an emptying Mediterranean theater. Churchill passed the lunch swatting flies and building a little fly mortuary beside his plate. Over and over the Prime Minister repeated the sentence: "It is all quite simple, there are just three areas . . ." Then he would swat a fly; the sentence was never completed. It was the first sign of the Prime Minister's complete physical collapse which shortly followed the Tehran Conference.[9]

6. The asterisk and following phrase are in the source text; see ibid., pp. 812–13.
7. Sherwood, *Roosevelt and Hopkins*, pp. 798–9.
8. Wilson, *Churchill*, p. 153.
9. Bryant, *Triumph in the West*, pp. 78–9.

CONCLUSION

W inston Churchill called the relationship which existed between America, Great Britain, and the Soviet Union during the Second World War the Grand Alliance. When applied to the cooperation of Washington and London, the phrase had some justification, though there were unshared secrets and periods of tension and sharp disagreement. When applied to relations between the Soviet Union and her Anglo-American partners, Churchill's designation, as he well knew, was almost meaningless. Despite contrary wartime propaganda, from Pearl Harbor to the summer of 1943, the Anglo-Americans and the Russians were at best uneasy cobelligerents, and during the summer of 1943 conditions further deteriorated. Stalin recalled Maisky from Great Britain and Litvinov from the United States. London was informed that Maisky's replacement as Ambassador would be one of the better junior men in the Soviet Foreign Ministry. And in a personal message to Roosevelt and Churchill, Stalin virtually accused his allies of watching Germany and the Soviet Union cripple each other in a war without mercy while they husbanded their resources and waited for the moment when intervention would make America and Britain the arbiters of an exhausted Europe.

Tensions among powers so ideologically diverse as the United States, Great Britain, and the Soviet Union were inevitable. But it was what Stalin regarded as broken promises and false dealings by his cobelligerents, not ideology, that produced the crisis of 1943. In three areas particularly Stalin felt that Roosevelt and Churchill, sometimes acting together and sometimes acting separately, had deceived him. These were the American refusal to recognize the Soviet Union's western frontier, a prolonged reduction in the number of lend-lease convoys to Murmansk and Archangel during a crucial stage of the war in Russia, and the often promised but never fulfilled mounting of an Anglo-American cross-channel assault on Hitler's Europe. The last was incomparably the most important issue, and the admission by Roosevelt and Churchill that no such attack would be made in 1943 provoked Stalin's denunciation. What the Soviet Premier failed to see, or would not admit, was that his own policy of isolation and suspicion contributed to the crisis.

In December, 1941, the Soviet Union asked Great Britain to agree to a Treaty of Alliance containing formal recognition of Russia's European frontier as it existed on the day of the German attack. This frontier made all of Latvia, Lithuania and Estonia, as well as large parts of prewar Poland, Finland, and Rumania, Soviet territory. The total area amounted to 180,000 square miles. Its population was twenty-two million. Except for parts of Rumania, the land had been defined as the Soviet Union's sphere of influence by a secret protocol to the Nazi-Soviet Non-Aggression Treaty of 1939. Despite this dubious provenance, London early in 1942 indicated that it was willing to accept the frontier.

The American State Department opposed any wartime territorial settlements. Washington further implied that if the Soviet Union retreated on the frontier question, her allies would launch a cross-channel attack probably in 1942 and certainly in 1943. Washington had its way, and the Anglo-Soviet Treaty of Alliance signed by Molotov and Eden on May 26, 1942, said nothing about the Russian boundary. It pledged the parties to no separate peace with Hitler or his European satellites and to twenty-five years of future friendship. Although carrying the main burden of the war against Germany, the Soviet Union could not get agreement on her frontiers. Nor were there any cross-channel attacks in 1942 or 1943.

On October 1, 1941, and again on October 6, 1942, the Soviet Union, the United States, and Great Britain negotiated formal lend-lease protocols which allocated to Russia specific and massive amounts of military equipment and other supplies. The protocols stated that these goods would be made available at British and American centers of production, but her allies had a moral commitment to assist in their delivery. Three routes were used. Taking advantage of Japan's neutrality in the Russo-German war, one stretched across the Pacific from San Francisco to Vladivostok. Soviet flag vessels had to be used, and Japan could interrupt the traffic at any time. A second route traversed the South Atlantic and Indian Oceans to Iran. This was a relatively safe passage, but in 1942 and 1943 overland transportation facilities in Iran were limited. Distance constituted a further problem. With the Mediterranean closed, 14,000 miles separated New York and the unloading sites in the Persian Gulf. The third route, the Northern Convoys, passed through the North Atlantic and Arctic Oceans. The ports of entry were Murmansk and Archangel. In terms of proximity to the fighting front and shortness of the voyage, the northern route was the best of the three. Until the summer of 1942, it was also the most used. Then Russia's Allies reduced both the number and size of the Arctic convoys. Despite numerous protests, this reduction extended through most of 1943. Efforts to take up the slack by increased shipments through Iran and by flying planes from Alaska to Siberia were only partially successful. While the battle of Stalingrad raged, undelivered supplies piled up in Britain and America. Lend-lease, designed to be an instrument of unity, became a source of dispute.

Disagreements about frontiers and convoys, however, were of subsidiary importance when compared with the argument over a cross-channel assault. With varying degrees of qualification and sometimes with no qualifications at all, the Anglo-Americans kept promising to open a second front by attacking the Germans in northern France. In consecutive order, Stalin was told his allies would strike in the fall of 1942, in August or September, 1942, in the spring of 1943, in August or September, 1943, and, finally, in the spring of 1944. The first commitment was made by Roosevelt to Molotov on May 30, 1942, just six days after the signing of the Anglo-Soviet Treaty. The message announcing the decision to attack in the spring of 1944, and which by omission canceled earlier promises, arrived in Moscow on June 4, 1943. It was true that the threat of invasion caused Hitler to scatter troops from Norway to Crete; but during October, 1943, eleven of Eisenhower's Anglo-American divisions in Italy were in fighting contact with a slightly smaller number of German divisions. In that same month, Washington estimated enemy ground strength on the Russian front at 205 German and 14 satellite divisions. Stalin in his reply to the June dispatch listed the broken pledges, stated that his confidence in the Alliance was shaken, and categorized the contribution of Anglo-American armies to the winning of the war as insignificant.

Although Stalin's complaints were justified, it was not true that America and Great Britain plotted to cripple the Soviet Union. British talk of territorial commitments and Anglo-American agreements about lend-lease and the cross-channel assault were not simply hollow devices to keep Russia in the struggle. They were intended as real and effective programs. If the Soviet Union did not obtain what she wanted or was promised in 1942 and 1943, it was because of the fortunes of war and Anglo-American policy differences. These differences, particularly the ones on European military strategy and the Soviet boundary, drew Washington and London into sharp dispute. Marshall and Brooke argued passionately about the Mediterranean and the Channel, while Eden and Hull, though in more moderate language, disagreed over the merits of the Soviet boundary.

Eden and the British Foreign Office favored recognition of the 1941 frontier because it would give Russia what she wanted when the sound of German guns could be heard in Moscow. As the sound diminished, London reasoned that the wants might rise. Except in the case of the four million people living in the Baltic States, the boundary roughly followed ethnographic lines. The new frontier line in Poland was in this respect much better than the prewar boundary, which exploited Soviet weakness after the First World War. Also it was more or less the familiar line of demarcation, the boundary of 1815 to 1914, the frontier of Europe's longest peace.

Cordell Hull and the American State Department strongly opposed any commitment on the Soviet boundary. Territorial aggrandizement was specifically renounced by the Atlantic Charter, which supposedly defined the peace aims of the Alliance. The frontier also violated the principles of self-determination and nationality guaranteed by the charter and rewarded what Hull regarded as the Soviet Union's abuse of power in 1939 and 1940. The State Department was further concerned with the lessons to be learned from the peacemaking in 1919. One of these lessons alleged that boundary questions should be postponed until after the conclusion of hostilities.

When it came to the cross-channel attack, Anglo-American positions were reversed. Washington, or rather George Marshall and the War Department, believed in it. London had doubts about the operation's practicality and utility. Washington, which wanted to attack strength, not exploit weakness, saw it as the quickest way to defeat Germany: cross-channel assault hurled Pittsburgh at the Ruhr along a straight line passing through Great Britain. No attention in Washington was given to the diplomatic or political ambience of the operation.

Churchill disliked the American strategy. A frontal attack on the beaches of northern France to be followed by a march to the Rhine and beyond resembled British military policy in the First World War. It was the direct approach to victory, the drive through Flanders, and the last time this had been tried Britain suffered three million casualties. Churchill lived with memories of the Somme and Passchendaele and of his own fruitless efforts to stop the slaughter. Churchill also felt concern over postwar relations between Britain and Western Europe. The German campaign of 1940 had left most of France, Belgium, and Holland physically undamaged. Liberation by devastation was a poor formula for future friendship.

Despite these reservations, the British in April, 1942, accepted the American proposal. France would be invaded, the second front opened, in the spring of 1943. The intervening time allowed for a substantial American buildup of men and supplies in England. Marshall was surprised by the ready agreement to his ideas. Probably Churchill and Brooke wanted to seal Washington to the primacy of the European theater. Marshall's plan also provided American troops for the defense of Great Britain should the Soviet Union collapse.

It was Stalin, however, who first linked the military question of the timing of a cross-channel assault and the diplomatic issue of the Soviet frontier. Without consulting the British, though aware that they had approved Marshall's strategy, Roosevelt asked the Soviet Premier to send Molotov to Washington to hear the military plans of his allies. Stalin replied that Molotov would stop first in London for an exchange of views. He also called for a second front in the near future. Roosevelt correctly interpreted this to mean that Molotov would press London for some sort of territorial agreement and Washington for a cross-channel attack in 1942. With the link established, the result was obvious though not entirely honorable. Roosevelt decided to offer Stalin a second front in France in the fall of 1942 in return for an innocuous Anglo-Soviet Treaty.

Molotov arrived in London, asked what was expected, but after a conversation with the American Ambassador substituted twenty-five years of friendship for the boundary agreement. In Washington, Roosevelt kept his part of the bargain. On his way back to Moscow, Molotov again stopped in London. Churchill supplied him with an *aide-mémoire* summarizing the military program as viewed by Great Britain. The British, said Churchill, were concentrating their maximum effort on the organization of an invasion of Europe by over a million men in 1943. They were also preparing for a landing in August or September, 1942, but could give no promise on this operation. Stalin, for whom the second front might be vital while the territorial agreements were only important, was content.

George Marshall and the American Chiefs of Staff tried very hard to keep Roosevelt's promises. Unfortunately, the fortunes of war, Churchill, the British Chiefs of Staff, and, eventually, even Roosevelt himself turned against them. During the summer of 1942, a brilliant German general, Erwin Rommel, defeated a competent British general, Neil Ritchie, in North Africa. The Middle East appeared endangered and the British believed the Middle East had to be held. London proposed joint operations in 1942 to clear the African shore of the Mediterranean. The plan had long been favored by Churchill. The decision was theirs to make as the British would have to provide the bulk of the forces. London, nevertheless, chose to exercise the art of persuasion. Roosevelt became a ready convert; Marshall never did. Marshall argued that operations in the Mediterranean had the effect of canceling any cross-channel attack in both 1942 and 1943. The British believed an assault in the channel in 1942 was a military impossibility. Rommel also had to be defeated, and the Anglo-Americans could not afford simply to stand idle for a year. Roosevelt overruled his professional adviser, and North African operations were undertaken.

Each side was right. During the Dieppe raid of August 1942, a cross-channel reconnaissance in force, 5,000 Canadians were unable to go much farther than the seawall despite the fact that they had tanks, tactical surprise, and the Royal

Air Force secured local air supremacy. The casualties amounted to 3,372 killed, wounded, or missing. But as Marshall had predicted, there was no cross-channel assault. Instead the North African, Sicilian, and Italian campaigns followed each other through 1942 and 1943. A British strategy of encirclement replaced the American strategy of direct attack on Europe.

In contrast to the questions of territorial recognition and cross-channel attack, London and Washington did agree on the necessity of military supplies for Russia. And until the summer of 1942, such aid as was available was sent. It moved by the route the Russians preferred—the Arctic convoys. The Germans, however, were able to concentrate sufficient air and naval power in Norwegian waters to make the cost of the convoys prohibitive. They were reduced. The demands on shipping incurred by operations in the Pacific, the U-boat war in the Atlantic, and the Mediterranean campaigns extended the reduction well into 1943. The Soviet Government correctly protested in September, 1943, that so far that year they had received through Murmansk less than a third of the aid they had gotten in 1942, and in 1942 unloadings had dried to a trickle after July; but this was not due to any conspiracy. Tanks rusting on the bottom of the Arctic Ocean were of no use to anybody.

Stalin complained bitterly about the confusions, cross-purposes, and broken promises of 1942 and 1943. The situation was compounded by his own isolation and suspicion. Except for the Eden and Molotov missions, the Soviet Union refused to engage in military or diplomatic discussions with either Great Britain or the United States. Normal diplomatic channels were sterile. The reports of the American Ambassador to Moscow, Admiral William H. Standley, consisted largely of intelligent deductions from the Soviet press. Frustration and isolation best described his lot. To obtain an exit visa for a member of his staff sometimes required his personal intervention at the Soviet Foreign Office, and even then success might take months. He never could find out what happened to lend-lease deliveries, and on one of the few occasions he talked with an ordinary Russian, the constant presence of the secret police tended to have an inhibiting effect; he was told that the Soviet Union paid for all aid in gold.

Though living in a freer atmosphere, Soviet ambassadors serving abroad felt similar frustrations. After two years in Washington, Maxim Litvinov complained to Sumner Welles that his work could have been done by an intelligent file clerk. Litvinov said his reports provoked no response from Moscow. A more chilling glimpse into the life of a Stalinist diplomat was provided by Ivan Maisky, the Soviet Ambassador to Great Britain. After his recall to the Soviet Union, Maisky asked Molotov that he be allowed to go back to London briefly to collect his wife. Maisky believed this would counter British opinion that he was about to vanish without a trace. He noted that such treatment was frequent for returning Soviet ambassadors during the days of the personality cult.

Efforts to transcend normal diplomatic channels were equally sterile. Churchill's visit to Moscow in 1942 was unproductive because Stalin simply subjected the Prime Minister to a drumfire of recriminations over the broken promise of a cross-channel attack. Only in the final hours of his visit did the mood become more friendly, when Stalin informed Churchill that enforcing collectivization had proved harder than fighting the Germans. Despite numerous invitations, Stalin always wanted to, but never could, attend a meeting with Churchill and Roosevelt. His excuse was that he directed Russia's war effort and could not be absent from Moscow for a single day.

Roosevelt particularly wanted Stalin to attend what became the Casablanca Conference. The President offered to fly to any site in Africa, including Khartoum, pledged complete secrecy, said vital strategic decisions were involved, and provided a range of dates stretching from January through March, 1943. Stalin refused to come, and the strategy of cross-channel attack in 1943 foundered. Even when Roosevelt said he would go to Alaska for a few days of private conversations with the Soviet Premier and had the message delivered by so fervent an admirer of the Soviet Union as Washington's former Ambassador to Moscow, Joseph Davies, the answer ultimately was the same. Stalingrad made no difference. In defeat or in victory, Stalin would only talk to those who made the pilgrimage to Russia, and his constant theme was the second front.

Despite everything Roosevelt remained optimistic. Co-operation with the Soviet Union was necessary to win the war and secure the peace. Contrary evidence was considered false or ignored. William Bullitt, Washington's first Ambassador to the Soviet Union and an intimate of Roosevelt's, warned of the dangers in the President's policy. He argued that the Soviet Union intended to create a Communist sphere of influence in Europe. His warning became known as the Bullitt thesis. He ceased to be an intimate and ended the war serving in the French Army. Ambassador Standley wanted greater recognition by the Soviet Union of American lend-lease efforts and fewer special emissaries from Washington. Roosevelt sent Davies to Moscow with his invitation to Stalin. Davies believed that continuous praise of all things Soviet constituted a policy. Standley decided to retire. Charles Bohlen, First Secretary to the Embassy in Moscow, merely listed known Soviet demands and expressed his opposition by asking this rhetorical question: What did they mean? The reports of American ambassadors or representatives serving in Sweden, Finland, and Turkey contain, as might be expected from the countries involved, many negative appraisals of Soviet policy, but all are carefully attributed to someone other than the sender. De Gaulle, who was poorly briefed, won no favor from Roosevelt when in a letter to the President he presented himself as the alternative to Communism in France.

If many in Washington made optimism about the Soviet Union their guiding rule, London by the summer of 1943 was becoming increasingly pessimistic. The British were willing to try for an accommodation with Russia, but they wanted it defined by specific agreements. They regretted Washington's seeming determination to postpone everything until the war had ended. The British were also upset by other American attitudes: the obvious lack of coordination between the President and his Secretary of State; Hull's determined efforts to make the price of lend-lease to Great Britain be the dismantling of the Imperial tariff system; the pervasive anticolonialism current in both the White House and the State Department; the cheerful fecklessness of Roosevelt as he talked of disarming most of the world, partitioning Yugoslavia, or uniting Belgium, Luxembourg, Alsace-Lorraine and parts of northern France in the new nation of Wallonia. The latter suggestion may have been a playful one, but the President appeared serious when he nominated himself, Chiang, Churchill, and Stalin as the creators and Policemen of some sort of new world order.

If Washington indulged in uncongenial and unrealistic speculation, it was, nevertheless, the Soviet Union's actions which most alarmed the British. The news of the Katyn Forest massacre, sundered relations between Russia and the Polish Government-in-Exile, Stalin's bitter denunciations over the second front, and Maisky's recall followed each other in rapid succession during April, May, and June, 1943. It seemed the twenty-five years of friendship between Great Britain and the Soviet Union would not survive its first anniversary. Then in August came one of those swift reversals characteristic of Stalinist diplomacy. Though the request was still couched in admonitory language, the Soviet Premier asked for a Foreign Ministers' meeting to be followed by a conference with Roosevelt and Churchill.

The reasons for this change were paradoxical. Stalin's anger was provoked by the success, not the failure, of cross-channel strategy. George Marshall had finally won the President's full support, and although Mediterranean operations would continue until the war's end in Europe, the British in May, 1943, committed themselves to a cross-channel assault in 1944. For so long in the limelight, the Mediterranean theater was now to be gradually closed down and the center of attention would shift to the beaches of northern France. What caused the invective from Moscow, the scurrying of ambassadors, the atmosphere of crisis, turned out to be the very news the Soviet Premier most wanted to hear. Though now two years late, the second front was on its way.

Shortly after the Anglo-American decision had been taken, however, Churchill's indirect strategy, the probing of weakness and the avoidance of strength, scored what appeared to be its greatest victory. Mussolini fell and Italy offered to change sides. With great difficulty Churchill persuaded the Americans to open an Italian theater of war. The Prime Minister's own ambitions were more far-reaching. Italian troops garrisoned large areas in the Balkans. Resistance movements, admittedly fractured and strife-ridden, existed in Greece and Yugoslavia. Vague peace feelers were received in London from parties in Hungary and Rumania who wanted to follow the Italian precedent. Sketchy in outline, shapeless in detail, there emerged a Balkan alternative to the cross-channel assault. With its eyes fixed on France, Washington ignored the possibilities of the situation.

Stalin could not be so profligate. Lacking any agreement on his frontiers, excluded from the Italian surrender negotiations and with the bulk of the German Army tied down on his front, no one was more alive to what could happen than the Soviet Premier. Italian defection might presage the complete collapse of the German satellite system in the Balkans and a sudden end to the war. He needed to know the intentions and, if possible, influence the actions of his partners. He called for a Big Three meeting. The British hoped that Stalin might be willing to postpone the distant cross-channel attack and ask for more immediate relief through Anglo-American operations in the eastern Mediterranean. Roose-

velt wanted to establish a warm personal relationship with
the Soviet Premier. Stalin, Roosevelt, and Churchill began
moving toward Tehran.

The Tehran Conference lasted just four days. Except for the
development of the atomic bomb, it was probably the most
important event in the Second World War. By acts of
commission and omission, it has shaped nearly three decades
of postwar history. The straight line of Stalin's crayon en-
dures on the present map of Poland. It follows no rivers or
hills or the calculations of ethnographer or the whims of
voters. A frozen gesture of power exercised, and accepted, the
line runs for one hundred miles across what used to be
Prussia. It transformed Koenigsberg into Kaliningrad, and
that was its only function—a territorial memorial to the
triumph of the Slav over the German. The line, drawn in
seconds and now locked into political geography, might be
taken as a symbol of Tehran. Not Yalta, not Potsdam, but
here was the seat and center of decision.

Churchill's hope for Stalin's support on military matters
died the first day. The Russians had the measure of the
German Army. Slowly, inexorably, and at a terrible cost in
life they were driving the attacker from the Soviet Union.
American strategy assured the Russians that they would be
the conquerors and liberators of Eastern Europe. It also
assured that the Germans would have to divide their forces
and fight on two widely separated fronts. From a Soviet
perspective, the American plan was excellent both militarily
and politically. It spelled out in detail exactly what Moscow
had been calling for all along. Stalin must have found
Churchill's proposals for an Anglo-American presence in the
Balkans disquieting. The Soviet Premier did not come to
Tehran expecting to be made the arbiter of Anglo-American
strategy in Europe, but when the role was thrust upon him
he knew what was best for the Soviet Union.

While the Americans congratulated themselves over the

good sense being shown by Uncle Joe, Churchill continued to press his own views on the Mediterranean for an additional twenty-four hours. Though everyone was aware of the political basis of his proposals, the Prime Minister had to argue within a strictly military framework. Churchill alleged that the Anglo-Americans possessed a manpower redundancy in the Mediterranean and that it should be put to work to assist the cross-channel attack. Since neither shipping nor time permitted their transfer to Great Britain, the Prime Minister said that the troops should attack the Germans in Greece, Yugoslavia, and Rumania. He also wanted Turkey drawn into the war. According to Churchill, the price of all this activity would be only a short delay in the cross-channel assault.

Marshall listened with amazement. Hopkins found Churchill's efforts gallant, but Stalin proved his skill as a negotiator. He suggested that the Prime Minister's redundant manpower not assist Tito's Partisans but instead invade southern France. This immediately became part of the American credo, and invade southern France they did. Stalin also subjected the Prime Minister to increasingly bitter attacks. Finally, on his sixty-ninth birthday, Churchill surrendered. The thought of American and Soviet Armies meeting in the middle of a devastated continent gave him cold comfort. No one at Tehran thought that they would still be standing there twenty-six years later, but the possibility of Europe's partition had clearly been raised.

Stalin scored an equal triumph in the political discussions. Churchill and his matchsticks moved Poland to where Stalin wanted it. Roosevelt and Churchill watched together as the Soviet Premier drew Poland's eastern boundary. They also agreed to a western frontier which followed the Oder and Neisse Rivers. Roosevelt and Churchill, still together, entered no caveat against Stalin's claims to Finnish lands. Roosevelt, in private, acceded to the Soviet annexation of Latvia, Lithuania, and Estonia. The President did ask for future plebiscites in the former Baltic States, but when Stalin bristled Roosevelt retreated. Soviet territorial acquisitions from Rumania were not mentioned, but this omission must have occurred through oversight, not as a matter of policy. The President and Prime Minister both made it very clear that they accepted the Soviet Union's territorial claims in Europe, including the absorption of Koenigsberg. This was the settled British approach to the question, but for Washington it constituted an apparent reversal of attitude.

In other matters there were divisions among the Big Three. Stalin and Churchill did not share Roosevelt's enthusiasm for China. Stalin and Churchill had reservations about the President's ideas on a future world organization to replace the League of Nations. Stalin rejected Churchill's proposed revival of Austria-Hungary. Churchill disliked Roosevelt's and Stalin's constant denigration of France. Churchill wanted to weaken Germany. Stalin and Roosevelt seemed prepared to undertake the nation's destruction. Churchill blocked any precipitate action by having the whole issue of partition referred to the new European Advisory Commission for further study. The Prime Minister was assisted by meteorologists and doctors, whose predictions and decisions limited the political talks to a single day. Differences were exposed, but shortness of time prevented any resolution.

Churchill left Tehran more anxious than when he arrived. He still doubted the feasibility of a cross-channel assault. Even if it succeeded, Soviet armies would be deployed deep in Europe at the war's end. Although he met privately with Stalin, Roosevelt had refused to meet with the Prime Minister. Roosevelt, indeed, played the role of courtier to the Soviet Premier. Churchill's sole victory was a promise from Stalin that if the London Poles accepted the Tehran frontier, the Soviet Union might, but only might, consider restoring diplomatic relations. The good news of Russia's eventual entry into the war against Japan had to be balanced with the information that such action would be accompanied by more territorial demands. Given Roosevelt's attitude, the Prime Minister could not doubt that these demands would be satisfied. Churchill's efforts to secure some sort of Anglo-American presence in the Balkans had been blocked. Later attempts to make Anglo-American armies the liberators of Prague and Vienna or the conquerors of Berlin were also to be frustrated by Washington. But Tehran remained the focus of decision. America and Britain were there committed to the invasion of France. Half of Europe would be occupied by the Soviet Union. Washington and London might talk a great deal, but, short of an unthinkable war, Moscow alone could determine the nature and duration of her tenure.

If Churchill felt troubled and depressed, Roosevelt by all accounts appeared delighted with the results of the conference. The President was still the happy warrior and at the height of his powers. The marked physical deterioration of 1944 and 1945 lay in the future. Stalin had proved to be a hard bargainer. But if Soviet Premier Stalin discounted Chiang Kai-shek, he also discounted General de Gaulle. Stalin criticized the policy of unconditional surrender while supporting, and this was far more important, American strategy for the defeat of Germany. Stalin renewed the Soviet pledge to enter the war against Japan once the struggle in Europe ended. He accepted the Cairo communiqué which awarded Manchuria, Formosa, and the Pescadores to China. The Soviet Premier might have quibbled about the distribution of the Italian fleet, but so did Churchill. Roosevelt was upset by the animosity which developed between the Prime Minister and Stalin, yet it enabled the President both to assume the role of mediator and to demonstrate the separateness and independence of British and American policies. Roosevelt, moreover, greatly appreciated Stalin's public recognition of the contribution of American production to the winning of the war. Knowing Hull's opposition to the territorial agreements, Roosevelt decided to solve that difficulty by not telling his Secretary of State what he had done. The President's fear that Stalin might support Churchill's schemes in the Balkans had also proved unwarranted. Certainly there were differences on many issues between the President and the Premier, but as Hopkins told Lord Moran, Roosevelt found Stalin to be a reasonable man.

Svetlana Alliluyeva said her father returned to Moscow in a particularly good, almost boisterous, frame of mind. He had every reason to be happy. But it was Stalin who during a brief exchange with Roosevelt revealed the basic weakness in the Tehran decisions. When the President agreed to the Soviet Union's annexation of Latvia, Lithuania, Estonia, and half of prewar Poland, he stated that the American public neither knew nor understood the issues involved. Stalin replied that some good propaganda work should be done. Except for the Polish frontier, and even here the real position was misrepresented, no propaganda work in Stalin's sense ever occurred.

Instead American statements about the peace remained rooted to the Wilsonian principles of the Atlantic Charter. After the Yalta Conference in 1945, Roosevelt and Churchill declared themselves in favor of the new home for Poland. They further said Poland would be free, independent, and democratic. Roosevelt did not really anticipate an independent Poland, nor did he mention the Asian concessions to Russia which were also agreed to at Yalta. He deceived Cordell Hull and his fellow countrymen. He permitted, even encouraged, a gap to open between what the American and other Allied peoples thought would be the nature of the peace settlement and an already arranged and far different actuality.

Wilsonianism, national self-determination, no territorial changes until the Peace Conference and then only in accordance with the freely expressed wishes of the peoples concerned—these things were deeply entrenched in the thinking of Americans of the right and of the left and of the postwar planners in the State Department. According to the Office of War Information, these principles and their defense were what the Second World War was all about. Perhaps Roosevelt believed that his personal stature and his revelation of the historical background and practical necessity of the concessions would clear the way for their acceptance. More likely, Roosevelt gave his commitments to Stalin without thinking too much about the problems of implementation. Stalin had, however, in that brief exchange with the President raised two of the fundamental issues of the war: Would America accept the reality of Soviet power, and if it did when would the adjustment of American ideology to that reality take place? Roosevelt died leaving both questions unanswered.

After the President's death, Washington's foreign policy gradually reversed itself. Truman said he would follow Roosevelt's attitude toward the Russians, but he also believed in the rightness of Wilson's ideals and in the strength of the United States. He was suspicious of Soviet intentions. When the Soviet Union occupied Eastern Europe, the Americans demanded that free elections take place to organize postwar governments. Free elections, as Stalin found out when one was held in Hungary, resulted in regimes covertly hostile to the Soviet Union. The Soviet Premier accelerated the transformation of the area into a protective glacis. Stalin's actions confirmed Truman's doubts. The inconsistency between the principles of the Atlantic Charter and Roosevelt's personal diplomacy was resolved. America stood by its interpretation of the charter.

Washington now set out to undo what it with Soviet help had just accomplished. Germany and Japan, then in ruins, must be revived to contain the Ally turned enemy. Leahy, who once admired the way the Russians argued down the British, applauded Truman's standing up to Stalin. Churchill became aware of the new mood at the opening session of the Potsdam Conference in July, 1945. He watched with delight as the new President introduced one position paper after another, many of which challenged the known views of the Soviet Union. Churchill became even happier when

Truman told him about the successful explosion of the atomic bomb. The Prime Minister had always wanted to channel American military power into Europe in such a way as to limit Soviet expansion. He believed the shift had come too late, but he supported it. Seven months later, out of office but with Truman in the audience, Churchill delivered his iron curtain speech at Fulton, Missouri, and challenged the actions of the Soviet Union.

The weakness of American foreign policy in the mid-twentieth century was its refusal to face unwelcome realities. Roosevelt believed in an Uncle Joe who never existed. Truman's approach constituted an opposite but equally illusory policy. Stalin was never the leader of a monolithic conspiracy. The role of diplomacy is the peaceful solution of differences between nations. Stalin wanted to create a Soviet sphere of influence in Eastern Europe. Tehran and the strength of Soviet arms made this inevitable. Roosevelt refused to face the issue. His last message to Churchill urged the Prime Minister to play down differences with the Russians. Hope replaced diplomacy. When the Soviet Union created its sphere of influence, Truman again rejected reality. Instead of dealing with what was, America launched itself into an increasingly costly and frustrating struggle to create what could not be. Washington fought the Second World War as a crusade against Germany and Japan. It entered the cold war as a crusade against Stalin. The positive object of both crusades was the concrete realization of the Atlantic Charter. This has proved to be beyond our power. It does not mean that we were wrong.

A Glossary of Code Names

ACCOLADE   British plan for the capture of Rhodes and other Aegean islands garrisoned by the Italians.

ACROBAT   British plan for the capture of Libya in 1942.

ANAKIM   Combined Chiefs' plan for the recapture of all of Burma in 1944.

ANVIL   Early Combined Chiefs' plan for invasion of southern France.

ARCADIA   U.S.-British conference held in Washington, December 1941–January 1942.

AVALANCHE   Combined Chiefs' plan for invasion of Italy at Salerno.

AXIS   German plan for the occupation of Italy.

BAYTOWN   Combined Chiefs' plan for invasion of Italy at Calabria.

BOLERO   Buildup of U.S. forces in England for cross-channel attack.

BRIMSTONE   Combined Chiefs' plan for invasion of Sardinia.

BUCCANEER   Combined Chiefs' plan for invasion of the Andaman Islands.

CHAMPION   Late 1943 Combined Chiefs' plan for the recapture of Burma.

CULVERIN   British plan for the invasion of Sumatra.

EUREKA   Conference of Roosevelt, Churchill, and Stalin at Tehran, November, 1943.

GYMNAST   British plan for invasion of French Northwest Africa.

HABAKKUK   British plan for aircraft carriers made out of ice.

HADRIAN   British plan for a landing on the Cotentin Peninsula in Normandy in 1943.

HARDIHOOD   Military aid to Turkey.

HUSKY   Invasion of Sicily, July, 1943.

JUPITER   British plan for invasion of northern Norway.

OVERLORD   Combined Chiefs' plan for cross-channel attack, May–June, 1944.

POINTBLANK   Combined Chiefs' plan for bomber offensive against Germany.

QUADRANT   U.S.-British conference at Quebec, August, 1943.

RANKIN   Plans for return to the Continent in the event of deterioration of the German position.

ROUNDUP   Plan for major U.S.-British cross-channel operation in 1943.

SAUCY   Limited offensive to reopen land route from Burma to China.

SEXTANT   International conference at Cairo, November and December, 1943.

SLEDGEHAMMER   Plan for limited cross-channel attack in 1942.

SUPER-GYMNAST   Combined Chiefs' plan for the invasion of French Northwest Africa in 1942.

SYMBOL   Casablanca Conference, January 14–23, 1943.

TORCH   Allied invasion of northwest Africa.

TRIDENT   U.S.-British conference held at Washington, May, 1943.

BIBLIOGRAPHY
AND INDEX

BIBLIOGRAPHY

Documents and Official Histories

Butler, James R. M., and Gwyer, J. M. A.: *Grand Strategy, June 1941–August 1942.* ("Grand Strategy," III.) London: H.M. Stationery Office; 1965.

Carnegie Endowment for International Peace: *International Conciliation: Documents for the Year 1943.* New York: Carnegie Endowment for International Peace; 1943.

———: *International Conciliation: Documents for the Year 1944.* New York: Carnegie Endowment for International Peace; 1944.

Cline, Ray S.: *Washington Command Post: The Operations Division.* ("United States Army in World War II.") Washington, D.C.: U.S. Government Printing Office; 1951.

Coakley, Robert W., and Leighton, Richard M.: *Global Logistics and Strategy, 1940–1941.* ("United States Army in World War II.") Washington, D.C.: U.S. Government Printing Office; 1955.

Ehrman, John: *Grand Strategy, August 1943–September 1944.* ("Grand Strategy," V.) London: H.M. Stationery Office; 1956.

———: *Grand Strategy, October 1944–August 1945.* ("Grand Strategy," VI.) London: H.M. Stationery Office; 1956.

Garland, Albert N., and Smyth, Howard M.: *The Mediterranean Theater of Operations: Sicily and the Surrender of Italy.* ("United States Army in World War II.") Washington, D.C.: U.S. Government Printing Office; 1965.

General Sikorski Historical Institute: *Documents on Polish-Soviet Relations, 1939–1945.* Vol. I: 1939–1943. London: Heinemann; 1961.

Great Britain: *Parliamentary Papers.* Vol. IX (*Accounts and Papers*). Cmd. 6335. 1941–42. "Treaty of Alliance between the United Kingdom and the Soviet Union and Iran (with notes)," p. 725.

————: *Parliamentary Papers.* Vol. IX (*Accounts and Papers*). Cmd. 6368. 1941–42. "Treaty for an Alliance in the War against Hitlerite Germany and her Associates in Europe and providing also for collaboration and mutual assistance thereafter, concluded between the United Kingdom and the Union of Soviet Socialist Republics," p. 633.

Harrison, Gordon A.: *Cross-Channel Attack.* ("United States Army in World War II.") Washington, D.C.: U.S. Government Printing Office; 1951.

Howe, George F.: *Northwest Africa: Seizing the Initiative in the West.* ("United States Army in World War II.") Washington, D.C.: U.S. Government Printing Office; 1957.

Matloff, Maurice: *Strategic Planning for Coalition Warfare, 1943–1944.* ("United States Army in World War II.") Washington, D.C.: U.S. Government Printing Office; 1959.

Matloff, Maurice, and Snell, Edwin M.: *Strategic Planning for Coalition Warfare, 1941–1942.* ("United States Army in World War II.") Washington, D.C.: U.S. Government Printing Office; 1953.

Morton, Louis: *The Fall of the Philippines.* ("United States Army in World War II.") Washington, D.C.: U.S. Government Printing Office; 1953.

————: *The War in the Pacific. Strategy and Command: The First Two Years.* ("United States Army in World War II.") Washington, D.C.: U.S. Government Printing Office; 1962.

Motter, T. H. Vail: *The Persian Corridor and Aid to Russia.* ("United States Army in World War II.") Washington, D.C.: U.S. Government Printing Office; 1952.

Notter, Harley A.: *Postwar Foreign Policy Preparation, 1939–1945.* Washington, D.C.: U.S. Government Printing Office; 1949.

Pogue, Forrest C.: *The Supreme Command.* ("United States Army in World War II.") Washington, D.C.: U.S. Government Printing Office; 1954.

Romanus, Charles F., and Sunderland, Riley: *Stilwell's Command Problems.* ("United States Army in World War II.") Washington, D.C.: U.S. Government Printing Office; 1956.

————: *Stilwell's Mission to China.* ("United States Army in World War II.") Washington, D.C.: U.S. Government Printing Office; 1953.

Roskill, Stephen W.: *The War at Sea, 1939–1945.* 3 vols. London: H.M. Stationery Office; 1954–58.

U.S. Department of the Army: *American Military History,* Washington, D.C.: U.S. Government Printing Office; 1959.

U.S. Department of State: *Treaties and Other International Acts Series 1604, Armistice with Italy, 1943.* Washington, D.C.: U.S. Government Printing Office; 1947.

————: *Foreign Relations of the United States. Diplomatic Papers, 1941.* 6 vols. Washington, D.C.: U.S. Government Printing Office; 1956–58.

————: *Foreign Relations of the United States. Diplomatic Papers, 1942.* 6 vols. Washington, D.C.: U.S. Government Printing Office; 1960–63.

————: *Foreign Relations of the United States. Diplomatic Papers, 1943.* 6 vols. Washington, D.C.: U.S. Government Printing Office; 1963–65.

————: *Foreign Relations of the United States. Diplomatic Papers, 1942, China.* Washington, D.C.: U.S. Government Printing Office; 1956.

————: *Foreign Relations of the United States. Diplomatic Papers, 1943, China.* Washington, D.C.: U.S. Government Printing Office; 1957.

————: *Foreign Relations of the United States. Diplomatic Papers. The Conferences at Cairo and Tehran, 1943.* Washington, D.C.: U.S. Government Printing Office; 1961.

————: *Foreign Relations of the United States. Diplomatic Papers. The Conferences at Washington, 1941–1942, and Casablanca, 1943.* Washington, D.C.: U.S. Government Printing Office; 1968.

————: *Foreign Relations of the United States. Diplomatic Papers. The Conferences at Washington and Quebec, 1943.* Washington, D.C.: U.S. Government Printing Office; 1970.

————: *Nazi-Soviet Relations, 1939–1941: Documents from the Archives of the German Foreign Office.* ed. by R. J. Sontag and J. S. Beddie. Washington, D.C.: U.S. Government Printing Office; 1948.

U.S. House of Representatives: Select Committee on the Katyn
          Forest Massacre. *The Katyn Forest Massacre.* Hear-
          ings before the Select Committee, 82nd Congress,
          1st and 2nd Sessions. Washington, D.C.: U.S.
          Government Printing Office; 1952.
U.S. Senate and House of Representatives, Joint Committee on the
          Investigation of the Pearl Harbor Attack: *The
          Pearl Harbor Attack.* Hearings and Exhibits of the
          Joint Committee, 79th Congress, 1st and 2nd
          session. 39 pts. Washington, D.C.: U.S. Govern-
          ment Printing Office; 1946.
U.S.S.R. Ministry of Foreign Affairs: *Correspondence Between the
          Chairman of the Council of Ministers of the
          U.S.S.R. and the Presidents of the U.S.A. and the
          Prime Ministers of Great Britain During the Great
          Patriotic War of 1941–1945.* 2 vols. Moscow:
          Foreign Language Publishing House; 1957.
———: *Documents and Materials Relating to the Eve of the Second
          World War.* 2 vols. Moscow: Foreign Language
          Publishing House; 1948.
———: *Soviet Foreign Policy During the Patriotic War, Documents
          and Materials.* Translated by Andrew Rothstein. 2
          vols. London: Hutchinson; 1944–45.
———: "Tehran Conference of the Leaders of the Three Great
          Powers (November 28 to December 1, 1943),
          Documents." *International Affairs, A Monthly
          Journal of Political Analyses* (Moscow). No. 7
          (July, 1961), pp. 133–45; No. 8 (August, 1961),
          pp. 110–22.
Vigneras, Marcel: *Rearming the French.* ("United States Army in
          World War II.") Washington, D.C.: U.S. Govern-
          ment Printing Office; 1957.
Watson, Mark S.: *Chief of Staff: Prewar Plans and Preparations.*
          ("United States Army in World War II.") Wash-
          ington, D.C.: U.S. Government Printing Office;
          1950.
Webster, Charles, and Frankland, Noble: *The Strategic Air Offen-
          sive Against Germany, 1939–1945.* 4 vols. London:
          H.M. Stationery Office; 1961.
Williams, Mary H.: *Chronology, 1941–1945.* ("United States Army
          in World War II.") Washington, D.C.: U.S.
          Government Printing Office; 1960.
Woodward, Llewellyn: *British Foreign Policy in the Second World
          War.* London: H.M. Stationery Office; 1962.

Books

Acheson, Dean: *Present at the Creation: My Years in the State Department.* New York: Norton; 1969.

Alliluyeva, Svetlana: *Only One Year.* Translated by Paul Chavchavadze. New York: Harper and Row; 1969.

————: *Twenty Letters to a Friend.* Translated by Priscilla McMillan. New York: Harper and Row; 1967.

Anders, Wladyslaw: *An Army in Exile: The Story of the Second Polish Corps.* London: Macmillan; 1940.

Armstrong, Anne: *Unconditional Surrender: The Impact of the Casablanca Policy upon World War II.* New Brunswick, N.J.: Rutgers University Press; 1961.

Arnold, Henry H.: *Global Mission.* New York: Harper and Bros.; 1949.

Badoglio, Pietro: *Italy in the Second World War: Memories and Documents.* Translated by Muriel Curvey. London: Oxford University Press; 1948.

Barghoorn, Frederick C.: *The Soviet Image of the United States: A Study in Distortion.* New York: Harcourt, Brace; 1950.

Beneš, Eduard: *Memoirs of Dr. Eduard Beneš: from Munich to New War and New Victory.* London: Allen and Unwin; 1954.

Bor-Komorowski, Tadeusz: *The Secret Army.* New York: Macmillan; 1951.

Bouscaren, Anthony T.: *Soviet Foreign Policy: A Pattern of Persistence.* New York: Fordham University Press; 1962.

Bryant, Arthur: *A History of the War Years Based on the Diaries of Field Marshal Lord Alanbrooke, Chief of the Imperial General Staff,* Vol. I: *The Turn of the Tide.* Garden City, N.Y.: Doubleday; 1957.

————: *A History of the War Years Based on the Diaries of Field Marshal Lord Alanbrooke, Chief of the Imperial General Staff,* Vol II: *Triumph in the West.* Garden City, N.Y.: Doubleday; 1959.

Buchanan, A. Russel: *The United States and World War II.* 2 vols. New York: Harper and Row; 1964.

Bullitt, William C.: *The Great Globe Itself: A Preface to World Affairs.* New York: Charles Scribner's Sons; 1946.

Burns, James M.: *Roosevelt: The Soldier of Freedom.* New York: Harcourt, Brace and World; 1970.

Butcher, Harry C.: *My Three Years with Eisenhower: The Personal Diary of Captain Harry C. Butcher, USNR, Naval*

        Aide to General Eisenhower, 1942 to 1945. New
        York: Simon and Schuster; 1946.

Byrnes, James F.: *Speaking Frankly.* New York: Harper and Bros.;
        1947.

Chandler, Alfred D., ed.: *The Papers of Dwight David Eisenhower:
        The War Years.* 5 vols. Baltimore, Md.: Johns
        Hopkins University Press; 1970.

Churchill, Sir Winston S.: *The Second World War.* 6 vols. Boston:
        Houghton Mifflin; 1948–53.

Ciano, Count Galeazzo: *Ciano's Diaries, 1939 to 1943.* Translated
        and edited by Malcolm Muggeridge. London:
        Heinemann; 1946.

Ciechanowski, Jan: *Defeat in Victory.* Garden City, N.Y.: Double-
        day; 1947.

Clark, Alan: *Barbarossa: The Russian-German Conflict, 1941–45.*
        New York: William Morrow; 1965.

Clark, Mark W.: *Calculated Risk.* New York: Harper and Bros.;
        1950.

Cunningham, Sir Andrew B. C.: *A Sailor's Odyssey: The Autobiog-
        raphy of Admiral of the Fleet, Viscount Cunning-
        ham of Hyndhope.* London: Hutchinson; 1951.

Dallin, David J.: *The Big Three: The United States, Britain, and
        Russia.* New Haven: Yale University Press; 1945.

Davies, Joseph E.: *Mission to Moscow.* New York: Simon and
        Schuster; 1941.

Dawson, Raymond H.: *The Decision to Aid Russia, 1941.* Chapel
        Hill: University of North Carolina Press; 1959.

Deane, John R.: *The Strange Alliance: The Story of Our Efforts at
        Wartime Co-operation with Russia.* New York:
        Viking Press; 1957.

de Gaulle, Charles: *Mémoires de Guerre.* 3 vols. Paris: Plon; 1954–59.

The War Memoirs of Charles de Gaulle. Translated by Joyce
        Murchie and Hamish Erskine as 6 vols. New York:
        Simon and Schuster; 1960.

Dennett, Raymond, and Johnson, Joseph E., eds.: *Negotiating with
        the Russians.* Boston: World Peace Foundation;
        1951.

Deutscher, Isaac: *Stalin: A Political Biography.* London: Oxford
        University Press; 1949.

Djilas, Milovan: *Conversations with Stalin.* New York: Harcourt,
        Brace and World; 1962.

Eden, Sir Anthony: *The Memoirs of Anthony Eden, Earl of Avon.*
        3 vols. Boston: Houghton Mifflin; 1960–65.

Eisenhower, Dwight D.: *Crusade in Europe.* Garden City, N.Y.:
        Doubleday; 1948.

Falls, Cyril: *The Second World War*. London: Methuen; 1948.

Feis, Herbert: *Between War and Peace: The Potsdam Conference.* Princeton, N.J.: Princeton University Press; 1960.

———: *Churchill, Roosevelt, Stalin: The War They Waged and the Peace They Sought*. Princeton, N.J.: Princeton University Press; 1957.

———: *The China Tangle: The American Effort in China from Pearl Harbor to the Marshall Mission*. Princeton, N.J.: Princeton University Press; 1953.

———: *The Road to Pearl Harbor: The Coming of the War Between the United States and Japan*. Princeton, N.J.: Princeton University Press; 1950.

Fischer, George: *Soviet Opposition to Stalin: A Case Study in World War II.* Cambridge: Harvard University Press; 1952.

Fleming, Denna F.: *The Cold War and Its Origins*. 2 vols. Garden City, N.Y.: Doubleday; 1961.

Fuller, John F. C.: *The Second World War, 1939–45: A Strategical and Tactical History*. London: Eyre and Spottiswoode; 1948.

Gallagher, Matthew P.: *The Soviet History of World War II: Myths, Memories, and Realities*. New York: Praeger; 1963.

Giraud, Henri: *Un Seul But, la victoire: Alger 1942–1944*. Paris: René Julliard; 1949.

Goebbels, Joseph: *The Goebbels Diaries*. Edited and translated by Louis P. Lochner. Garden City, N.Y.: Doubleday; 1948.

Graebner, Norman, ed.: *An Uncertain Tradition: American Secretaries of State in the Twentieth Century*. New York: McGraw-Hill; 1961.

Greenfield, Kent R.: *American Strategy in World War II: A Reconsideration*. Baltimore: Johns Hopkins University Press; 1963.

Greenfield, Kent R., ed.: *Command Decisions*. New York: Harcourt, Brace; 1959.

Greiner, G. K. E. Helmuth: *Die Oberste Wehrmachtführung, 1939–1943*. Wiesbaden: Limes Verlag; 1951.

Guderian, Heinz: *Erinnerungen eines Soldaten*. Heidelberg: Vorwinckel Verlag; 1951.

———: *Panzer Leader*. Translated by Constantine Fitzgibbon. New York: E. P. Dutton; 1957.

Hammond, Thomas T.: *Soviet Foreign Relations and World Communism: A Selected, Annotated Bibliography of*

7,000 Books in 30 Languages. Princeton, N.J.: Princeton University Press; 1965.

Hayes, Carlton J. H.: *Wartime Mission in Spain, 1942–45.* New York: Macmillan; 1945.

Healey, Denis, ed.: *The Curtain Falls: The Story of the Socialists in Eastern Europe.* London: Lincolns-Prager; 1951.

Higgins, Trumbull: *Hitler and Russia: The Third Reich in a Two-Front War, 1937–1943.* New York: Macmillan; 1966.

———: *Winston Churchill and the Second Front, 1940–1943.* New York: Oxford University Press; 1957.

Hoare, Sir Samuel: *Complacent Dictator.* New York: Knopf; 1947.

Hull, Cordell: *The Memoirs of Cordell Hull.* 2 vols. New York: Macmillan; 1948.

Ismay, Sir Hastings: *The Memoirs of General the Lord Ismay.* New York: Viking Press; 1960.

Jacobsen, Hans-Adolf, and Rohwer, Jürgen, eds.: *Decisive Battles of World War II: The German View.* Translated by Edward Fitzgerald. London: André Deutsch Ltd.; 1965.

Kecskemeti, Paul: *Strategic Surrender: The Politics of Victory and Defeat.* Stanford, Calif.: Stanford University Press; 1958.

Kennan, George F.: *Memoirs, 1925–1950.* Boston: Little, Brown; 1967.

———: *Russia and the West Under Lenin and Stalin.* Boston: Little, Brown; 1961.

———: *Soviet Foreign Policy, 1917–1941.* New York: Van Nostrand; 1960.

Kesselring, Albert: *A Soldier's Record.* Translator not named. New York: William Morrow; 1954.

———: *Gedanken zum Zweiten Weltkrieg.* Bonn: Athenäum Verlag; 1955.

King, Ernest, and Whitehill, Walter: *Fleet Admiral King: A Naval Record.* New York: W. W. Norton; 1952.

Kleist, Peter: *Zwischen Hitler und Stalin, 1939–1945.* Bonn: Athenäum Verlag; 1950.

Knatchbull-Hugessen, Sir Hugh: *Diplomat in Peace and War.* London: Murray; 1949.

Kogan, Norman: *Italy and the Allies.* Cambridge: Harvard University Press; 1956.

Kolko, Gabriel: *The Politics of War: The World and United States Foreign Policy, 1943–1945.* New York: Random House; 1968.

Kot, Stanislaw: *Conversations with the Russians and Dispatches.* New York: Oxford University Press; 1959.

Langer, William L.: *Our Vichy Gamble.* New York: Alfred A. Knopf; 1947.

Leahy, William: *I Was There.* New York: McGraw-Hill; 1950.

Liddell-Hart, Basil H.: *The German Generals Talk.* New York: Morrow; 1948.

Lukacs, John A.: *A History of the Cold War.* Garden City, N.Y.: Doubleday; 1961.

——: *The Great Powers and Eastern Europe.* New York: American Book; 1953.

MacArthur, Douglas: *Reminiscences.* New York: McGraw-Hill; 1964.

Maclean, Fitzroy: *Escape to Adventure.* Boston: Little, Brown; 1950.

——: *The Heretic: The Life and Times of Josip Broz-Tito.* New York: Harper and Bros.; 1957.

Macmillan, Harold: *The Blast of War, 1939–1945.* New York: Harper and Row; 1967.

Maisky, Ivan M.: *Journey into the Past.* Translated by Frederick Holt. London: Hutchinson; 1962.

——: *Memoirs of a Soviet Ambassador: The War, 1939–43.* Translated by Andrew Rothstein. New York: Charles Scribner's Sons; 1968.

McNeill, William H.: *America, Britain, and Russia: Their Cooperation and Conflict, 1941–1946.* ("Survey of International Affairs, 1939–1946.") London: Oxford University Press for the Royal Institute of International Affairs; 1953.

Mikolajczyk, Stanislaw: *The Rape of Poland: Pattern of Soviet Aggression.* New York: McGraw-Hill; 1948.

Millspaugh, Arthur C.: *Americans in Persia.* Washington: The Brookings Institution; 1946.

Montgomery, Sir Bernard: *The Memoirs of Field-Marshal the Viscount Montgomery of Alamein, K.G.* New York: World Publishing; 1958.

Morgan, Sir Frederick: *Overture to Overlord.* London: Hodder and Stoughton; 1950.

Morison, Samuel E.: *History of the United States Naval Operations in World War II.* 15 vols. Boston: Little, Brown; 1947–57.

——: *Strategy and Compromise.* Boston: Little, Brown; 1958.

Murphy, Robert: *Diplomat Among Warriors.* Garden City, N.Y.: Doubleday; 1964.

Neumann, William L.: *Making the Peace, 1941–1945: The Diplo-*

macy of the Wartime Conferences. Washington:
    Foundation for Foreign Affairs; 1950.

Nicolson, Nigel, ed.: Harold Nicolson, Diaries and Letters, Volume
    II: The War Years, 1939–1945. New York: Athe-
    neum; 1967.

Pawle, Gerald: The War and Colonel Warden; Based on the Recol-
    lections of Commander C. R. Thompson, Personal
    Assistant to the Prime Minister, 1940–1945. New
    York: Alfred A. Knopf; 1963.

Pogue, Forrest C.: George C. Marshall. 2 vols. New York: Viking
    Press; 1963.

Roberts, Henry L.: Foreign Affairs Bibliography: A Selected and
    Annotated List of Books on International Relations,
    1942–1952. New York: Harper and Bros.; 1955.

———: Foreign Affairs Bibliography, 1952–1962. New York:
    Bowker; 1964.

Roosevelt, Elliott: As He Saw It. New York: Duell, Sloan and Pearce;
    1946.

Rozek, Edward J.: Allied Wartime Diplomacy: A Pattern in Poland.
    New York: John Wiley and Sons; 1958.

Russell, Ruth, and Muther, Jeannette: A History of the United Na-
    tions Charter: The Role of the United States,
    1940–1945. Washington, D.C.: Brookings Institu-
    tion; 1958.

Saunders, Hilary A. S. G.: Combined Operations. New York: Mac-
    millan; 1943.

Seton-Watson, Hugh: The East European Revolution. London:
    Methuen; 1950.

Sherwood, Robert: Roosevelt and Hopkins: An Intimate History.
    Revised Edition. New York: Harper and Bros.; 1950.

Shulman, Marshall D.: Stalin's Foreign Policy Reappraised. Cam-
    bridge: Harvard University Press; 1963.

Smith, Gaddis: American Diplomacy During the Second World War,
    1941–1945. New York: John Wiley and Sons; 1965.

Smith, Walter Bedell: Eisenhower's Six Great Decisions: Europe,
    1944–1945. New York: Longmans Green; 1956.

Snell, John L.: Illusion and Necessity: The Diplomacy of Global
    War, 1939–1945. Boston: Houghton Mifflin; 1963.

———: Wartime Origins of the East-West Dilemma over Germany.
    New Orleans: Hauser Press; 1959.

Snell, John L., ed.: The Meaning of Yalta: Big Three Diplomacy and
    New Balance of Power. Baton Rouge: Louisiana
    State University Press; 1956.

Stalin, Joseph: *On the Great Patriotic War of the Soviet Union.* Moscow: Foreign Language Publishing House; 1946.

————: *War Speeches, Orders of the Day, and Answers to Foreign Press Correspondents During the Great Patriotic War.* London: Hutchinson; 1946.

Standley, William H., and Ageton, Arthur A.: *Admiral Ambassador to Russia.* Chicago: Regnery; 1955.

Stettinius, Edward R., Jr.: *Lend-Lease: Weapon for Victory.* New York: Macmillan; 1944.

————: *Roosevelt and the Russians: The Yalta Conference.* Edited by Walter Johnson. Garden City, N.Y.: Doubleday; 1949.

Stilwell, Joseph W.: *The Stilwell Papers.* Arranged and edited by Theodore H. White. New York: William Sloane; 1948.

Stimson, Henry L., and Bundy, McGeorge: *On Active Service in Peace and War.* New York: Harper and Bros.; 1948.

Strong, Sir William: *Home and Abroad.* London: André Deutsch Ltd.; 1956.

Tedder, Arthur W.: *With Prejudice: The War Memoirs of Marshal of the Royal Air Force Lord Tedder.* London: Cassell; 1966.

Toynbee, Arnold, and Ashton-Gwatkins, Frank, eds.: *The World in March 1939.* ("Survey of International Affairs, 1939–1946.") London: Oxford University Press for the Royal Institute of International Affairs; 1952.

Toynbee, Arnold, and Toynbee, Veronica, eds.: *Hitler's Europe.* ("Survey of International Affairs, 1939–1946.") London: Oxford University Press for the Royal Institute of International Affairs; 1954.

————: *The Eve of War, 1939.* ("Survey of International Affairs, 1939–1946.") London: Oxford University Press for the Royal Institute of International Affairs; 1958.

————: *The Initial Triumph of the Axis.* ("Survey of International Affairs, 1939–1946.") London: Oxford University Press for the Royal Institute of International Affairs; 1958.

————: *The Realignment of Europe.* ("Survey of International Affairs, 1939–1946.") London: Oxford University Press for the Royal Institute of International Affairs; 1955.

Viorst, Milton: *Hostile Allies: F.D.R. and Charles de Gaulle.* New York: Macmillan; 1965.

von Einsiedel, Heinrich: *Tagebuch der Versuchung*. Berlin: Pontes Verlag; 1950.
von Papen, Franz: *Die Wahrheit einer Gasse*. Munich: Pontes Verlag; 1952.
von Ribbentrop, Joachim: *Zwischen London und Moskau: Erinnerungen und Letzte Aufzeichnungen*. Leoni am Starnberger See: Druffel Verlag; 1953.
von Schlabrendorff, Fabian: *Offiziere gegen Hitler*. Zurich: Europa Verlag; 1945.
Welles, Sumner: *Seven Decisions That Shaped History*. New York: Harper and Bros.; 1951.
Werth, Alexander: *Russia at War, 1941–1945*. New York: E. P. Dutton; 1964.
Wilmot, Chester: *The Struggle for Europe*. New York: Harper and Bros.; 1952.
Wilson, Sir Charles: *Churchill: The Struggle for Survival, 1940–1965*. Taken from the Diaries of Lord Moran. Boston: Houghton Mifflin; 1966.
Wilson, Sir Maitland: *Eight Years Overseas: 1939–1947*. London: Hutchinson; 1948.
Winant, John G.: *Letter from Grosvenor Square, An Account of a Stewardship*. Boston: Houghton Mifflin; 1947.
Zawodny, Janusz K.: *Death in the Forest: The Story of the Katyn Forest Massacre*. Notre Dame, Indiana: University of Notre Dame Press; 1962.

Articles and Periodicals

Acheson, Dean: "Morality, Moralism and Diplomacy." *Yale Review*, Vol. XLII (December 1958), 481–93.
Armstrong, John A.: "Recent Soviet Publications on World War II." *American Slavic and East European Review*, Vol. XXI (September 1962), 508–19.
Baudot, Marcel: "L'Opinion publique devant l'invasion de la Russie." *Revue d'Histoire de la Deuxième Guerre Mondiale*, Vol. LXIV (October 1966), 63–80.
Bergman, Alexander: "The Soviet Version of World War Two." *East Europe*, Vol. XII (April 1963), 23–8.
Blumenthal, Henry: "Les Perspectives historiques de la diplomatie américaine." *Revue Politique et Parlementaire*, Vol. CCXVI (April–June 1955), 281–93.
Bullard, Sir Reader: "Persia in the Two World Wars." *Royal Central Asian Journal*, Vol. L (January 1963), 6–20.

Burdick, Charles: "Planungen für das Einrücken deutscher Kräfte in Spanien in den Jahren 1942–1943: Die Unternehmen Ilona und Gisela." *Wehrwissenschaftliche Rundschau,* Vol. XIII (March 1963), 164–78.

Calvet, Henri: "Roosevelt et la reddition inconditionnelle." *Revue d'Histoire de la Deuxième Guerre Mondiale,* Vol. XX (October 1955), 43–9.

Campbell, John C.: "Negotiating with the Soviets: Some Lessons of the War Period." *Foreign Affairs,* Vol. XXXIV (January 1956), 305–19.

Cantril, Hadley: "Evaluating the Probable Reactions to the Landing in North Africa in 1942: A Case Study." *Public Opinion Quarterly,* Vol. XXIX (Fall 1965), 400–10.

Castellan, Georges: "La Politique allemande de l'U.R.S.S., 1941–1945: d'après les mémorialistes anglo-saxons." *Revue d'Histoire de la Deuxième Guerre Mondiale,* Vol. XXI (January 1956), 38–54; Vol. XXII (April 1956), 31–46.

Chase, John L.: "Unconditional Surrender Reconsidered." *Political Science Quarterly,* Vol. LXX (June 1955), 258–79.

Cherniavsky, Michael: "Corporal Hitler, General Winter, and the Russian Peasant." *Yale Review,* Vol. LI (June, 1962), 547–58.

Deutscher, Isaac: "Der Generalissimus." *Wehrwissenschaftliche Rundschau,* Vol. XII (July 1962), 381–90.

Dincic, Kruno M.: "Les Alliés et la résistance yougoslave." *Revue d'Histoire de la Deuxième Guerre Mondiale,* Vol. XLII (April 1961), 27–48.

———: "Tito et Mihailovitch: leur conflit et ses suites." *Revue d'Histoire de la Deuxième Guerre Mondiale,* Vol. XXIX (January 1958), 3–31.

Duroselle, Jean-Baptiste: "Le conflit stratégique anglo-américain de juin 1940 à juin 1944." *Revue d'Histoire Moderne et Contemporaire,* Vol. X (July–September 1963), 161–84.

———: "L'Évolution des États-Unis vers la guerre." *Revue d'Histoire de la Deuxième Guerre Mondiale,* Vol. XVIII (April 1955), 1–10.

Emerson, William: "Franklin Roosevelt as Commander-in-Chief in World War II." *Military Affairs,* Vol. XXII, No. 4 (Winter 1958–59), 181–207.

Erickson, John: "The Soviet Union at War (1941–1945): An Essay on Sources and Studies." *Soviet Studies,* Vol. XIV (January 1963), 249–74.

Fischer, Fritz: "Das Verhältnis der USA zu Russland von der Jahrhundertwende bis 1945." *Historische Zeitschrift,* Vol. CLXXXV (1958), 300–47.

Fischer, George: "Genesis of United States–Soviet Relations in World War II." *Review of Politics,* Vol. XII (July 1950), 363–78.

Franklin, William M.: "Zonal Boundaries and Access to Berlin." *World Politics,* Vol. XVI (October 1963), 1–31.

Gause, Alfred: "Der Feldzug in Nordafrika im Jahre 1941." *Wehrwissenschaftliche Rundschau,* Vol. XII (October 1962), 594–618.

——: "Der Feldzug in Nordafrika im Jahre 1942." *Wehrwissenschaftliche Rundschau,* Vol. XII (November 1962), 652–80.

——: "Der Feldzug in Nordafrika im Jahre 1943." *Wehrwissenschaftliche Rundschau,* Vol. XII (December 1962), 720–8.

Greene, Fred: "The Military View of American National Policy, 1904–1940." *American Historical Review,* Vol. LXVI (January 1961), 354–77.

Hutchings, Robert: "Comment on the Soviet Population: Wartime Losses and the Postwar Recovery." *Soviet Studies,* Vol. XVIII (July 1966), 81–2.

Jacobsen, Hans: "Les Buts et la politique de guerre de Hitler de 1939 à 1943." *Revue d'Histoire de la Deuxième Guerre Mondiale,* Vol. LXIII (July 1966), 23–40.

Juhasz, Gyula: "La Politique extérieure de la Hongrie de 1939 à 1943." *Revue d'Histoire de la Deuxième Guerre Mondiale,* Vol. LXII (April 1966), 19–36.

Kennan, George F.: "An Historian of Potsdam and His Readers." *American Slavic and East European Review,* Vol. XX (April 1961), 289–94.

Kent, George O.: "Britain in the Winter of 1940–41 as Seen from the Wilhelmstrasse." *Historical Journal,* Vol. VI (1963), 120–30.

Kochan, Lionel: "L'U.R.S.S. et le partage de l'Allemagne en zones d'occupation." *Revue d'Histoire de la Deuxième Guerre Mondiale,* Vol. XLVI (April 1962), 13–27.

Kulski, Wladyslaw W.: "Soviet Diplomatic Techniques." *Russian Review,* Vol. XIX (July 1960), 217–26.

——: "The Lost Opportunity for Russian-Polish Friendship." *Foreign Affairs,* Vol. XXV (July 1947), 667–84.

Leighton, Richard M.: "Overlord Revisited: An interpretation of American strategy in the European War, 1942–1944." *American Historical Review*, Vol. LXVIII (July 1963), 919–38.

May, Ernest R.: "The United States, the Soviet Union, and the Far Eastern War, 1941–45." *Pacific Historical Review*, Vol. XXIV (May 1955), 153–74.

Morton, Louis: "Soviet Intervention in the War against Japan." *Foreign Affairs*, Vol. XL (July 1962), 653–62.

Mosely, Philip E.: "Dismemberment of Germany: The Allied Negotiations from Yalta to Potsdam." *Foreign Affairs*, Vol. XXVIII (April 1950), 487–98.

———: "Hopes and Failures: American Policy toward East-Central Europe, 1941–47." *Review of Politics*, Vol. XVII (October 1955), 461–85.

———: "The Occupation of Germany: New Light on How the Zones Were Drawn." *Foreign Affairs*, Vol. XXVIII (July 1950), 580–604.

Néré, Jean: "Logistique et stratégie de l'alliance anglo-américaine: les temps difficiles (1939–mars 1943)." *Revue d'Histoire de la Deuxième Guerre Mondiale*, Vol. XXVII (July 1957), 1–18.

New York Times, The, 1941–43.

Presseisen, Ernst L.: "Prelude to 'Barbarossa': Germany and the Balkans, 1940–1941." *Journal of Modern History*, Vol. XXXII (December 1960), 359–70.

Rubin, Seymour J.: "American Diplomacy: the Case for 'Amateurism.'" *Yale Review*, Vol. XLV (March 1956), 321–35.

Times, The (London), 1941–43.

Villate, Robert: "Roosevelt contre De Gaulle." *Revue d'Histoire de la Deuxième Guerre Mondiale*, Vol. XXIII (July 1956), 17–31.

Vloyantes, John P.: "The Significance of Pre-Yalta Policies Regarding Liberated Countries in Europe." *Western Political Quarterly*, Vol. XI (June 1958), 209–28.

Waters, Maurice: "Special Diplomatic Agents of the President." *American Academy of Political and Social Science Annals*, No. 307 (September 1956), 124–33.

Weinberg, Gerhard: "Hitler's Image of the United States." *The American Historical Review*, Vol. LXIX (July 1964), 1006–21.

Wiesner, Franz: "Überlegungen zur Bedeutung von Konferenzen als Führungselement bei Koalitionskriegen aufgezeigt an der Tehran-Konferenz." *Wehrwissenschaftliche Rundschau,* Vol. XII (April 1964), 215–40.

Woodward, Llewellyn: "The place of diplomatic history in the study of international relations during the twentieth century." *American Philosophical Society, Proceedings,* Vol. XCVII (1953), 151–8.

Wright, Theodore F.: "The Origins of the Free Elections Dispute in the Cold War." *Western Political Quarterly,* Vol. XIV (December 1961), 850–64.

Zemskov, Igor N.: "Diplomatic History of the Second Front." *International Affairs* (August 1961), 48–55.

————: "Diplomatic History of the Second Front." *International Affairs* (September 1961), 49–57.

INDEX

ABDA Command (America, Great Britain, Netherlands, Australia), 22–3, 30

ACCOLADE (Brit. plan for the capture of Rhodes and Aegean islands), 162, 189–90, 238–9, 272–3, 278–9, 288, 313, 335

Acikalin, Cvar, 244

ACROBAT (Brit. plan to capture Libya), 16, 34

Aegean islands: see ACCOLADE

Afrika Corps (German), 31

Alamein, battle of, 65

Alaska, 43

Albania, 259

Alexander, Harold, 64, 87, 113, 212–13, 256, 259

Algiers, 65

Algiers Commission: see Italian Advisory Commission

Allen, George, 202, 203, 226

Ambrosio, Vittoria, 119

American Signal Intelligence Service, 4–5

Andaman Islands, 272, 306, 362–4; see also BUCCANEER

Anders, Wladyslaw, 244 and n.

Anglo-Soviet Treaty of Alliance: see Great Britain, Anglo-Soviet Treaty of Alliance

Antonescu, Ion, 155

ANVIL (Combined Chiefs' plan for invasion of southern France), 312, 319, 327, 335, 362–4

ARCADIA (Roosevelt-Churchill conference, Jan. 1942, Washington): see Washington Conference (Jan. 1942)

Army Group B, 119–20

Arnold, Henry, 15, 83, 96, 304, 311

Athlone, Earl of, Canadian Governor General, 124, 126

Atlantic, battle of, won, 103

Atlantic Charter, 9, 38

Auchinleck, Claude, 16, 31, 34, 40, 43, 46, 50, 64

Australia, 13, 20, 32, 43, 49

Austria, 8, 198, 352

AVALANCHE (Anglo-Am. plan to invade Italy in Naples area), 105, 116, 128; see also Quebec Conference (Aug. 1943)

B-29, 275

Badoglio, Pietro, 118, 119, 189

Balkan Confederations, 166; see also Great Britain, and Danubian Confederation

Baltic States, annexation by Soviet Union approved at Tehran, 346–7; see also Estonia; Latvia; Lithuania

Basra, 258

Bataan, fall of, 29

BAYTOWN (Anglo-Am. plan to invade Italy at Strait of Messina), 105, 128

Beaverbrook, Lord, 12, 19–20, 255

Beneš, Eduard, 223

Benghazi, 31

Berezhkov, Valentin, 303, 322, 329

Berio, Alberto, 119

Bessarabia, 8

Birse, Arthur, 311, 329

Bizerte, 65

Boettiger, John, 303

A Note About the Author

Robert Beitzell is an assistant professor of history at the University of Maine. Born in Elizabeth, N.J., in 1930, he received his B.A. from Wesleyan University, his M.A. from Columbia University, and his Ph.D. from the University of North Carolina. He taught at the University of Massachusetts before joining the Maine faculty in 1967. He lives in Bangor with his wife and son.

A Note on the Type

This book was set on the Linotype in Electra, a type face designed by W. A. Dwiggins. The Electra face is a simple and readable type suitable for printing books by present day processes. It is not based on any historical model, and hence does not echo any particular time or fashion.

This book was composed, printed, and bound by H. Wolff Book Manufacturing Company, New York, New York. Typography and binding design by Anthea Lingeman.